DALE BOISSELLE

CS

Elementary Computability, Formal Languages, and Automata

ROBERT McNAUGHTON
Rensselaer Polytechnic Institute

PRENTICE-HALL, INC., Englewood Cliffs, New Jersey 07632

Library of Congress Cataloging in Publication Data

McNaughton, Robert.
   Elementary computability, formal languages, and
automata.

   Bibliography: p. 388
   Includes indexes.
   1. Computable functions.   2. Formal languages.
3. Sequential machine theory.   I. Title.
QA9.59.M35   511   81-10618
ISBN 0-13-253500-9   AACR2

Editorial/production supervision
   and interior design by *Linda M. Paskiet*
Cover design by *Infield/D'Astolfo*
Manufacturing buyer: *Gordon Osbourne*

Printed in the United States of America

10   9   8   7   6   5   4   3   2   1

ISBN 0-13-253500-9

PRENTICE-HALL INTERNATIONAL, INC., *London*
PRENTICE-HALL OF AUSTRALIA PTY. LIMITED, *Sydney*
PRENTICE-HALL OF CANADA, LTD., *Toronto*
PRENTICE-HALL OF INDIA PRIVATE LIMITED, *New Delhi*
PRENTICE-HALL OF JAPAN, INC., *Tokyo*
PRENTICE-HALL OF SOUTHEAST ASIA PTE. LTD., *Singapore*
WHITEHALL BOOKS LIMITED, *Wellington, New Zealand*

FOR VIVIEN

Contents

Preface

This book is an introduction to theoretical computer science emphasizing two interrelated areas: the theory of computability (how to tell whether problems are algorithmically solvable) and the theory of formal languages (how to design and use special languages, as for algorithms). Automata (idealized computer devices) are used as precise models of computation in studies that have actual computers as their primary application. Other areas, such as semantics and computational complexity, are treated briefly, in an attempt to bring all of theoretical computer science into view.

There are many excellent books in theoretical computer science for the graduate student and the more advanced undergraduate. These are, for the most part, too advanced for students without previous exposure to theoretical issues, even those with experience in programming: The main difficulty is that there are not enough exercises suitable for students confronting theory for the first time.

This book seeks to provide a well-rounded and elementary explanation of the issues, and, more important, an adequate supply of exercises at the right level, integrated with the text. A number of groups of exercises are particularly appropriate for beginning students, but exercises for the more advanced or more mathematically inclined students are provided throughout.

Together with the exercises accommodating above-average ingenuity, there are some advanced expository sections, but the predominating level is consistently that of an elementary text. The student who has mastered a course using this book should be capable of going on to a more advanced course in computability, formal languages, automata, or any one of a number of other theoretical areas of computer science. On the other hand, the material provides both useful skills and appropriate orientation for the majority of computer science students who (experience indicates) will not go on to more advanced theory courses. The bibliography emphasizes volumes and articles that serve an expository purpose, rather than original research papers.

Content

Chapter 1 presents the concept of algorithm and other similar concepts, and ends with a descriptive outline of the book suitable for the uninitiated reader.

Chapter 2, on Turing machines, can be omitted without loss of continuity. On the other hand, the Turing-machine model of computation is particularly helpful in clarifying the concept of algorithm. Several Turing machines are designed and then universal Turing machines are discussed.

Chapter 3 presents two foundational programming languages, the GOTO language and the WHILE language, providing a foundation for the theory of computability suitable for computer science students. The halting problem is discussed in some detail, and the method for writing programs that compute partial and total functions is shown. The chapter ends with the introduction into the WHILE language of the DO-TIMES command, which controls a loop by a simple count.

Chapter 4 contains the heart of the book's material on computability. It tells how to define functions by explicit definition (taking the place of composition in some books), primitive recursion, and mu-recursion. It proves that programs can be written for functions so defined, provided that programs are available for the functions used in the definitions. Ackermann's function, formal computations, and general equational definitions are also treated. The chapter ends with a discussion of the class of primitive-recursive functions as a subclass of the class of computable functions.

Chapter 5 turns back to the general concept of algorithm as it was discussed informally in Chapter 1, and argues that for every algorithm there is a mu-recursive function over the nonnegative integers whose computation, in effect, does the work of the algorithm. The argument for this proposition, known in part as Church's thesis, is due to Kleene and is based on the technique of Gödel numbering.

Chapter 6 demonstrates that certain problems are unsolvable, that is to say, have no algorithms. It begins by proving relative to Church's thesis that the halting problem for the GOTO language is unsolvable, and goes on to prove that certain other apparently unrelated problems are also unsolvable.

Chapters 7, 8, and 9 focus on formal grammars for formal languages. (The syntax of formal languages is treated informally in previous chapters.) Chapter 7 investigates, quite extensively and in an elementary fashion, how context-free grammars can be written for various formal languages. Chapter 8 investigates how a string in the language of a given context-free grammer can be parsed. Ambiguity is discussed, and a parsing automaton is put forth that is capable of parsing a string by making one pass on the string from left to right. This automaton uses a one-dimensional tape in an action that is similar to that of a pushdown machine. Our parsing automaton is introduced without the concept of finite automaton, making our presentation quite elementary.

Chapter 9 deals with regular languages and the automata especially capable of dealing with them: finite automata. Regular languages constitute an important subclass of the class of context-free languages, for which special techniques of manipulation are available. Transition graphs, state graphs, and regular expressions are also treated. The chapter closes with a technique for proving that certain languages are not regular.

Appendices I and II are correctness proofs, respectively, for the Euclidean algorithm and the labyrinth algorithm of Chapter 1.

Appendix III explains the basic issues of formal languages relevant to the various formal languages that appear in the book. It discusses the nature of formal languages, their syntax, semantics, and pragmatics. It closes with a special section on the semantics of commands, providing background for parts of Chapter 3.

Appendix IV serves to round out the discussion of algorithms in Chapter 1 by investigating criteria, other than correctness, by means of which algorithms are judged. The largest part of this appendix contains a brief description of computational complexity, showing its relation to the theory of computability.

Appendix V explains the many proofs by mathematical induction (especially course-of-values induction) that appear in the book. Appendix VI is an excursus from Chapter 6, illustrating proofs by the diagonal method in mathematical logic and computational complexity, similar to the proof of the unsolvability of the halting problem.

Students who wish to find out what this book is all about are advised to read Section 1.1 and then the brief description of the text's contents in Section 1.3. Those using the book for independent study are advised to work out the exercises, if only the first few (the easiest) in each section. All students using this book should be prepared to find Chapter 4 and the chapters beyond—both text and exercises—more difficult than Chapters 2 or 3, although the book on the whole is more elementary than most others covering the same topics.

The original stimulus to write this book dates back to some conversations in 1964 with Jack B. Dennis of M.I.T. about a course he was then planning, conversations I recalled when I undertook a course of my own at Rensselaer Polytechnic Institute three years later. After teaching that course for eight consecutive years, I began, in January 1975, to write this book as its text and to use drafts of certain chapters in teaching. A sabbatical granted by the Institute during the year 1976–1977 enabled me to write a complete draft of the book.

The Department of Mathematical Sciences at Rensselaer has encouraged and materially aided my work, and I thank the former chair, Richard C. DiPrima, his secretary, Lorraine Morin, the executive officer, James A. Voytuk, and the entire office staff.

Bobby F. Caviness, who taught the course at Rensselaer in 1976, using draft materials as a text, was particularly helpful. His numerous suggestions and comments have resulted in a book that is more attentive to the needs of computer science students. My colleague M.S. Krishnamoorthy also made several useful comments when he taught from this material at Rensselaer in 1979. He taught from it again in 1980, as did Heinrich Rolletschek and, in 1981, my colleague Moon-Jung Chung.

Anthony J. Dos Reis, who assisted in the course for two years, was responsible for several expository improvements. My colleague S. Kamal Abdali, exceptionally alert to the issues of theoretical computer science, was constantly available for informal discussion. Ross Stenstrom provided some valuable consultation in connection with the parsing automaton of Chapter VIII, and helped in the final stages by reading proofs.

I enjoyed my consultation with the late Edwin B. Allen and with Ronald S. Calinger (Department of History and Political Science at Rensselaer) on matters connected with the history of mathematics used in Section 1.1.7. My wife Vivien Leonard (Department of Language, Literature, and Communication) contributed a substantial improvement of the exposition especially in Chapter 1.

To Steven S. Muchnick of the University of California at Berkeley and the University of Kansas, who read almost every word of three drafts, I am grateful for expert and helpful criticism, with which I almost always came to agree. In many places he kept me from saying things that I did not mean, and in at least one place he kept me from making a false statement.

Several anonymous readers were helpful, as was the late David T. Atwater, who gave an intelligent reading of an early version of Section 1.1 from the point of view of someone well on the outside of computer science.

I have appreciated the patient consideration and material assistance that Karl V. Karlstrom of Prentice-Hall has given to my efforts during several years of partial drafts. Thanks also to Stephen E. Cline, James Fegen, and Linda Paskiet.

I thank Barbara Hale for typing the entire manuscript, and Ava Biffer, Kathy Kuslansky, Jane Lewis, Lorraine Morin, and Virginia Steffen for earlier typing efforts.

ROBERT MCNAUGHTON

The Concept of Algorithm 1

This book is an introduction to the theoretical aspects of computer science, focusing on the three topics that form its title. The first of these, the theory of computability, embodies the central objective, namely to distinguish between what is computable and what is not computable. The pursuit of this objective will take us outside the theory of computability to formal languages and automata, and to other topics of theoretical computer science as well.

A descriptive outline of the book will be given at the end of this chapter (Section 1.3). Meanwhile, we begin our study by defining and discussing the concept of algorithm, which is at the basis of the theory of computability and of all computer science.

Although algorithms have existed for thousands of years, their use in stored-program computers has recently increased their importance and somewhat changed their character. Machines working at electronic speeds must often be told precisely what to do in all possible circumstances—before they even begin. For this reason it has become necessary to articulate algorithms with great precision.

But although the concept of algorithm has become important because of large-scale electronic digital computers, its meaning does not rest in any essential way on any concept of computing machine. For this reason, our definition will be worded so as to make no reference to computers or computer programs.

"ALGORITHM" DEFINED 1.1

We cannot adequately communicate the meaning of this term by a simple definition without discussion. In rough terms, an *algorithm* is a method of answering a question taken from a class of questions, the class being known as a *problem*. Accordingly, we shall begin with some discussion of questions and problems, then define the term *algorithm*, and describe generally how an algorithm is executed to answer a question.

1.1.1 Questions and Problems

We shall depend on everyone's ordinary concept of the question–answer relationship, noting that a question and an answer must both be expressed in some language or other, which we assume to be a written language.

We also assume that there is an understanding, explicit or implicit, that makes it definite whether something is or is not a correct answer to a question, even though we may not be capable of ascertaining either that it is correct or that it is incorrect. A question may have no correct answers at all. (For example, "For what real number x is $x^2 + 36 = 25$?") It may have several correct answers, or even infinitely many. ("For what fraction p/q is $|\pi - p/q| < 0.002$?") Or it may have just one correct answer. ("What is the smallest prime number greater than 20?")

As much as possible, a question should be phrased so as to indicate precisely what is acceptable as an answer. Consider the question, "For what positive real number x is $x^2 = 2x + 1$?" Unless there is a clear understanding, this phrasing causes difficulties. Just by reading it we don't know if $1 + \sqrt{2}$ is an acceptable answer (the person asking may not find radicals acceptable), or if 2.414 is an acceptable answer (although it is a useful approximation, 2.414 is not a root of the equation).

There are really (at least) two questions here, acceptable phrasings of which might be: (1) "What expression in radicals denotes the positive root of the equation $x^2 = 2x + 1$?" (2) "What decimal expression with three places to the right of the point is the closest approximation to the positive root of $x^2 = 2x + 1$?" The second of these is more likely to be rendered, "What is the positive root of $x^2 = 2x + 1$ to the nearest thousandth?"

Our insistence that questions and answers be expressible in a written language implies, among other things, that they be finite expressions. Thus the following question (or pseudoquestion) is not tolerated: "For what positive real number x, expressed as an infinite decimal, is $x^2 = 2x + 1$?"

Although each question and each answer must have a certain finite size, we place no finite bound on all questions and answers. We allow arbitrarily large positive integers, for example, which require arbitrarily large representations in any language.

An algorithm must be capable of answering not merely a single question but a class of questions, which brings us to the definition of our first two technical terms.

Definition: A *problem* is a class of questions. Each question in the class is an *instance* of the problem.

Generally, an interesting problem is an infinite class of questions that can be phrased as a single interrogative sentence. For example, "What is the (positive) square root of a given positive integer x to nearest thousandth?" Here the phrase "a given positive integer x" indicates that a question is determined only when a particular positive integer is specified. If we take $x = 17$, we get the question: "What is the square root of 17 to the nearest thousandth?" This question is an instance of the problem, which actually consists of infinitely many questions, one for each positive integer.

To the extent that a problem is interesting, it becomes interesting to find an algorithm that is capable of answering any of the questions on demand.

Most problems in the mathematical sciences are of two kinds. The first is to obtain the value of a *function* for a given argument. Often, but not always, the function is a numerical function. For example, if we define $f(x)$, for x a positive integer, to be the smallest prime number greater than x, then we have the problem: "For a given positive integer x, what is the smallest prime number p such that $p > x$?"

The second kind of problem is one whose answers are "yes" and "no." (Such a problem could be considered to be a problem about a function, but we find it worthwhile to make the distinction.) An example is the problem: "For a given positive integer n, for a given vector V in R^n (where R is the field of the rational numbers), and for a given set E of linear equations with integral coefficients and constant terms, is V a solution to E?" (More briefly, "Does a given vector satisfy a given set of linear equations?")

Many examples of both kinds of problem will be considered in this book. Many of these problems, unlike all the examples chosen in this subsection, will be nonnumerical.

(Although the terms "question" and "problem" are used as above in much of the literature, there are deviations: One can find the word "question" in places where we would use the word "problem," and vice versa. We shall use these words consistently as we have defined them, although occasionally we shall say, for emphasis, "class of questions" in place of "problem," and "instance of a problem" in place of the shorter term "question.")

The Definition   1.1.2

Most of the definitions in this book will make the defined term clear without further explanation. Our definition of the term *algorithm*, however, is not and could not be of this kind, since the concept requires extensive explanation.

The following, therefore, will require for its clarification the informal discussion that follows in the remainder of this section. Some of the terms in the definition (e.g., *deterministic*, *step*, *simple*) are terms that we have not yet discussed and require for their clarification the passages that follow. (Even with the explanation in the remainder of this chapter, we do not claim that we have given a complete or precise definition. Perhaps by the very nature of the concept a precise definition is impossible.)

Definition: An *algorithm* for a problem is an organized set of commands for answering on demand any question that is an instance of the problem, subject to the following stipulations:

1. The algorithm is actually written, or is capable of being written, as a finite expression A, in some language.

2. Exactly which question is answered by the execution of the algorithm is determined by setting the *inputs* of the algorithm before execution begins.

3. It is possible to regard an execution of the algorithm as a step-by-step process, where the total result of the action during any one step is simple.

4. The action at each step, including possibly a decision to terminate, and all results of this action relevant to the execution of the algorithm are strictly determined by the written expression A, from the inputs and the results of the previous steps. (In short, an algorithm must be *deterministic*.)

5. Upon termination the answer to the question is a clearly specified part, called the *output*, of the result of the execution.

6. Whatever the values of the inputs, the execution will terminate after some finite number of steps.

We begin our informal discussion by pointing out that the written expression A must be in some language or other. It may simply be written in ordinary English with mathematical symbolism, or it may be written in some formal language, such as a programming language.

It should be understood that our definition permits certain aspects of the execution of an algorithm to be left to the option of the executor (the person or machine that executes the algorithm) or else to be determined by the circumstances of the mode of execution, provided that they do not affect the outcome in any essential way. Such things we lump together under the phrase, "allowable implementational variations." As a human executor may choose between writing on paper and writing on a blackboard, may pause for lunch between any two steps, and may execute quickly or slowly, so an algorithm may be programmed on a computer in different ways. If the computer's time is shared, the execution of the program may be interrupted at any time. What is required is that two executions starting with the same input values must go along in essentially the same way, step by step, and produce the same answer. Since the algorithm itself determines exactly what variations are allowable, this matter can be fully clarified only when we discuss specific computational models.

An algorithm may be used informally by people, and perhaps there may be a person who uses it but is incapable of articulating it (e.g., someone who is capable of coming up with the right answer every time, but cannot readily instruct anyone else in the method). In our work, however, we are interested in written algorithms, articulated at least well enough so there are no questions about how things are done. Moreover, we are interested in formalisms in which many algorithms can be expressed. In the chapters that follow, we shall present several formalisms (the concept of Turing machines, two foundational programming languages, and the formalism of functional expressions), each of which will be capable of expressing algorithms for all problems that have any algorithms at all.

Condition 3, although it states that execution of an algorithm is a step-by-step process, does not say anything specific about how we can break things down into steps. Indeed, this is a question that can best be answered in terms of a specific formalism. As we deal with each of the algorithmic formalisms in turn, we shall have a precise idea of what a step is. But we shall make no effort to stipulate in general terms how the execution of an algorithm is to be broken into steps. Nor shall we try to specify precisely how "simple" the action of a single step must be.

The significance of stating in condition 3 that the action of each step is simple is that we should not consider as a single step something that is really a long sequence of actions. For example, if a human executor is multiplying a 10-digit number by a 1-digit number on paper, we should not regard the entire multiplication as a single step. It would be more appropriate to regard it as composed of perhaps 10, 20, or 30 steps.

It may be convenient for some purposes to think of this entire multiplication as a unit, as for example when it is part of the execution of a more elaborate algorithm. The algorithm may be written in a way to suggest that the multiplication is a single step, which is permissible if, say, a human executor is capable of doing the multiplication without the need of detailed verbal instructions. However, a detailed analysis of the situation must regard the execution of the multiplication as taking several steps.

Although the definition of algorithm makes no mention of measurements of time, condition 3 tells us that the amount of time that it takes to execute an algorithm for a given input has something to do with the number of steps, since there is a limit on the amount of time required to execute a single step. It tells us also that, as a result of a single step, only a limited amount of information is added. Therefore, as a consequence of condition 3 and the fact that the input is finite, there is only a finite amount of information after any finite number of steps, and in particular, upon termination. An output of infinite size is therefore impossible.

In analyzing and designing algorithms we must be careful to acknowledge all necessary actions that are relevant to execution. For example, suppose that an algorithm directs the executor to add 2 to a number if that number is divisible by 317 without remainder, and to subtract 2 otherwise. If the number is large, each step in the procedure used to determine whether the number is divisible by 317 would have to be regarded as a separate step in the execution of the algorithm.

1.1.3 Determinism

Condition 4 in the definition states more than that the executor does what the algorithm directs and that the executor is not permitted to make choices relevant to execution. It also states that an algorithm, by definition, will not tell the executor to make such a choice. It cannot say, for example, "Pick an integer between 1 and 5." A human executor may have freely chosen the algorithm, the input values, and the mode of implementation; but once these choices have been made, no other choices relevant to execution are available.

Note also that condition 4 does not permit an algorithm to direct that a pair of dice be thrown at any step, since the result of such an action is not determined. Another consequence is that Monte Carlo programs, important in computer applications, are not algorithmic. (A detailed discussion of this point would be complicated by the fact that most Monte Carlo programs on computers use pseudo-random numbers rather than numbers selected in truly random fashion.)

In summary, condition 4 of the definition, the condition of determinism, implies three things: (1) the action taken by an executor is mandatory; (2) the executor has no options relevant to the execution of the algorithm; and (3) the relevant outcome of any action taken is determined absolutely and not merely probabilistically.

There is an important consequence of the condition of determinism. If on two different occasions two different executors execute the same algorithm for the same input values, then the same thing, within an allowable implementational variation, will happen step by step. In particular, the number of steps taken will be the same, and the answer will be the same.

1.1.4 Further Discussion

Condition 6, that any execution of an algorithm terminates, implies that the question is always answered. The difficulty in verifying that an alleged algorithm satisfies condition 6 is a focal point in the theory of computability, known as the *halting problem*.

Although execution of an algorithm must eventually terminate, the definition does not tell us how many steps will be required, saying only that the number of steps must be finite. For some familiar algorithms, one can quickly estimate the number of steps that an execution requires. But for other algorithms this is not possible, which means that the only way to estimate this number is either to carry through the execution, or else to do something equally laborious.

A computation that is directed by an algorithm may possibly require too much time for practical completion. In Section 4.4 we shall see some algorithms whose execution, for some small inputs, requires an extremely large number of steps; so large, in fact, that even if we assume a step could be executed in a billionth of a second, the amount of time needed for execution, although finite, would exceed any estimate of time ever made in the study of the physical universe.

Furthermore, algorithms for infinite classes of questions will admit inputs of arbitrarily large size. (A finite bound on the input size implies that there are only finitely many possible input values.) It follows that for most algorithms of interest, there will be input values that require more space to write down than we have available, whatever the implementation.

The theory of computability sets no finite bound on practicality. Although it does not allow a computation that takes an infinite amount of any resource (time, space, energy, etc.), it does allow any computation that limits itself to a finite amount of resources, however large that may be.

One of the benefits we shall derive from this study is the knowledge that certain problems have no algorithms. Results to this effect (discussed in Chapter 6) would lose their force if we did not entertain a concept of an algorithm that is broad enough to include anything anyone would ever think of as an effective computation method. It does not detract from these results that the concept is broad enough to include algorithms that we judge to be practically impossible, as long as the concept also includes all those that are practically possible.

In studying the theory of computability, we shall also learn something about how algorithms for all solvable problems can be designed according to a uniform style. If we attempted to limit ourselves to a study of only practical algorithms (whatever that may mean), it is doubtful that we could get such an insight.

With regard to this matter of theoretical computability versus practicality, computational complexity (discussed briefly in Appendix IV) can be said to begin where the theory of computability leaves off. But even computational complexity cannot offer a precise theoretical distinction between the practical and the impractical. After all, as computers get larger, some algorithms that are impractical one year may become practical the next.

The most important results in the theory of computability state that certain problems have no algorithms. To say that an algorithm does not exist for a given problem is to say more than that we do not know of any such algorithm. Moreover, it is possible to know that an algorithm exists without knowing what the algorithm is, which is true in some cases covered by the following:

THEOREM 1.1.1: For every finite class of questions all having answers, there exists an algorithm.

PROOF: A question and its answer are both finite expressions. Hence the expression consisting of all the questions and answers, where each answer is written right after its question, is a finite expression. This expression, in effect a table of questions and answers, is an algorithm that would enable an executor to answer any question in the class. The executor would simply look up the question in the table, which could be done in a finite number of steps, and read off the answer following it. ∎

The sign ∎ is an end-of-proof sign that will be found at the end of all proofs in this book, with the exception of proofs of lemmas inside larger proofs.

Although this theorem tells us that an algorithm exists for any finite class of questions having answers, it does not say that we can necessarily know what that algorithm is. After all, there are many questions whose answers we do not know. Before we can use any algorithm to learn an answer, we must know the algorithm.

The algorithm of Theorem 1.1.1 is often called a "table look-up." There are many situations in which such an algorithm is not desirable, simply because the table is enormous and unwieldy. We generally like to think of each problem we study as an infinite class of questions, sometimes enlarging a finite class of questions to an interesting infinite class, so that the algorithm that results may have greater simplicity and generality.

1.1.5 *Three Similar Definitions*

In this subsection and the next we shall look at some related concepts.

Definition: A *procedure* for a problem is an organized set of commands that satisfies conditions 1 to 5 of the definition of *algorithm* (but does not necessarily terminate after a finite number of steps for every choice of inputs).

For a given set of inputs the execution of a procedure may halt after a finite number of steps. Then by condition 5 the question is answered correctly by the output. But it may go on forever without halting. In this case the question is never answered and, what may be worse, there may never be any way of knowing that it will never halt, as we shall see in Chapter 6.

Although an algorithm is better than a procedure that is not an algorithm, there is no way of studying the class of algorithms without also studying the larger class of procedures. And (as we shall prove in Chapter 6) there is no way of knowing whether a given procedure is an algorithm.

Definition: An *incompletely specified algorithm* is an organized set of commands satisfying conditions 1 to 3, 5, and 6 of the definition of "algorithm" (i.e., all the conditions except the condition of determinism), and containing at certain junctures in place of a categorical command, a command to take one of several courses of action freely chosen by the executor. (Whichever choices the executor makes at such junctures, execution will eventually terminate with the question correctly answered.)

An incompletely specified algorithm can generally be converted into an algorithm by replacing each free choice by a categorical command to execute one of the commands in the set of alternatives.

Incompletely specified algorithms are widely found in informal work. An example of one to sort a pile of cards alphabetically is the following:

INCOMPLETELY SPECIFIED ALGORITHM: Try to find two adjacent cards that are out of order. If it is certain that no two can be found, halt. If two are found, interchange them, and repeat from the beginning. In the search for two adjacent cards that are out of order, never examine a pair of cards a second time if they were examined once and found to be in order and, since that time, neither has been moved.

There is no specification of exactly how the search is to be made for two adjacent cards out of order, but an important implicit assumption is that there does exist a way of looking through the pile of cards to verify that no two cards are out of order. One could convert this incompletely specified algorithm into an algorithm as follows:

CORRESPONDING COMPLETELY SPECIFIED ALGORITHM: Compare the first card with the seocnd, then the second with the third, and so on, until either (case I) two adjacent cards are found to be out of order, or (case II) all the cards have been so examined (with no two out of order), whichever comes first. In case I, interchange the two adjacent cards found, and repeat from the beginning. In case II, halt.

Although this is not the most efficient sorting algorithm, it does illustrate what must be done to pass from an incompletely specified algorithm to an algorithm proper. The fact that the former can be given with less detail makes it convenient in cases where (1) we do not wish to execute the algorithm, but merely appreciate that an algorithm exists, and (2) it is perfectly clear that one could convert the incompletely specified algorithm into an algorithm proper. Incompletely specified algorithms will be presented in various parts of this book. The reader must be reminded of the danger in such a practice: one often has the feeling that one can fill in details, only to realize when pressed to do so that one cannot.

Some high-level programming languages permit programs that are incompletely specified algorithms. The advantage to the programmer is that steps need not be specified completely at times when, if they did, the programmer would be distracted from the crucial considerations of the problem. Needless to say, when a machine translates such a program into its own language for execution, it must transform the algorithm into a completely specified algorithm.

Definition: A *nondeterministic procedure* is an organized set of commands satisfying conditions 1 to 3, and 5 (but is not necessarily deterministic, and does not necessarily terminate). A nondeterministic procedure is a *nondeterministic solution* to a problem if, for every set of input values, there is a possible execution that does terminate and answer the question.

This concept is a strange one, but it plays an important role in theoretical computer science. It will come up in Chapters 8 and 9, where some nondeterministic procedures will be considered in the form of nondeterministic automata.

For many mathematically precise algorithmic languages actively studied in the theory of computability, one can prove that if a problem has a nondeterministic solution in that language, then it has an algorithm in that language. One can usually construct a rather clumsy algorithm that, for each instance of the problem, traces through all possible executions of the nondeterministic procedure up to the point (provably reachable) where the question is answered. (The outline of such a construction for Turing machines is given as the proof of Theorem 7.3, p. 164, of Hopcroft and Ullman [1979].)

Although a nondeterministic solution to a problem can be converted into an algorithm in this way, there seems to be no general method to make the resulting algorithm less clumsy. This difficulty appears in many forms and in many problem areas of computer science.

1.1.6 Related Concepts

Definition: An *effective operation* for obtaining some result from something given is an operation according to an algorithm whose input is the given and whose output is the result. In this case the result is obtained *effectively* from the given.

Definition: A problem is *solvable* if there exists an algorithm for it. Otherwise, it is *unsolvable*.

Definition: A *decision procedure* is an algorithm for a class of questions each of whose answers is "yes" or "no." A problem is *decidable* if it has a decision procedure. A problem with yes–no answers is *undecidable* if it is unsolvable (i.e., if it has no decision procedure).

Definition: A set σ is a *recursive set* (or *decidable set*), with respect to a language L, if there is a decision procedure to tell whether any given object as named in the language L is or is not in σ. When the language L is understood, we speak of σ as simply a *recursive set*. (The use of the word "recursive" for this concept has to do with the study of recursive functions.)

For example, the set of even nonnegative integers and the set of primes are both recursive sets (assuming a language whose set of named objects is the set of nonnegative integers).

Definition: A set σ is *recursively enumerable* (or *effectively enumerable*) if either it is the empty set or else there is an algorithmically computable function f, called an *enumerating function*, mapping the set of positive integers onto the set, that is,

$$\sigma = \{f(i) \mid i \text{ a positive integer}\}$$

Note that this definition allows the possibility that $f(i) = f(j)$ for $i \neq j$. In this case we say that the set σ is *enumerated with repetition*. It follows that every finite set (whose objects can be named in some specified language) is recursively enumerable. For example, take $\sigma = \{s_1, \ldots, s_n\}$, where $n \geq 1$. An enumerating function for σ is the function defined as follows: For each i, $1 \leq i \leq n$, $s_i = f(i) = f(n + i) = f(2n + i) = \ldots$. Clearly, this function f is algorithmically computable. (There are other enumerating functions for this set that are just as good.)

(Strictly speaking, the empty set cannot be enumerated. For many purposes, however, it is convenient to classify it as a recursively enumerable set.)

There is another way to regard a nonempty recursively enumerable set. Think of a computer that runs forever and every so often prints out some member of σ, possibly with repetitions, but in such a way that every member of σ is eventually printed at least once. The computer is acting deterministically, but never stops. The enumerating function here is given by the order in which the members of σ are printed out: $f(1)$ is the first, $f(2)$ the second, and so on. (If the computer does not print anything at all, then σ is the empty set.)

Although they will not be studied in this book, recursively enumerable sets are widely discussed in the theory of computability. The relationship between recursive sets and recursively enumerable sets is summarized in the following three propositions, which are theorems in the theory of computability. We shall not give proofs, but we shall give intuitive arguments for two of the three.

PROPOSITION 1.1.1: If σ is a recursive set of objects (with respect to some language), then σ is recursively enumerable.

Intuitive argument: Effectively enumerate all the names in the language. Test each of these in turn for membership in σ. Form a new enumeration of those that pass the test, which is an effective enumeration of σ.

PROPOSITION 1.1.2: There exists a recursively enumerable set σ such that there is no decision procedure for telling whether an object (as named in an appropriate language) is in σ.

Putting together Propositions 1.1.1 and 1.1.2, we see that the concept of recursively enumerable set is a sort of generalization of the concept of recursive set.

PROPOSITION 1.1.3: If σ is a recursively enumerable set of objects named in a language L, and the complement of σ with respect to the set of all objects named in L is also recursively enumerable, then σ is also a recursive set.

Intuitive argument: The decision procedure to tell whether or not a given object x as named in L is in the set σ works as follows. Enumerate σ and simultaneously enumerate the complement of σ. Eventually, x will appear in one enumeration or the other, telling us whether x is in σ or its complement.

1.1.7 Etymology

Algorithms have always been important in mathematics, but the word "algorithm" was not used before medieval times. The term originated from the name of the great Islamic mathematician, Abù Ja'far Muhammad ibn Mūsā al Khwārizmī, who died about A.D. 847. Many historical works refer to this man simply as "Al-Khwarizmi," an epithet that normally would indicate that he was a native of Khwarizm in the Islamic Empire, now the city of Khiva and environs, about 150 miles south of the Aral Sea in Soviet Uzbekistan. It is known that he lived briefly in Khwarizm, but mostly in or near Baghdad, the capital of the Islamic Empire and the great center of learning at the time.

From the seventh to the thirteenth centuries, Islamic thinkers made many contributions to the development of mathematics. Al-Khwarizmi's principal work was a book on elementary practical mathematics, partly original and partly a transmission of important ideas of Greek and Hindu mathematicians, entitled, "The Compendious Book on Calculation by Completion and Balancing." It contained, together with material on the Hindu number system, a complete system of rules for algebraic manipulation (the appellation "al-jabr" in its title is the source of our word "algebra"). Translated into Latin in the twelfth century, the book was so influential in Europe that in the thirteenth and fourteenth centuries the new arithmetic using the Hindu number system (as opposed to Roman numerals) was identified with Al-Khwarizmi, and the Latin form of his name, "algorismus," was given to any treatise on that topic. The word "algorithm" and its present meaning can be traced to that usage. (Grateful acknowledgement is made to the late Edwin B. Allen and to Ronald S. Calinger, both of Rensselaer Polytechnic Institute, for historical information. See Boyer [1968], pp. 251–257.)

1.2 EXAMPLES OF ALGORITHMS

We now discuss a select set of examples to help clarify the concept that was defined and discussed abstractly in the preceding section.

1.2.1 Algorithms from Our Childhood

After we became familiar with the decimal number-representation system, one of the first algorithms we learned was that for adding two one-digit decimal numbers. This algorithm was a table for a finite class of questions, which we eventually memorized. We went on to learn an algorithm for adding two non-negative decimal integers of arbitrary size. This algorithm was for an infinite class of questions, and it contained as a part the algorithm for adding single digits.

Two things are illustrated here. First, it is convenient for instructional purposes to teach algorithms that have other previously taught algorithms as parts. Second, the execution of an algorithm may involve repetition of steps. In the second of these two algorithms, the repeated sequence of steps might be verbalized as follows:

Add the ith (from the right) addend digit to the $(i - 1)$st carry (which is zero if $i = 1$). Add this result to the ith augend digit. If this result is a one-digit decimal number, the ith sum digit is this digit and the ith carry is zero. But if the result is a two-digit decimal number, the right digit is the ith sum digit and the ith carry is 1 (which is the left digit).

This sequence of steps is repeated an appropriate number of times.

In Section 1.1 we mentioned that an interesting algorithm is one for an infinite class of questions, which implies that inputs can be arbitrarily large. Since the execution must (in general) take longer for larger inputs, and since the algorithm must be a finite expression, it follows that some of its commands must be repeated more and more times for larger inputs.

The term "loop" (undoubtedly familiar to the reader) is used, somewhat vaguely, to signify a set of commands in an algorithm that is executed repeatedly. Without trying to clarify the term at this point, we can say that if one wishes to understand algorithms, one must understand loops; and if one wishes to write algorithms, one must learn to design loops that work precisely for an intended purpose.

We went on, in our early school years, from addition to subtraction and then multiplication. Next came short division, by means of which we could divide any dividend by a divisor whose multiplication table we had memorized. Long division, for larger and harder-to-manage divisors, was the most complicated of all. Several algorithms exist for long division, involving multiplication and subtraction as parts in essentially the same way. Some people (myself, for example) have no precise rule for estimating the new quotient digit each time they go from left to right in the dividend and therefore execute (at best) an incompletely specified algorithm for long division.

Another thing that we learned early (probably without explicit instruction) is comparison of two positive decimal numbers to determine which of the two, if either, is larger.

Engineers who design computers must reexamine these operations that we all learned in our early school life, but predominantly in terms of the binary, rather than the decimal number-representation system. Computer arithmetic is a fascinating topic, but is outside the scope of this book.

Another type of algorithm that we are all familiar with is a formula. Most formulas are incompletely specified algorithms, there being no indication of the exact order in which some operations are to be performed. If $b + c + d$ is part of a formula, for example, one can compute its value either by adding b to c first, then adding d, or else by adding d to c first, then adding b. If all additions are done with perfect precision, the results are the same (although it is well known that if b, c, and d are floating-point numbers inside a machine, the two results can sometimes vary significantly).

Formulas are important, but they pose no challenge for us in our general study of algorithms. An algorithm based on a formula depends on previously established algorithms for the arithmetic operations already discussed and others, such as taking the square root. Most formulas involve no loops; the only loops in their computation are those that are parts of the basic operations As a consequence, most algorithms based on formulas are not very interesting.

1.2.2 The Euclidean Algorithm

This well-known algorithm for finding the greatest common divisor of two positive integers (i.e., the greatest positive integer that divides each of the two without remainder) is fairly elementary and yet has certain features that make it typical of a wide variety of algorithms.

EUCLIDEAM ALGORITHM, SUBTRACTION VERSION: Compute integers $x_1, x_2,$ ..., as follows. x_1 and x_2 are, respectively, the first and second inputs. For each $i \geqq 2$, when the sequence has been computed as far as x_i:

     1. If $x_i = 0$, halt and take x_{i-1} as output.
     2. Otherwise, if $x_{i-1} < x_i$, put $x_{i+1} = x_{i-1}$.
     3. Otherwise, put $x_{i+1} = x_{i-1} - x_i$.

For example, if the two inputs are 352 and 154, the sequence of x's will come out to be

$$352, \quad 154, \quad 198, \quad 154, \quad 44, \quad 110, \quad 44, \quad 66, \quad 44, \quad 22, \quad 22, \quad 0$$

and thus the output will be 22, which is therefore the greatest common divisor of 352 and 154.

EUCLIDEAN ALGORITHM, REMAINDER VERSION: The same as the subtraction version, except that alternative 3 is replaced by:

     3′. Otherwise, put $x_{i+1} =$ the remainder when x_{i-1} is divided by x_i.

For this version of the algorithm, the two inputs 352 and 154 will yield the following sequence of x's:

$$352, \quad 154, \quad 44, \quad 22, \quad 0$$

Again the output is 22. In general, the remainder version will produce a sequence of x's that is a subsequence of the sequence of x's produced by the subtraction version, and (of course) the same output, which is the greatest common divisor of the two inputs. (One could say that remainders are actually computed in the subtraction version by continued subtraction of the divisor from the dividend. For example, 44 must be subtracted from 154 three times before 22 is obtained, which is the remainder when 154 is divided by 44.)

Note that the subtraction version presupposes two algorithms as parts, one for comparison and one for subtraction. Thus what has been written is not the fully written algorithm.

The remainder version is more efficient because the sequence it produces is generally shorter. (Repeated subtraction is generally an inefficient way to do division.) On the other hand, it makes use of a division algorithm which is more involved than either subtraction or comparison. It should be noted that, in the remainder version, alternative 2 never arises for $i > 2$, since the remainder of a division is less than the divisor. Furthermore, alternative 2 could be eliminated completely, since if $x_1 < x_2$, then the remainder when x_1 is divided by x_2 is x_1.

We have stated these algorithms in a way that is convenient for our theoretical, expository purpose. If one has an actual implementation in mind, one can make suitable variations. For one thing, after x_{i+1} has been computed, x_{i-1} can be discarded since it is no longer needed.

The Euclidean algorithm has certain important features that the more elementary algorithms discussed in Section 1.2.1 do not have. In execution, one does not proceed by doing a predictable number of steps clearly foreseen in advance. After each step, one must make an observation that determines which of three things to do. Consequently, one cannot tell simply by looking at the two numbers precisely how long the execution will take, as one can when one adds two numbers or evaluates a formula made up from the elementary mathematical operations.

Many books on computer programming use the Euclidean algorithm as an example in their first chapter. It is indeed an excellent example. We focus on the subtraction version because it is conceptually simpler than the remainder version, which contains the involved division algorithm as a part.

The theory of computability is concerned not only with finding algorithms for problems, but also with proving in each case that what is found is an algorithm for the problem as posed. We give such a proof for the Euclidean algorithm in Appendix I.

A Labyrinth Algorithm 1.2.3

Two widespread preconceptions are that algorithms are about numbers and that algorithms are run on computers. The fact is that there are many practical algorithms that have nothing to do with numbers; algorithms having to do with alphabetic characters, such as sorting and searching, are examples, as are algorithms for dealing with structures, including data structures, graphs, and character strings. Computer applications of such algorithms are prevalent and well known.

A computer program may be an algorithm, and many algorithms can be conveniently written as computer programs. There are, however, algorithms covered by our definition that for one reason or another are not intended, and are not suitable, for use on a computer.

Next, we present an algorithm for ascertaining whether or not a certain object is in a labyrinth, an algorithm that is not about numbers and, although it could be programmed, would be quite inefficient on a computer. The algorithm is suitable only in situations where the entire labyrinth cannot be read into the memory of a computer; one must get the answer to the question by actually searching in the labyrinth.

In order to gain mathematical precision, we depict the labyrinth as a graph. We must begin with a few graph-theoretic definitions.

Definition: A *graph* is an ordered pair (N, E), where N is a finite set of *nodes* and E is a finite set of *edges*. Each edge connects two distinct nodes.

For example, Fig. 1.2.1 is a graph whose nodes and edges are labeled by numbers and letters, respectively. However, by this definition Fig. 1.2.2 is not a graph, since one of the edges connects a node to itself. For most purposes (including the representation of labyrinths) we can get by with Fig. 1.2.3 in place of Fig. 1.2.2.

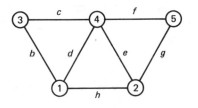

Figure 1.2.1

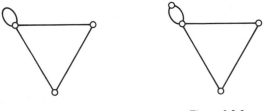

Figure 1.2.2   *Figure 1.2.3*

Definition: A *walk* in a graph is a sequence $N_0, E_1, N_1, \ldots, E_n, N_n$, where $n \geq 0$ and each E_i is an edge connecting nodes N_{i-1} and N_i. We say that this is a walk *from N_0 to N_n*. If $n = 0$, then the walk is the *null walk* from N_0 to N_0.

Definition: A *path* from node N_0 to node N_n in a graph is a walk $N_0, E_1,$ $N_1, \ldots, E_n, N_n$, where, for $i \neq j$, $N_i \neq N_j$. If $n = 0$, the path is the *null path* at N_0.

Definition: A graph is *connected* if for any two nodes there is a path from one to the other.

(We shall deal with graphs in several places in this book. Our use of the terms *walk* and *path* are in accord with Harary [1969]. A *path* is defined as a "direct" walk from one node to another without "side trips." The word "walk" suggests an activity, and the word "path" suggests a part of the graph on which this activity takes place. In many books and papers, the term "path" is used in the way we use the term "walk.")

We assume that the graph representing the labyrinth is connected, that there is an origin node labeled A, and that one of the edges from A is clearly identified as the *leading edge*. There may or may not be a target node labeled T. We wish to have an algorithm for a person who travels through the graph beginning at A, determines whether or not there is a node labeled T, and returns to A with the answer. We assume that the person has no overall view of the graph and no idea of its size except that it is finite and connected.

The person going through the graph needs to keep track of where he has been so that (1) he does not search the same places over and over again, and (2) he does not leave some places unvisited. Furthermore, he must be able to get back to A at the end. We must keep in mind that the graph is too large for person to learn, the nodes may not be distinguishable from one another by their appearance, and the same for the edges.

All this would be feasible if the person could lay out a string along his journey, and at certain times go back along the string. This idea has merit, but we prefer to substitute the idea of coloring edges in the search process.

Thus we assume that the person can color and recolor the edges, using the two colors yellow and red, and that these colors are not present in the graph before he begins.

We assume, furthermore, that the graph is on a flat surface, and that the person when he reaches a node can order the edges leading away from that node in some fashion, beginning with the edge he has just traversed; to be definite we shall assume that this order is the clockwise ordering. (Any other order on all the edges touching a node would serve as well. Planarity is not necessary if some other ordering is available.)

A step in this algorithm begins at a node; the person remembers which edge he has just traversed, observes the colors of the edges touching the node, and then decides either to halt or else to traverse one of the edges (coloring it as he goes) to an adjacent node, where the next such step begins.

The algorithm has two phases; a search phase and a return phase. The latter is entered only after a node labeled T has been found.

LABYRINTH ALGORITHM: At the beginning, at *A*, observe whether or not this node is also labeled *T*. If it is, halt with an affirmative answer. If not, traverse the leading edge, painting it yellow, and enter the search phase.

Search phase: At each step, go through the following list of five possibilities, in order, determining your move by the first possibility in the list that fits.

    1. If the node is labeled *T*, go to the return-affirmative phase.

    2. Otherwise, if the edge just traversed and in addition at least one other edge at the node are yellow, then return along the edge just traversed, coloring it red.

    3. Otherwise, if there is at least one uncolored edge leading from the node, traverse the first such edge clockwise from the edge just traversed, coloring it yellow.

    4. Otherwise, if the node is labeled *A*, halt. The answer is that there is no node labeled *T* in the graph.

    5. Otherwise, traverse the unique yellow edge leaving the node, coloring it red.

Return-affirmative phase: If the node is not labeled *A*, traverse the one and only one yellow edge, coloring it red. If the node is *A*, halt: the answer is "yes."

(This algorithm is taken from Chapter III of Trakhtenbrot [1963], where it is related to the Greek myth of the hero Theseus and his attempt to find and kill the Minotaur in a labyrinth, aided by the goddess Ariadne.)

1.2.4 Labyrinth Algorithm : Discussion

In Appendix II, this organized set of commands is proved to be an algorithm for the problem of determining whether some node in a given graph is labeled *T*. It should be observed that there is more to be proved here than in the case of the Euclidean algorithm. It is not obvious that the so-called labyrinth algorithm is a procedure, let alone an algorithm. That is, it is not obvious that it determines a course of action for each step. Before we can conclude that it does, we must prove that whenever the person is at a node *N*, either in the search phase when none of the conditions 1 to 4 hold, or in the return-affirmative phase with $N \neq A$, there does exist a unique yellow edge leaving that node. For unless such an edge exists in those situations, there is no direction for him.

    One helpful lemma in the proof states that the yellow edges in the order in which they were colored always constitute (i.e., are the edges of) a walk from *A* to the person's present position. To understand the ordering of possibilities in the search phase, it is helpful to imagine in place of the yellow coloring a string with one end fixed at node *A*. The person has the spool containing this string, sometimes unwinding it as he traverses a new edge, and other times rewinding it (traversing already covered ground). But when he rewinds, he must color the edge red to indicate that he has been there.

After checking to see whether T is at that node, the person checks for the presence of another part of the string, indicating that he has just created a loop in the string. If so, he rewinds—one of the guiding principles behind the algorithm is to keep order by not allowing such loops to remain. If he does not find another part of the string, he checks to see if there is an unvisited edge, in which case he traverses that edge unwinding the string. If not, he checks for the label A, in which case he concludes that he has visited the entire graph without finding T. In the event that all four of these checks turn out to be negative, he does the only thing he can do, namely go back along the string and rewind.

When the person is at A in the search phase, with all the string rewound and no untraveled edges from A, he knows that the whole graph has been searched. The justification for this inference is that, while he was in the search phase, there were only two circumstances when he would leave a node with an unvisited edge by way of an already visited edge. One is the circumstance of being at the node labeled T (in which case he would have left the search phase with the answer "yes"), and the other is the circumstance of a loop in the string. In the latter circumstance he would leave the node by rewinding, knowing that he would return there later with the string unlooped, at which time he could traverse one of the unvisited edges leading from that node.

As an example, assume that the graph is as in Fig. 1.2.4, in which no node is labeled T. The edges are numbered to show the journey. Note that numbers 2, 3, 7, 8, 9, 10, 11, and 13 were in response to condition 3; numbers 4, 12, and 14 were in response to condition 2; and numbers 5, 6, 15, 16, 17, and 18 were in response to condition 5.

To help clarify this example, we show in Fig. 1.2.5 the graph with edge

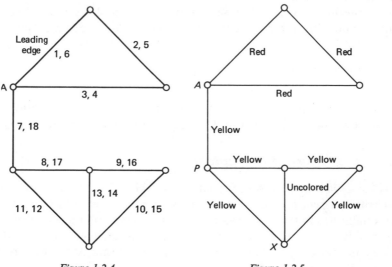

Figure 1.2.4   Figure 1.2.5

coloring indicated just after step 11, with the person's present position labeled
P and his immediately preceding position labeled X. Finding yellow corridors
at node P, besides the one just traversed, the person will act on condition 2,
returning to node X, coloring the edge red.

When the person follows the command of possibility 3, he must traverse
an uncolored edge. From the point of view of the efficacy of the algorithm, it
does not matter which uncolored edge is traversed if there are more than one.
The only reason for picking the first such edge (clockwise from the one just
traversed) is to have a definite command in order to satisfy the condition of
determinism. It is for a similar reason that we have one of the edges leaving
node A designated as the *leading edge*.

If we omit the leading-edge condition and allow the agent to make a free
choice of which uncolored edge to traverse at the beginning and later in possibility 3, we would have an incompletely specified algorithm.

This algorithm is appropriate only in a situation in which the input, which
is the entire graph, cannot be read into a computer, onto a piece of paper, or
into a person's mind. The very word "input" (which shows our bias in terminology toward computer application) is inappropriate in this situation because
it is not *put* into anything. If the graph representing the labyrinth were read into
a computer, the computer would not need such an elaborate algorithm to tell
whether or not there is a node labeled T. Even if we made the problem more
difficult, such as by requiring that there be a printout of the path from A to T,
an efficient algorithm for computer application would be quite different.

A significant fact about this algorithm is that the person need not remember
anything as he travels for any indefinite length of time, except the algorithm
itself. The only other demand the algorithm places on his memory is that he
keep track for the moment of which edge he traversed last. If we decide to
replace the person by a robot, then we could get by with quite a simple robot.
(More precisely, once the sensory and motor problems are solved for the
construction of the robot, the computer part of the robot could be quite simple.)

1.3   DESCRIPTIVE OUTLINE OF THE BOOK

Having discussed the concept of algorithm rather thoroughly in Sections 1.1 and
1.2, we are now in a position to describe the contents of the book as a whole.

1.3.1   The Theory of Computability

This theory is concerned with formalisms in which algorithms can be expressed,
and with mathematical characterizations of computable functions. It became
well established in the 1930s when several mathematically precise definitions of
the intuitive notion of *algorithmically computable function* were offered. It was
proved mathematically that a function over the nonnegative integers is com-

putable by a Turing machine if and only if it is definable by a set of equations in a certain way (*equationally definable*). Then it was argued convincingly, although it was not subject to mathematical proof, that any algorithmic function is computable by a Turing machine and equationally definable (Church's thesis). Finally, it was proved that Church's thesis implies that certain specific problems are undecidable. This exciting contribution to the mathematical logic of the 1930s has become one of the foundations of the theoretical computer science of today.

(A third mathematically precise definition, not discussed in this book, was that of being computable in the lambda calculus, which has received attention recently in the area of programming-language semantics and program verification.)

We shall present these results in this book, departing in some ways from the treatment of the 1930s. Two types of formalisms for algorithms will be presented, Turing machines (Chapter 2) and the foundational programming languages (Chapter 3), the latter receiving more attention than the former. In Chapter 4 we study certain ways of defining computable functions of nonnegative integers, and prove that all functions so definable are computable in the foundational programming languages. In Chapter 5 we discuss the proof of the converse to this result and go on to a variant of Church's thesis, which lays the basis for the proof in Chapter 6 that certain problems are unsolvable.

Our treatment is brought up to date by the foundational programming languages of Chapter 3, which differ from programming languages used in actual computing in being greatly simplified for theoretical purposes. Many contemporary computability theorists favor the use of these foundational programming languages over Turing machines, because they are closer to the computing practice of today and more convenient for writing algorithms.

On the other hand, Turing machines are still widely used for many theoretical purposes, and for that reason we treat them briefly in Chapter 2. They represent the simplest known model of computation that offers a complete picture of what happens during the execution of an algorithm.

Although many important algorithms deal with nonnumerical subject matter, in Chapters 2 to 4 we confine our attention exclusively to the domain of the nonnegative integers. The fact that all data in digital computers are represented by bit patterns, which in turn represent numbers in binary, gives partial justification for our restriction. Complete justification is given in Chapter 5 with the demonstration that Gödel numbers can be assigned to any organized set of discrete structures, so that algorithms about the latter can be readily constructed from algorithms about the former.

We do get a biased view of algorithms by considering only a numerical domain, but this disadvantage is offset by the advantage of having a brief elementary survey of the important facts about the theory of computability. Later in the book, in Chapters 7 to 9, we examine some interesting nonnumerical algorithms.

Some computer scientists think of the theory of computability as linked to computational complexity, a study that has emerged more recently. Although computational complexity is outside the scope of this book, its general nature is discussed in Appendix IV, together with the various criteria by which algorithms are generally judged.

1.3.2 Formal Languages and Automata

The importance of languages and formalisms for algorithms makes it desirable to extend the scope of this book beyond computability to formal languages and automata.

An *automaton* is a computational model such as a computer, except that the word is usually reserved for machine models of which there are no existing physical instances. The Turing machine is a good example of an automaton, the first of many to be discussed in this book. Other types of automata will emerge in Chapters 3, 8, and 9.

The word "automaton" suggests the idea of a robot; indeed, *automata theory* embraces many things that will not be discussed in this book, such as robotics and cellular models for growth and reproduction. Only those automata having to do with the problems of computability and formal languages will be discussed, and even then the selection will be quite limited.

Formal languages are, roughly speaking, specially constructed languages with precise sets of rules, two common types being programming languages and the formal systems of symbolic logic. The main objective of our treatment of formal languages (Appendix III, Chapters 7 to 9) is to present those fundamental aspects that have a bearing on the functioning of programming languages, relative to a user and relative to a machine.

Appendix III is a philosophical introduction to formal languages. In Chapter 7 we discuss the concept of a context-free grammar for a formal language; in Chapter 8, the problem of ambiguity and various ways of parsing strings (including a special automaton) in terms of these grammars; in Chapter 9, a well-known subclass of the class of context-free languages, namely the regular languages, and their relationship to finite automata, transition graphs, and regular expressions.

It is to be emphasized that although formal languages are investigated intensively in the later chapters, language considerations will be important in the earlier chapters as well. The difference, one might say, is that in the earlier chapters on computability we are concerned about formal languages for algorithms, whereas in the later chapters we are concerned with algorithms for formal languages. (Thus Appendix III is as relevant to Chapters 3 and 4 as it is to Chapters 7 and 8.)

Turing Machines 2

Each of Chapters 2 to 4 presents a certain formalism for expressing algorithms. The present brief chapter on Turing machines can be omitted without loss of continuity.

Alan Mathieson Turing put forth his concept of computing machine in his famous 1936 paper, which was an integral part of the formation of the theory of computability. These machines are still the subject of research in computer science, even though they are not suitable for practical computing.

As an explication of the concept of algorithm, the concept of Turing machine is particularly helpful in offering a clear and realistic demarcation of what constitutes a single step of execution. The problem of how to separate the steps from one another in a step-by-step procedure could be discussed only vaguely in Chapter 1. But when a previously vague algorithm is put into the form of a Turing-machine table, all the vagueness disappears: exactly what the executor must do in execution is made perfectly precise.

DESIGNING SIMPLE TURING MACHINES 2.1

In this section we explain the rudiments of Turing machines and their operation. We then design a machine that copies a string of characters, and machines to compute some arithmetic functions.

The Model 2.1.1

A Turing machine consists of two parts, an active machine with a reading and writing head, and a passive tape from which the machine reads and on which it writes. The one-dimensional tape is divided into squares and is conceived of as being infinite in both directions: that is, it has no left end and no right end. The machine proper is capable of assuming any of a finite number of states. Looking at a square of the tape which may or may not have symbol written upon it, the machine either halts or acts, according to what it reads and the state that it is in at the time that it reads. Its action consists of at most four things: (1) it may or may not erase the symbol that it sees at the square that it is scanning; (2) having erased or having found the square blank, it may or may not print a new symbol on that square; (3) it may move one square to the left or one square to the right, or it may stay where it is on the tape; and (4) it may change to a new state. We think of the machine's head moving on a stationary tape, although most machinery moves the tape with the head stationary.

The interval of time during which the machine does these (at most) four things is a *time cycle*. After it completes a time cycle, it begins a new one, again looking at a square of the tape in one of its states. The complete action during a time cycle, which might be a halt, is determined by the state that the machine is in at the beginning of the cycle, and the symbol that is read. (Thus the Turing machine we consider is the *deterministic Turing machine*, and is to be distinguished from the nondeterministic Turing machine, which is also found in the literature.)

Thus, during a time cycle, the Turing machine executes at least one and at most four steps of its step-by-step procedure. In the remainder of this chapter, we shall no longer refer to the steps of a computation, referring instead to time cycles.

The set of characters that the machine is capable of reading or writing on the squares of the tape is called the *machine alphabet*, which must be finite. For convenience, the blank is assumed to be one of these characters. The set of states assumed by the active machine is also finite, so that a summary of the rules by means of which the machine acts can be given as a table. Figure 2.1.1 is our first example; it is a table for a Turing machine for addition.

Character State	B	/	*
q_1			Rq_2
q_2		R	Rq_3
q_3	Lq_4	R	
q_4		BLq_5	Bq_6
q_5		L	$/q_6$
q_6			

Figure 2.1.1

This machine has six states and an alphabet of three characters, including the blank, which is symbolized by the capital B. Throughout this chapter "B" is used in this way; thus it is never a character is the machine alphabet, but a symbol we use to represent a blank square.

A place in the table with no entry means that, when the machine is in that state scanning the indicated character, it halts. Thus it halts whenever it is in state q_6, whenever it is scanning a blank square in any state other than q_3, in state q_1 scanning a stroke /, or in state q_3 scanning an asterisk *. In all other cases, it begins a time cycle; what happens during that time cycle is indicated precisely by what is written in the entry opposite the state and under the character scanned.

When it is in state q_4 scanning a stroke, it will erase the stroke, move one square to the left, and go into state q_5. The notation of the table ignores the difference between erasing and writing. Both are examples of something more general, namely changing a character from something to something else.

When the machine is in state q_5 scanning an asterisk, it changes the asterisk to a stroke, and goes into state q_6, without moving left or right (since neither L nor R appears in that entry table). In certain other entries, no new character is written, which means that the machine leaves the character unmodified. For example, the machine in q_2 scanning an asterisk leaves the asterisk there and goes to the right in state q_3. The machine in q_2 scanning a stroke simply moves right; it neither changes the character nor changes state.

Total Configurations; Computations   2.1.2

Definition: The *total configuration* of a Turing machine at a given time is the information about what is written on every square of the tape, which square the head of the machine is scanning, and which state the machine is in.

We shall present the total configuration in diagrammatic form by showing the tape, square for square, assuming that only finitely many of them are nonblank, with an arrow pointing to the scanned square, and with the state written beneath the arrow (e.g., Figs. 2.1.2, 2.1.4, and 2.1.5).

We now give a sample history of the machine of Fig. 2.1.1, beginning with the total configuration shown in Fig. 2.1.2.

The action of the machine during the first eight time cycles consists of a general movement to the right, ending with a movement one square to the left, without any change of characters on any of the squares. This movement is indicated in Fig. 2.1.3, which actually shows nine consecutive total configurations.

The machine is now scanning the rightmost nonblank square in state q_4. This time the machine erases and moves one square to the left in q_5 (Fig. 2.1.4).

Again the machine moves left until it reaches the asterisk. It thereupon changes the asterisk to a stroke, and halts in state q_6 (Fig. 2.1.5).

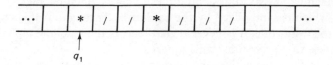

Figure 2 1.2

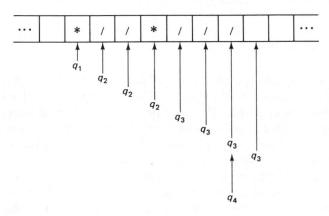

Figure 2.1.3

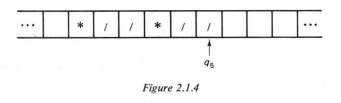

Figure 2.1.4

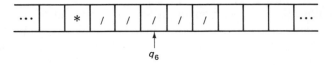

Figure 2.1.5

Definition: A *computation* of a Turing machine is a sequence of total configurations occurring in the operation of the machine, ending in a halt. The first total configuration is called the *initial configuration* of the computation; the string that is then on that portion of the tape beginning with the first non-blank square and ending with the last nonblank square is the input to the computation. The *output*, correspondingly, is the string on the tape when the machine halts, beginning with the first nonblank square and ending with the last nonblank square. (We shall never have occasion to begin a Turing machine on a tape with infinitely many characters written on it.)

As we shall explain in Section 2.1.4, the sample computation just considered is a computation of $2 + 3 = 5$.

Copying 2.1.3

When one designs a Turing machine to accomplish something, one is forced to become aware of everything that is involved in successful accomplishment in all possible cases. We shall now see how to design a Turing machine that can copy what is written on its tape onto a blank portion of the same tape. The difficulty in our design problem is that the Turing machine may have only a certain fixed number of states, but still must be able to copy strings that are arbitrarily long.

In order to remove some of the complications of our task, without obscuring the essential difficulties, we assume that what is written on the tape is a string over the two-letter alphabet $\{b, c\}$.

We first ask: How would a human being copy a string of b's and c's written on a portion of the tape onto another portion of the tape? One method that works up to a certain point is: Read it, remember it, and then write it from memory. For most people this method becomes difficult or impossible for a string of about 15 or more characters.

If the string is much longer than that, the best method seems to be the following: Read and remember the first (say) five characters, go to where they are to be written, and write them from memory. Then do the same to the next five characters, and so forth, until the whole string is copied. (Some people will make mistakes if they repeatedly attempt to retain more than five characters.) If the string is long, the person must be able to leave a mark on the original string each time (say a check mark just above the last character in the set of five that he is copying) so that he can know where to come back to next time. With this device, a person should be able to copy a string of any length, limited only by his ability to sustain an interest in the task.

In designing the Turing machine to do this job, we shall try to get as simple a Turing machine as possible and not worry about how efficient the operation is. We shall not, for example, be concerned with how long the copying operation takes—except to make one brief remark after we have completed our design.

To simplify the machine, we shall have it remember only one character at a time, which will mean that it will have to make a complete round trip on the tape from the reading area to the copy area for each character that it copies. It will check off each character that it is about to copy, so that it knows where to come back to next time.

The machine alphabet will include besides the b and c of the original string, the characters y (which means a checked b) and z (a checked c), and an asterisk that will separate the portion of the tape containing the original string from the copy. In effect, when the machine changes b to y, it is doing what the human agent does in checking the b. At the end the machine will change all the y's to b's and all the z's to c's, corresponding to the human operation of going through and erasing all check marks.

The Turing machine that copies is given in Fig. 2.1.6. We leave it to the reader to verify that, if the machine is given a tape with a string W of b's and c's written on it, with the head left-justified on the string and the machine in state q_1, then the machine will compute and eventually halt with W*W on the tape, the second W having been copied from the first. Note that if the machine is begun in state q_1 with an empty tape, it will halt with a single asterisk on an otherwise blank tape; this computation is the copying of the null string, with the asterisk indicating as usual the marker between the original string and the copy.

Informal description		b	c	y	z	B	*
Place asterisk	q_1	R	R			*Lq_2	
Return	q_2	L	L	L	L	Rq_3	L
Look for unchecked b or c	q_3	yRq_b	zRq_c	R	R		Lq_4
Copy b	q_b	R	R	R	R	bLq_2	R
Copy c	q_c	R	R	R	R	cLq_2	R
Erase checks	q_4			bL	cL		

Figure 2.1.6

This machine, therefore, does the task we set out to construct it to do, but we should also note that there are certain restrictions that we must place on the input tape to ensure correct operation. The strings of b's and c's must be on consecutive squares of the tape, with no blanks intervening. For this machine "assumes" that the string has ended when it sees the first blank square. If there are any more b's and c's anywhere to the right of this blank square, it will not count them as part of the string to be copied. Furthermore, we must make sure that only b's and c's appear in the string to be copied. The machine simply does not "know" what to do if it should see a d, for example.

2.1.4 Nonnegative Integers

Because we are not concerned with the efficiency of Turing machines, we shall represent numbers by the tally code, which is sometimes called the "unary number system." In our version of this code, the numeral representing the integer i is a string consisting of an asterisk followed by i strokes. Thus the number zero is represented by asterisk alone, one by */, two by *//, and so on. A finite sequence of nonnegative integers is represented on a tape by the numerals side by side, with no spaces or commas between. For example, the sequence 2, 5, 0, 1 is represented by the tape as

$$* / / * / / / / / * * /$$

and the sequence 0, 0 is represented by the tape as

$$* *$$

(Strictly speaking, these are not tapes but strings. We shall follow the practice of indicating a tape by writing the string of characters beginning with the first nonblank square and ending with the last nonblank square.)

Definition: A Turing machine M with a designated *initial state* q_1 *computes* a function f on n nonnegative integral arguments if M behaves as follows for each ordered n-tuple of nonnegative integers $(i_1, i_2, \ldots, i_n)$: M beginning in the initial state left-justified on an input tape representing the sequence $i_1, i_2, \ldots, i_n$ will eventually halt, at which time the output tape will contain a single numeral representing the function value $f(i_1, i_2, \ldots, i_n)$.

For example, the Turing machine of Fig. 2.1.1 represents the two-argument addition function. When this machine is begun left-justified on a tape representing (i_1, i_2), it will eventually halt with the numeral representing $i_1 + i_2$ written on it and nothing else. We carried this computation through for $i_1 = 2$ and $i_2 = 3$ in Section 2.1.2. We leave it to the reader to see that the computation is carried out by the machine for all values of i_1 and i_2, even when i_1 or i_2 or both are zero.

The operation of the Turing machine of Fig. 2.1.1 is quite simple. It either erases a stroke at the right end and replaces the second asterisk by a stroke, or else simply erases that asterisk if the second argument is zero. We now construct a Turing machine to compute the *floored subtraction function* (which will be dealt with in more detail in Chapter 4), defined as follows:

$$\dot-(i, j) = \begin{cases} i - j & \text{if } i \geq j \\ 0 & \text{if } i < j \end{cases}$$

Note that if i and j are nonnegative integers, then $\dot-(i, j)$ is also a nonnegative integer.

Our machine to compute this function in effect goes through a cancellation loop for every stroke in the numeral representing j. Each time that the machine goes through this loop it erases a stroke from the j numeral and then a stroke from the i numeral, if any. It decides to come out of this loop when there are no more strokes in the j numeral.

The machine is given by the table of Fig. 2.1.7. It begins in the initial state q_1, by placing an asterisk at the right end of the tape. (The purpose of this third asterisk will be explained below.) Then it goes in state q_2 to the middle asterisk. Thereafter the machine is generally in a loop in which it erases first a stroke from the right of the middle asterisk and then a stroke from its left.

The loop consists of the states q_{11}, q_{12}, q_{13}, and q_{14} which the machine goes through in that order. In q_{11} the machine looks for and erases a stroke from the j numeral. Then in q_{12} it goes left, changing to q_{13} at the asterisk. In state q_{13} it goes left, looking for either the first asterisk or a stroke, in the latter case erasing the stroke that it finds. Then in q_{14} it goes right, looking for the second asterisk again, whereupon it goes right again in q_{11}.

		B	/	*
Beginning	q_1	$*Lq_2$	R	R
	q_2		L	Rq_{11}
Cancellation loop	q_{11}	R	BLq_{12}	BLq_{21}
	q_{12}	L	L	Lq_{13}
	q_{13}	L	BRq_{14}	Rq_{14}
	q_{14}	R	R	Rq_{11}
End	q_{21}	L		BLq_{22}
	q_{22}	L	L	

Figure 2.1.7

While the machine is going right in state q_{11} looking for a stroke in the j numeral, if it encounters instead the third asterisk, then it leaves the loop of states. Here we see why the third asterisk is necessary: It enables the machine to "know" that all the strokes in the j numeral have been erased. This third asterisk is in effect a right end marker. Sometimes the first blank square to the right can be used as a right end marker; in this case it cannot, because a blank square may be a square from which a stroke has been erased with further strokes to its right.

In state q_{21} (having left the loop and having erased the third asterisk) it goes left, looking for the second asterisk and erases that. It then goes into the last state q_{22}, in which it goes left to halt at the first asterisk.

We leave it to the reader to verify that this machine computes floored subtraction by considering three cases: (1) $i \geq j = 0$, (2) $i \geq j > 0$, and (3) $i < j$.

The cancellation idea that we used in designing the Turing machine for floored subtraction in Section 2.1.4 is, in a way, just the opposite of the idea of copying that we developed in Section 2.1.3. There is another idea that is quite useful in designing Turing machines, namely the idea of iteration. We shall now use this idea to construct a Turing machine to compute multiplication.

We use the well-known fact that multiplication is iterated addition. Four times five, for example, equals the sum of four fives. We begin by redesigning the addition machine of Fig. 2.1.1 as machine A of Fig. 2.1.8, which does not quite satisfy the definition in Section 2.1.4 of the computation of a function, but which will be useful as part of a machine that multiplies.

		B	/	c	*
Go to second asterisk	q_A				Rq_{10}
	q_{10}		R		Lq_{11}
Copy cycle	q_{11}		cRq_{12}	L	Rq_{21}
	q_{12}			R	Rq_{13}
	q_{13}	$/Lq_{14}$	R		
	q_{14}		L		Lq_{11}
Change c's to strokes	q_{21}			/R	Lq_{22}
Halt at first asterisk	q_{22}		L		

Figure 2.1.8

The initial state of machine A is q_A. This machine is more like the copying machine of Fig. 2.1.6 than the addition machine of Fig. 2.1.1. It adds two numbers by copying the strokes in the first into the squares just after the strokes of the second, using the auxiliary character c, to indicate a stroke that it has copied. After it has finished this copying operation, it changes the c's back to strokes.

We leave it to the reader to verify (by hand-simulating the machine for a few sample inputs) that if machine A is begun in state q_A left-justified on a tape containing the input representing the sequence i, j, it will eventually halt with the output representing the sequence $i, j + i$ on the tape. For example, if it begins with the tape $* / / / * / / / /$, it will eventually halt with $* / / / * / / / / / / /$

on the tape. It is important also to observe that the machine halts left-justified on the tape in state q_{22}, never having gone to the left of the left asterisk.

We are now ready to construct machine M to compute multiplication, using machine A as a part. We explain our plan for machine M in terms of an example. If the machine is given the tape * / / / * / / / /, we shall have the machine compute "four times three" by beginning at zero and then adding 4 three times. Placing an asterisk at the right end of the tape gives us the initial zero: * / / / * / / / / *. The machine now has a sequence of three numerals on its tape: 3, 4, 0. It now erases one of the strokes from the first numeral and goes to the second asterisk in state q_A. The result is that the machine will eventually come back to this second asterisk in state q_{22}. having added the four to the zero. The tape will then be as follows:

$$* \ / \ / \ B \ * \ / \ / \ / \ / \ * \ / \ / \quad /$$

It now erases another stroke and again adds the four to the third numeral. The result is the tape

$$* \ / \ B \ B \ * \ / \ / \ / \ / \ * \ / \ / \ / \ / \ / \ / \ /$$

Doing this the third time the tape becomes

$$* \ B \ B \ B \ * \ / \ / \ / \ / \ * \ / \ / \ / \ / \ / \ / \ / \ / \ / \ / \ / \ /$$

It remains only to erase everything to the left of the third asterisk, so that just the numeral for 12 will be on the tape.

The table for machine M is given in Fig. 2.1.9. The states q_A through q_{22} inclusive represent the part of machine M that is almost identical to machine A. The exceptions are that q_A is no longer the initial state, and halting does not occur in q_{22}. Machine M will get into state q_A when it "wants" to perform an addition. When it reaches state q_{22} and is scanning an asterisk, it "knows" that this addition is complete; hence the new entry in the q_{22} row under the asterisk heading.

It is left to the reader to verify that machine M computes multiplication for all appropriate inputs. The reader interested in economy will note that states q_2 and q_{22} are exact duplicates, so one of them can be disposed of. A bit more subtle is the fact that states q_4 and q_A can be merged together into a single state. Thus the 14-state machine M can be readily simplified to a 12-state machine.

This method of construction of a machine using another as part is used in the advanced theory to prove that a whole class of functions is computable by Turing machines. Such proofs for the foundational programming languages rather than Turing machines will be given in Section 4.5. Meanwhile we note that a Turing machine that computes exponentiation can be constructed from M in the same way that M is constructed from A (Exercise 12), since exponentiation is iterated multiplication.

		B	/	c	*
Prepare	q_1	*Lq_2	R		R
	q_2		L		Lq_3
Delete stroke	q_3	L	BRq_4		⟨BRq_{31}⟩ *3 a3..*
To second asterisk	q_4	R			q_A
Machine A part	q_A				Rq_{10}
	q_{10}		R		Lq_{11}
	q_{11}		cRq_{12}	L	Rq_{21}
	q_{12}			R	Rq_{13}
	q_{13}	/Lq_{14}	R		
	q_{14}		L		Lq_{11}
	q_{21}			/R	Lq_{22}
	q_{22}		L		Lq_3
Clean up tape and halt	q_{31}	R *⁄R*			⟨BRq_{32}⟩
	q_{32}		⁄BR		*4\0 8*

Figure 2.1.9

Exercises 2.1.6

Group I

These computations are similar to the copying machine of Section 2.1.3. In each case, design a Turing machine which, when given a string W over the alphabet $\{c, d\}$, will transform the tape into the output tape as indicated. The input string W is to be written on consecutive squares of an otherwise blank tape, and your machine is to begin in state q_1 on the leftmost nonblank square. Make sure that your machine computes correctly for every string W of length one or more over the alphabet $\{c, d\}$.

There is no restriction on how much tape you may use in the computation, or on which particular set of squares in reference to the input location the output string appears on. However, the output must appear exactly as specified, which may require that the machine "clean up" excess characters before halting. Nothing but the output should be on the tape at the halt.

1. The output is the string W written backwards on consecutive squares.

2. The output is a string written on consecutive squares with the same number of c's, and with the same number of d's, as the input W; but all the c's in the output string are to the left of all the d's. (In other words, the output is the input string with the characters put into alphabetic order.)

3. The output is the string W written on the tape with a single blank space between each pair of adjacent characters. Sample input and output are given in Fig. 2.1.10.

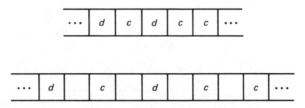

Figure 2.1.10

4. The output consists of the string W (as written as input) followed without a blank by (1) *MORE, if there are more c's than d's in W, (2) *EQUAL, if there are as many c's as d's, or (3) *LESS, if there are fewer c's than d's.

The input alphabet for Exercises 5 to 7 is extended to include the asterisk. The input is a string of the form

$$*W_1*W_2*W_3* \ldots *W_n$$

written on consecutive squares, where $n \geq 4$ and each W_i is a nonnull string over the alphabet $\{c, d\}$. The input is to be thought of as a sequence of strings over alphabet $\{c, d\}$.

5. The output is $*W_1*W_3*W_2*W_4* \ldots *W_n$ written on consecutive squares. (In other words, the second and third strings of the sequence are interchanged.)

6. The output is $*W_1*W_2* \ldots *W_n*// \ldots /$, where the number of strokes equals the length of the longest string among the W_i's.

7. (*Long and difficult*) The output is $*W_{i_1}*W_{i_2}* \ldots *W_{i_n}$ written on consecutive squares, where the sequence $W_{i_1}, W_{i_2}, \ldots, W_{i_n}$ is the sequence $W_1, W_2, \ldots, W_n$ sorted into alphabetic order.

Group II

Design Turing machines to compute the following functions according to the conventions laid down in Section 2.1.4.

8. Absolute difference:

$$|i_1 - i_2| = \begin{cases} i_1 - i_2 & \text{if } i_1 \geq i_2 \\ i_2 - i_1 & \text{if } i_1 < i_2 \end{cases}$$

9. $\mathrm{QU}(i_1, i_2) =$ the quotient when i_1 is divided by i_2. [Sometimes written as $[i_1/i_2]$ or $\lfloor i_1/i_2 \rfloor$, the quotient is the greatest integer not greater than i_1/i_2. You may assume what you like about the values of $\mathrm{QU}(i_1, i_2)$ for $i_2 = 0$.]

10. REM(i_1, i_2) = the remainder when i_1 is divided by i_2. You may assume what you like about the values of REM(i_1, i_2) for $i_2 = 0$. [For $i_2 \neq 0$, REM(i_1, i_2) = $i_1 - i_2$ QU(i_1, i_2).]

11. MIN($x_1, \ldots, x_n$) = the smallest value among $x_1, \ldots, x_n$. (Your Turing machine should work for any value of $n \geqq 2$, a generalization of the definition in Section 2.1.4.)

12. Exponentiation: $i_1^{i_2}$. Assume that $0^0 = 1$. (*Hint:* Observe that exponentiation is the iteration of multiplication, and imitate the construction method in Section 2.1.5.)

13. (*Long and difficult*) The greatest common divisor: GCD(i_1, i_2). Assume that GCD(i_1, i_2) = 0 if either i_1 or i_2 is zero. Use the Euclidean algorithm. (We suggest the subtraction version. See the rather neat solution for positive-integer inputs on p. 63 and pp. 71–73 of Trakhtenbrot [1963].)

Group III

A knowledge of binary arithmetic is presupposed by these exercises. Here we represent the nonnegative integers by *0, *1, *10, *11, *100, *101, and so on. Sequences of these are formed by juxtaposition, as with the tally code. (In effect, the asterisk is a separator.) The definition of computation parallels exactly the definition given for the tally code in Section 2.1.4. Design Turing machines to compute the following functions in binary.

14. Addition. Sample input and output:

$$\ldots \text{*}101\text{*}1001 \ldots \qquad \ldots \text{*}1110 \ldots$$

15. Floored subtraction.

16. Multiplication. Determine how many time cycles are required by your machine to multiply two integers m and n, and for comparison determine the same for the tally-code machine M of Fig. 2.1.9.

17. Quotient.

18. Remainder.

19. Minimum value of n arguments.

20. (*Long and difficult*) Greatest common divisor, using the Euclidean algorithm.

21. Design a Turing machine that will convert a tally-code numeral into an equal binary numeral.

22. Design a Turing machine that will convert a binary numeral into an equal tally-code numeral.

THE UNIVERSAL TURING MACHINE 2.2

Having presented the rudiments of Turing machines in Section 2.1, we now discuss them from a rather broad point of view. Most of this section is devoted to a sketch of the universal Turing machine, which in some ways resembles a general-purpose stored-program computer.

2.2.1 Turing Machines Versus Computers

If a Turing machine were to be built in the way in which we normally conceive it, it certainly would be an inefficient gadget to do computing. The chief reason is that the mechanical action of moving on the tape (or moving the tape relative to the machine) would be required at almost every step of a computation. Furthermore, since all storage is along a one-dimensional tape, the machine would be forced to go back and forth long distances to pick up and store data that it needs.

How much faster is the stored-program computer with which we are all familiar! It is capable of doing all of its internal operations at electronic speeds. The input and output steps, which do involve mechanical action and therefore take longer, are generally executed in parallel with the ongoing computation so that they do not slow it down. Thus there are many computations that it can do at electronic speeds, measurable in fractions of microseconds.

Moreover, the design of the stored-program computer is efficient. Even if the Turing machine were to be built electronically, including an electronic simulation of the tape action, the design would still be much too awkward for most practical computing.

However, in spite of its practical advantages, there is something about the stored-program computer that makes it unsuitable as a model for the study of algorithms: its limitation of size. The machine is just so large, as measured for example in the total number of bits of storage (or, if you prefer, bytes). Most machines, furthermore, have a fixed word size, which makes it difficult to deal with integers greater than a certain size.

In contrast, the Turing machine is a good model for the study of algorithms, since we can conceive of computations with arbitrarily large inputs on their tapes, using an arbitrarily large amount of intermediate storage during a computation, and taking an arbitrarily large amount of time.

Turing machines are universal, in the sense that every known algorithm can be executed by a Turing machine. This statement may seem surprising, because it implies that it is possible to execute algorithms dealing with graphs on a Turing machine. After all, graphs are multidimensional and the Turing machine tape is one-dimensional. The fact is that any information structure, however many dimensions it seems to require, can be coded on a tape. In Chapter 5 we offer some clues as to how this is possible, and argue more generally that any algorithm can be executed on a Turing machine. In this sense the Turing-machine model is universal. So, by the way, are the models we study in Chapters 3 and 4.

2.2.2 Coded Quintuples

One apparently odd feature about the Turing-machine model is that each new algorithm requires an entirely new machine. It is interesting that in the very paper in which he introduced his concept of machine computation, Turing also introduced the concept now known as the universal Turing machine. From a certain point of view, this machine was the precursor of the modern stored-program computer, which was designed 10 years later.

It is clear that any Turing machine is a procedure. Indeed, given a Turing machine table and an input tape, we can hand-simulate execution; the machine is not necessary for implementation. All the conditions in the definition of "algorithm" hold, except possibly the condition that there be a halt. If the machine halts for every input, then it is an algorithm.

The procedure of simulating a Turing machine is a uniform one. Whatever the Turing machine, we simulate it by a sequence of steps, each of which consists of looking up what to do in the table, and then carrying through a rather simple operation on the tape. Thus we can say that there is a procedure for simulating any Turing machine given by a table, on any given tape. From this observation, it is not difficult to construct a universal Turing machine to execute this procedure.

We shall not complete the construction of a universal Turing machine here, but we shall carry it through far enough to see the important issues involved in its construction. Readers who are interested can either complete the construction on their own or can read about it elsewhere (e.g., Hennie [1977], pp. 90–102; Minsky [1967], Chap. 7; or Turing's original 1936 paper, Secs. 6 and 7).

Two obstacles must be overcome before we can design our universal Turing machine, which we shall call U. First each Turing-machine table is two-dimensional. Somehow the information of each such table must be written on U's one-dimensional tape. Second, U must be capable of simulating any Turing machine however large. We have stipulated that each Turing machine have a finite alphabet, but we have placed no finite limit on the number of characters in any alphabet. Thus U must be capable of simulating machines with an arbitrarily large alphabet. On the other hand, U itself can have only a fixed finite alphabet. It follows that however big we make U, it will still have to be capable of simulating machines with larger alphabets.

We seek a way of coding every finite set of states and every finite alphabet using a fixed alphabet, which is to be part of U's alphabet. It turns out that we can do this using a two-letter alphabet $\{0, 1\}$. If U is to simulate a Turing machine T whose set of states is $\{q_1, q_2, \ldots, q_m\}$, we shall let each of these states q_i be represented by the string $10^{2i+3}1$ (i.e., the string that begins with the character 1, continues with $2i + 3$ occurrences of the character 0, and ends with the character 1). Then, if T has k characters in its alphabet, designated by $s_1, \ldots, s_k$, respectively, we shall let s_i be represented by the string $10^{2i+2}1$. We shall assume that s_1 is the blank, but it does not matter which character s_i is for $i \geq 2$.

Thus the initial state q_1 is represented by 1000001 and the blank s_1 is represented by 100001.

The strings 101, 1001, and 10001 will mean, respectively, "move left on the tape," "stay on the same square," and "move right on the tape."

Having provided a way of coding an arbitrarily large alphabet and an arbitrarily large state set in the alphabet of U, we must now overcome the other obstacle: to present the information of a Turing-machine table on a one-dimensional tape. Accordingly, we convert a Turing-machine table into a set of quintuples. Consider, for example, the table of Fig. 2.1.1. Note the entry BLq_5 in the q_4 row under the stroke. This entry is a command to the Turing machine: "When scanning a stroke in state q_4, erase the stroke, move to the left on the tape, and go into state q_5." We represent this command by the quintuple

$$\langle /, q_4, B, L, q_5 \rangle$$

Assuming that s_1 is B, s_2 is /, and s_3 is *, we represent this quintuple on U's tape as

$$1000000110000000000011000011011000000000000001$$

In general, each nonempty entry of the Turing-machine table is represented by a quintuple. The elements of the quintuple are, in order: old character, old state, new character, direction, and new state. In many cases, the new character or new state will be the same as the old.

The key observation is that the total information given by the Turing-machine table can be given in terms of a set of quintuples of this form. For example, Fig. 2.1.1 can be given as a set of nine quintuples, since there are nine nonblank entries in that table. We can simply write all nine quintuples on U's tape. Since there are exactly five coded items in every quintuple, we need not be concerned with separating one quintuple from another. The machine U can count items and tell when one quintuple ends and another begins. The entire string representing the machine of Fig. 2.1.1 (with repeated zeros abbreviated) begins as follows:

$$10^8110^5110^8110^3110^7110^6110^7110^6110^3110^7110^8110^7110^8110^3110^91 \ldots$$

Actually shown here are the first three quintuples (i.e., those from the first two rows of the table).

Let us now designate the machine that U is to simulate as Turing machine T, and assume that U has on its tape the list of T's quintuples. U will require many time cycles to simulate one of T's time cycles. If the latter begins with T scanning character s_i in state q_j, U will have to search through the list of T's quintuples to find one that begins $10^{2i+2}110^{2j+3}1 \ldots$. There is at most one such quintuple in the list, since T is deterministic. If it finds that quintuple, it learns from it what to do in simulating T, as we shall see in the next subsection. On the other hand, if the search discloses that there is no such quintuple, then U knows that it should halt.

2.2.3 Coded Configurations

In simulating the machine T, the universal Turing machine U has a copy of T's state table, coded as in Section 2.2.2, which it keeps on its tape throughout the operation. It must also keep information about the entire total configuration after each step of T's operation: It must have all the information about the characters appearing on all the squares, together with the information about which square is being scanned and what state T is in.

Before introducing U, we introduce a method of representing a total configuration of T by a string of characters, exactly one of which represents a state of T, all the others representing characters of T's alphabet. We select p consecutive squares of T's tape which, at a certain moment in T's history, include all the nonblank squares and also the scanned square. Suppose that the characters on these squares are, respectively, $s_{i_1}, s_{i_2}, \ldots s_{i_p}$, and that the machine is scanning the jth of these squares in state q_k. Then we represent the total configuration at the moment by the string

$$s_{i_1} s_{i_2} \ldots s_{i_j} q_k s_{i_{j+1}} \ldots s_{i_p}$$

The placement of the state symbol tells us not only what state the machine is in at that moment, but also where the head is: namely, scanning the character immediately to its left.

Generally, if W is a string representing a total configuration, one can append any number of blanks to either end of W, and the result B . . . BWB . . . B is a string that also represents the same total configuration. E.g., each of the strings *q_1 / / * / / / and BBB*q_1 / / * / / /B represents the configuration of Fig. 2.1.2 and it does not matter for U's purpose which string it uses. The first of these is the shortest string representing the configuration and by the code of Section 2.2.2 is put on U's tape as:

$$10^8 110^5 110^6 110^6 110^8 110^6 110^6 110^6 1$$

The machine U operates with both the coded table of the Turing machine T and also the coded version of T's total configuration on it at the same time, separated by an asterisk. The table portion of the tape is to the left of the asterisk and the total-configuration portion is to the right of the asterisk, which always remains fixed on a square of U's tape.

In general, the nonblank portion of the tape of the machine T grows. Sometimes it grows at the right end, but at other times it grows at the left end. In simulating the movement of T's head to the left onto a blank square that is not one of the squares represented by the string on U's tape, U must go through the laborious task of moving the whole total-configuration portion of its tape to the right to make room to represent another square at the left. This is one of several difficulties that we would have to face if we were to design U's table, which we shall not begin to do in this book.

We have come to the end of our discussion of the design of a universal Turing machine U. The design we have presented here is close to Turing's original idea. More recent books use a modification of this design that makes things a bit easier for the actual construction.

2.2.4 The Stored-Program Computer

Although this book is not concerned with computer design, we find it interesting to discuss the general design of a computer in connection with the universal Turing machine.

All large-scale electronic digital computers that are in operation today, as well as some hand calculators, are stored-program computers. Programs are read into computers and stored there in the same way that the data upon which the programs operate are read in and stored. There is a close analogy here to U, the universal Turing machine. The list of quintuples of the simulated machine, which is in effect a program for U to execute, is stored on the tape in exactly the same way that any other data used in the computation are stored.

The first high-speed, large-scale electronic digital computer, the ENIAC (Electronic Numerical Integrator and Computer), was not a stored-program computer, but was programmed manually, mostly by plugboard wiring. Completed at the Moore School of Electrical Engineering at the University of Pennsylvania in 1946 (10 years after the publication of Turing's paper), its great innovation was the use of electronics. Previous digital computers had all been mechanical or electromechanical—computing, more or less, by the turning of notched wheels. The ENIAC could compute much faster than any previous computer because it used electronic switching, free from mechanical action.

But very high speeds made programming even more essential. (To use the high speeds efficiently, the electronic machine had to act most of the time without step-by-step human supervision.) The designers of the ENIAC soon realized that plugboard wiring was too long and difficult a process to have to go through to prepare the machine for each new job. Accordingly, certain individuals on or associated with the ENIAC project devised in detail the computer structure that is used in all large-scale digital computers today. Although there appears to be no causal connection between Turing's idea and the design of the stored-program computer, there is a strong philosophical similarity. (For the history of the ENIAC and the design of the stored-program computer, see Burks [1980]; Eckert [1980]; Goldstine [1972], pp. 148–210; and Mauchly [1980].)

This ends our brief treatment of Turing machines. This has been our first investigation in the theory of automata, and also our first formal scheme for presenting algorithms. In many books, Turing machines play the role that the foundational programming languages of Chapter 3 will play in this book. In effect, the foundational programming languages constitute a variant of the Turing-machine model of computation: In place of Turing's concept, there is the concept of a simple variable-word-length computer, with an unlimited number of registers. Like the Turing machine, this machine lacks the size limitation of the actual digital computer. Although it is not quite as simple conceptually as a Turing machine, it will have the advantage of being closer to the machines with which most readers are familiar.

The Foundational Programming Languages 3

Because programs are the most important examples of algorithms in the contemporary world, it is appropriate for us to develop as much of our study of algorithms as possible in programming terms. Any practical computing language, however, is far too complicated for our purposes. We shall use instead two languages that have been selected to facilitate the study of the foundations of computing. These languages, which are quite similar to languages used in other books about theoretical computer science, are made up of command types that are present in practical programming languages.

Both languages deal exclusively with nonnegative integers, and both are simple enough to lack even an addition command: One must write programs to do addition and the other more involved arithmetic operations many programming languages take for granted. The only arithmetic operations that the two foundational programming languages have as single commands are incrementing a number by one and decrementing a number by one.

We name each of these languages after the command type that is responsible for the construction of loops. In the first language, the GOTO language, loops are constructed by means of transfer commands that tell the machine to jump to another part of the program for the command it is to execute next.

In the second language, the WHILE language, loops are constructed by a command that tells the machine to execute repeatedly a certain segment of the program *while* a certain variable is greater than zero. Although not present in all programming languages, the while command (in forms that are more general than ours) is popular with some programmers who think it can encourage the writing of well-structured programs. However, it is included in this chapter not because of its value in structured programming, but because of its closeness to many important ideas in the theory of computability. Since the while command is a convenient and powerful way of programming certain abstractly defined functions, the WHILE language will be used in some crucial proofs in Chapter 4.

We make no claim that the material in this chapter will be helpful in practical programming; both foundational programming languages are too simple. On the other hand, the very simplicity is an aid in our exposition of important theoretical issues, linguistic as well as computational.

3.1 THE SYNTAX OF THE GOTO LANGUAGE

The objective of this section is to stipulate precisely which strings of characters are programs in the GOTO language, which has five syntactic categories: numeral, name, unlabeled command, labeled command, and (the chief syntactic category) program. (Syntactic categories are like the parts of speech of English grammar. See Appendix III.)

This section will deal with syntax, except for the first subsection, in which the distinction between semantics and syntax is not sharply drawn. In the next section we deal with semantics, which includes how programs are executed by the machine.

3.1.1 Informal Description

A programming language needs numerals (i.e., symbols representing numbers) and also variables ranging over numbers. The GOTO language also has a need for labels, which under certain situations can refer to commands in a program.

A programming-language variable is to be physically realized by a storage position in a computer containing different numbers at different times. However, we find it convenient to depart from realism at this point and to assume that there are no scaling restrictions on a number in a storage position. We imagine a computer in which each storage position can hold a decimal number written as an arbitrarily long string of decimal digits. As explained in Chapter 1, our theory of computability draws no line on sizes of written expressions except the line between the infinite and the finite. Thus the GOTO language admits no scaling limitation.

The language has only two arithmetic commands: incrementing by one and decrementing by one. Since zero cannot be decremented by one in the domain of the nonnegative integers, we stipulate that that operation applied to zero produces zero. The term "decrement" is therefore a slight misnomer.

The three control commands are unconditional transfer (GOTO . . .), conditional transfer (IF $V = 0$ GOTO . . .), and HALT. The sequencing of commands in execution of a program is as it is in most programming languages.

We begin by enumerating all the single characters used in the GOTO language. First, there are all the decimal digits, 0, 1, 2, 3, 4, 5, 6, 7, 8 and 9. Then there are all the capital letters from our Roman alphabet, A through Z. The colon, the semicolon, the equal sign, and parentheses complete the list. The blank (or space) is not part of the alphabet. In spite of this, we shall often insert spaces in what we write for visual clarity. Such blank spaces will have no syntactical significance.

We must proceed by explaining several syntactic categories. The first syntactic category is that of *numeral* (or *number symbol*). A *numeral* is either a single digit by itself or else a string of digits beginning with a digit other than zero.

Next is the syntactic category of *name*. A name is any string of letters and digits beginning with a letter (with no restriction on length). Names have two uses, as variables and as labels of commands. However, for the present syntactic task, we officially ignore the distinction between the two uses, and insist merely on a clear understanding of which strings of characters are names.

Next are the two syntactic categories of *unlabeled command* and *labeled command*. (The word "command" will be used in this book to mean an imperative sentence in the two programming languages, in place of the words "instruction" and "statement.")

There are seven types of unlabeled commands. First, an *unlabeled variable-assignment command* consists of a name followed by a colon, equals, and then a name. Example:

$$XX1 := Y$$

Second, an *unlabeled numerical-assignment command* consists of a name, colon, equals, then a numeral. Example:

$$X := 17$$

Third, an *unlabeled increment command* consists of INCR, followed by a left parenthesis, followed by a name, followed by a right parenthesis. Example:

$$INCR(XX2)$$

Fourth, an unlabeled decrement command consists of DECR, followed by an open parenthesis, followed by a name, followed by a close parenthesis. Example:

$$DECR(Y)$$

Fifth, an *unlabeled unconditional transfer command* consists of GOTO followed by a name. Example:

GOTO LOCUS

Sixth, an *unlabeled conditional transfer command* consists of IF, followed by a name, followed by an equals sign, followed by zero, followed by GOTO, followed by a name. Example:

IF XX1 = 0 GOTO LOCUS

Seventh is the *unlabeled halt* command:

HALT

Of these seven unlabeled commands, the first four (variable assignment, numerical assignment, increment, and decrement) are *unlabeled operational commands*, and the last three (unconditional transfer, conditional transfer, and halt) are *unlabeled control commands*. The significance of these terms will be made clear in the next section.

A colon together with the equals sign immediately following it is conveniently regarded as a single symbol, called an *assignment symbol*. In some programming languages this symbol is rendered by the equals sign alone; in others, it is rendered by an arrow pointing leftward. The assignment symbol should not be read "equals" but as "set equal to" (or, more correctly, "Assign— the value of—"). The equal sign in the conditional transfer command, on the other hand, should be read "equals."

A *labeled command* (the next syntactic category) consists of a name, followed by a colon, followed by anything in the syntactic category of unlabeled command. We use the term *command* to denote anything that is in either the syntactic category of unlabeled command or the syntactic category of labeled command.

The final syntactic category is that of *program*, which is either a single command or a sequence of commands separated by semicolons.

3.1.3 Discussion

Following is an example of a program:

REPEAT: IF Y = 0 GOTO EXIT;

DECR(Y);

INCR(X);

GOTO REPEAT;

EXIT: Z := X;

HALT

(This program, as will be explained in Section 3.2.2, computes the addition function.)

It should be noted that the following is also a program, as "program" has been defined:

$$Z: \quad GOTO \ X;$$
$$Z: \quad X := X;$$
$$Z: \quad GOTO \ GOTO;$$
$$GOTO: \quad INCR(IF);$$
$$X: \quad GOTO \ Z;$$
$$GOTO \ BLANK$$

There are several things apparently wrong here. (1) The name X is used both as a label and as a variable. (2) GOTO is used as a label. (When does GOTO mean "go to" and when does it mean the command of which GOTO is the label?) (3) The name Z is the label of three different commands. (Where should the machine go when it is told GOTO Z?) (4) IF is used as a variable. (When does IF mean "if" and when does it refer to the storage location?) (5) There is no command labeled BLANK to go to; the last command cannot be executed.

We shall see that, in spite of all these anomalies, not only is this a program according to the foregoing definition, but it will run, assuming an appropriate machine. It serves no conceivable purpose, but it will run. Any sequence of commands is a program, however unrelated the parts are to one another.

But not everything we write down by chance is a program: for example,

$$X: \quad GOTO \ Y: \quad GOTO \ Z$$

If this string were a program, it would have to be a single command, since there is no semicolon. Certainly, it is not an unlabeled command since it fits none of the seven patterns that were listed above. If it were a labeled command, X would have to be the label. But then the remainder of the string

$$GOTO \ Y: \quad GOTO \ Z$$

would have to be an unlabeled command, which it is not since it does not fit any of the seven patterns. Clearly, therefore, this example is not a program, even though we might be able to guess what its author intended to write.

For visual ease, spaces are placed between symbols although they are not officially part of the syntax; for example, they are placed to the left and right of GOTO and IF, to the left and right of an assignment symbol, to the left and right of an equals sign that is not part of an assignment symbol, and after a colon following a command label. Although the syntax of the GOTO language is such as to allow unique interpretation without regard to spaces, we use them for legibility. They have no significance to the machine but their use facilitates human reading.

Similarly, the arrangement of a program line by line has no syntactic significance and no significance to the machine. We generally write programs with one command per line for human visual ease, although the semicolons make this unnecessary for the machine.

We shall now describe how a program can be parsed mechanically. First, by means of the semicolons, one can separate a program into its commands. Next, one can easily tell whether any occurrence of a colon is part of an assignment symbol, namely, when it is immediately followed by an equals sign. Otherwise, the colon is being used to separate the label part from the command part of the labeled command, and a name must occur before this colon, which is the label.

A command without parentheses or an assignment symbol must be a control command; if it is not HALT, it must be either a conditional transfer or an unconditional transfer. If it has $=$, it is a conditional transfer; there must be a name (which is a variable) between the IF that begins the command (or comes right after a colon) and the equals sign; and there must be a name (which is a label) between

$$= 0 \ \text{GOTO}$$

and the end of the command. If it has no equals sign, it is an unconditional transfer consisting of GOTO followed by a name (which is a label).

If the command has an assignment symbol or parentheses, it is an operational command. Similar determinations can be made. Apart from the label of the command, names that occur must be variables.

A name can occur in a program as both variable and label. The machine can tell which is which, and in the next section we describe exactly how the machine responds. (Sometimes this double use of a name occurs in a well-written program. However, we should guard against doing it inadvertently, not because it confuses the machine but because it may confuse a human reader.)

Note also that this method of parsing a program makes no reference to spaces between characters or to the lines of the program. Thus we were justified above in asserting that spaces and line breaks are not needed for machine comprehension.

The reader should be convinced at this point that there is a parsing algorithm for the GOTO language, although our discussion has been informal. One thing that a parsing algorithm is usually expected to do is to reveal when an intended program fails syntactically to be a program: for example,

$$3: \ \ \text{GOTO X}$$

(what occurs before the colon is not a name). The method we have just outlined is easily extended to perform this function. Parsing algorithms will be the subject of Chapter 8.

The GOTO language is similar to an early foundational programming language put forth in Shepherdson and Sturgis [1963].

THE ELEMENTARY SEMANTICS 3.2
OF THE GOTO LANGUAGE

Section 3.1 had as its goal the specifications of which strings of symbols are programs. It did so by defining certain syntactic categories, which are sets of strings. A person could learn to tell whether any given string is in any given syntactic category (including the syntactic category of program) without having heard of algorithms, computers, or computing.

Now, after having given a complete treatment of the syntax, we offer a complete and precise treatment of the elementary (or operational) semantics.

Basic Exposition 3.2.1

We begin by postulating a machine, the likes of which will never be built. This machine has an inexhaustible supply of storage positions. It prepares itself to run a program given to it by assigning a storage position to each variable appearing in the program. The human agent loads arbitrary numbers (i.e., nonnegative integers) into these storage locations and then signals the machine to begin. Thereupon the machine begins to execute the program, which it does by executing the commands in a certain order, to be described below.

We describe how the first four command types are executed as isolated commands. The machine executes a variable assignment command, for example,

$$Y := XX1$$

by taking the number in storage position XX1 and loading it into storage position Y; the number that was in storage position Y is destroyed in the process, but the number in XX1 remains there (destructive write-in and nondestructive readout).

The numerical assignment command, for example,

$$X := 17$$

is executed by setting the storage position X to 17, destroying whatever number was there previously.

The increment command, for example,

INCR(XX1)

is executed by adding one to the number in storage position XX1. Similarly, the decrement command, for example,

DECR(XX1)

is executed by subtracting 1 from the number in XX1, unless this number is zero, in which case it is left at zero.

Note that in each of the four operational commands there is a storage position that may be modified by the execution of the command, namely the storage position for the variable to the left of the assignment symbol or inside the parentheses. The execution of a control command, on the other hand, leaves all the storage positions unchanged. The sole function of a control command is to determine which, if any, command is to be executed next.

To explain the control commands we must explain the general way in which commands are sequenced for execution. (It is useful to give a thorough account even though most readers will find it to be something they already know.) Let the commands of the program be, in order, $I_1, I_2, \ldots, I_p$. The machine begins a program by executing I_1. What it executes next depends on the general rule of sequencing. Let us suppose that at a certain time the machine is executing I_j. If I_j is an operational command, the next command it executes will be I_{j+1} provided that $j \neq p$; if $j = p$, the machine halts, since there is no I_{p+1}.

If I_j is an unconditional transfer command, for example,

GOTO LL36

the next command to be executed is the command in the program whose label is LL36, or the first such command if there are more than one. If LL36 is a *dummy label* (i.e., if there is no command in the program labeled LL36), the machine will halt. The machine does nothing other than this in response to the command I_j.

(Although we have stipulated what the machine will do in these cases, we advocate programs in which no two commands have the same label and in which there are no dummy labels.)

If I_j is a conditional transfer, for example,

IF X = 0 GOTO D36

the machine looks at the number currently stored in the storage position assigned to the variable X. If this number is 0, the machine executes next the first command in the program labeled D36, halting if there is no such command. If this number is not 0, the machine next executes the command I_{j+1} if $j \neq p$, and halts if $j = p$.

The halt command causes the machine to halt. Note that there are two other ways the machine can halt, which we call *halting by default*. After executing the last command of a program the machine will halt, unless that command causes a transfer. Also, as mentioned above, if the machine is seeking to execute a transfer where the label in that command occurring after the GOTO is a dummy label, the machine will halt.

(A well-written program does not halt by default. If halting can occur only in response to a halt command, the program is more intelligible for human reading and checking.)

If a name occurs in one place in a program as a label and in another place as a variable, the machine will interpret these as if they were two distinct symbols.

To sum up some of these remarks in a single example: In the GOTO language, you can tell the computer

$$\text{IF GOTO} = 0 \text{ GOTO GOTO}$$

and it will be able to tell that there are three distinct senses of the string "GOTO." But human readers may become confused.

Time Cycles; Run Histories   3.2.2

To think of how the machine operates, we think of a time cycle during which the machine executes a single command. Since integers can be arbitrarily large, the time cycle during which an assignment statement is executed could reasonably be expected to be arbitrarily long. Although practical time considerations are of no concern to us, we should note that the execution of a single command in our programming language cannot always be regarded as a single step in the execution of an algorithm in the sense discussed in Section 1.1.2. However we divide the operation of the machine into steps, there will be no upper bound on the number of steps taken in the execution of an assignment command. Thus a time cycle is not to be identified with a step in the sense of Section 1.1.2.

The first time cycle we call time one; the next, time two; the next, time three, and so on. At the beginning of a time cycle each of the storage positions has a number in it and a command is taken up. If that command is an operational command, there is one storage position whose number may change as a result of its execution, all other storage positions remaining the same. And the command taken up at the beginning of the next time cycle is the next command, as explained in Section 3.2.1.

If the command taken up is a halt, or if either of the other two halting situations occurs, we say that there is no next time cycle.

Although we suppose that the machine has an unlimited number of storage positions, a given program must be finite and hence can use only finitely many storage positions. Thus we can associate with each time cycle a storage vector, whose entries are the numbers in the respective storage positions; this idea presupposes only that we have assigned a certain order to the storage variables of a program.

Let us illustrate all the foregoing ideas with the simple program of Fig. 3.2.1. The commands of the program are numbered for reference purposes; these numbers are not part of the program in the GOTO language. The program adds the initial values of X and Y, placing the sum in the storage position Z at the end, with both the original values of X and Y destroyed in the process.

		Time cycle	Command	X	Y	Z
(1)	REPEAT:	IF $Y = 0$ GOTO EXIT;	1	(1)	3	2	1066
(2)		DECR(Y);			–	–	–
(3)		INCR(X);	2	(2)			
(4)		GOTO REPEAT;	3	(3)	–	1	–
(5)	EXIT:	$Z := X$;			4	–	–
(6)		HALT	4	(4)			

Time cycle	Command	X	Y	Z
1	(1)	3	2	1066
		–	–	–
2	(2)			
		–	1	–
3	(3)			
		4	–	–
4	(4)			
		–	–	–
5	(1)			
		–	–	–
6	(2)			
		–	0	–
7	(3)			
		5	–	–
8	(4)			
		–	–	–
9	(1)			
		–	–	–
10	(5)			
		–	–	5
11	(6)	5	0	5

Figure 3.2.1

Figure 3.2.1 also has a table that gives a run history for this program, in which X, Y, and Z are initially set to 3, 2, and 1066, respectively. (The initial value in the Z storage position is clearly immaterial to the outcome of the program.) The run history shows the command that is executed during each time cycle, and shows the number in each storage position at the beginning and at the end of each time cycle. A dash indicates that no change has taken place in that storage position, and therefore the number there is the same as what it was just before.

A run history can be given in this way for any program and for any initial setting of the storage positions corresponding to each variable of the program. A run history, which in effect is a detailed hand simulation, tells the whole story of what happens during execution. At the end of Section 3.4 are given some exercises in making run histories in tabular form. Although they may seem tedious, and are certainly not challenging, these exercises make clear what goes on inside a machine when it executes a program.

We have shown how any program in the GOTO language will run. For some purposes we restrict the programs that can be written, so that they become easier to deal with conceptually:

Definition: A *proper program* is a program in the GOTO language that satisfies the following conditions:

1. For every label that occurs at the end of a control command (which will be after a "GOTO") there is one and only one labeled command in the program having that label.

2. The last command in the program as written is either a halt command or an unconditional transfer.

It should be noted that a proper program cannot halt by default. It will halt only in response to a halt command. An example of a program that satisfies neither condition 1 nor condition 2 of this definition is

$$Z: \quad \text{GOTO } Z; \quad Z: \quad \text{DECR}(X)$$

Unsuitability for Practical Programming   3.2.3

The simplicity of the foundational programming languages makes them ideally suited for the things we are most interested in in this book. However, they are quite inadequate for practical programming, and for many theoretical pursuits.

One feature of a practical programming language that our languages lack has some significance in the theory of computability, namely arrays. We can write X1, X2, X3, and so on, as variables, but we cannot write X(I) as a variable. And, apparently, we have no way of getting the effect of creating dynamically (i.e., in the run of a program) an array $X(1)$, $X(2)$, . . . , satisfying, say, the condition

$$X(I + 1) = F(X(I))$$

even when F is a function that is computable. (In Section 4.4, we remark on how helpful this would be in a certain computation of theoretical interest. Then in Chapter 5 we show how the effect of an array can be obtained in our foundational programming languages as they are, by a mathematical trick. Thus although arrays are useful, they are theoretically unnecessary.)

We note also that both of our languages lack the ability to pick out a decimal digit from a number in a storage position. There is no direct way, for example, to operate on the rightmost decimal digit. Any program to obtain the rightmost digit is roundabout, with an execution time proportional to the number itself.

Because our two foundational programming languages lack the ability to manipulate digits, arithmetic functions generally take longer than they do under optimal conditions. Addition, for example, takes an amount of time proportional to the second of the two numbers (in the worst case) with either of our languages. The well-known addition algorithm requires time proportional to the logarithm of the second number (in the worst case), but cannot be realized in either language. For this reason, we cannot use the foundational programming languages as they are in any significant study of computational complexity.

Finally, we note the complete lack of attention given to input and output problems in the foundational programming languages. As everyone who has written any substantial program knows, making arrangements for input and output is often a challenging part of a programming task. These arrangements, however, are not generally of concern in the theory of computability.

3.3 *THE* WHILE *LANGUAGE*

All programming languages must relate both to a machine and to a user, although some are closer in their mode of expression to one than to the other. The GOTO language is quite close in its features to an imaginary and quite peculiar machine; indeed, we might think of it as the assembly language of such a machine.

The WHILE language is almost as simple as the GOTO language, but is closer to the user. Although it lacks the common arithmetic commands, such as addition and multiplication (which must be programmed, as in the GOTO language), it has commands that reflect certain ideas of computation that are universal and are popular among many programmers. These are the ideas of "while" and "if." Ultimately, the WHILE language will be quite helpful to us in understanding the theory of computability.

3.3.1 *Syntax*

The alphabet of the WHILE language is the alphabet for the GOTO language augmented by the three characters

$$>, [,]$$

(greater than, left bracket, right bracket).

The syntactic categories of *numeral* and *name* are exactly as they are in the GOTO language.

There are no labels in the WHILE language. All commands are unlabeled.

The syntactic categories of *command* and *program* are divided into infinitely many subcategories, called *levels*. This bit of complication is necessary to avoid circularity in the definition of the categories. Generally, a program of level i will be a sequence of commands of level i or less. But for $i \geqq 1$, a command of level i will itself have a program of level $i - 1$ as part of it.

The syntactic category of *command* includes seven types. The first four (variable assignment command, numerical assignment command, increment command, and decrement command) are exactly the same as the first four unlabeled command types in the GOTO language. These commands are all and only all the commands of level zero in the WHILE language.

A *program of level zero* is either a command of level zero or else a sequence of commands of level zero separated by semicolons.

In the following descriptions we shall use the phrase "bracketed program" to mean a left bracket, followed by a program, followed by a right bracket.

The fifth command type is the *unilateral conditional command*. A unilateral conditional command of level $i + 1$ ($i \geqq 0$) consists of IF followed by a name followed by $= 0$, followed by THEN, followed by a bracketed program of level i. An example of level 1 is:

$$\text{IF ALPHA} = 0 \text{ THEN}$$
$$\text{[DECR(BETA)};$$
$$\text{INCR(GAMMA)]}$$

A *bilateral conditional command* (the sixth command type) *of level $i + 1$* consists of IF, followed by a name, followed by $= 0$ THEN, followed by a bracketed program of level j, followed by ELSE, followed by a bracketed program of level k, where $\text{MAX}(j, k) = i$. An example of level 1 is

$$\text{IF ALPHA} = 0$$
$$\text{THEN [ALPHA} := \text{BETA]}$$
$$\text{ELSE [INCR(GAMMA)};$$
$$\text{DECR(ALPHA)]}$$

The *while command* (the seventh command type) of level $i + 1$ consists of WHILE, followed by a name, followed by > 0 DO, followed by a bracketed program of level i. An example of level 1 is

$$\text{WHILE ALPHA} > 0 \text{ DO}$$
$$\text{[DECR(ALPHA)};$$
$$\text{INCR(BETA)]}$$

A *program of level i* is either a command of level i or a sequence of commands of maximum level i separated by semicolons.

It should be observed that we have just completed, in effect, infinitely many definitions. It is as if we have first defined *command of level zero*, then *program of level zero*, then *command of level 1*, then *program of level 1*, then *command of level 2*, then *program of level 2*, and so on. Our procedure here has been that of a recursive definition (see the definition of *binary tree* in Section AV. 3).

Examples of higher-level commands and higher-level programs will be found in Section 3.3.3.

We can now define a *unilateral conditional, bilateral conditional,* or *while command* to be a unilateral conditional, bilateral conditional, or while command (respectively) of any positive integer level. And we can define a *program* to be a program of any level. Thus a program is any sequence of commands, separated by semicolons if there are more than one.

In Chapter 7 we introduce the notion of a context-free grammar, by means of which the syntax of the WHILE language can be described without reference to the notion of level. This technique is essentially the same as that known as Backus–Naur form for describing the syntax of programming languages.

Taking an overview of the syntax of the two foundational programming languages, we see that it is the matter of bracketed programs (which are, in effect, subprograms of larger programs) that makes the syntax of the WHILE language more complex than the GOTO language. In effect the "GOTO" commands of the latter make it unnecessary to deal with bracketed programs. But there is an advantage in using the WHILE language with its more complex syntax. The structure of a WHILE-language program is self-revealing: If it is written line by line, and if the lines are properly indented, its structure is visible at a glance. There seems to be no comparable way of writing a GOTO-language program: No matter how it is written, the reader must draw its flowchart (partially, at least) to discern its structure.

3.3.2 Elementary Semantics

In a WHILE-language program, each command is executed in turn. After the last command has been executed, the machine halts; there is no halt command in the language.

The conditional and while commands, however, involve difficulties in our description of the semantics. Before we can describe how these commands are executed, we must explain the execution of the programs that occur between the brackets.

The machine executes a command of level zero (assignment, increment, or decrement) as explained in Section 3.2 for the GOTO language. A program of level zero is executed by executing the commands in order.

Assuming that it is understood how programs of level i are executed, we explain the execution of a command of level $i + 1$.

The execution of a unilateral conditional command of level $i + 1$ is explained in terms of a typical example. We assume that the bracketed program in the following is of level i:

$$\text{IF } X = 0 \text{ THEN } [\ldots]$$

The machine executes this command by first examining X. If X is not zero, the execution is complete. But if X equals 0, the machine executes the bracketed program, after which the execution of this unilateral conditional of level $i + 1$ is complete.

The bilateral conditional of level $i + 1$, for example,

$$\text{IF } X = 0 \text{ THEN } [\ldots] \text{ ELSE } [\ldots]$$

is executed by first examining X. If X equals 0, the machine executes the first bracketed program, after which the execution of the entire command is complete, the second bracketed program being ignored completely. On the other hand, if the examination of X shows it to be nonzero, the machine ignores the first bracketed program and executes the second bracketed program.

In executing either of these conditional commands, any changes that occur to X (the test variable) during the execution of a bracketed program can in no way affect the test itself, since the latter occurs before the former in time.

The while command of level $i + 1$, for example,

$$\text{WHILE } X > 0 \text{ DO } [\ldots]$$

is executed by doing the following in order. First, X is tested. If X is zero, the execution is complete, the bracketed program being completely ignored. But if $X > 0$, the machine executes the bracketed program, after which it tests X again. If X is now zero, the execution of the entire command is complete. But if X is still not zero, the bracketed program is executed again, after which X is tested again. And so on.

The execution of a while command is not complete until a test reveals that X is zero. It is possible that this will never happen, in which case the program of which the while command is a part will never halt.

A program of level $i + 1$ is executed by executing its commands in turn.

This completes our description of the elementary semantics of the WHILE language, or how the machine executes a program. In this account, we have not made reference to time cycles in the machine execution. For the purpose of giving a precise account of a run history, we can assume that the assignment, increment, and decrement commands take one time cycle, and that the testing of the test variable of the other commands takes one time cycle. From these two assumptions, the number of time cycles in a program run is determined.

3.3.3 A Sample Run

Figure 3.3.1 shows a sample run of a sample program of level 2. This program, with X as input, Z as output, and U as an auxiliary variable, adds all the positive integers between input X and 1 inclusive, in decreasing order. (If X is zero, the result is zero.)

①   Z := 0;

②   WHILE $X > 0$ DO

③   [U := X;

④   DECR(X);

⑤   WHILE $U > 0$ DO

⑥   [DECR(U);

⑦   INCR(Z)]]

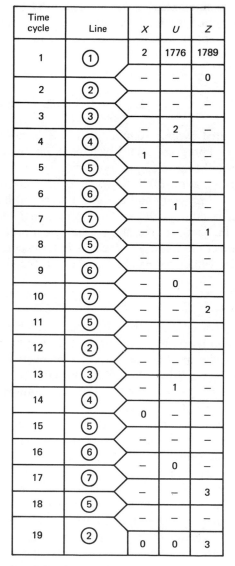

Time cycle	Line	X	U	Z
1	①	2	1776	1789
		−	−	0
2	②			
		−	−	−
3	③			
		−	2	−
4	④			
		1	−	−
5	⑤			
		−	−	−
6	⑥			
		−	1	−
7	⑦			
		−	−	1
8	⑤			
		−	−	−
9	⑥			
		−	0	−
10	⑦			
		−	−	2
11	⑤			
		−	−	−
12	②			
		−	−	−
13	③			
		−	1	−
14	④			
		0	−	−
15	⑤			
		−	−	−
16	⑥			
		−	0	−
17	⑦			
		−	−	3
18	⑤			
		−	−	−
19	②			
		0	0	3

Figure 3.3.1

In the right column of Fig. 3.3.1 the run of this program is shown (Cf. Fig. 3.2.1) with X, U, and Z originally set to 2, 1776, and 1789, respectively. (Clearly, the initial values of U and Z are immaterial to the ouptut of the program.)

The Two Languages Compared 3.3.4

Given a program in the WHILE language, it is an easy matter to rewrite the program in the GOTO language. The effect of an if–then, if–then–else, or while command can be gotten quite easily using conditional and unconditional transfers. Thus a WHILE-language program can be translated into the GOTO language (the details are left as an exercise) in such a way that the result is, in a manner of speaking, the "same" program: indeed, the programs have identical flowcharts.

Translating a program in the GOTO language into the WHILE language is more difficult. There is apparently no way of carrying through the translation in such a way that the resulting program always has the same flowchart.

Our options for writing programs are therefore broader in the GOTO language than in the WHILE language. If we think of a flowchart as a potential program that we would like to write in some programming language or other, then the class of potential programs that can be written in the WHILE language is a proper subclass of the class of those that can be written in the GOTO language. The class of functions computed, however, is the same for both languages.

However, although there are in this sense more programs in the GOTO language than in the WHILE language, those programs that do exist in the WHILE language are quite suitable for our purpose. When we prove in Chapter 4 that certain kinds of functions have programs in the WHILE language, we find that the proofs are clear and insightful.

Exercises 3.3.5

1. Consider the following WHILE-language program of level 3 in which X and Y are inputs, Z is an output, and U is an auxiliary variable.

```
Z := 0;
INCR(Y);
WHILE  X > 0 DO
     [U := X;
      DECR(Y);
```

IF Y = 0

    THEN [DECR(X);

        WHILE U > 0 DO

        [DECR(U);

        INCR(Z)]]

    ELSE [DECR(X);

        DECR(X);

        DECR(X);

        WHILE U > 0 DO

        [DECR(U);

        INCR(Z);

        INCR(Z)]]]

Translate this program into a GOTO-language program, in executing which the machine will do the same things in order for each value of the inputs X and Y. Your program must have exactly the same variables, inputs, and outputs, and at the halt the value of the output must be the same.

[The program of this exercise computes the function $Z = f(X, Y)$, where $f(X, Y)$ is the sum of the positive terms in the sequence

$$2X, 2(X - 3), 2(X - 6), \ldots, 2(X - 3(Y - 1)),$$
$$(X - 3Y), (X - 3Y - 1), (X - 3Y - 2), \ldots$$

For Y = 0 this is the sequence $X, X - 1, X - 2, \ldots$.]

2. Give an algorithm to translate any WHILE-language program into a GOTO-language program in the manner of Exercise 1. No new variables should be introduced into the new program. It should halt under exactly the same input conditions, with the resulting values of all variables exactly the same. The new program must be such that the machine, in execution, will do the same things in the same order as it would in executing the old program for the same input conditions.

3. (*Difficult*) Give an algorithm for drawing, for a given WHILE-language program, a flowchart with the following properties: (1) there is exactly one begin circle and exactly one halt circle; and (2) for every box of the flowchart there is a path from the begin circle to that box, and a path from that box to the halt circle. (*Hint:* The algorithm we have in mind is the natural way of drawing a flowchart from a given program in the WHILE language.) Prove that the flowchart constructed by your algorithm has these two properties.

3.4 FLOWCHARTS

Many programmers find it easier to write a program if they draw a flowchart first, and find it easier to read someone else's program if it is presented as a flowchart. We shall find that certain theoretical ideas become clearer when they are presented in terms of flowcharts.

For these reasons we now introduce flowcharts into our discussion of the foundational programming languages, and establish a convention that will make a certain type of flowchart the precise equivalent of a program in the GOTO language.

Schematic and Detailed Flowcharts 3.4.1

The reader is probably more familiar with flowcharts than with directed graphs. Nevertheless, the former is a variety of the latter, which must be defined first.

Definition: A *directed graph* is an ordered pair (N, A), where N is a finite set of nodes, A a finite set of arcs, and each arc *goes from* (or *leaves*) a node and *goes to* (or *enters*) a node which may be the same or distinct from the first.

A directed graph differs from a graph (see Section 1.2.3) in that its edges, so to speak, are directed and are called *arcs*. Furthermore, an arc may go from one node to the same node, and more than one arc may go from one node to another. Walks and paths in a directed graph must go in the right direction along each arc:

Definition: A *walk* in a directed graph is a sequence $N_0, A_1, N_1, \ldots, N_n$, where each N_i is a node and each A_i is an arc going from N_{i-1} to N_i.

Definition: A *path* is a walk $N_0, A_1, N_1, \ldots, N_n$ in which, for $i \neq j$, $N_i \neq N_j$.

Definition: A *flowchart* is a directed graph whose nodes are circles, rectangular boxes, and diamonds. There is one arc leaving each rectangular box; there are two arcs leaving each diamond, one labeled *yes*, the other labeled *no*. It has one circle with BEGIN (or IN, etc.) written inside, with one arc leaving it and no arcs entering it. All other circles have HALT (or OUT, etc.) written inside and have no arcs leaving them. A rectangular box has a command (or a sequence of commands, occurring from top to bottom) to be executed (in order); and a diamond has written in it a single question that has a *yes* or *no* answer.

If each question inside a diamond has a clear answer at any moment it is asked, and if each command can be clearly executed at any moment, then a flowchart is a procedure. A computation is a certain kind of walk: One begins at the begin circle, follows the arrows, executes the statements as they come up, answers the questions inside the diamonds, taking the "yes" or "no" arc depending on the answer to the question, and finally halts upon reaching a HALT circle. If a HALT circle is never reached, no walk and no computation are determined (see Section 3.5).

In particular, if the commands and questions are appropriate, a flowchart represents a program. A run is determined from the values of the variables at the beginning.

We assume that the reader is familiar enough with flowcharts not to need further explanation. Figure 3.4.1 is a flowchart for the short program in the GOTO language from Fig. 3.2.1.

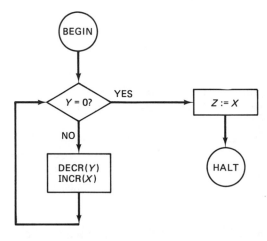

Figure 3.4.1

Definition: A *detailed flowchart* is one in which every line in a rectangular box is an operational command of the GOTO language (assignment, increment, or decrement), and every question in a diamond asks whether a variable is equal to zero. A *schematic flowchart* is a flowchart that is not a detailed flowchart.

Although our flowcharting technique will be directed toward the GOTO language, we shall be able to convert most detailed flowcharts that we would care to write, perhaps with some modifications, into programs in the WHILE language. For example, a WHILE-language program for Fig. 3.4.1 is as follows:

$$\text{WHILE } Y > 0 \text{ DO}$$
$$[\text{DECR}(Y);$$
$$\text{INCR}(X)];$$
$$Z := X$$

3.4.2 Multiplication

As we have seen, addition can be programmed in the foundational programming languages. We now do the same for multiplication.

Knowing that multiplication is repeated addition and recalling the program of Fig. 3.4.1 for addition, we set out to write a program that multiplies. We first make a schematic flowchart, Fig. 3.4.2, containing a box standing for an addition, hoping that we can fill in the details later. Note that if Y = 0, then Y times X is 0. If Y is greater than 0, then Y times X equals the result of adding X to zero Y times. We need an extra storage position, W, for this purpose, since the value of X must be kept intact. Each time we add another X to W, we subtract 1 from Y. Thus when Y gets down to zero, the original value of Y times X will be in W, which we can take as the output.

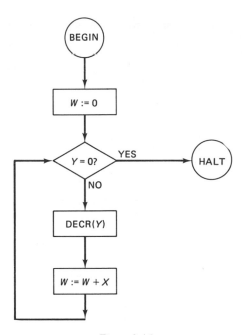

Figure 3.4.2

But how shall we replace the box W := W + X? Before setting out on this task, we must decide exactly what is to happen as a result of this box. One requirement is that, upon leaving the box at any time, the value of W must be X more than what it was at the time the box was entered. But there is another requirement: X and Y must have the same values upon leaving the box that they had when the box was entered. If we were to replace the box by a sequence of commands that modified X or Y, we would be guilty of producing an unwanted *side effect;* such a side effect would spoil the program as a whole.

What we want, then, is a subprogram that will cause X and Y to remain as they are and to increase W by the amount in X. A flowchart for the desired subprogram, with a new variable U, is given in Fig. 3.4.3.

The detailed flowchart for the multiplication program can now be composed by simply replacing the box W :=W + X in Fig. 3.4.2 by the flowchart of Fig. 3.4.3. The result is Fig. 3.4.4.

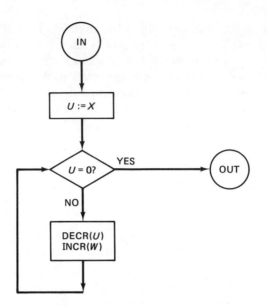

Figure 3.4.3

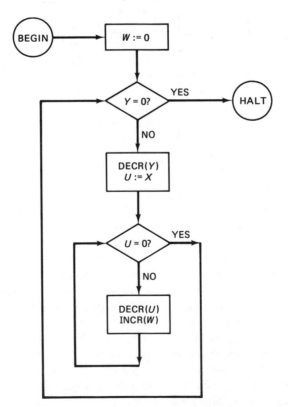

Figure 3.4.4

The technique of using a program that we have written before as part of a new program is one that we shall depend upon to prove rather sweeping results about the computability of functions in Chapter 4.

The GOTO-language program that results from the flowchart of Fig. 3.4.4 is as follows:

$$W := 0;$$

OUTER: IF Y $= 0$ GOTO EXIT;

DECR(Y);

U $:=$ X;

INNER: IF U $= 0$ GOTO OUTER;

DECR(U);

INCR(W);

GOTO INNER;

EXIT: HALT

A program in the WHILE language is easily written from the flowchart of Fig. 3.4.4:

$$W := 0;$$

WHILE Y > 0 DO

[DECR(Y);

U $:=$ X;

WHILE U > 0 DO

[DECR(U);

INCR(W)]]

Note the loop structure of Fig. 3.4.4, which is apparent from a mere inspection. There are two loops, one of which is part of the other. A loop in a flowchart means the iteration of a certain sequence of commands in a program. Each time through the outer loop generally involves several times through the inner loop. The loops in Fig. 3.4.4 are controlled by count-down: the outer loop by a count-down on Y, the inner loop by a count-down on U. In each case, the machine leaves the loop when the variable controlling the loop reaches zero.

What a Program Does   3.4.3

For some purposes it is good to take note of all the variables that appear in a program and tell exactly what happens to each as a result of the running of the program. Given that arbitrary numbers are loaded into these storage positions before the program is run, what number will be in each of them when the machine halts?

We have in mind the communication that sometimes takes place between a person who writes a program and another person who intends to use it. The latter is not interested in how the program works, but is interested in what happens as a result. For his or her purpose it suffices to know the total storage content at the halt as a function of the total storage content at the beginning of the run. In fact, for many purposes this may be too much information; what happens to the auxiliary variables may be of no interest.

Consider the GOTO-language program coded from the flowchart of Fig. 3.4.4. (For this purpose, we may look at the detailed flowchart and not bother with the actual program.) We are interested in the vector $\langle X, Y, W, U\rangle$ when the machine halts as a function of an arbitrary vector $\langle X, Y, W, U\rangle$ with which the machine begins. We see that, if the input vector is $\langle n_1, n_2, n_3, n_4\rangle$, where the n's are arbitrary numbers, then the output vector is $\langle n_1, 0, n_1 n_2, 0\rangle$. The same can be said for the WHILE-language program coded from the same flowchart.

Note that in both programs the values of W and U at the beginning are immaterial; they have no effect on any of the four values at the halt. This is because W and U are assigned other values in the program before the original values can have any effect at all. W is, of course, the output variable; at the halt it will contain the product that we wrote both programs to compute. Note also that the value of X is preserved in both programs but the value of Y is not, which is important to know if either of these programs is to be a subprogram of another program in which the original value of X or Y is to be used after the run of the subprogram.

Thus the answer to the question of what a program does is that it computes a function. We shall formalize this notion is Section 3.6. Experience indicates that the flowchart sometimes gives us quick insights into which function a program computes.

3.4.4 Exercises

1. (a) Give a run history in tabular form (see Section 3.2.2) for the multiplication program in the GOTO language which was given for the flowchart of Fig. 3.4.4, assuming that X, Y, W, and U are set at 3 and 2, 1914, and 1939, respectively. (You will thereby trace the multiplication of 3 by 2.) Number the commands in the program 1 through 9.

   (b) Do the same for the program in the WHILE language written from Fig. 3.4.4, numbering the commands (consecutively, by line) 1 through 7.

In each of the following, write a program to compute the function F that is indicated. Let X1, X2, X3, and so on, be your input variables, or simply X if there is only one, and let Y be your output variable, with auxiliary variables as you see fit. The values of your input variables may be destroyed in the working of the program. You may give your answer as a detailed flowchart, as a GOTO-language program, or as a

WHILE-language program, as you choose. We suggest that you use the following convenient abbreviations:

$+(X)$	for INCR(X)
$-(X)$	for DECR(X)
$++(X)$	for INCR(X);INCR(X)
$---(X)$	for DECR(X);DECR(X);DECR(X)
$-(X1,X2)$	for DECR(X1);DECR(X2)

In the first few of these exercises you are asked to give run histories in tabular form, which requires that you write out your program and number the commands (see Section 3.2.2). In each run history, set the input values as indicated, set the output $Y = 0$, and set each auxiliary variable at 1492.

2. F(X1, X2) is the maximum of the two values X1, X2 [e.g., F(3, 2) = 3, F(2, 2) = 2]. Give the run histories for X1 = 3, X2 = 1; for X1 = 2, X2 = 4; and for X1 = 2, X2 = 2.

3. $F(X) = \begin{cases} X & \text{if } X \leq 5 \\ 5 & \text{if } X > 5. \end{cases}$

Give the run histories for X = 3 and for X = 6.

4. $F(X) = \sum_{i=0}^{X} i$. Give the run histories for X = 0 and X = 2.

5. $F(X1, X2) = \begin{cases} 0 & \text{if } X1 \leq X2 \\ X1 - X2 & \text{if } X1 > X2 \end{cases}$

[e.g., F(5, 3) = 2; F(5, 5) = 0; F(5, 8) = 0]. (In Chapter 4 this function, called "floored subtraction," will play an important role and will be denoted by the symbol $\dot{-}$. The functions of Exercises 9, 11, and 12 will also play a significant role in Chapter 4.)

6. $F(X) = \begin{cases} X + 1 & \text{if } X < 2 \\ X & \text{if } X = 2 \\ X - 1 & \text{if } X > 2. \end{cases}$

7. $F(X) = \begin{cases} X & \text{if } X \text{ is divisible by 3} \\ X - 1 & \text{if } X \text{ is not divisible by 3.} \end{cases}$

8. $F(X) = \begin{cases} 2X & \text{if } X \text{ is even} \\ 3X & \text{if } X \text{ is odd.} \end{cases}$

9. $F(X1, X2) = \begin{cases} 0 & \text{if } X1 = X2 \\ 1 & \text{if } X1 \neq X2. \end{cases}$

10. $F(X) = 2^X$.

11. F(X1, X2) is the quotient when X1 is divided by X2 $\neq$ 0; F(X1, X2) = 0 if X2 = 0. [e.g., F(52, 5) = F(50, 5) = 10, F(49, 5) = 9]. (This function is similar to integer division in FORTRAN, etc.)

12. F(X1, X2) is the remainder when X1 is divided by X2 if X2 $\neq$ 0; F(X1, X2) = X1 if X2 = 0 [e.g., F(52, 5) = 2, F(50, 5) = 0, F(49, 5) = 4].

13. F(X1, X2, X3, X4) is the minimum value of X1, X2, X3, and X4.

14. F(X1, X2, X3, X4) is the maximum value of X1, X2, X3, and X4.

15. $F(X1, X2) = \begin{cases} 0 & \text{if } X1 = X2 = 0 \\ 1 & \text{if } X1 = 0 \text{ but } X2 \neq 0 \\ 2 & \text{if } X1 \neq 0 \text{ but } X2 = 0 \\ 3 & \text{if } X1 \neq 0 \neq X2. \end{cases}$

16. $F(X1, X2, X3, X4, X5) = \begin{cases} X3 & \text{if } X1 < X2 \\ X4 & \text{if } X1 = X2 \\ X5 & \text{if } X1 > X2. \end{cases}$

17. Let GCD(X1, X2) be the greatest common divisor of X1 and X2 if $X1 \neq 0 \neq X2$; you may pick your own value of GCD(X1, X2) when either X1 or X2 is zero.

  (a) Write a schematic flowchart for the subtraction version of the Euclidean algorithm to compute GCD(X1, X2).

  (b) From your schematic flowchart, write a program in the GOTO language to compute the function GCD.

  (c) From your schematic flowchart, write a program in the WHILE language.

18. The nonnegative real numbers can be coded in the foundational programming languages in unlimited finite precision by pairs of nonnegative integers. The pair (X1, X2) represents the number $X1*10^{-X2}$ (where * denotes multiplication). (X1, X2) is *normal* if either X2 = 0, or else X2 > 0 and X1 is not a multiple of 10 [e.g., the normal equivalents of (1070, 3), (0, 2), and (100, 1) are, respectively, (107, 2), (0, 0), and (10, 0) since $1070*10^{-3} = 107*10^{-2}, 0*10^{-2} = 0*10^{-0}$, and $100*10^{-1} = 10*10^{-0}$].

  (a) Write a schematic flowchart for real number multiplication that has inputs X1, X2, Y1, and Y2 and outputs Z1 and Z2, such that the output $Z1*10^{-Z2}$ at the end of a program run equals what $(X1*10^{-X2})*(Y1*10^{-Y2})$ was at the beginning of the run, and such that (Z1, Z2) is normal. Thus your program will do "floating-point" multiplication in unlimited finite precision. You may use the commands:

$$V3 := \text{QUOTIENT } (V1, 10)$$

$$V3 := \text{REMAINDER } (V1, 10)$$

$$V3 := V1 + V2$$

$$V3 := V1*V2$$

The first and second of these obtain the quotient and remainder, respectively, upon division by 10. And you may use in a decision box:

$$V1 \leq V2?$$

  (b) Using the instructions in part (a), write a schematic flowchart for "floating-point" addition. This time $Z1*10^{-Z2} = X1*10^{-X2} + Y1*10^{-Y2}$, and (Z1, Z2) is normal.

  (c) Thought question: How might you extend this system of representing the nonnegative reals to a system representing all the reals?

19. Let the WHILE II language be the result of adding the four command types of part (a) of Exercise 18, and another bilateral conditional command:

$$\text{IF } V1 \leq V2 \quad \text{THEN } [\ldots] \quad \text{ELSE } [\ldots]$$

Satisfy the requirements of Exercise 18 in terms of programs in this language.

In this section we examine some programs that, for certain input values, run forever. Although such programs should be avoided in practice, they play an important role in the theory of computability, as we now begin to explain. The halting problem will continue to occupy our attention in the next three chapters.

Subtraction **3.5.1**

Figure 3.5.1 is the detailed flowchart of a program in the GOTO language with input variables X and Y and output variable Z. If input Y is greater than input X, the program will keep decrementing X and Y until X is zero, at which point Y will be nonzero. It will then continue to loop, but this time it will short-circuit the portion in which X and Y are decremented. It will continue to do this forever; it will never halt.

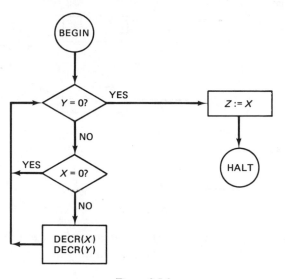

Figure 3.5.1

On the other hand, if input Y is less than or equal to input X, the machine will eventually halt. Upon halting, Y will be zero, and Z and X will each be the original value of X minus the original value of Y.

A program in the WHILE language written from this flowchart is as follows:

$$\begin{aligned}
&\text{WHILE } Y > 0 \text{ DO} \\
&\quad [\text{IF } X = 0 \text{ THEN } [X := X] \\
&\quad \text{ELSE } [\text{DECR}(X); \text{ DECR}(Y)]]; \\
&\text{Z} := \text{X}
\end{aligned}$$

In this program, the innocent command X := X is used because the flowchart directs that nothing be done if X = 0.

The discussion about nonhalting applies to this WHILE-language program. If input Y is greater than input X, the execution of the while command will never be completed, because Y will never become zero.

In practical programming situations it is never desirable to write a program that fails to halt in any situation. It is generally better for the programmer to foresee those situations and to put in an error return or to provide some other way to come out of the loop.

The program of Fig. 3.5.2 is a modification of Fig. 3.5.1 which always halts, at which point output Z equals the absolute difference of inputs X and Y.

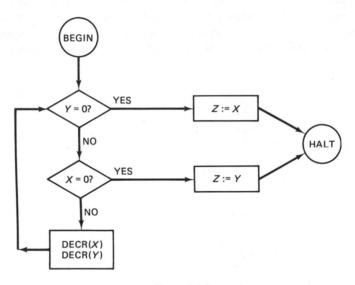

Figure 3.5.2

In writing a program in the WHILE language from Fig. 3.5.2, we need to compute a new quantity U equal to zero if and only if either X = 0 or Y = 0.

```
U := 1;
IF X = 0 THEN [U := 0];
IF Y = 0 THEN [U := 0];
WHILE U > 0 DO
     [DECR(X);
      DECR(Y);
       IF X = 0 THEN [U := 0];
       IF Y = 0 THEN [U := 0]];
IF Y = 0 THEN [Z := X] ELSE [Z := Y]
```

In studying the theory of computability, we must allow for the possibility of functions so difficult to compute that we cannot guarantee that our program for them will halt in all possible circumstances. More precisely, the situation is this: We shall find that all computable functions can be computed by programs in the GOTO language and that they can all be computed by programs in the WHILE language. But when we try to delimit the class of computable functions, we find that we cannot effectively classify all such programs without also including programs that sometimes fail to halt.

The reader may find it difficult to appreciate this point at the present moment. In hopes of making the halting problem less remote, we embark upon the following analogy. Let us imagine a person who is a good programmer, but whose mathematical knowledge is severely limited. We must imagine that this person lacks knowledge of two elementary mathematical facts. First, he believes that every nonnegative integer has an integral square root. Second, he is not aware that the square root of an integer, if it exists, must be less than or equal to that integer.

In his naïve state he writes the program of Fig. 3.5.3 to compute the square root of V with output R. The program squares each successive value of R, beginning at zero, and compares the result with V. When it discovers that value of R whose square equals V, it halts (see Engeler [1973], pp. 108–109).

This situation may seem absurd, since anyone with knowledge of computational procedures has at least some mathematical knowledge of squares and square roots. However, the writing of a mathematical program to find a number with a certain property, without knowing for certain that such a number exists, is quite a real possibility. What is unreal about the present example has to do with its simplicity. (We offer a more complicated and perhaps more gratifying example in Section 4.4.4.)

The detailed flowchart may be obtained from Fig. 3.5.3 by replacing the box $Z := |X - Y|$ by Fig. 3.5.2 and replacing the box $W := W*Y$ by Fig. 3.4.4 (In each case the begin and halt circles in Figs. 3.4.4 and 3.5.2 are deleted and the arrows connected in the obvious way. The composition is similar to the composition of Fig. 3.4.4 from Figs. 3.4.2 and 3.4.3.)

Let us trace through Fig. 3.5.3 to understand in detail what happens for two sample inputs, $V = 4$ and $V = 5$. For $V = 4$, the program tries successively, $R = 0$, $R = 1$, and $R = 2$. For $R = 0$, W becomes 0 and Z becomes $|0 - 4| = 4 \neq 0$, indicating that 0 is not the square root of 4. For $R = 1$, W becomes 1 and Z becomes 3, indicating that 1 is not the square root of 4. But for $R = 2$, W becomes 4 and Z becomes 0, indicating that 2 *is* the square root of 4, and the machine halts with $R = 2$.

When $V = 5$ is the input, the machine successively tries $R = 0$, $R = 1$, $R = 2$, $R = 3$, $R = 4$, $R = 5$, $R = 6$, and so on forever. Since there is no value of R that is the square root of 5, there is no value that will make Z go to zero, so the machine will never leave the loop.

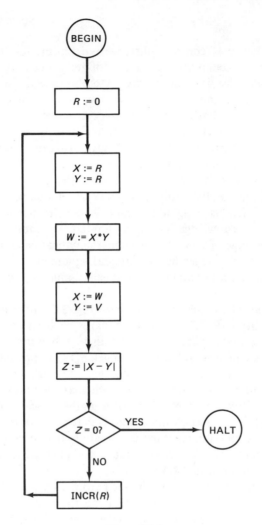

Figure 3.5.3

The program in the GOTO language written from Fig. 3.5.3 (and Figs. 3.5.2 and 3.4.4) is easy to write, and we shall omit it.

A program in the WHILE language is as follows, in which P_1 represents a sequence of lines to compute $W := X*Y$ and P_2 represents a sequence of lines to compute $Z := |X - Y|$.

$$R := 0; \quad X := R; \quad Y := R;$$
$$P_1;$$
$$X := W; \quad Y := V;$$
$$P_2;$$

WHILE Z > 0 DO

[INCR(R); X := R; Y := R;

P$_1$;

X := W; Y := V;

P$_2$]

Using some simple tricks of a clever programmer, it is possible to write a shorter program in the WHILE language from Fig. 3.5.3. We give this program without further explanation:

Z := 1; R := 0;

WHILE Z > 0 DO

[X := R; Y := R;

P$_1$;

X := W; Y := V;

P$_2$;

INCR(R)];

DECR(R)

Note that what we have said about halting and nonhalting in connection with Fig. 3.5.3 applies to these two WHILE programs as well.

Let us go back now to the good programmer with severely limited mathematical knowledge who designed the flowchart of Fig. 3.5.3. This imaginary person has written a program that successfully computes the square root, provided that the square root of the input is a nonnegative integer. But if the input is not a perfect square, then the program does not tell us this; it simply keeps on going forever. In this particular program for this particular problem, the failure of the program to halt in some cases could easily be corrected. But when we get sufficiently complicated programs, it will sometimes be impossible to tell that a program is not going to halt.

In fact, we shall prove that there can be no algorithm to tell whether or not a given program in the GOTO language halts for a given input; nor is there one for the WHILE language. This failure to be able to tell whether a program halts is not a peculiar property of the two languages; it is inherent in the theory of computability itself. Any language sufficiently rich to express all computable functions will have an unsolvable halting problem.

It is for this reason that we include exercises (at the end of the next section) to write programs that fail to halt in certain circumstances. Certainly, there is no practical value in having a program that will run forever for certain input values. The gain in carrying through these exercises is toward a theoretical understanding of the halting problem.

This program for finding the square root is more of a paradigm of programs that do not halt than the subtraction program of Fig. 3.5.1. The general pattern of a program that fails to halt is a program that searches for a number satisfying a certain relationship to certain given numbers (generally, the inputs). When there is no such number, the program fails to halt because it simply keeps on searching.

3.6 PROGRAMS FOR TOTAL
AND PARTIAL FUNCTIONS

As we mentioned in Section 3.4.3, we can describe what a program does by naming a mathematical function that the program computes. In this section we formalize this method of description in the case where we are interested only in one variable as program output.

3.6.1 Functions

Although the concept of function is one that pervades our mathematical education and application, and although we have used it in earlier sections of this chapter, we must at this point give a clear explanation of this concept as we use it in the remainder of this chapter and in the chapters that follow. To begin with, the universe of discourse is fixed for the next few chapters as the domain of the nonnegative integers (which, for simplicity, we call *numbers*). We say that an *n*-argument function f ($n \geq 1$) associates to each *n*-tuple of numbers $(x_1, \ldots, x_n)$ at most one number; if this number exists, it is called the value of f for the arguments $x_1, \ldots, x_n$, or $f(x_1, \ldots, x_n)$; if this number does not exist, we say that f has no value (or is *undefined*) for the arguments $x_1, \ldots, x_n$, or more simply that $f(x_1, \ldots, x_n)$ *has no value* (or *does not exist*, or is *undefined*). (The terms in parentheses are terms that occur in other books.)

Definition: An *n*-argument function f is a *total function* if it has a value for every *n*-tuple of numbers. Otherwise, f is a *partial function*.

We have already discussed several total functions: the one-argument successor function (computed by the increment command), the one-argument predecessor function (computed by the decrement command), two-argument addition, two-argument multiplication, and the two-argument absolute-difference function. The minus function, on the other hand, is a two-argument partial function: If $f(x, y) = x - y$, then f has a value for x and y if and only if $x \geq y$. The square-root function (which is computed in Fig. 3.5.3) is an example of a one-argument partial function: If $f(x) =$ the square root of x, then f has a value for x if and only if x is a perfect square.

(It should be noted that the lowercase letters used above—the letters x, y, and so on—are not variables of the programming languages. They are the ordinary variables of ordinary mathematical discourse, which we use in our discussion about the programming language.)

Definition: A program P *computes* a function f of n arguments with respect to a sequence S of $n + 1$ programming-language variables ($n \geqq 1$) if, for each n-tuple of numbers $x_1, \ldots, x_n$, when the program P is run after setting the storage positions corresponding to the first n variables of S (the *input variables*) to the numbers $x_1, \ldots, x_n$, respectively, and however the other storage positions are set, then (1) if $f(x_1, \ldots, x_n)$ has a value, the program will halt after some finite amount of time and the storage position corresponding to the $(n + 1)$st variable of S (the *output variable*) will have the number $f(x_1, \ldots, x_n)$ at the halt; and (2) if $f(x_1, \ldots, x_n)$ has no value, the program P will never halt.

In our study of the theory of computability we focus on the computation of functions. This may seem restrictive when we realize that many useful programs have several outputs and not just one. However, for theoretical purposes, a program with n outputs can simply be regarded as n different programs, one for each output.

Examples; Discussion   3.6.2

The program of Fig. 3.2.1 in the GOTO language, whose detailed flowchart is given as Fig. 3.4.1, computes the addition function with respect to the sequence of variables, X, Y, Z. In this case $n + 1 = 3$. Exactly the same is true, of course, of the program in the WHILE language written for Fig. 3.4.1.

By looking at the flowchart alone it can be seen that the two programs of Fig. 3.4.4, one in the GOTO language, the other in the WHILE language, compute multiplication with respect to the sequence X, Y, W. The programs of Fig. 3.5.1 compute the partial function minus with respect to the sequence X, Y, Z. The programs of Fig. 3.5.2 compute the total function absolute difference with respect to the sequence X, Y, Z. And, finally, the programs of Fig. 3.5.3 compute the partial one-argument square-root function with respect to the sequence V, R.

In general, a program has variables other than its input and output variables. For example, the programs of Fig. 3.4.4 have the auxiliary variable U in addition to the variables Z, Y, and W. The definition demands that the programs compute multiplication regardless of how W and U are set at the beginning, since neither is an input variable. We have already noted that the setting of W and U before the machine executes its first step is immaterial to the working of the program.

From the detailed flowchart (and often from a schematic flowchart) we can verify that a program computes the function it is supposed to compute, with respect to a specified sequence of variables. In going from a detailed flowchart to the program in the GOTO language, no new variables are added and the role each variable plays is unchanged. Although a program in the WHILE language sometimes uses a new auxiliary variable, as, for example, the variable U in the WHILE-language program (p. 68) written from Fig. 3.5.2, this makes no difference in the matter at hand since auxiliary variables do not occur in the sequence with respect to which a program computes a function.

The condition of the definition says nothing about the setting of any variables other than the output variable when the machine halts. The program may, for example, destroy some of the input values.

The relationship of a program to the function it computes is part of the advanced semantics of the programming language. This relationship is an important one and is related to the formulation of the semantics of an algorithmic command given in Section AIII.6; a command denotes a function mapping a total configuration of the computer to another total configuration, namely the total configuration that comes next. (See Section 5.2, which has a mathematically precise definition of "total configuration.")

The study of semantics of programming languages based on this idea is called *denotational semantics*. One of the problems in this area of the theory of computation is determining the function denoted by a program from the way the program is composed from individual commands.

3.6.3 Program Verification

In this and the next subsection we describe a well-known method of verifying that a program computes a certain function, namely Floyd's method of inductive assertions and well-founded sets (see Manna [1974], pp. 174, 185). As an example we use the multiplication program of Fig. 3.4.4. A flowchart is convenient and sufficient for our purposes; we need not decide which of the two programming languages the program is written in.

Accordingly, we revise the flowchart of Fig. 3.4.4 in two ways, resulting in Fig. 3.6.1. First, we revise the set of variables. X0 and Y0 are input variables; Y, W, and U are the other variables, of which W is the output variable. X0 and Y0 are not modified in the course of the program, and therefore have the same value at the halt that they do at the beginning. We can then think of the relationship at the halt of the value of W to the value of X0 and Y0 as the function computed by the program. Second, we place circled numbers at certain vertices in the flowchart and investigate the values certain variables have at times when execution passes through points of the program corresponding to these vertices.

Definition: A *verification flowchart* is one with certain nodes labeled (circled numbers are used in the figures) such that (a) there is a labeled node at the beginning and at every halt, and (b) there is a labeled node on every closed path (loop) of the flowchart; furthermore, the input variables in such a flowchart are not modified.

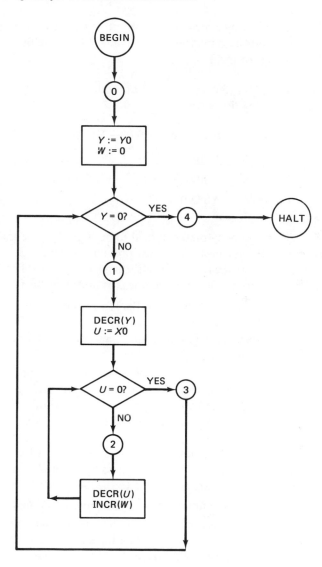

Figure 3.6.1

Note that Fig. 3.6.1 is a verification flowchart. We wish to verify that its program computes multiplication. More specifically, we wish to verify that if the machine is at node 0 (with X0 and Y0 set to the numbers to be multiplied) then at some later time the machine is at node 4 with W = X0*Y0.

Multiplication Program Verified   3.6.4

To prove that the program of Fig. 3.6.1 does compute multiplication, we prove two separate propositions: (I) if the machine is ever at node 4, then W = X0*Y0; and (II) eventually the machine will reach node 4.

(We note that breaking down our work into two parts in this way is in accord with the methods used in Appendices I and II to prove the correctness of informally written algorithms.)

LEMMA 1: Whenever the machine is at node i, $i = 1, 2, 3, 4$, assertion (Ai) in the following list is true:

> (A1) $Y > 0$ and $W = (Y0 - Y)*X0$
>
> (A2) $U > 0$ and $U + W = (Y0 - Y)*X0$
>
> (A3) $U = 0$ and $W = (Y0 - Y)*X0$
>
> (A4) $W = Y0*X0$

PROOF: The proof is by mathematical induction. Assume that Lemma 1 was true before the tth time cycle. We must prove for each $i = 1, 2, 3, 4$ that if the machine is at node i at the tth time cycle, then (Ai) is true. (The basis of the induction is vacuously true, since the machine is at node 0 at the first time cycle.)

Case 1. The machine is at node 1, and the last numbered node the machine visited was node 0. The machine came downward through the decision box, so $Y > 0$. Since W has been set to 0, and Y has been set to Y0, both sides of the equation in (A1) are zero, so (A1) is true.

Case 2. The machine is at node 1 and the last numbered node was node 3. By inductive hypothesis, at the time the machine was at node 3, $W = (Y0 - Y)*X0$. No variable has changed value, so the equation is still true. And $Y > 0$ since the machine came downward through the decision box. Again (A1) is true.

Note that cases 1 and 2 exhaust all the possibilities in which the machine is at node 1 at the tth time cycle. We shall not carry through the proof for the remaining cases, because they are all similar to the cases just given.

Case 3. The machine is at node 2 and the last numbered node was node 1.

Case 4. The machine is at node 2 and the last numbered node was node 2. (In this case the machine has gone around the inner loop. $U + W$ remains the same because U, which is greater than zero, has been decremented and W has been incremented.)

Case 5. The machine is at node 3 and the last numbered node was node 1.

Case 6. The machine is at node 3 and the last numbered node was node 2.

Case 7. The machine is at node 4, and the last numbered node was node 0.

Case 8. The machine is at node 4, and the last numbered node was node 3. ∎

Lemma 1 clearly implies proposition I. The method of proof used in the lemma is known as the *method of inductive assertions.*

The proof of proposition II is easy in this example. In fact, it follows from two easily proved lemmas.

LEMMA 2: If the machine is ever at node 1, then at some time later it will be at node 3.

PROOF: Each new time node 2 is visited (if at all), the value of U is decreased. Eventually, U will be zero, and then the machine will be at node 3. ∎

LEMMA 3: Eventually, the machine (which begins at node 0) will be at node 4.

PROOF: Any time the machine visits node 1 (if at all), at some time later it will be at node 3, by Lemma 2. The value of Y will be decreased. Thereafter the machine will be either at node 4 or at node 1 again.

Each new time it is at node 1, the value of Y is decreased, so eventually Y will be zero, and the machine will then go to node 4. ∎

This method of proving that a program terminates is called the *method of well-founded sets*. Generally, the method of proving that a program halts is to find, for each loop, a quantity that decreases each time around the loop, but that cannot be less than a certain amount.

The process of verifying a program, when one is given a program for calculating a function written by someone else, is difficult to the point of being practically impossible. What is feasible is that the person who writes a program can expend some extra effort to verify it in the very process of writing it. If he succeeds in coming up with a program for a given function then he should understand why the program works. He should therefore be able to find an appropriate set of labeled nodes in his flowchart, write inductive assertions for each of them, and (assuming that his program is indeed correct) prove them. He should also possess the insight of why the machine always comes out of every loop, and prove the equivalent of our Lemmas 2 and 3 for his program.

Whether or not the advocates of program verification will ever persuade any sizable group of programmers to write verified programs is another matter. Many programmers feel that program verification, as distinguished from debugging, is futile because of the immensity of most programs.

(For further information about this method of program verification, see Chapter III of Manna [1974].)

3.6.5 Exercises

Write a detailed flowchart, a program in the GOTO language, or a program in the WHILE language that computes the function described in each of the following. Use the input variables X1, X2, ... (or X itself if there is just one input), and use Y as output variable. Your program must be such as never to halt if the function has no value for a set of arguments. Use the abbreviations suggested for the exercises of Section 3.4.

1. $F(X) \begin{cases} = 0 & \text{if X is even} \\ \text{has no value} & \text{if X is odd.} \end{cases}$

2. $F(X1, X2) \begin{cases} = X1 & \text{if X1} = \text{X2} \\ \text{has no value} & \text{if X1} \neq \text{X2.} \end{cases}$

3. $F(X) \begin{cases} \text{has no value} & \text{if X} \leq 4 \\ = 0 & \text{if } 5 \leq X \leq 10 \\ = X - 10 & \text{if X} > 10. \end{cases}$

4. $F(X1, X2) \begin{cases} = X1/X2 & \text{if X2} \neq 0 \text{ and X1 is an integral multiple of X2} \\ \text{has no value} & \text{otherwise.} \end{cases}$

[Thus F(X1, X2) is the result of division, if this result is an integer.]

3.7 DO-TIMES

In this section we introduce a new command into the WHILE language, comparable to the "DO" of FORTRAN and the "FOR" of ALGOL. This DO-TIMES command can always be replaced by a certain kind of WHILE command, so that the WHILE language is not thereby enriched in computing power.

We consider programs in the WHILE language with DO-TIMES commands but without WHILE commands. These programs (first considered in Meyer and Ritchie [1967] and called "loop programs") have a significance in the theory of computability that is discussed in Section 4.8. In this section we prove that they always halt.

3.7.1 A New Command

We now allow ourselves to write in the WHILE language

DO X TIMES [. . .]

The variable X can be replaced by any other variable, and inside the brackets there is a program. We need no further discussion of the syntax of this command, since it is so similar to the other commands that have bracketed programs.

As for semantics, the machine responds to this command by attempting to execute the bracketed program a number of times equal to the value of X at the time it first examines the command. Even if the bracketed program modifies the value of X, it is the original value of X that determines the number of times the bracketed program is executed. (We say "attempting to execute," because, in the event that the bracketed program does not halt one of the times it is to be executed, the machine will not be able to execute it the required number of times.)

For example, the machine in executing the program

$$X := 2; \text{ DO } X \text{ TIMES } [\text{INCR(X)}]$$

will execute the bracketed program twice, and will halt when X has the value 4. The fact that X changes to 3 and 4 in the process has no effect on the number of times the bracketed program is executed.

If the machine executes the program

$$X := 0; \text{ DO } X \text{ TIMES } [\text{INCR(X)}]$$

it will not execute the bracketed program at all (i.e., it will execute it zero times) and will halt with X equal to zero.

A DO-TIMES command can always be rewritten as a WHILE command. If XX is a variable that does not occur in the program π, then

$$\text{DO } X \text{ TIMES } [\pi]$$

can be rewritten as

$$XX := X; \text{ WHILE } XX > 0 \text{ DO } [\text{DECR(XX)}; \pi]$$

Indeed, even if this DO-TIMES command occurs as part of a larger program, the rewriting is still possible, provided we are careful that the variable XX is one that does not occur anywhere in the larger program. Thus, in adding the DO-TIMES command to the WHILE language, we have not really added any new capability to the language.

We note that if π is a program that always halts whatever the initial values of its variables, then the program

$$\text{DO } X \text{ TIMES } [\pi]$$

will always halt whatever the values of X and other variables occurring in π.

Definition: A *DO-TIMES program* is a WHILE-language program in which no WHILE command occurs (but in which DO-TIMES commands may occur).

THEOREM 3.7.1: A DO-TIMES program always halts.

By the remark made just prior to the definition, the proof is quite straight-forward, using mathematical induction on the *level* of the program (a concept from Section 3.3.1 that is easily extended to DO-TIMES programs). We leave the details to the reader.

One consequence of this theorem is that not every WHILE-language program has an equivalent DO-TIMES program. It turns out that the WHILE command is much more powerful than the DO-TIMES command, as the next few chapters show.

We note that a WHILE-language program without any WHILE commands and without any DO-TIMES commands has no loops at all. That is, no command in any part of the program is ever executed more than once in any run. As a consequence, the class of mathematical functions computed by such programs is quite limited (see Exercises 6 to 9).

3.7.2 Discussion; Examples

Not all computable functions can be computed by DO-TIMES programs. The class of functions that can be so computed turns out to be an interesting class of functions, namely the class of primitive recursive functions, discussed in Section 4.8. Most functions that we deal with are in this class.

As we mentioned, the WHILE command is more powerful than the DO-TIMES command. Many programming languages (such as FORTRAN) do not contain any similar command as powerful as the WHILE, their various iteration commands being only as powerful as the DO-TIMES. Such languages can get the full power of the unrestricted WHILE command only by use of the GOTO.

Some programs with WHILE commands can be converted with effort into equivalent DO-TIMES programs. For example, the following program taken from Section 3.3 (Fig. 3.3.1) is akin to a DO-TIMES program in that both WHILE commands are such that their bracketed programs are executed a prescribed number of times:

$$Z := 0;$$
$$\text{WHILE } X > 0 \text{ DO}$$
$$[U := X; \text{ DECR}(X);$$
$$\text{WHILE } U > 0 \text{ DO } [\text{DECR}(U); \text{ INCR}(Z)]]$$

Making some minor adaptations, we can easily write an equivalent DO-TIMES program:

$$Z := 0;$$
$$\text{DO } X \text{ TIMES}$$
$$[U := X; \text{ DECR}(X);$$
$$\text{DO } U \text{ TIMES } [\text{INCR}(Z)]]$$

With a little reflection, we see that the auxiliary variable U can be dispensed with, and we get the following simpler equivalent program:

$$Z := 0;$$
DO X TIMES
   [DO X TIMES [INCR(Z)];
   DECR(X)]

Note that the decrementing of X affects the number of times the inner loop ([INCR(Z)]) is executed each successive time, but not the number of times the outer loop (i.e., the outer bracketed program) is executed.

A flowchart for a DO-TIMES program that computes

$$F(X) = \begin{cases} 0 & \text{if X is even} \\ 1 & \text{if X is odd} \end{cases}$$

with output Y is given in Fig. 3.7.1. A DO-TIMES program for this function adapted from this flowchart is as follows:

$$Y := 0;$$
DO X TIMES
   [IF Y = 0 THEN [Y := 1] ELSE [Y := 0]]

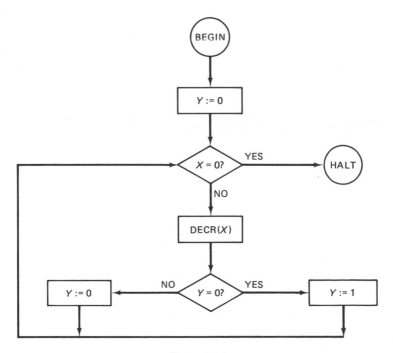

Figure 3.7.1

Compare a WHILE-language program for the same function:

Y := 0;

WHILE X > 0 DO

  [DECR(X);

   IF X = 0 THEN [Y := 1] ELSE [DECR(X)]]

The latter is probably more efficient than the DO-TIMES program: Y changes value at most once in it, but changes value X times in the DO-TIMES program.

Recall the WHILE-language program for the absolute-difference function written from Fig. 3.5.2. A DO-TIMES program for the same function with respect to X, Y, Z requires a completely different structure:

X1 := X;   Y1 := Y;

DO X1 TIMES [DECR(Y1)];

DO Y TIMES [DECR(X)];

IF Y1 = 0 THEN [Z := X] ELSE [Z := Y1]

Loosely speaking, this program subtracts X from Y, and then subtracts Y from X, yielding zero in place of negative values in each case. It then chooses the latter if the former is zero, and chooses the former otherwise. The program is not as efficient as the one written from Fig. 3.5.2. For example, if X = 100, Y = 2, the latter will need to decrement X and Y only twice, whereas the former will have to decrement Y1 100 times, and then decrement X twice. Although the DO-TIMES program can be improved, there seems to be no way of making it as efficient as the one written from Fig. 3.5.2.

DO-TIMES programs have an appealing simplicity, in that the DO-TIMES command is simpler than the WHILE command, but they are sometimes inefficient.

3.7.3 Exercises

1. Write DO-TIMES programs for Fig. 3.4.1.

2. Write DO-TIMES programs for Fig. 3.4.4.

3. Write DO-TIMES programs for the functions of Exercises 2 to 6 of Section 3.4. (If you have already written programs in the WHILE language for these exercises, at most a small effort will probably be needed to convert them.)

4. The same for Exercises 7 to 9 of Section 3.4.

5. The same for Exercises 10 to 12 of Section 3.4. (These will be more involved, but not too difficult if you master the technique of using a previously written program as a part of a new program.)

6. Write a program in the WHILE language without any WHILE or DO-TIMES commands that computes F with respect to X1, X2, Y, where

$$F(X1, X2) = \begin{cases} X2 & \text{if } X1 = 0 \\ X2 + 2 & \text{if } X1 = 1 \text{ or } 2 \\ X2 + 4 & \text{if } X1 \geq 3 \end{cases}$$

7. (*Difficult*) (a) Prove that if a program in the WHILE language that has only one variable X and no WHILE, DO-TIMES or conditional commands computes a function F with respect to X, X (i.e., X is both input and output), then there are nonnegative integers i and j such that either

$$(\text{type 1}) \quad F(X) = i \quad \text{for all } X$$

$$(\text{type 2}) \quad F(X) = \begin{cases} X \mid i & \text{for } X \geq j \\ j + i & \text{for } X < j \end{cases} \quad \text{or}$$

$$(\text{type 3}) \quad F(X) = \begin{cases} X - i & \text{for } X \geq j \\ j - i & \text{for } X < j \end{cases}$$

(*Hint:* Such a program has no brackets, and is simply a succession of assignments, increments, and decrements to X. Carry through your proof by mathematical induction on the length of the program.)

(b) Show how to construct a program of each type for a given i and j ($j \geq i$ in type 3, and j immaterial in type 1).

8. (*More difficult*) (a) Prove that, if a program in the WHILE language with only one variable X and no WHILE or DO-TIMES commands (but possibly having conditional commands) computes a function F with respect to the variable sequence X, X, then there are nonnegative integers i and j such that either

$$(\text{type 1}') \quad F(X) = i \quad \text{for all } X \geq j$$

$$(\text{type 2}') \quad F(X) = X + i \quad \text{for } X \geq j \quad \text{or}$$

$$(\text{type 3}') \quad F(X) = X - i \quad \text{for } X \geq j$$

[In each case, the values of F(X) for X < j are arbitrary.]

(b) Prove that every function of type 1', type 2', or type 3' can be computed by such a program ($j \geq i$ in type 3).

9. (*Difficult*) (a) Suppose that a program in the WHILE language without WHILE or DO-TIMES commands and with only the variables X1, ..., $X\Delta_n$ computes a function F with respect to X1, X2, ..., $X\Delta_n$, X1 (X1 is both input and output). Prove there exist i, j, and k, $1 \leq k \leq n$, such that either

$$F(X1, \ldots, X\Delta_n) = i \quad \text{for all } X1, \ldots, X\Delta_n \geq j$$

$$F(X1, \ldots, X\Delta_n) = X_k + i \quad \text{for all } X1, \ldots, X\Delta_n \geq j \quad \text{or}$$

$$F(X1, \ldots, X\Delta_n) = X_k - i \quad \text{for all } X1, \ldots, X\Delta_n \geq j$$

(Δ_n is the numeral for n; thus, if n = 12, $X\Delta_n$ is X12.)

(b) Prove that addition is not computable by a program without WHILE or DO-TIMES commands, using the result of part (a). (Not a surprising result, but it is interesting to have a rigorous proof of it.)

4 Computable Functions

Our objective in this chapter is to gain a broad understanding of the entire class of computable functions over the nonnegative integers. In order to approach such an ambitious goal, we must go beyond individual algorithms for individual functions to wholesale methods of generating, or defining, new computable functions.

Four types of formal function definition are presented in this chapter: explicit definition, primitive recursion, mu recursion, and general equational definition. By studying these (especially the first three) we shall be able to get a reasonable overview of the class of computable functions. In particular, we shall see that there are many functions of nonncgative integers that are computable (which means that they have an algorithm as we defined the term in Chapter 1) but are way beyond practical computation for all but a small set of arguments.

The vehicle for studying these four types of function definition is the formalism of functional expressions. In contrast to practically all programming languages, this formalism is a language of declaratives, or descriptive language. It will not be used for asserting mathematical theorems, but only for writing definitions of functions and, later, formal computations in the declarative mode.

4.1 EXPLICIT DEFINITION
AND PRIMITIVE RECURSION

In this section we present the first two of our definitional schemes. Later (Section 4.5) we prove that any function definable by either of these schemes in terms of functions computable in a foundational programming language is itself computable in the same foundational programming language. Various insights will be forthcoming about the class of computable functions in the course of our investigation of these two types of definition (Sections 4.1 to 4.3), but they alone without mu recursion (introduced in Section 4.4) are not enough to define all the computable functions.

Explicit Definition 4.1.1

In this, the simplest, type of function definition, the function is defined in a single equation, for example,

$$f(x, y, z) = +(*(x, y), *(z, 10))$$

Here the three-argument function f is defined in terms of the addition and multiplication functions, assumed to be known; the variables x, y, and z are used to represent the three arguments. In such a definition, variables other than the arguments are not allowed on the right side of the equation. The symbols $+$ and $*$ are allowed, because these functions are assumed as given; but certainly the function symbol f would not be allowed on the right side, lest the definition be circular.

The right side of this equation is called a *functional expression*, which is an expression made up of function symbols, variables, and numerals in the familiar way. In order to stipulate the general form of an explicit definition, we must characterize what a functional expression is in a formal way. We do this by means of a concept of level, similar to the level of a WHILE-language program in Section 3.3.1.

We begin by stipulating that a *numeral* is as it was defined in Chapter 3 for the foundational programming languages. A *variable* is either one of the letters x, y, or z, or one of these followed by a numeral subscript (e.g., x_1, y_0, or z_{17}).

A *function symbol* is either one of the letters f, g, or h, one of these followed by a numeral subscript, the letter S (the successor function: $S(x) = x + 1$ for all x), or a symbol introduced by means of a function definition. Not all such definitions introduce new function symbols, since we shall frequently use the letters f, g, and h, and these with subscripts to represent newly defined functions.

We are adopting the practice in our development of this formal system of allowing an expanding alphabet of characters, and expanding syntactic categories. For that reason, we do not list all the alphabetic characters in the formalism of functional expressions, because new characters will be added with some new definitions. The syntactic category of *function symbol* and any syntactic category depending on it (such as *functional expression* and *equation* to be described below) will also expand.

A *functional expression of level zero* is either a numeral or a variable. (Thus a functional expression of level zero is not a functional expression in the ordinary sense.) Now assume that functional expressions of levels $0, \ldots, i$ have been defined: A *functional expression of level* $i + 1$ is a function symbol followed by a left parenthesis followed by one or more functional expressions, separated by commas if there are more than one, followed by a right parenthesis; the functional expressions between the parentheses are all of levels no greater than i and there is at least one of level i. The number of functional expressions, called *arguments*, between these parentheses is exactly one in case the function symbol is S; and in the case of a symbol previously introduced in a function definition, the number of arguments must be the same as the number of arguments in that definition.

We now define a *functional expression* as a functional expression of level i, for any nonnegative integer i.

It is an easy matter to see the level of a functional expression: it is simply the maximum size of a set of nested parentheses (e.g., the level of the expression in Fig. 4.1.1 is four, the arrows indicating the nested set). Henceforth we shall talk about functional expressions without explicit reference to their level.

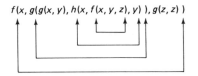

Figure 4.1.1

An *equation*, finally, is a functional expression followed by an equals sign followed by a functional expression.

We have in effect outlined the syntax of a formal language. A short discussion of some linguistic issues is given in Section 4.1.3. Meanwhile, we proceed with the matter at hand.

Definition: An *explicit definition* of an n-argument function $(n \geq 1)$ is a single equation whose left side consists of the function symbol for that function followed by n distinct variables, and whose right side is a functional expression with no variables other than those n variables and having only known function symbols. (In particular, the symbol denoting the function being defined may not appear on the right side.)

Subsequently, we shall adopt a procedure to ensure that function symbols used on the right side are known. Although we may use *only* the variables occurring on the left, we need not use all of them. Thus

$$f(x, y, z) = +(*(2, x), y)$$

is an acceptable explicit definition. The function f so defined is a three-argument function whose third argument has no effect on the value. Another similar definition is that of the constant-zero function Z of one argument:

$$Z(x) = 0$$

Quite obviously, a function defined explicitly in terms of computable functions is itself computable.

We shall have occasion to define partial functions by explicit definition. Our understanding is that if any of the given functions in an explicit definition is a partial function then the function defined is a partial function; moreover, for any set of values for which the given function has no value, the defined function has no value. For example, suppose that we have the following definition of f:

$$f(x, y, z) = h(g(z, x), y, x)$$

If $g(0, 4)$ has no value, then $f(4, j, 0)$ has no value for any value of j. And if $g(1, 2) = 3$ but $h(3, 2, 2)$ has no value, then $f(2, 2, 1)$ has no value.

Primitive Recursion   4.1.2

Explicit definition, although it may seem like the most natural kind of definition, is much too limited. In this subsection we introduce formally a kind of recursive definition known as primitive recursion. Perhaps the best example of this type of definition is the manner of defining multiplication of nonnegative integers in terms of addition. We first stipulate that the product of any nonnegative integer and zero equals zero. We then stipulate, for any nonnegative integer y, how the product of x by $y + 1$ is related to the product of x by y. In symbols we write this definition as follows:

$$\begin{cases} *(x, 0) = 0 \\ *(x, y + 1) = +(*(x, y), x) \end{cases}$$

Under the assumption that we can numerically compute $+(x, y)$ whenever any numerals are substituted for the variables x and y (addition itself will be defined by a primitive recursion below), these two equations tell us how to compute multiplication. For example, from the equations

$$*(3, 0) = 0$$
$$*(3, 1) = +(*(3, 0), 3)$$
$$*(3, 2) = +(*(3, 1), 3)$$
$$*(3, 3) = +(*(3, 2), 3)$$
$$*(3, 4) = +(*(3, 3), 3)$$

we can use addition to successively compute

$$*(3, 1) = 3$$
$$*(3, 2) = 6$$
$$*(3, 3) = 9$$
$$*(3, 4) = 12$$

The function of addition by one, which we call the *successor* function, is important in our work, and so we use the special symbol S for it. Thus $S(0) = 1$, $S(1) = 2$, and so on. Note that this function corresponds exactly to the incrementing operation of Chapter 3.

We are now ready for the formal definition of a primitive-recursive definition, which must be presented in a rather abstract way. To make the reading easier, we suggest that the reader focus on the following example of the primitive-recursive definition of the function f from functions g and h, which are assumed to be known:

$$\begin{cases} f(x_1, \ldots, x_{n-1}, 0) = g(x_1, \ldots, x_{n-1}) \\ f(x_1, \ldots, x_{n-1}, S(x_n)) = h(x_1, \ldots, x_n, f(x_1, \ldots, x_n)) \end{cases}$$

Definition: For $n \geq 1$, a *primitive-recursive definition* of an n-argument function (or *primitive recursion*) is a pair of equations

$$\begin{cases} L1 = R1 \\ L2 = R2 \end{cases}$$

where L1 consists of the symbol for the function being defined followed by $n - 1$ distinct variables, and 0 in the nth argument place; L2 consists of the same function symbol followed by the same $n - 1$ variables, respectively, but in the nth argument place the successor of an nth variable; R1 is a functional expression in which only the first $n - 1$ variables and only known function symbols may occur; and R2 is a functional expression in which only the n variables, and only known function symbols and the symbol for the function being defined may occur, but in each occurrence in R2 the function symbol for the function being defined must appear with precisely the n variables in order.

For example, if the foregoing definition of * is rewritten to fit the formalism ($n = 2$), it becomes

$$\begin{cases} *(x, 0) = 0 \\ *(x, S(y)) = +(*(x, y), x) \end{cases}$$

Note that the symbol * itself occurs on the right side of the second equation with the arguments x, y. Thus $*(x, S(y))$ is defined in terms of $*(x, y)$. The restriction that the function symbol being defined be followed by precisely the right set of variables prevents the definition from being circular.

We note the primitive recursive definition of addition in terms of successor alone:

$$\begin{cases} +(x, 0) = x \\ +(x, S(y)) = S(+(x, y)) \end{cases}$$

We assume here that successor is more fundamental than addition. In our work, we shall never attempt to define successor, but ultimately, we shall define all our other functions in terms of it. (For example, since multiplication is defined in terms of addition, and addition is defined in terms of successor, multiplication is defined indirectly in terms of successor.)

We give another example to illustrate the definition of a one-argument function ($n = 1$), the factorial function (conventionally written $x!$):

$$\begin{cases} f(0) = 1 \\ f(S(x)) = *(f(x), S(x)) \end{cases}$$

Many more examples are presented in Section 4.2.

The Formalism of Functional Expressions 4.1.3

In the process of setting up schemes for defining functions, we have set up a formalism about which we should make a few general comments before going on. The reader may skip this subsection without sacrificing understanding of any material through Section 4.5.

The formalism of functional expressions has the following characters: the 10 decimal digits, the letters S (representing the successor function), x, y, z, f, g, h, parentheses, the comma, the equals sign, and symbols for various functions (such as $+$ and $*$). The alphabet of characters will expand in later sections.

In Section 4.1.1, the terms *numeral*, *variable*, *function symbol*, *functional expression*, and *equation* were introduced. These were syntactic categories, but it should be noted that explicit definition and primitive recursive definition were also characterized syntactically.

Since the formalism of functional expressions is a language of declaratives, the three semantic concepts for it are denotation, truth, and validity. Its semantics, which we now present in some detail, will differ from that of programming languages, which are languages of commands. (See Appendix III.)

Function symbols denote functions, and nothing other than function symbols in our formalism denotes a function. Second, numerals denote nonnegative integers, as we have already mentioned. A variable denotes a number ambiguously; its denotation is always a number, but which number it denotes varies. Our convention is that a variable in every equation must be capable of denoting any nonnegative integer. For example, when we write

$$+(x, 0) = x$$

we mean for this to be true for any nonnegative integer.

The function symbols f, g, and h (with or without subscripts) have no fixed meaning, but are used to denote different functions in different contexts. Some authors call these *function variables*, which might be misleading. When we write $f(x)$ in an equation, that one occurrence of the letter x has a varying denotation, ranging over all nonnegative integers, whereas the letter f in that equation and other equations associated with it denotes just one function.

If all its function symbols denote total functions, then a functional expression with variables denotes a number, depending on the numbers denoted by the variables occurring in the expression. For example, the expression

$$+(*(x, y), y)$$

denotes a number depending on what numbers the variables x and y denote. If they denote 3 and 2, respectively, the expression denotes the number 8; but if they denote 6 and 7, respectively, the expression denotes 49. Thus the denotation of a functional expression varies with the denotation of the variables, generally speaking.

A functional expression without variables, in which all function symbols denote total functions, denotes a number unambiguously. For example, the functional expression

$$+(+(3, 0), +(1, 4))$$

denotes the number 8.

All our technical semantics, so far, is in accord with common sense, since we have been talking about total functions. When a functional expression contains function symbols that denote partial functions, the expression may not denote a number even when the variables in the expression do. For example, if h is the partial minus function,

$$h(x, y) \begin{cases} = x - y & \text{if } x \geq y \\ \text{has no value} & \text{if } x < y \end{cases}$$

then the functional expression

$$h(x, y)$$

does not denote anything when the variables x and y denote 3 and 5, respectively. It does denote something (the number 2) when they denote 5 and 3, respectively.

Finally, an equation is *true* if the left side and the right side denote the same number, or if neither of them denotes any number. Thus, if h denotes the partial minus function, the equation

$$h(S(x), S(y)) = h(x, y)$$

is true whatever the variables x and y denote. The equation

$$h(x, y) = +(z, y)$$

is true if x, y, z denote 5, 2, 1, respectively, but is false if x, y, z denote 2, 2, 2, and false if they denote 3, 4, 5. Finally, $h(1, 3) = h(1, 2)$ is true.

In Section 4.6, our study of formal computation makes use of this discussion of syntax and semantics.

DEFINITIONS OF SOME USEFUL 4.2 FUNCTIONS

The functions we formally define in this section, some of which are quite well known, will play an important role in our work in the theory of computability. The list was started in the preceding section with the one-argument constant-zero function (Z), the one-argument successor function (S), the two-argument addition function $(+)$, the two-argument multiplication function $(*)$.

Some More Definitions 4.2.1

Frequently, we wish to use an addition or multiplication function that has several arguments. Such functions are now easily defined by explicit definition from the two-argument functions already defined. For example, three-argument addition is defined by the following line:

$$+(x, y, z) = +(+(x, y), z)$$

A peculiar thing about this line is that the symbol $+$ seems to be defined in terms of itself. In reality, this definition is not circular, because the function symbol $+$ denotes a different function when it is followed by three arguments than when it is followed by two arguments. This definition is necessary: the functional expression $+(x, y, z)$ would have no meaning just from a definition of two-argument addition.

Similarly, we have the following definitions

$$+(w, x, y, z) = +(+(w, x, y), z), \text{ etc.}$$
$$*(x, y, z) = *(*(x, y), z)$$
$$*(w, x, y, z) = *(*(w, x, y), z), \text{ etc.}$$

Note that the "etc." here means that we can write down more definitions for multiargument addition and multiplication if we like. We could never write them all down in the formalism since there are infinitely many such functions, which would require infinitely many definitions. The formalism of functional expressions has no way of defining all these functions at once, although intuitively we have a clear idea what they are.

Observing how multiplication and addition were defined, we can say that addition is an iteration of the successor function whereas multiplication is an iteration of the addition function. What function from our mathematical education is the iteration of multiplication? The answer is exponentiation: x to the y power is the number 1 multiplied by x, y times. It seems that it should be possible to use primitive recursion to define exponentiation from multiplication.

Now, although zero to the zero power is traditionally not defined, it is convenient to arbitrarily set this value to be 1. Then, adopting the symbol $\uparrow$ for this function, we can give the following primitive recursive definition of it:

$$\begin{cases} \uparrow(x, 0) = 1 \\ \uparrow(x, S(y)) = *(\uparrow(x, y), x) \end{cases}$$

Sample computations, for example, a computation of $\uparrow(2, 3)$, are all it should take to make it clear that this is a definition of exponentiation. We leave this to the reader.

We now define the predecessor function, corresponding to the decrementing operation of Chapter 3:

$$\begin{cases} P(0) = 0 \\ P(S(x)) = x \end{cases}$$

This primitive recursive definition could not be replaced by an explicit definition. Still, it is a degenerate type of primitive recursive since the function symbol P does not appear on the right side of the second equation.

As we have already noted (Section 3.5.1), minus is not a total function over the nonnegative integers. There are two useful total functions that serve in its place. One is *floored subtraction* (sometimes called *proper subtraction*, and sometimes *monus*) definable as follows:

$$\begin{cases} \dot{-}(x, 0) = x \\ \dot{-}(x, S(y)) = P(\dot{-}(x, y)) \end{cases}$$

Note that $\dot{-}(x, y) = x - y$ if $x \geqq y$; but $\dot{-}(x, y) = 0$ if $x < y$. The other substitute for minus is the better known *absolute-difference* function:

$$\text{ABD}(x, y) = +(\dot{-}(x, y), \dot{-}(y, x))$$

It is easily seen that $\text{MAX}(x, y)$, $\text{MAX}(x, y, z)$, and so on, as defined below, always equal the maximum value assumed by their arguments; also that $\text{MIN}(x, y)$, $\text{MIN}(x, y, z)$, and so on, always equal the minimum value assumed by their arguments.

$$\text{MAX}(x, y) = +(x, \dot{-}(y, x))$$
$$\text{MAX}(x, y, z) = \text{MAX}(x, \text{MAX}(y, z)), \text{ etc.}$$
$$\text{MIN}(x, y) = \dot{-}(x, \dot{-}(x, y))$$
$$\text{MIN}(x, y, z) = \text{MIN}(x, \text{MIN}(y, z)), \text{ etc.}$$

Frequently, we wish to define a function as follows:

$$f(x) = \begin{cases} 2x & \text{if } x \leq 3 \\ 2x - 2 & \text{if } x > 3 \end{cases}$$

Next, we define five functions that will make it possible to write explicit definitions for such functions:

$$\begin{cases} \text{SG}(0) & = 0 \\ \text{SG}(S(x)) = 1 \end{cases}$$
$$\begin{cases} \text{ISG}(0) = 1 \\ \text{ISG}(S(x)) = 0 \end{cases}$$
$$\text{GT}(x, y) = \text{SG}(\dot{-}(x, y))$$
$$\text{GE}(x, y) = \text{GT}(S(x), y)$$
$$\text{EQ}(x, y) = *(\text{GE}(x, y), \text{GE}(y, x))$$

The function SG is the well-known signum (or sign) function restricted to nonnegative integers: argument 0 yields the value 0, but all positive arguments yield the value 1. The function ISG is the logical inverse of SG. Both definitions are degenerate primitive recursions, although they could have been defined explicitly thus:

$$\text{ISG}(x) = \dot{-}(1, x)$$
$$\text{SG}(x) = \text{ISG}(\text{ISG}(x))$$

Note that $\text{GT}(x, y) = 1$ or 0, according to whether or not $x > y$. We can think of the function as expressing the greater-than relationship.

Similarly, $\text{GE}(x, y) = 1$ or 0, according to whether or not $x \geq y$, so the function GE expresses the greater-than-or-equal-to relationship.

Finally, EQ expresses the equals relationship since $\text{EQ}(x, y) = 1$ or 0, according to whether or not $x = y$.

[In these terms, we can think of $\text{SG}(x)$ as saying that x is positive, and $\text{ISG}(x)$ as saying that x is zero.]

With these functions, we can convert many definitions given by cases into explicit definitions. For example, an explicit definition for the function presented at the beginning of this subsection is as follows:

$$f(x) = +(*(2, x, \text{GE}(3, x)), *(\dot{-}(*(2, x), 2), \text{GT}(x, 3)))$$

Explanation: If $x \leq 3$, then $\text{GE}(3, x) = 1$ and $\text{GT}(x, 3) = 0$ and the expression as a whole equals $2x$. But if $x > 3$, $\text{GE}(3, x) = 0$ and $\text{GT}(x, 3) = 1$ and we get $\dot{-}(*(2, x), 2)$, which equals $2x - 2$ in this case.

At this point we notice that expressions in strict functional notation get rather awkward. We can improve things a bit by allowing ourselves to depart from the formalism by representing addition and multiplication in the conventional way (i.e., in operator notation rather than in functional notation), writing $x + y + z$ for $+(x, y, z)$; xy or $x*y$ for $*(x, y)$; $xy + z$ for $+(*(x, y), z)$; and so on. The definition of the function f just given is then rewritten as something more easily read:

$$f(x) = 2x*\text{GE}(3, x) + \dot{-}(2x, 2)*\text{GT}(x, 3)$$

[One is tempted to write $\dot{-}$ in operator notation: $x \dot{-} y$ for $\dot{-}(x, y)$, and so on. However, this practice requires caution: Parentheses must be kept in cases where we do not keep them with the minus sign. For example $(x + y) - z$ $= x + (y - z)$ in ordinary algebra, and is normally written $x + y - z$. However, $\dot{-}(x + y, z)$ and $x + \dot{-}(y, z)$ are sometimes unequal (e.g., when $x = 1$, $y = 0, z = 1$). Thus we could not write either of these as $x + y \dot{-} z$ without some clear resolution of the ambiguity. In this book $\dot{-}$ will always be rendered in functional notation.]

The technique for converting a definition by cases into an explicit definition is rather simple. Suppose that the definition by cases is as follows:

$$f(x_1, \ldots, x_n) = \begin{cases} g_1(x_1, \ldots, x_n) & \text{if (case I)} \\ g_2(x_1, \ldots, x_n) & \text{if (case II)} \\ \cdot \\ \cdot \\ \cdot \\ g_m(x_1, \ldots, x_n) & \text{if (case m)} \end{cases}$$

We first find for each case i a function h_i such that $h_i(x_1, \ldots, x_n) = 1$ in case i and 0 in all other cases. The explicit definition is then a sum of products:

$$f(x_1, \ldots, x_n) = g_1(x_1, \ldots, x_n)*h_1(x_1, \ldots, x_n) + \ldots$$
$$+ g_m(x_1, \ldots, x_n)*h_m(x_1, \ldots, x_n)$$

Another example: For all nonnegative integers x and y,

$$f(x, y) = \begin{cases} 3x + y & \text{if } x > y + 2 \\ 2x + 2y & \text{if } y - 2 \leqq x \leqq y + 2 \\ x + 3y & \text{if } x < y - 2 \end{cases}$$

A function characterizing the middle case is

$$h_2(x, y) = \text{GE}(x, \dot{-}(y, 2))*\text{GE}(y + 2, x)$$

[A subtle point: For all nonnegative integers x and y, $x \geq y - 2$ if and only if $x \geq \div(y, 2)$.] Note that the value of h_2 is 0 in each of the other two cases. The other two cases are easily characterized, and so we get the following explicit definition:

$$f(x, y) = (3x + y)*GT(x, y + 2) + (2x + 2y)*GE(x, \div(y, 2))*GE(y + 2, x)$$
$$+ (x + 3y)*GT(\div(y, 2), x)$$

A final example:

$$f(x, y) = \begin{cases} 7 & \text{if } x = y = 0 \\ 0 & \text{if } x = 0, y \neq 0 \\ 15 & \text{if } x \neq 0, y = 0 \\ MAX(x, y) + 11 & \text{if } x \neq 0 \neq y \end{cases}$$

A solution:

$$f(x, y) = 7*ISG(x)*ISG(y) + 15*SG(x)*ISG(y)$$
$$+ (MAX(x, y) + 11)*SG(x)*SG(y)$$

Quotient and Remainder   4.2.3

Two functions that are useful in work with nonnegative integers are the quotient and remainder functions. Assuming for the moment that $y \neq 0$, the quotient q and remainder r when x is divided by y must be such that

$$(1) \quad x = yq + r$$
$$(2) \quad 0 \leq r \leq y - 1$$

As is well known, q and r are uniquely determined nonnegative integers, given any nonnegative integer x and positive integer y.

To have total functions, we must decide what to do in the case $y = 0$, in which (2) is impossible, although it is still desirable to keep (1). What seems convenient is to put $q = 0$ and $r = x$ in this case; this is customary in books on computability.

To get the remainder function REM as a primitive recursion, let the first argument be the recursion argument. We define first a function f where $f(y, x)$ is to be equal to $REM(x, y)$:

$$\begin{cases} f(y, 0) &= 0 \\ f(y, S(x)) = S(f(y, x)) * ISG(EQ(S(f(y, x)), y)) \end{cases}$$
$$REM(x, y) = f(y, x)$$

Thus we have solved our problem of defining remainder by first defining f by primitive recursion in terms of other known functions and then defining remainder by an explicit definition in terms of f. To justify the second line in the definition of f, note that for $y \neq 0$ either $REM(x + 1, y) = REM(x, y) + 1$ or else $REM(x + 1, y) = 0$; and that $REM(x + 1, y) = 0$ precisely when $REM(x, y) + 1 = y$.

For $y = 0$, note that $REM(x, 0) = f(0, x) = x$: in the second equation $S(f(y, x))$ is never equal to $y = 0$, so $f(0, S(x))$ always equals $S(f(0, x))$.

Note also that the primitive-recursive definition of f is legitimate since each time f appears on the right side of the second equation it is followed by the arguments y, x in order.

The definition of the quotient function uses a similar technique. Where $QU(x, y)$ is to be the quotient when x is divided by y, it is again feasible to do recursion on the first argument. Supposing for the moment that $y \geq 2$, we note that either $QU(x + 1, y) = QU(x, y)$ or $QU(x + 1, y) = QU(x, y) + 1$; and that the latter condition holds if and only if $x + 1$ is a multiple of y. The remainder function just defined is useful here, because $REM(x + 1, y) = 0$ if and only if $x + 1$ is divisible by y. To summarize,

$$QU(x + 1, y) = \begin{cases} QU(x, y) & \text{if } REM(x + 1, y) \neq 0 \\ QU(x, y) + 1 & \text{if } REM(x + 1, y) = 0 \end{cases}$$

(The remainder function is not really needed here. See Exercise 48.)

Since we wish to do recursion on x, we first define a function g with arguments x and y reversed, and then define QU explicitly in terms of g:

$$\begin{cases} g(y, 0) = 0 \\ g(y, S(x)) = g(y, x) + ISG(REM(S(x), y)) \end{cases}$$
$$QU(x, y) = g(y, x)$$

Since $REM(x, 0) = x, g(0, x) = 0$, for all x; hence $QU(x, 0) = 0$.

We call the technique used in defining g the *step-function technique*; it is often useful in defining a function whose value is either the same as the preceding value or else is the preceding value plus a certain step size (equal to 1 in this example).

4.2.4   Summary List of Functions

An important type of exercise will be that of defining functions. Certain functions defined in this chapter are useful in defining other functions. A summary list of those, with informal explanations, is now given:

$$Z(x) = 0 \text{ (constant-zero function)}$$
$$+(x_1, \ldots, x_n) = \text{sum of the arguments}; n \geq 2$$
$$*(x_1, \ldots, x_n) = \text{product of the arguments}; n \geq 2$$
$$\uparrow(x, y) = x^y, \text{ fixing } \uparrow(0, 0) = 1$$
$$P(x) = \text{predecessor of } x, \text{ for } x > 0; P(0) = 0$$
$$\dot{-}(x, y) = \begin{cases} 0 & \text{if } x < y \\ x - y & \text{if } x \geq y \text{ (floored subtraction)} \end{cases}$$
$$\text{ABD}(x, y) = \text{absolute difference of } x \text{ and } y$$
$$\text{MAX}(x_1, \ldots, x_n) = \text{maximum value assumed by the arguments}$$
$$\text{MIN}(x_1, \ldots, x_n) = \text{minimum value assumed by the arguments}$$
$$\text{SG}(x) = \begin{cases} 1 & \text{if } x > 0 \\ 0 & \text{if } x = 0 \text{ (signum of } x) \end{cases}$$
$$\text{ISG}(x) = \begin{cases} 0 & \text{if } x > 0 \\ 1 & \text{if } x = 0 \text{ (inverse signum of } x) \end{cases}$$
$$\text{GT}(x, y) = \begin{cases} 1 & \text{if } x > y \\ 0 & \text{otherwise (greater-than)} \end{cases}$$
$$\text{GE}(x, y) = \begin{cases} 1 & \text{if } x \geq y \\ 0 & \text{otherwise (greather-than-or-equal-to)} \end{cases}$$
$$\text{EQ}(x, y) - \begin{cases} 1 & \text{if } x = y \\ 0 & \text{otherwise (equals)} \end{cases}$$
$$\text{REM}(x, y) = \begin{cases} x & \text{if } y = 0 \\ \text{remainder when } x \text{ is divided by } y & \text{if } y \neq 0 \end{cases}$$
$$\text{QU}(x, y) = \begin{cases} 0 & \text{if } y = 0 \\ \text{quotient when } x \text{ is divided by } y & \text{if } y \neq 0 \end{cases}$$

Sample exercise: Suppose that $D(x)$ is the number of positive-integer divisors of x, for $x > 0$; $D(0) = 0$ [e.g., $D(10) = 4$, since the positive-integer divisors of 10 are 1, 2, 5, and 10]. Define D by using explicit definition or primitive recursion or both, from the foregoing list of functions.

In order to define D, it is convenient to define first an auxiliary two-argument function f, where, for $x > 0$, $f(x, y) = $ the number of positive-integer divisors of x less than or equal to y. The new variable y will enable us to count the divisors of x by primitive recursion thus:

$$f(x, 0) = 0$$

$$f(x, S(y)) = \begin{cases} f(x, y) & \text{if } S(y) \text{ is not a divisor of } x \\ S(f(x, y)) & \text{if } S(y) \text{ is a divisor of } x \end{cases}$$

We make this a legitimate primitive recursion, and then define D explicitly in terms of f:

$$\begin{cases} f(x, 0) = 0 \\ f(x, S(y)) = f(x, y) + \text{ISG(REM}(x, S(y))) \end{cases}$$
$$D(x) = f(x, x)$$

Note that $D(0) = f(0, 0) = 0$, which is correct. Thus these three equations are the solution to the exercise.

When one has a function to define, one should in general prefer an explicit definition over a primitive recursion, since the latter is a more complex kind of definition. Of course, there are trade-offs; a primitive recursion with two simple lines one might regard as simpler than a lengthy explicit definition.

4.2.5 Exercises

Group I

Define the function described in each exercise by using primitive recursion or explicit definition or both, from the functions listed in Section 4.2.4. If possible, define the function entirely by means of explicit definition.

1. $\text{MUL}(x, y) = 1$ if x is an integral multiple of y; $\text{MUL}(x, y) = 0$ if not. [Note that $\text{MUL}(0, y) = 1$, but $\text{MUL}(x, 0) = 0$ if $x \neq 0$.]

2. $\text{CON}(x, y, z) = 1$ if $\text{REM}(x, z) = \text{REM}(y, z)$; $\text{CON}(x, y, z) = 0$ if $\text{REM}(x, z) \neq \text{REM}(y, z)$. [For $x \neq 0$, $\text{CON}(x, y, z) = 1$ if and only if x is congruent to y modulo z, as the term is used in number theory; in conventional symbols, $x \equiv y \pmod{z}$.]

3. $\text{SD}(x)$ is the sum of the positive-integer divisors of x for $x \neq 0$; $\text{SD}(0) = 0$. [For example, $\text{SD}(1) = 1$; $\text{SD}(3) = 4$; $\text{SD}(6) = 12$; $\text{SD}(10) = 18$. *Hint:* See the sample exercise of Section 4.2.4.]

4. $\text{PR}(x) = 1$ if x is a prime; $\text{PR}(x) = 0$, otherwise. [Thus $\text{PR}(0) = \text{PR}(1) = \text{PR}(4) = 0$; $\text{PR}(2) = \text{PR}(3) = 1$. *Hint:* See the sample exercise of Section 4.2.4.]

5. $\text{WSX}(x) = 1$ if $x = 14, 34, 42, 72,$ or 96; $\text{WSX}(x) = 0$, otherwise (the Manhattan-West-Side-Express function).

6. $f(x) = 1$ if either $10 \leq x \leq 19$ or $30 \leq x \leq 39$; $f(x) = 0$, otherwise.

7. $f(0) = 0$; for $x > 0, f(x) = $ the number of y's, $0 \leq y \leq x - 1$ such that $h(y) \neq h(y + 1)$. h is a given total function.

8. $h(0) = 3$; $h(x + 1) = 2^*h(x)$ if x is even; $h(x + 1) = 3^*h(x)$ if x is odd.

9. $f(0) = 1$; for all $x, f(x + 1) = \uparrow(2, f(x))$ if x is even, and $f(x + 1) = \uparrow(f(x), 2)$ if x is odd.

10. $f(x_1, x_2, x_3, x_4) = x_3$ if $x_1 \geq x_2$; $f(x_1, x_2, x_3, x_4) = x_4$ if $x_1 < x_2$.

11. $h(x) = 0$ if either $g(x) \geq 3$ or $g(x) = 0$; $h(x) = 1$ if $g(x) = 1$ or $g(x) = 2$. g is a given total function.

12. $f(x, y, z) = x + y$ if $100 \geq x + y*z \geq 50$; $f(x, y, z) = z$, otherwise.

13. $g(x_1, x_2, x_3, x_4)$ is the number of distinct numbers among the arguments x_1, x_2, x_3, and x_4 [e.g., $g(1, 0, 4, 0) = 3$; $g(6, 6, 6, 6) = 1$].

14. $f(x) = 0$ if $x < 12$. For $x \geq 12$, $f(x) = 7$ if x is a number of the form $3i$; $f(x) = 8$ if x is of the form $3i + 1$; and $f(x) = 3$ if x is of the form $3i + 2$, for i an integer.

15. $\text{MED}(x, y, z)$ is the median of x, y, and z (i.e., the middle number when x, y, z are arranged in order of magnitude). [For example, $\text{MED}(1, 2, 3) = \text{MED}(2, 3, 1) = 2$; $\text{MED}(0, 1, 0) = 0$; and $\text{MED}(3, 3, 3) = 3$.]

16. $g(x) = 7$ if $x = 0$ or if x is odd; $g(x + 2) = 2*g(x)$ if x is even. (*Hint:* There are at least two approaches. First, you may analyze the function mathematically and give an explicit definition. The second approach is to define by primitive recursion an auxiliary function from which g can be defined explicitly.)

Group II

Assume that $f, f_1, f_2, \ldots$ are given total functions of one argument, whose mathematical nature you do not know. In each case, a one-argument function h is described intuitively in terms of these. Define h by means of a primitive recursion or explicit definition.

17. $h(x) = \sum_{i=0}^{x} f(i)$. (Note that $\sum$, the symbol for summation, is not in the formalism.)

18. $h(x) = \prod_{i=1}^{x} f(i)$. ($\prod$ is the informal symbol for product.)

19. $h(x) = \min_{i=1}^{x} (f(i))$, that is, the smallest of the values $f(0), f(1), \ldots, f(x)$.

20. (*Difficult. Do Exercise 19 first.*) $h(x)$ is the smallest y, $0 \leq y \leq x$, such that $f(y) = \min_{i=0}^{x} (f(i))$.

21. (*Difficult. Do Exercise 19 first.*) $h(x)$ is the largest y, $0 \leq y \leq x$, such that $f(y) = \min_{i=0}^{x} (f(i))$.

22. $h(x) = 1$ if both $f_1(x) = 1$ and $f_2(x) = 1$; $h(x) = 0$, otherwise.

23. $h(x) = 1$ if $f_1(x) = 1$ or $f_2(x) = 1$ or both; $h(x) = 0$, otherwise.

24. $h(x) = 1$ if either $f_1(x) = 1$ or $f_2(x) = 1$ but not both; $h(x) = 0$ if either $f_1(x) = 1 = f_2(x)$ or $f_1(x) \neq 1 \neq f_2(x)$.

25. $h(x) = 1$ if neither $f_1(x) = 1$ nor $f_2(x) = 1$; $h(x) = 0$, otherwise.

26. $h(x) = 1$ if there is at least one y, $0 \leq y \leq x$, such that $f(y) = 1$; $h(x) = 0$, otherwise.

27. $h(x) = 1$ if for all y, $0 \leq y \leq x$, $f(y) = 1$; $h(x) = 0$, otherwise.

28. $h(x) = 1$ if there are at least two distinct values y_1 and y_2 between 0 and x inclusive such that $f(y_1) = f(y_2) = 1$; $h(x) = 0$, otherwise.

29. $h(x)$ is the sum of those y, $0 \leq y \leq x$, such that $f(y) = 1$. [For example, $h(0) = 0$ whatever f may be. If $f(1) = f(4) = 1$ and $f(2) = f(3) = f(5) = 0$, then $h(1) = h(2) = h(3) = 1$; $h(4) = h(5) = 5$.]

Group III

Define the function described by an explicit definition. Use of REM and QU is advised in these.

30. $g(x, 0) = 0$; for $y \neq 0$, $g(x, y)$ is the result of integer division with roundoff of x by y. More explicitly, for $y \neq 0$, $g(x, y)$ is the nearest integer to the fraction x/y; if x/y is halfway between two consecutive integers, $g(x, y)$ is the larger of these two. [Thus, $g(35, 8) = g(32, 8) = 4$; but $g(36, 8) = g(37, 8) = g(40, 8) = 5$.]

31. $f(x, y)$ is the digit in the xth place from the right in the decimal representation of y, counting the rightmost place as the zeroth place. [For example, $f(x, 0) = 0$ for all x; $f(0, 174) = 4$; $f(1, 174) = 7$; $f(2, 174) = 1$; and $f(x, 174) = 0$ for all $x \geq 3$.]

32. $h(x)$ is the xth digit in the (infinite) decimal expansion $1.111246246246246 \ldots$ (sometimes written $1.111\overline{246}$). Take $h(0) = h(1) = h(2) = h(3) = 1$, $h(4) = 2$, $h(5) = 4$, $h(6) = 6$, $h(7) = 2$, and so on.

Group IV

Follow the same instructions for Group I, although these are more difficult. (*Hint:* Some of these can be solved by defining an auxiliary function with an extra variable, as in the sample exercise in Section 4.2.4.)

33. $g(x, y)$ is the greatest common divisor of x and y provided that $x \neq 0 \neq y$. You may pick your own values for $g(x, y)$ when either x or y is 0.

34. $EXP(x, y)$ is the exponent of the greatest power of x that divides y for $x \geq 2$ and $y \geq 2$; $EXP(0, y) = EXP(1, y) = EXP(x, 0) = EXP(x, 1) = 0$. [For example, $EXP(2, 22) = 1$, $EXP(2, 23) = 0$, $EXP(2, 24) = 3$.]

35. (Do Exercise 4 first.) $f(x)$ is the smallest prime greater than x. [*Hint:* Use the fact that $f(x) \leq x! + 1$. The latter is proved by a simple and famous argument due to Euclid.]

36. (Do Exercises 4 and 35 first.) $PRIME(x)$ is the xth prime in order of magnitude, counting 2 as the zeroth prime. [Thus, $PRIME(0) = 2$; $PRIME(1) = 3$; and so on.]

37. (Do Exercise 4 first.) $f(0) = f(1) = 0$; for $x \geq 2$, $f(x)$ is the number of distinct prime numbers dividing x [e.g., $f(4) = f(2) = 1$; $f(84) = 3$].

38. $f(x, 0) = f(x, 1) = 0$. For $y \geq 2$, $f(x, y)$ is the number of z's, $0 \leq z \leq x$, such that z is divisible by at least one of the numbers $2, 3, \ldots, y$. [For example, $f(7, 3) = 5$, since the numbers ≤ 7 that are divisible by 2 or 3 are 0, 2, 3, 4, and 6.]

39. WSQ(x) is the whole part of the square root of x: in conventional symbols, $[\sqrt{x}]$. [Thus WSQ(0) $= 0$, WSQ(1) $=$ WSQ(2) $=$ WSQ(3) $= 1$, WSQ(4) $=$ WSQ(5) $= 2$, and so on. *Hint:* Note that this function is a step function with step size 1.]

40. MED(x_1, x_2, x_3, x_4, x_5) is the median of x_1, x_2, x_3, x_4, x_5 (see Exercise 15).

41. $f(0) = 0$; for $x > 0, f(x)$ is the characteristic of the logarithm of x to the base 2. In other words, for $x > 0, f(x)$ is the largest integer y such that $2^y \leqq x$.

42. $h(x)$ is the xth digit in the (infinite) decimal expansion of the fraction $\frac{106}{93}$ $= 1.1397\ldots$. Take $h(0) = 1, h(1) = 1, h(2) = 3, h(3) = 9, h(4) = 7$, and so on.

43. $g(x)$ is the xth digit to the right of the decimal point in the infinite decimal expansion of $\sqrt{2} = 1.4142\ldots$. Take $g(0) = 1, g(1) = 4, g(2) = 1, g(3) = 4$, and so on. You may use the function WSQ of Exercise 39 as a given function.

44. $f(x, y)$ is the smallest $z \leqq y$ such that $h(x, z) = 0; f(x, y) = y + 1$ if there is no such z. h is a given total function.

45. $h(x, y, z)$ is the number whose decimal representation (possibly with superfluous zeros at the left) consists of the xth through the yth digit from the right, inclusive, in the decimal representation of z, counting the rightmost digit as the zeroth digit; if $x < y, h(x, y, z) = 0$. [For example, if $z = 1973428$, then $h(4, 2, z) = 734; h(9, 5, z)$ $= h(6, 5, z) = 19; h(10, 8, z) = 0; h(0, 0, z) = 8; h(7, 1, 100000001) = 0$.]

46. $g(x) = 7$ if $x = 0$ or if x is odd; $g(x + 2) = h(g(x))$ if x is even. h is a given total function.

47. $f(0) = 0$; for $x > 0, f(x)$ is the number of y's, $0 \leqq y \leqq x - 1$, such that $h(y) \neq h(x)$. h is a given total function.

48. Define QU without using REM, but using any of the functions other than QU and REM listed in Section 4.2.4. Then give an explicit definition of REM in terms of QU. (Your solution will then be an alternative to the development in Section 4.2.3.)

ACKERMANN'S FUNCTION 4.3

In this section we define an infinite sequence of function $\phi_0, \phi_1, \phi_2, \ldots$, by primitive recursion, and see that only the first few of these are practically computable. We shall thereby become aware for the first time of some rather surprising things covered by the concept of algorithm as it was defined in the opening pages of this book.

The Function ϕ_4 4.3.1

Let us return now to the observation (Section 4.2.1) that exponentiation bears the same relationship to multiplication that multiplication bears to addition and that addition bears to the successor function. What function bears this relationship to exponentiation?

Let us prepare to deal with this and other questions by introducing some notation. Put

$$\phi_0(x, y) = S(y)$$
$$\phi_1(x, y) = +(x, y)$$
$$\phi_2(x, y) = *(x, y)$$
$$\phi_3(x, y) = \uparrow(x, y)$$

This notation is justified by the fact that each of these functions after ϕ_0 is defined by a primitive recursion from the preceding function in the sequence and that all three primitive recursions are somewhat alike.

Recalling how ϕ_3 was defined from ϕ_2, we offer by analogy the following definition of ϕ_4:

$$\begin{cases} \phi_4(x, 0) = 1 \\ \phi_4(x, S(y)) = \uparrow(x, \phi_4(x, y)) \end{cases}$$

Let us examine this function by doing some sample substitutions, writing x^y instead of $\uparrow(x, y)$:

$$\phi_4(x, 1) = x^1 = x$$
$$\phi_4(x, 2) = x^x$$
$$\phi_4(x, 3) = x^{x^x}$$

In general, we can write informally:

$$\phi_4(x, y) = x^{\cdot^{\cdot^{\cdot^x}}}$$

where there are y occurrences of x on the right side.

Trying some sample computations, we find that

$$\phi_4(2, 0) = 1$$
$$\phi_4(2, 1) = 2^1 = 2$$
$$\phi_4(2, 2) = 2^2 = 4$$
$$\phi_4(2, 3) = 2^4 = 16$$
$$\phi_4(2, 4) = 2^{16} = 65{,}536$$

We then give up when we discover that $\phi_4(2, 5) = 2^{65,536}$. Clearly, for all $y \geq 5$, $\phi_4(2, y)$ is going to be much greater than 2^y. Actually, we can make stronger assertions: $\phi_4(2, y)$ is greater than 2^{2^y} for all $y \geq 5$ (and is generally much greater). Furthermore, $\phi_4(2, y)$ exceeds $2^{2^{2^y}}$ for all $y \geq 6$ (and is generally much greater). Indeed, it turns out that for any one-argument function f defined explicitly in terms of exponentiation, there is an i such that, for all $y \geq i$, $\phi_4(2, y) > f(y)$, although the proof of this assertion is not given in this text.

A Family of Functions 4.3.2

We now consider the following definition:

$$\begin{cases} \phi_5(x, 0) = 1 \\ \phi_5(x, S(y)) = \phi_4(x, \phi_5(x, y)) \end{cases}$$

The function ϕ_5 is defined from ϕ_4 just as ϕ_4 is defined from exponentiation. Fixing x at some integer that is 2 or more, we find that $\phi_5(x, y)$ increases with y so fast that it does not even have an intuitive rendition. The only way to communicate an understanding of ϕ_5 is to say that it bears the same relation to ϕ_4 as ϕ_4 bears to exponentiation.

To see how fast ϕ_5 increases, we again fix x at 2:

$$\phi_5(2, 0) = 1$$
$$\phi_5(2, 1) = \phi_4(2, 1) = 2$$
$$\phi_5(2, 2) = \phi_4(2, 2) = 4$$
$$\phi_5(2, 3) = \phi_4(2, 4) = 65{,}536$$

Nothing spectacular so far. But the next value, $\phi_5(2, 4) = \phi_4(2, 65{,}536)$, is way out of the range of our desire and need to do further computation. We need say nothing to describe how large this value is after we point out that we already decided to quit computing values of $\phi_4(2, y)$ when y got to be 5.

We can then go on to define ϕ_6, ϕ_7, and so on. For $i > 3$, the general definition of ϕ_{i+1} from ϕ_i is

$$\begin{cases} \phi_{i+1}(x, 0) = 1 \\ \phi_{i+1}(x, S(y)) = \phi_i(x, \phi_{i+1}(x, y)) \end{cases}$$

We call attention to the fact that i is not a variable in the formalism, but a variable in the metalanguage (i.e., the informal language in which we talk about the formalism; see Section AIII.3). Thus the above is not a single formal definition, but a schematic representation of infinitely many definitions in the formalism, giving us an infinite sequence of functions.

We have seen that, for a fixed $x \geq 2$, $\phi_4(x, y)$ increases with y faster than $\uparrow(x, y)$, and $\phi_5(x, y)$ increases faster than $\phi_4(x, y)$. In general, for each $i \geq 1$ and for each fixed $x \geq 2$, $\phi_{i+1}(x, y)$ increases with y faster than $\phi_i(x, y)$; in fact, generally much faster, although the proof is beyond this text (see, e.g., Hermes

[1969], pp. 82–88, or Brainerd and Landweber [1974], pp. 252–259). For $i = 1$ and $i = 2$, this assertion comes to the well-known facts that $*(x, y)$ increases faster than $+(x, y)$ (for a fixed $x \geq 2$) and $\uparrow(x, y)$ increases much faster than $*(x, y)$.

On the other hand, there is the relatively trivial fact that, for all $i \geq 1$, $\phi_i(2, 2) = 4$, a generalization of a fact many of us discovered with a feeling of curiosity in our early mathematical education, namely that $2 + 2 = 2*2 = 2^2$.

This sequence $\phi_0, \phi_1, \phi_2, \ldots$ is an interesting infinite sequence of functions. It begins with functions that we know well. The relationship between each function and the next in the sequence is quite clear, and is at least related to something in our common mathematical experience. But very quickly, as we progress forward in the sequence, we reach functions that are quite strange, if for no other reason than the magnitudes of their function values for small arguments. It is safe to say that no one has ever encountered any of the functions after ϕ_4 outside the theory of computability—or possibly in some other branch of mathematics in which recursive definitions were focused on critically and abstractly. Even the function ϕ_4 is rarely found.

4.3.3   The Function Defined by Ackermann

Definitions by means of explicit definition and primitive recursion are important in the theory of computability; for the same reason, the class of functions they determine, called the *class of primitive-recursive functions* (see Section 4.8), is an important class of functions, even though this class is not the class of all computable functions. The functions $\phi_0, \phi_1, \phi_2, \ldots$ are all in this class, although not all functions in the class are in this sequence. Furthermore, this sequence gives us an insight into how extensive the class is; at any rate, they certainly show that the class contains functions that are well beyond our ordinary mathematical experience.

We are now in a position to look at a function that is computable but is not in the class of primitive-recursive functions. In the 1920s a German logician and mathematician, Wilhelm Ackermann, studied the sequence $\phi_0, \phi_1, \phi_2 \ldots$, being motivated by a problem in the foundations of mathematics that had no direct bearing on problems of computation. Nevertheless, the results of Ackermann's research, reported in Ackermann [1928], were to be recognized for their significance in the theory of computability which took shape in the 1930s.

Ackermann defined a three-argument function, which we shall call A, by putting $A(i, x, y) = \phi_i(x, y)$, for each i, x, and y. This definition we cannot accept as a definition in our formalism since i is not a formal variable. But if we are willing to go beyond primitive recursion and explicit definition, we can set up (as Ackermann did) a kind of definition of the function A in the formalism, as follows:

$$\begin{cases} A(0, x, y) = S(y) \\ A(1, x, y) = +(x, y) \\ A(2, x, y) = *(x, y) \\ A(SSS(z), x, 0) = 1 \\ A(SSS(z), x, S(y)) = A(SS(z), x, A(SSS(z), x, y)) \end{cases}$$

We write $SSS(z)$ here for clarity instead of $S(S(S(z)))$. Since the first argument in the fourth and fifth lines is $SSS(z)$, we are assured that no substitution from either of these lines could result in a first argument less than 3. (This kind of definition will be studied in Section 4.7. The function A defined here is a trivial variation of the function that appeared in Ackermann [1928].)

It is easy to verify that, for each i, $A(i, x, y) = \phi_i(x, y)$. It is curious to note that, although there is a uniform way of defining ϕ_i from ϕ_{i-1} that works for all $i \geq 3$, the manner in which ϕ_1 and ϕ_2 are defined is different from all of these and also different from each other. The difference consists in the value at $y = 0$: $\phi_1(x, 0) = x$, $\phi_2(x, 0) = 0$, but for all $i \geq 3$, $\phi_i(x, 0) = 1$. This curious fact leads to an awkwardness in the definition of the function A, but does not have much bearing on the broad issues that we wish to focus upon now.

The last equation in this definition is a new variety of recursion. In primitive recursion there is one and only one recursion argument, which as a formal requirement is the last argument of the function. In this last equation, we see a recursion not only on the third argument, but a recursion at the same time on the first argument. Such functional definitions are known in the literature as *double recursions*. (As a curiosity, note the triple recursion of Exercise 9 of Section 4.7.)

The function A is computable from the set of equations consisting of two equations in the definition of $+$, the two equations in the definition of $*$, and these five equations. However, as we discuss in Section 4.8, Ackermann proved that his function is not in the class of primitive-recursive functions. He proved, moreover, that if he defined

$$h(x) = A(x, x, x)$$

the function h increases faster than any one argument function in the class of primitive-recursive functions.

It is interesting to observe that we could already get from ϕ_5 a function that increased much faster than any function we have come across in our ordinary mathematical experience. We then found that ϕ_5 was quite low in an infinite hierarchy of functions, each of which yields functions that increase faster than functions preceding it in the hierarchy. And now we find that h, defined in terms of Ackermann's function, increases faster than any of the functions in this hierarchy. But we can still go on. There is in the advanced literature an infinite hierarchy of computable functions (Péter [1967]), each much faster increasing than the preceding functions, in which this function h is rather low.

In this section so far we have offered a significant insight into what functions are computable. We introduced the class of primitive-recursive functions all of which are computable. We have shown that there are many functions in this class that are beyond our ordinary mathematical experience, in that they have enormous function values for rather small arguments. Then we examined a computable function (i.e., Ackermann's function) that is not even in the class of primitive-recursive functions, which is certainly way beyond ordinary mathematical experience. And finally we pointed out the existence of computable functions that are way beyond Ackermann's function.

Certainly, the class of computable functions cannot be identified with the class of *practically* computable functions. It is for this reason that many theoretical computer scientists focus on computational complexity rather than on the theory of computability.

4.3.4 The Ackermann–Péter Function

Functions that are theoretically computable but beyond our ordinary mathematical experience are interesting, perhaps in the same way that science fiction is interesting. They reveal certain attributes of computation processes that we would perhaps never know about if we insisted on paying attention only to practically computable functions. Ackermann's function serves such a purpose, but that purpose is perhaps better served by a more neatly defined function of two arguments devised by the Hungarian mathematician Rósza Péter. It is a trivial variation of the function that appeared in her 1935 paper that is called "Ackermann's function" in most contemporary textbooks. We shall call it the *Ackermann–Péter function*, and designate it as AP to distinguish it from the three-argument function A. Its definition, which includes a double recursion, is as follows:

$$\begin{cases} (1) \ \ \text{AP}(0, y) = S(y) \\ (2) \ \ \text{AP}(S(x), 0) = \text{AP}(x, 1) \\ (3) \ \ \text{AP}(S(x), S(y)) = \text{AP}(x, \text{AP}(S(x), y)) \end{cases}$$

It can be proved that, for every ordered pair of numerals (i_1, i_2), one and only one evaluation of $\text{AP}(i_1, i_2)$ can be computed from this set of equations (Exercise 1). The mathematical relationship between Ackermann's function and the Ackermann–Péter function is given by the equation

$$\text{AP}(x, y) = A(x, 2, y + 3) - 3$$

which is valid for all x and y (Exercises 2 and 3). A slight bit of generality is lost in foreshaking the function A for the function AP, but AP with its simpler definition has all the interesting properties of A.

Just as a curiosity, let us begin an attempt to compute AP(102, 33). We would first obtain, by substitution in (3), AP(102, 33) = AP(101, AP(102, 32)). Again, by substitution in (3), we get AP(102, 32) = AP(101, AP(102, 31)), from which we then get AP(102, 33) = AP(101, AP(101, AP(102, 31))). Noting a pattern here, we see that eventually we get an equation

(4) AP(102, 33) = AP(101, AP(101, . . . , AP(102, 0) . . .))

where there are 34 pairs of parentheses and 34 occurrences of the function symbol AP on the right side.

By (2) and (3), AP(102, 0) = AP(101, 1) = AP(100, AP(101, 0)). Similarly, AP(101, 0) = AP(99, AP(100, 0)), and so on. Thus AP(102, 0) − AP(100, AP(99, AP(98, . . . , AP(0, AP(1, 0)) . . .))). Replacing AP(102, 0) in (4), we thus get

(5) AP(102, 33) = (AP(101, . . . , AP(101, AP(100, AP(99, . . . ,

$$\text{AP}(0, \text{AP}(1, 0) \ldots))) \ldots)$$

Looking back at what we have done so far, we see that we have obtained a sequence of equations all having a certain pattern,

$$\text{AP}(102, 33) = \text{AP}(i_1, \text{AP}(i_2, \text{AP}(i_3, \ldots, \text{AP}(i_m, i_{m+1}) \ldots)))$$

The next equation in the sequence is obtained from this expression by first obtaining that equation of the form

$$\text{AP}(i_m, i_{m+1}) = R$$

which is obtained by substituting from whichever of the equations (1), (2), or (3) in the definition of AP is appropriate, and then by replacing AP(i_m, i_{m+1}) by R. Note that if equation (3) is used, the next equation in the sequence will be longer. If equation (2) is used, it will be just as long (approximately), and if (1) is used it will be shorter. Equation (5) is quite long because, so far, we have used (3) often but have never used (1).

However, the equation following (5) is obtained by replacing AP(1, 0) by AP(0, 1). Then we use the substitution instance of (1) for the first time, namely AP(0, 1) = S(1) = 2. We thus find that the next equation in the sequence is shortened and is, in fact,

$$\text{AP}(102, 33) = \text{AP}(101, \ldots, \text{AP}(101, \text{AP}(100, \ldots, \text{AP}(0, 2) \ldots)$$

But then we see that we are going to lengthen the expression again before we get to shorten it again, raising a question: When will the expression be shortened down to a single numeral and thus an evaluation of AP(102, 33)? The answer is that the amount of time needed is beyond any way we talk about time; we are very, very far beyond practicality. But let us continue.

If we actually wish to use this procedure to compute the function, we see there is a certain amount of 'wasted writing. By virtue of the uniformity in the right side in the sequence of equations, all that we need record is the sequence of numbers

$$i_1, i_2, \ldots, i_m, i_{m+1}$$

The computation consists in modifying this sequence at the right end depending on the values of i_m and i_{m+1}. If i_m is zero, i_m, i_{m+1} is replaced by $i_{m+1} + 1$. If i_m is nonzero but i_{m+1} is zero, these are replaced by $i_m - 1, 1$. If both are nonzero, they are replaced by $i_m - 1, i_m, i_{m+1} - 1$.

4.3.5 Programmability of AP

When this algorithm is executed, not only do the numbers get hopelessly large, the sequences get hopelessly long. How, then, could this algorithm be expressed in the foundational programming languages? We are not discussing the practical problem here; we have already seen that it is practically impossible. What we are discussing is a theoretical question: Does there exist a program in the GOTO language or in the WHILE language that (theoretically) executes this algorithm? The theoretical problem is that, by definition, any such program has a fixed finite number of variables, but the sequences of numbers get arbitrarily long. More precisely, given any program there is a finite number of variables for number storage; let this number be k. But in computing $AP(k + 10, k + 10)$, the length of the sequences will be much longer than k. Thus, for any given program that anyone says is a program to compute the function AP, we can find numbers i_1 and i_2 such that the storage needed in the computation of $AP(i_1, i_2)$ apparently exceeds the number of variables in the program. We appear to have proved that there is no such program.

However, there does exist a program in each of the two languages to compute the function AP. The program gets by with a certain finite set of variables because it uses a technique to code a finite sequence as a single number, which works for all finite sequences regardless of length. Recall the assumption that a storage position can assume as a value any nonnegative integer, without limit. If we code the sequence $i_1, i_2, \ldots, i_m, i_{m+1}$ as the number

$$2^{i_1+1} * 3^{i_2+1} * \ldots * PRIME(m - 1)^{i_m+1} * PRIME(m)^{i_{m+1}+1}$$

where $PRIME(j)$ is the jth prime in order of magnitude assuming that $PRIME(0) = 2$, we see that every finite sequence has a code number, and no two sequences have the same code number. (By the elementary theory of numbers, every positive integer can be expressed uniquely as a product of primes, up to order.) Furthermore, with some effort we can compute with these numbers to get the effect of computing with the sequences. This coding is an example of the technique of Gödel numbering which will be discussed in Chapter 5.

As a curiosity, we note that if we extend the WHILE language to include one-dimensional arrays (with unlimited dimensioning), we can easily write a program to compute the function AP, using the idea of Section 4.3.4. Letting SEQ(1), SEQ(2), . . . be the sequence mentioned at the end of Section 4.3.4, and letting M + 1 be its length, a program that computes AP with respect to X, Y, Z (i.e., Z will equal AP(X, Y)) is as follows:

$$M := 1;$$
$$SEQ(1) := X;$$
$$SEQ(2) := Y;$$
WHILE $M > 0$ DO
    [M1 := M
    INCR(M1);
    M2 := M1;
    INCR(M2);
    IF SEQ(M) = 0 THEN
        [SEQ(M) := SEQ(M1);
        INCR(SEQ(M));
        DECR(M)]
    ELSE
        [IF SEQ(M1) = 0 THEN
            [DECR(SEQ(M));
            SEQ(M1) := 1]
        ELSE
            [SEQ(M2) := SEQ(M1);
            DECR(SEQ(M2));
            SEQ(M1) := SEQ(M);
            DECR(SEQ(M));
            INCR(M)]]];
  Z := SEQ(1)

We present this program in a casual spirit and without further explanation, for the benefit of those readers who can puzzle it out for themselves. It does not seem worthwhile to discuss this extension of the WHILE language in any detail. (For an alternative program in a similar programming language, see Manna [1974], pp. 200–202.)

Incidentally, if the programming language is made still more powerful by including recursive procedures, then a program can be written for the function AP right from the equations. (See Manna [1974], p. 321.)

Discussing the computation of the Ackermann–Péter function is certainly a bit of science fiction. In the next section, we return to practicality and discuss another practically important method of defining functions. In this section we have presented for the first time in this book an extensive view of the class of computable functions, which we could do only by considering functions that were well beyond practical computation.

4.3.6 Exercises

These are all *theoretical and difficult*, involving skill in the use of mathematical induction.

1. Prove that, for each ordered pair of numerals (i_1, i_2), a value is determined for $AP(i_1, i_2)$ from the equations defining AP.

2. Prove the following assertions in turn:
(a) For all y, $AP(0, y) = y + 1 = A(0, 2, y + 3) - 3$.
(b) For all y, $AP(1, y) = y + 2 = A(1, 2, y + 3) - 3$.
(c) For all y, $AP(2, y) = 2y + 3 = A(2, 2, y + 3) - 3$.
(d) For all y, $AP(3, y) = 2^{y+3} - 3 = A(3, 2, y + 3) - 3$.
(e) For all y, $AP(4, y) = A(4, 2, y + 3) - 3$.

3. Prove that, for all x and y, $AP(x, y) = A(x, 2, y + 3) - 3$. [*Hint:* First prove that, for all $x \geq 3$, $A(x, 2, 2) = 4$.]

4. Prove that if f is a function of n arguments $(n \geq 1)$ defined explicitly from $+$, then there exist nonnegative integers $i_1, \ldots, i_{n+1}$ such that, for all $x_1, \ldots, x_n$,

$$f(x_1, \ldots, x_n) = i_1 x_1 + \ldots + i_n x_n + i_{n+1}$$

5. (a) Prove that if $f(x_1, x_2) = i_1 x_1 + i_2 x_2 + i_3$, for all x_1 and x_2, then there exist m_1 and m_2 such that, for all $x_1 \geq m_1$ and $x_2 \geq m_2$,

$$*(x_1, x_2) > f(x_1, x_2)$$

(b) Conclude from Exercise 4 that multiplication is not explicitly definable in terms of addition.

6. Prove that if a function f of n arguments is defined explicitly in terms of addition and multiplication, then there are positive integers $m, a_1, \ldots, a_n$ and nonnegative integers i_{jk} $(1 \leq j \leq m$ and $1 \leq k \leq n)$ such that

$$f(x_1, \ldots, x_n) = \sum_{j=1}^{m} \left(a_j \prod_{k=1}^{n} x_k^{i_{jk}} \right)$$

7. (a) Prove that the equation for f in Exercise 6 for $n = 2$ implies that there exist p and q such that, for all $x_1 \geq p$ and $x_2 \geq q$,

$$\uparrow(x_1, x_2) > f(x_1, x_2)$$

(b) Conclude from Exercise 6 that exponentiation is not explicitly definable in terms of addition and multiplication.

8. At the beginning of this section, we had to decide how to define ϕ_4 from ϕ_3 (i.e., $\uparrow$). Suppose that we had used

(a) $\begin{cases} \phi_4'(x, 0) = 1 \\ \phi_4'(x, Sy) = \uparrow(\phi_4'(x, y), x) \end{cases}$

(b) $\begin{cases} \phi_4''(x, 0) \quad = x \\ \phi_4''(x, Sy) = \uparrow(\phi_4''(x, y), x) \end{cases}$

Prove that in each case a function results that is explicitly definable in terms of $\uparrow$.

DEFINITION BY MU RECURSION 4.4

In this section we allow a function to be defined by stating that the function value equals the least number satisfying a certain relationship to the arguments. As an example, the least common multiple of two positive integers x and y can be defined to be the least positive z such that both $\text{REM}(z, x)$ and $\text{REM}(z, y)$ equal zero. We shall formalize this type of function definition and call it *mu recursion*. (The word "recursion" here is perhaps badly chosen, but the term "mu recursion" is well entrenched in the literature.) This type of function definition is related to a common computational procedure, that of searching for a number satisfying a certain property, by first testing 0, then 1, then 2, and so on.

Mu recursions play an important role in the theory that cannot be completely clarified in this section, where we shall be concerned mainly with showing how they work and how we can construct them to define functions. Their theoretical significance will be revealed in Chapter 5.

A New Definition Scheme 4.4.1

To begin with, we add the character μ (the Greek lowercase mu, to suggest "minimum") and square brackets to our formalism. The character μ is not a function symbol; in fact, it is an operator unlike any other symbol in the formalism, since it will have the unique effect of converting an equation into a functional expression. We shall stipulate that if V is a variable and E a functional expression, then

$$(\mu V)[E = 0]$$

is a mu expression, which is a new kind of functional expression. For simplicity we stipulate that no mu expressions occur inside E.

For example,

$$(\mu z)[g(x, y, z) = 0]$$

is a mu expression, V being the variable z and E being the expression $g(x, y, z)$. The meaning of this mu expression is "the smallest nonnegative integer z such that $g(x, y, z) = 0$."

If g is a known function, we can use our mu expression to define a new function as follows:

$$f(x, y) = (\mu z)[g(x, y, z) = 0]$$

If, for example, $g(1, 3, 0) = 1$, $g(1, 3, 1) = 3$, and $g(1, 3, 2) = 0$, then $f(1, 3)$ is defined to be 2 (since 2 is the smallest z such that $g(1, 3, z) = 0$). If g is a computable total function, then $f(x, y)$ can be computed as follows. Compute in order $g(x, y, 0), g(x, y, 1), g(x, y, 2)$, and so on, until the first time a value of zero is computed; the number then used as the third argument to produce this zero value for g is the value of $f(x, y)$.

Definition: A *mu-recursive definition* (or *mu recursion*) of an n-argument function, $n \geq 1$, is a single equation whose left side consists of the function symbol for that function followed by n distinct variables as arguments, and whose right side is a mu expression; the variable following the mu is distinct from the arguments; inside the brackets there is an equation whose right side is the numeral zero and whose left side is a functional expression containing only given function symbols, whose only variables are the argument variables and the variable following the mu.

We shall apply this definitional scheme only in cases where the function symbols occurring in E denote total functions. Advanced texts specify a meaning to this mu expression even in cases where the function symbols denote partial functions, but the matter is complicated and not worthwhile for the purposes of this book. (Actually, even in advanced texts, there is not much advantage in allowing partial functions to occur in E.)

Let us consider five examples:

$$f_1(x, y) = (\mu z)[\text{ISG}(\text{EQ}(y*z, x)) = 0]$$
$$f_2(x, y) = (\mu z)[y*\text{GE}(x, y*S(z)) = 0]$$
$$f_3(x, y) = (\mu z)[S(x)*S(y)*S(z) = 0]$$
$$f_4(x, y) = (\mu z)[\dot{-}(x, y) = 0]$$
$$f_5(x, y) = (\mu z)[\dot{-}(x, z) = 0]$$

Note that $f_1(x, y)$ is the smallest z such that $y*z = x$. Thus if x is a multiple of y, then $f_1(x, y)$ is the quotient of x divided by y. But if x is not a multiple of y (e.g., $x = 10$, $y = 3$), there is no z making $\text{ISG}(\text{EQ}(y*z, x))$ equal to zero. Hence $f_1(x, y)$ in that case has no value.

We see, then, that definitions by mu recursion sometimes result in partial functions, even when the given functions are total. In this respect, mu recursion differs from both explicit definition and primitive recursion, which always define total functions from given total functions.

On the other hand, f_2 as defined is a total function. In fact, we now verify that $f_2(x, y) = \mathrm{QU}(x, y)$ for all x and y: Let E be the expression

$$y*\mathrm{GE}(x, y*S(z))$$

If $y = 0$, $E = 0$ whatever the value of z; so 0 is the smallest value of z for which $E = 0$. If $y \neq 0$, then the smallest z making E zero is the smallest z such that $y*(z + 1) > x$ (i.e., the quotient). In both cases, therefore, $f_2(x, y) = \mathrm{QU}(x, y)$.

Definition by primitive recursion is to be regarded as more of an achievement than definition by mu recursion. When a function is defined by explicit definition or primitive recursion from the list of functions in Section 4.2.4, that means that we have proved that the function is in the class of primitive recursive functions, which has many important properties to be discussed in Section 4.8. Since we have already given a primitive recursive definition of the quotient, this alternative definition by mu recursion is merely an illustration.

It is easy to see that $f_3(x, y)$ has no value for any pair of values x, y.

For all x and y, $f_4(x, y)$ either equals 0 (when $x \leq y$) or has no value (when $x > y$). Since z does not appear inside the brackets, it does not influence the value of the expression.

Clearly, $f_5(x, y) = x$, for all x and y.

We reiterate that in a definition by mu recursion

$$f(\ldots) = (\mu z)[\ldots]$$

all the variables other than z that occur inside the brackets must occur in the list of arguments of f. However, z itself is not an argument of f. The situation is similar to the definition of a function by an integral

$$f(x, y) = \int_0^1 g(x, y, z)\, dz$$

where the variable z is not listed as an argument of the function being defined.

We shall find it convenient to liberalize our definition by mu recursion. Note that the definition of f_1 could be abbreviated to the following:

$$f_1(x, y) = (\mu z)[y*z = x]$$

In general we shall allow ourselves to write

$$(\mu z)[E_1 = E_2]$$

knowing that this mu recursion could be expanded to

$$(\mu z)[\mathrm{ISG}(\mathrm{EQ}(E_1, E_2)) = 0]$$

which is in accord with the definition of *mu recursion*.

4.4.2 More Examples

EXAMPLE 1. We return to the problem of defining the least common multiple, which we discussed briefly at the beginning of this section. Since this is a function over the positive integers, we must first decide how we shall extend its domain to include cases with one or both arguments zero. Let f be the function we wish to define and stipulate that $f(x, y)$ is to be equal to the least common positive multiple of x and y when x and y are both positive, but equal to zero when either x or y is zero. We can then use the following mu recursion as a formal definition:

$$f(x, y) = (\mu z)[x^*y^*(\text{ISG}(z) + \text{REM}(z, x) + \text{REM}(z, y)) = 0]$$

If either x or y is zero, the entire expression inside the brackets is zero, regardless of the value of z. Zero is then the smallest value of z for which the expression is zero. If neither x nor y is zero, both remainders must be zero and z must be nonzero in order to make the entire expression zero. Note that we are using + and * for their logical effect: $*(u, v)$ is zero if and only if either u or v is zero; $+(u, v)$ is zero if and only if both are zero.

For clarity, it is sometimes better to use a mu expression with a simpler functional expression inside the brackets. To this end, we can first define an appropriate function by explicit definition

$$g(x, y, z) = x^*y^*(\text{ISG}(z) + \text{REM}(z, x) + \text{REM}(z, y))$$

and then write the mu recursion

$$f(x, y) = (\mu z)[g(x, y, z) = 0]$$

EXAMPLE 2. Alternative definition of quotient. Suppose that we wish to define the quotient by using the idea that, when $y > 0$, $\text{QU}(x, y)$ is the largest w such that $w^*y \leq x$. We can do so by means of the mu operator by taking $z = \dot{-}(x, w)$; when z and w are so related, the smallest z will yield the largest w. Furthermore, $w = \dot{-}(x, z)$, so that the expression $\dot{-}(x, z)$ can be used in place of w. Accordingly, we can write the following definitions, f giving us the smallest z, and QU, in effect, defining the w that is related to this z:

$$f(x, y) = (\mu z)[\dot{-}(\dot{-}(x, z)^*y, x) = 0]$$
$$\text{QU}(x, y) = \dot{-}(x, f(x, y)) * \text{SG}(y)$$

The quotient is generally found by subtracting $f(x, y)$ from x; however, if y is zero the quotient must be taken as zero regardless. For example, $f(90, 20) = 86$, so $\text{QU}(90, 20) = \dot{-}(90, 86)^*\text{SG}(20) = 4$. $f(90, 10) = 81$, so $\text{QU}(90, 10) = \dot{-}(90, 81)^*\text{SG}(10) = 9$. $f(90, 0) = 0$, so $\text{QU}(90, 0) = \dot{-}(90, 0)^*\text{SG}(0) = 0$.

This solution illustrates a general technique for using mu recursions to find a number, given that it is the greatest number having a certain property. As in many examples, we must treat the case $y = 0$ specially.

EXAMPLE 3. A third definition of quotient. We illustrate another method of defining a function by mu recursion given to us by the idea of the greatest number satisfying some property. Since we wish to find the largest w such that $w*y \leq x$, we can instead find the smallest z such that $z*y > x$, and then subtract one from z to get w. The formal definitions are as follows:

$$g(x, y) = (\mu z)[y*\text{ISG}(\text{GT}(z*y, x)) = 0]$$
$$\text{QU}(x, y) = P(g(x, y))$$

A factor of y occurs inside the brackets so that $g(x, 0) = 0$ for all x, and thus $\text{QU}(x, 0) = P(0) = 0$. If this factor of y were omitted, $g(x, 0)$ and hence $\text{QU}(x, 0)$ would have no value.

Of the three mu-recursive definitions of the quotient function, probably the definition of it as f_2 in Section 4.4.1 is the simplest. But each of the other two is illustrative of a general technique.

EXAMPLE 4. Greatest common divisor. Again we have the problem of extending the meaning of a function over the positive integers so as to include cases with one or both arguments zero. Letting g be the function we wish to define, we stipulate that $g(x, y)$ is to be the greatest common divisor of x and y when x and y are positive and $g(x, 0) = g(0, y) = 0$.

Formally, an explicit definition of g in terms of the function f of Example 1 is

$$g(x, y) = \text{QU}(x*y, f(x, y))$$

This definition makes use of the well-known law that the product of two positive integers equals the product of the least common multiple and the greatest common divisor. Note that the function as defined is also correct for zero arguments.

We also wish to define g without using the f of Example 1. Since we wish to get the notion of the *greatest* from the mu operator, which represents the notion of the *least*, we use the technique of our solution to Example 2. We first find the smallest z such that

$$\dot{-}(\text{MAX}(x, y), z)$$

is both a divisor of y and a divisor of x. We define the auxiliary function h to give us this z:

$$h(x, y) = (\mu z)[\text{REM}(x, \dot{-}(\text{MAX}(x, y), z))$$
$$+ \text{REM}(y, \dot{-}(\text{MAX}(x, y), z)) = 0]$$

We note that if x and y are both positive, then $h(x, y)$ is $\text{MAX}(x, y)$ minus the greatest common divisor. But if x or y is zero then $h(x, y)$ is zero. Accordingly, we now define g explicitly in terms of this h:

$$g(x, y) = SG(x) * SG(y) * \dot{-}(MAX(x, y), h(x, y))$$

[$MAX(x, y)$ cannot be replaced by x, y or $MIN(x, y)$ here. See Exercise 16.]

4.4.3 Partial Functions

In Section 4.5 we shall see the precise relationship between a partial function defined by mu recursion and the program constructed to compute it, which does not always halt. In Chapter 5 we shall indicate that partial functions, of the utmost importance in the theory of computability, often arise either from mu-recursive definitions or from situations that give rise to mu-recursive definitions. The problem of whether a given function defined by mu recursion has a value for a given set of arguments turns out to be equivalent to the halting problem for programs. For these reasons, we now study mu-recursive definitions of partial functions.

Examples 5 and 6, which follow, are mu-recursive definitions of partial functions that were computed by programs given in Section 3.5. It is interesting to compare the programs with the definitions.

EXAMPLE 5. $f(x, y) = (\mu z)[y + z = x]$. The function as defined is the partial minus function over the nonnegative integers (see Section 3.5.1). Thus

$$f(x, y) \begin{cases} = x - y & \text{if } x \geqq y \\ \text{has no value} & \text{if } x < y \end{cases}$$

EXAMPLE 6. $g(x) = (\mu z)[\uparrow(z, 2) = x]$. The function g is the partial square-root function (see Section 3.5.2). Thus

$$g(x) \begin{cases} = \sqrt{x} & \text{if } \sqrt{x} \text{ is an integer} \\ \text{has no value} & \text{if } \sqrt{x} \text{ is not an integer} \end{cases}$$

It is instructive to see that this mu recursion suggests a procedure similar to the programs of Section 3.5.2. The procedure is to see first if zero squared equals x, then to see if 1 squared equals x, and so on. It tries each nonnegative integer z in turn until it finds that value of z whose square equals x. If there is no z, the procedure never halts and, correspondingly, the function defined by the mu recursion has no value.

We shall consider examples of mu recursions for partial functions and offer exercises that call for such mu recursions according to specification. These exercises are offered in the same spirit as the exercises at the end of Section 3.6, which called for programs that do not always halt. We hope they will provide some insight into the general halting problem and the general problem of partial functions. Examples 7 and 8 are samples of such exercises.

Another more practical reason for this work with partial functions is that quite often we can define in a simple manner a partial function that is a

halfway station to the additional objective of writing a more complicated definition of a given total function. Example 7 will illustrate this strategy.

EXAMPLE 7. Define a two-argument partial function g_2 such that $g_2(x, y)$
is the least common positive multiple of x and y if there is such, and has no
value if there is no such. Thus $g_2(x, y)$ has a value if and only if x and y are both
positive. A straightforward solution is

$$g_2(x, y) = (\mu z)[\text{ISG}(z) + \text{REM}(z, x) + \text{REM}(z, y) = 0]$$

This solution might be a halfway step to the solution of the problem posed in
Example 1.

EXAMPLE 8. Define a two-argument partial function h_2 such that $h_2(x, y)$
is the greatest common divisor of x and y if both x and y are positive, but has
no value if $x = 0$, $y = 0$, or both. A solution can be given as an explicit definition in terms of the function g_2 of Example 7, again using the fact that the
product of two positive integers equals the product of their least common multiple and their greatest common divisor:

$$h_2(x, y) = \text{QU}(x*y, g_2(x, y))$$

Since $g_2(x, y)$ has no value if x or $y = 0$, by this formal definition, $h_2(x, y)$ has
no value in those cases either.

The solution to Example 8 illustrates the fact mentioned in Section 4.1.1
that, when a function is defined explicitly in terms of a partial function, the
defined function is also a partial function. (If part of a functional expression has
no value for a certain set of arguments, then the entire functional expression
can have no value for that set of arguments.) In this book, partial functions
occur as given functions in explicit definitions, but not in primitive recursions
or in mu recursions.

To define h_2 without using the solution to Example 7, we find the smallest
z such that $\doteq(x, z)$ is a divisor of both x and y provided that these are nonzero.
If either of these is zero, we arrange things so that no value of z is found. If a
value of z is found, the greatest common denominator actually equals $\doteq(x, z)$.
Imitating the style of Example 2, we write

$$h_3(x, y) = (\mu z)[\text{ISG}(x) + \text{ISG}(y) + \text{REM}(x, \doteq(x, z)) + \text{REM}(y, \doteq(x, z)) = 0]$$
$$h_2(x, y) = \doteq(x, h_3(x, y))$$

Fermat's Last Theorem 4.4.4

We now seek to illustrate in a meaningful way the "halting" problem for functions defined by mu recursion. Almost everyone has heard of Fermat's last
theorem, which is still a conjecture. We phrase the problem in the following
way. Given an integer $x \geq 3$, do there exist positive integers z_1, z_2, z_3 such that

$$z_1^x + z_2^x = z_3^x?$$

To convert this problem into the computation of a function, let us find a way of representing the ordered triple (z_1, z_2, z_3) as a single number z. Our method of representation must be such that each ordered triple (z_1, z_2, z_3) of positive integers is represented by some nonnegative z; but the representation need not be unique.

To arrange for dealing with ordered triples in this way, we make use of the function EXP, where $EXP(x, y)$ equals the exponent of the highest power of x that divides y, for $x, y \geq 2$. [$EXP(x, y) = 0$ for x or $y = 0$ or 1.] By Exercise 34 of Section 4.2 this function is definable by means of primitive recursion and explicit definition. We define

$$h_1(z) = EXP(2, z) + 1$$
$$h_2(z) = EXP(3, z) + 1$$
$$h_3(z) = EXP(5, z) + 1$$

We then let $z_1, z_2,$ and z_3 be $h_1(z), h_2(z),$ and $h_3(z)$, respectively.

The functions EXP, $h_1, h_2,$ and h_3 are total functions and the h's have positive values. So each (z_1, z_2, z_3) is an ordered triple of positive integers. Since 2, 3, and 5 are prime, for every such (z_1, z_2, z_3) there exists a z representing this ordered triple. One value of z is

$$2^{z_1 - 1} * 3^{z_2 - 1} * 5^{z_3 - 1}$$

[e.g., to get (3, 1, 4) we can take $z = 500$]. The z obtained in this way is the smallest z representing (z_1, z_2, z_3).

We define a function f such that $f(x)$ in the smallest z such that $z_1^x + z_2^x = z_3^x$:

$$f(x) = (\mu z)[\uparrow(h_1(z), x) + \uparrow(h_2(z), x) = \uparrow(h_3(z), x)]$$

We then define:

$$f_1(x) = h_1(f(x))$$
$$f_2(x) = h_2(f(x))$$
$$f_3(x) = h_3(f(x))$$

Now if there exists a triple (z_1, z_2, z_3) such that

$$z_1^x + z_2^x = z_3^x$$

one such triple is obtained by taking $z_1 = f_1(x), z_2 = f_2(x),$ and $z_3 = f_3(x)$. But if there is no such triple, $f(x)$ has no value, and therefore each of $f_1(x), f_2(x),$ and $f_3(x)$ has no value. So $f, f_1, f_2,$ and f_3 are partial functions.

In the event that, for a given $x, f(x)$ has no value and there is no solution to

$$z_1^x + z_2^x = z_3^x$$

it may be that neither we nor anyone else alive may know it. All we know to do, generally, is to try successive values of z. But there is no general way known of determining that there is no such z in cases where there is none.

(As a matter of fact, number theorists by now have been able to prove for many values of x that no such z exists; that is, there is no solution to

$$z_1^x + z_2^x = z_3^x$$

The fact remains that there are still infinitely many values of x for which this question is open.)

Note there is a procedure here for finding z if z exists. But if no z exists, the procedure will simply never halt, without our ever knowing for sure that it never will. In situations like this, the halting problem is a very important problem indeed.

Exercises 4.4.5

In all exercises calling for the definition of a function, use the functions listed in Section 4.2.4 as given functions.

Group I

1. Assume as given the function **PR**, where $PR(x) = 1$ if x is a prime, and $PR(x) = 0$ if x is not a prime. (See Exercise 4 of Section 4.2.) (a) Define f from **PR** by mu recursion, where $f(x)$ is the smallest prime number greater than x. (b) Define g by mu recursion, possibly with the help of explicit definition, where $g(x)$ is the greatest prime number less than x. Note that g is a partial function since $g(0)$, $g(1)$, and $g(2)$ have no values. (c) By means of primitive recursion from f, define the one-argument function **PRIME**, where $PRIME(x) =$ the xth prime in order of magnitude, counting 2 as the zeroth prime. [Thus $PRIME(0) = 2$, $PRIME(1) = 3$, $PRIME(2) = 5$, and so on.] Note that, since there are infinitely many primes, f and **PRIME** are total functions. [Part (c) is identical to Exercise 36 of Section 4.2.]

2. Using both primitive recursion and mu recursion, and possibly also explicit definition, define the function g where $g(x)$ equals the largest integer y such that the sum of the squares of the first y positive integers is no greater than x; in particular, $g(0) = 0$ and $g(1) = 1$. [For example, $g(30) = g(31) = 4$ and $g(29) = 3$, since $1^2 + 2^2 + 3^2 + 4^2 = 30$.]

3. Define each of the two functions by mu recursion, possibly with the help of explicit definition: (a) $g(x) = 0$ if x is a perfect square; otherwise, $g(x)$ has no value. (b) $h(x) = 0$ if x is not a perfect square; otherwise, $h(x)$ has no value.

Group II

In each exercise, define the two functions described by using mu recursion, possibly with the help of explicit definition, but without using primitive recursion. The function you define in part (a) of each exercise must not have a value precisely where the specification calls for it not to have a value. The function you define in part (b) must be a total function.

4. (a) $f(x) = z$ if $x = 3z^2 - 2z + 1$, and $f(x)$ has no value if there is no such nonnegative integer z. [Note that for any x there is at most one z satisfying that relationship. Thus $f(0)$ has no value, $f(1) = 0, f(2) = 1, f(3), f(4), \ldots, f(8)$ have no value, $f(9) = 2$, and so on.] (b) $g(0) = 0$ and, for $x > 0$, $g(x)$ equals the largest value of z such that $x \geq 3z^2 - 2z + 1$.

5. (a) $f(x, y) = x + 2y$ if $x \neq y$; $f(x, y)$ has no value if $x = y$. (b) $g(x, y) = x + 2y$ if $x \neq y$; $g(x, y) = 0$ if $x = y$.

6. (a) Where h is a given one-argument total function, $f(x, y)$ is the smallest $z \leq x$ such that $h(z) = y$; $f(x, y)$ has no value if there is no such $z \leq x$. (b) $g(x, y) = f(x, y)$ if the latter has a value; otherwise, $g(x, y) = x + 1$.

7. (a) Where h is a given one-argument total function, $f(x, y)$ is the largest $z \leq x$ such that $h(z) = y$; $f(x, y)$ has no value if there is no such $z \leq x$. (b) $g(x, y) = f(x, y)$ if the latter has a value; $g(x, y) = 0$, otherwise.

Group III—Total Functions

Define the following without using primitive recursion. (The technique of Example 3 of Section 4.4.2 will be useful in some of these.)

8. $f(0) = 0$; for $x > 0$, $f(x)$ is the characteristic of the logarithm of x to the base 2. In other words, for $x > 0$, $f(x)$ is the largest nonnegative integer y such that $2^y \leq x$.

9. $h(0, y) = h(1, y) = h(x, 0) = h(x, 1) = 0$; and for $x, y \geq 2$, $h(x, y)$ is the smallest positive integer that is not divisible by x, is not divisible by y, is not a divisor of x, and is not a divisor of y.

10. $\text{EXP}(x, y)$ is the exponent of the greatest power of x that divides y, for $x \geq 2$ and $y \geq 2$; $\text{EXP}(0, y) = \text{EXP}(1, y) = \text{EXP}(x, 0) + \text{EXP}(x, 1) = 0$. [For example, $\text{EXP}(2, 22) = 1$; $\text{EXP}(2, 23) = 0$; $\text{EXP}(2, 24) = 3$.]

11. $\text{WSQ}(x)$ is the whole part of the square root of x (i.e., the greatest integer not greater than the square root of x). (Defining this total function by mu recursion is easier than Exercise 39 of Section 4.2, which asked for a primitive recursion. On the other hand, this exercise is more difficult than Example 6 of Section 4.4.3, since a total function is required here.)

12. $f(x)$ is the whole part of $\sqrt[5]{x^{17}}$.

13. $f(w, x, y)$ is the whole part of $\sqrt[w]{x^y}$ for $w \geq 0$; $f(0, x, y) = 0$.

14. (a) $g(x)$ is the number of digits in the decimal representation of x [e.g., $g(0) = g(1) = g(9) = 1, g(10) = 2, g(1000001) = 7$]. (b) $f(0) = 0$; for $x > 0$, $f(x)$ is the leftmost (nonzero) digit in the decimal representation of x [e.g., $f(3) = f(3142) = 3$].

Group IV—Miscellaneous

15. For the function f of Section 4.4.4 (Fermat's last theorem), what are $f(0)$, $f(1)$, and $f(2)$? What are the values of f_1, f_2, and f_3 for these arguments?

16. In Example 4 of Section 4.4.2, why could not $\dot{-}(\text{MIN}(x, y), z)$ be used instead of $\dot{-}(\text{MAX}(x, y), z)$?

17. Define by mu recursion the function h, where $h(x, y)$ equals the greatest common divisor of x and y if both x and y are positive, $h(x, 0) = h(0, x) = x$ if x is positive, but $h(0, 0)$ has no value. (Since every nonnegative integer is a divisor of zero, this function does have as its value the greatest common divisor, literally, even when one of the arguments is zero. Only when both arguments are zero, when the set of common divisors has no maximum, does this function have no value.)

18. Recall the function ϕ_i of Section 4.3. Let $\mathrm{PH}_i(x, y)$ be the largest z such that $\phi_i(x, z) \leqq y$ if there is such z; $\mathrm{PH}_i(x, y) = 0$ if there is no such z. (a) Define PH_i by mu recursion, assuming ϕ_i as a given function. (b) What are the functions PH_1, PH_2, and PH_3 in terms of your mathematical experience, or in terms of functions previously mentioned in this book either in the text or in the exercises?
Put $f(y) = \mathrm{PH}_4(2, y)$. (c) Prove that f is weakly monotonic [i.e., that $i < j$ implies $f(i) \leqq f(j)$]. (d) Prove that f is unbounded [i.e., that, for all k, there is an i such that $f(i) > k$]. (e) Compute $f(10^i)$ for each i from 1 to 10; then compute $f(10^{50^i})$ for each i from 1 to 10, using the fact that 2^{10} is approximately equal to 10^3. (f) What impresses you about this function f as compared to other weakly monotonic unbounded functions that you know?

19. (*Difficult*) Define by any of the three modes of definition or combination thereof: $f(x)$ is the second smallest z such that $g(x, z) = 0$; $f(x)$ has no value if there are not at least two distinct values of z such that $g(x, z) = 0$. Here g is a given total two-argument function. [*Caution:* The following solution is not acceptable:

$$h_1(x) = (\mu z)[g(x, z) = 0]$$
$$h_2(x, z) = g(x, z) + \mathrm{EQ}(z, h_1(x))$$
$$f(x) = (\mu z)[h_2(x, z) = 0]$$

The reason is that although g is a total function, h_1 and hence h_2 may not be, so the last line may not be an acceptable mu recursion.]

20. (*Difficult*) The same instructions (and the same words of caution) as for Exercise 19: $h(x)$ is the second largest $z \leqq x$ such that $g(x, z) = 0$; $h(x)$ has no value if there are not at least two distinct values of $z \leqq x$ such that $g(x, z) = 0$. g is a given total function.

PROGRAMS FOR DEFINED FUNCTIONS 4.5

We have indicated in our presentation that all three definition schemes are such as to allow computation of the function being defined, provided that the given functions can be computed. In this section we make a link with Chapter 3 by showing, for each of the definition schemes, how to construct a WHILE-language program computing a defined function from WHILE-language programs computing the given functions. These algorithms could easily be converted to algorithms for constructing GOTO-language programs from GOTO-language programs, and (perhaps with added complication) to algorithms for constructing Turing machines from Turing machines.

4.5.1 Explicit Definition

If a function f is explicitly defined from functions that are computable by WHILE-language programs, a program for computing f in the WHILE language can be constructed from these other programs in a straightforward manner. However, the algorithm is difficult to describe in words, so we shall simply exhibit the construction in terms of a specific example, namely the following explicit definition of f in terms of $g_1, g_2, g_3,$ and g_4:

$$f(x_1, x_2, x_3) = g_1(g_2(x_1, 17), g_3(g_4(x_1), g_2(x_3, x_2)))$$

We assume that there are WHILE-language programs $P_1, P_2, P_3,$ and P_4 such that:

1. P_1 computes g_1 with respect to W11, W12, W13.
2. P_2 computes g_2 with respect to W21, W22, W23.
3. P_3 computes g_3 with respect to W31, W32, W33.
4. P_4 computes g_4 with respect to W41, W42.

(Recall from Section 3.7.1 that this means that the outputs of these programs are, respectively, W13, W23, W33, and W42. The other variables mentioned are the inputs in the order given.)

5. No two of these use any variable in common.
6. None of them uses a variable beginning with the letter X or Y.

(These assumptions are justified, since programs can always be rewritten using other variables.)

We now present the program that computes the function f with respect to the variable sequence X1, X2, X3, Y5. The program uses the variables Y1, Y2, Y3, and Y4 to hold the values, respectively, of:

$$g_2(X1, 17)$$
$$g_4(X1)$$
$$g_2(X3, X2)$$
$$g_3(g_4(X1), g_2(X3, X2))$$

The program is:

W21 := X1; W22 := 17; P_2; Y1 := W23;
W41 := X1; P_4; Y2 := W42;
W21 := X3; W22 := X2; P_2; Y3 := W23;
W31 := Y2; W32 := Y3; P_3; Y4 := W33;
W11 := Y1; W12 := Y4; P_1; Y5 := W13

(The construction corresponding to this for the GOTO language is a bit more complicated, in that HALT commands inside P_1, P_2, P_3, and P_4 must be converted into transfers to the first command outside the subprogram.)

The construction uses no WHILE commands other than those already present in P_1, P_2, P_3, and P_4. In this sense, the construction is loopless. Any set of input values for which P_i does not halt ($i = 1, 2, 3$ or 4) is a set of arguments for which the function g_i has no value. If these values are involved in a computation of f for a set of arguments, the program will not halt and the function f has no value for those arguments. On the other hand, if g_1, g_2, g_3, and g_4 are total functions, then P_1, P_2, P_3, and P_4 always halt, and P always halts for all its input values.

We note that if the programs P_1, P_2, P_3, and P_4 are all DO-TIMES programs (see Section 3.7), then P as constructed is a DO-TIMES program.

Primitive Recursion 4.5.2

Suppose that a function f is defined by the primitive recursion

$$\begin{cases} f(x_1, \ldots, x_n, 0) = E_1 \\ f(x_1, \ldots, x_n, S(x_{n+1})) = E_2 \end{cases}$$

where (1) no variables other than $x_1, \ldots, x_n$ and no function symbols other than the given function symbols occur in E_1; (2) no variables other than $x_1, \ldots, x_{n+1}$ and no function symbols other than f and the given function symbols occur in E_2; (3) each occurrence of f in E_2 is in the context $f(x_1, \ldots, x_n, x_{n+1})$; and (4) each of the given functions is computable in the WHILE language.

In preparation for writing the program for f, we define

$$h_1(x_1, \ldots, x_n) = E_1$$

Next, we rewrite E_2 as E_2' by replacing each occurrence of $f(x_1, \ldots, x_n, x_{n+1})$ by the variable z. Note that E_2' does not contain the function symbol f, and contains only the variables $x_1, \ldots, x_n, x_{n+1}, z$. We then define

$$h_2(x_1, \ldots, x_n, x_{n+1}, z) = E_2'$$

The functions h_1 and h_2 are defined by explicit definition from functions that can be computed by WHILE-language programs. WHILE-language programs P_1 and P_2 can therefore be written for h_1 and h_2, respectively, by the construction method of Section 4.5.1. Then the primitive recursion defining f can be modified to the following:

$$\begin{cases} f(x_1, \ldots, x_n, 0) = h_1(x_1, \ldots, x_n) \\ f(x_1, \ldots, x_n, S(x_{n+1})) = h_2(x_1, \ldots, x_n, x_{n+1}, f(x_1, \ldots, x_n, x_{n+1})) \end{cases}$$

We assume that P_1 computes h_1 with respect to the variable sequence $W1, \ldots, W\Delta_n, W\Delta_{n+1}$, and that P_2 computes h_2 with respect to the variable sequence $V1, \ldots, V\Delta_{n+2}, V\Delta_{n+3}$. ($\Delta_n$ is the numeral in the WHILE-language for the nonnegative integer n, whatever n may be; for example, $W\Delta_{12}$ is W12.) We assume that neither P_1 nor P_2 has any of the variables R, U, Z, nor any variables beginning with the letter X; we further assume that P_1 and P_2 have no variables in common.

We use the DO-TIMES command of Section 3.7. (Recall that a DO-TIMES command can be replaced by a WHILE command.) The program for computing f with respect to the variable sequence $X1, \ldots, X\Delta_{n+1}, Z$ is as follows:

$$W1 := X1; \ldots; W\Delta_n := X\Delta_n; P_1; Z := W\Delta_{n+1};$$

$$R := 0;$$

DO $X\Delta_{n+1}$ TIMES

> $[V1 := X1; \ldots; V\Delta_n := X\Delta_n;$
>
> $V\Delta_{n+1} := R; V\Delta_{n+2} := Z; P_2; Z := V\Delta_{n+3};$
>
> INCR(R)$]$

Note that R has the value 0 first, is incremented each time, and equals the value of $X\Delta_{n+1}$ at the end.

To verify that this program does compute the function f, we must verify that if the program is run with input values set to $i_1, \ldots, i_n, i_{n+1}$, respectively, the program will eventually halt with the value of Z equal to $f(i_1, \ldots, i_n, i_{n+1})$.

It is helpful to abbreviate $f(i_1, \ldots, i_n, k)$ as $f(k)$; $h_1(i_1, \ldots, i_n)$ as h_1; and $h_2(i_1, \ldots, i_n, k, m)$ as $h_2(k, m)$. In discussing runs of the program it is convenient to ignore all commands in which the values of the variables $W1, \ldots, W\Delta_n, V1, \ldots, V\Delta_n$ are set.

Assume first that $i_{n+1} = 0$. In this case, the machine goes through P_1, sets R to zero, and halts without executing the loop at all, since $X\Delta_{n+1}$ equals 0. Since P_1 computes h_1, Z has the value $h_1 = f(0)$, which is what we want.

Next assume that $i_{n+1} \neq 0$. This value does not affect the running of P_1. When the machine gets through P_1, Z gets the value $h_1 = f(0)$ and R is set to 0. This time the loop is entered: $V\Delta_{n+1}$ is set to 0, $V\Delta_{n+2}$ is set to $f(0)$, and then P_2 is gone through for these values. After the machine comes out of P_2 the first time, it has $f(1) = h_2(0, f(0))$ as the value of Z. Then R is incremented to 1 and the loop is finished for the first time.

The loop is executed i_{n+1} times (the value of $X\Delta_{n+1}$). The kth time through the loop, the machine computes $f(k)$ from $f(k-1)$. Therefore, the last time through the loop, it computes $f(i_{n+1})$, which is in Z when the machine halts.

This concludes the verification that the program computes the function f. We note that if P_1 and P_2 are DO-TIMES programs, then P as constructed is a DO-TIMES program. Theorem 7.1 of Section 3.7 tells us that under this circumstance the program halts for all input settings.

The construction in Section 4.5.1 of a program for a function defined by explicit definition called for no new loops (no new WHILE commands and no new DO-TIMES commands). Thus, both construction methods result in the construction of DO-TIMES programs. It follows that if we have defined a function by means of a sequence of explicit definitions and primitive recursions from the given function S, then we can be sure that the function is computable by a DO-TIMES program. The number of DO-TIMES commands in the program will equal the number of times primitive recursion is used in the sequence of definitions.

We shall offer further comments on the significance of our constructions as DO-TIMES programs in Section 4.8. Meanwhile we note that, as remarked in Section 3.7, the DO-TIMES command corresponds to the DO statement of FORTRAN and the FOR statement of ALGOL. It is interesting to observe that functions definable by explicit definition and primitive recursion are computable by FORTRAN programs and ALGOL programs in which the only loops are DO loops and FOR loops, respectively.

Mu Recursion 4.5.3

We show now how to construct a WHILE-language program to compute a function defined by mu recursion (from a total function having a WHILE-language program). Unlike the other two constructions of this section, this one possibly results in a program that does not halt for all possible input values. But this is as it should be, because such a program computes a partial function.

Assume that g is a total $(n + 1)$-argument function computable by a WHILE-language program P_1 with respect to the variable sequence $W_1, \ldots,$ $W\Delta_{n+2}$, and has no variables beginning with the letter X or Z. Assume that f is defined from g by the mu recursion

$$f(x_1, \ldots, x_n) = (\mu z)[g(x_1, \ldots, x_n, z) = 0]$$

We shall construct a program P to compute f with respect to the variable sequence $X_1, \ldots, X\Delta_n, Z$.

Recall what it means to say that a program computes a function (Section 3.6.1). For a given set of inputs, if the function has a value, then the program, when the input variables have been set accordingly, eventually halts with the correct output. But if the function has no value, the program never halts for that input setting. Thus P_1 always halts, since g is a total function. But since f may not be a total function, the program P as constructed may not always halt.

The program P that computes f is as follows:

$$Z := 0; \ W\Delta_{n+2} := 1;$$
$$\text{WHILE } W\Delta_{n+2} > 0 \text{ DO}$$
$$[W1 := X1; \ \ldots; \ W\Delta_n := X\Delta_n;$$
$$W\Delta_{n+1} := Z; \ P_1; \ \text{INCR}(Z)];$$
$$\text{DECR}(Z)$$

We must show that, for each n-tuple of numerals $(i_1, \ldots, i_n)$, if $f(i_1, \ldots, i_n)$ has a value, then this program when run with $X1, \ldots, X\Delta_n$ set at $i_1, \ldots, i_n$, respectively, will eventually halt with $f(i_1, \ldots, i_n)$ as the value of Z; and that if $f(i_1, \ldots, i_n)$ does not have a value, the program will never halt. We abbreviate $f(i_1, \ldots, i_n)$ as f and $g(i_1, \ldots, i_n, k)$ as $g(k)$.

Assume first that f has the value m. Then $g(0), \ldots, g(m-1)$ are all non-zero, and $g(m) = 0$. P_1 will successively compute $g(0), g(1)$, and so on, with the result in $W\Delta_{n+2}$ each time. For each j, it computes $g(j)$ with the value j in Z. If $g(j) \neq 0$, then $W\Delta_{n+2}$ is nonzero; the machine, having incremented Z to $j + 1$, goes back and computes $g(j + 1)$. So it will successively compute $g(0)$, $g(1), \ldots, g(m-1)$, each time going back to reenter P_1 with a new value of Z. However, when it computes $g(m)$, 0 is thereby put into $W\Delta_{n+2}$, which causes the machine to exit from the loop (i.e., the evident WHILE command). Since Z is incremented to $m + 1$ before leaving the loop, it is decremented to m after leaving, which is the correct value of f.

On the other hand, if f does not have a value, then $g(j)$ is nonzero for every j. The variable $W\Delta_{n+2}$ will never have the value 0 at the conclusion of P_1, so the machine will never halt.

4.5.4 Programs and Function Definitions

We have shown how to construct programs in the WHILE language to compute the functions defined by our three types of definition, provided that we already have programs for the given functions. Thus any function that can be defined in a series of such definitions from the successor function has a program to compute it.

We have almost proved a theorem to the effect that all functions definable by the three types of definition are computable in the WHILE language. The same is true of the GOTO language or any programming language that has the features of one of these languages and has no bound on the size of integers that it can represent. We shall be able to state this theorem in a precise way in Section 4.8.

The formalism of functional expressions could be thought of as a high-level programming language, even though it is a language of declaratives. The constructions of programs that we have presented here suggest how some equations defining functions could be compiled. The question naturally arises: Is this possible for other types of functional definition besides the three we have so far considered? The next two sections in effect begin to consider this question for general equational definitions.

In advanced texts in the theory of computability, there are theorems that go the other way. It is proved, for example, that every function computed by a DO-TIMES program is in the class of primitive recursive functions, which means (see Section 4.8) that such a function can be defined from the successor function by a sequence of explicit definitions and primitive recursions. Also, it is proved that any function, total or partial, that is computed by any program in the WHILE language can be defined by means of repeated application of explicit definition, primitive recursion, and mu recursion. This result applies to the GOTO language and other programming languages. These matters are discussed in more detail in Section 4.8 and Chapter 5.

Thus, what we can do with programs, we can do by our definitions, and vice versa.

However, we must be careful not to see equivalences that are not really there. For example, suppose that f is a one-argument function defined by three given one-argument functions g_1, g_2, and g_3 by explicit definition as follows:

$$f(x) = \text{ISG}(g_1(x))^*g_2(x) + \text{SG}(g_1(x))^*g_3(x)$$

We are inclined to verbalize this definition by saying that $f(x) = g_2(x)$ if $g_1(x) = 0$, and $f(x) = g_3(x)$ if $g_1(x) \neq 0$. This verbalization is fully accurate if g_1, g_2, and g_3 are total functions. In the event that they are not all total functions, we must go on to say that if, for any x, $g_1(x)$ or $g_2(x)$ or $g_3(x)$ has no value, then $f(x)$ has no value. In particular, if $g_1(x) = 0$ and $g_2(x) = 19$ and $g_3(x)$ has no value, then $f(x)$ has no value, although we are inclined to look at the definition in this case and think as follows: Since $g_1(x) = 0$, $\text{SG}(g_1(x)) = 0$; therefore, whatever we multiply this expression by must be zero, so $f(x) = \text{ISG}(g_1(x))^* g_2(x) = 19$. This reasoning ignores our understanding (see the end of Section 4.1.1) that if a given function in an explicit definition has no value for any values of the arguments, then the defined function has no value for those values of the arguments. Thus, for any x, if $g_3(x)$ has no value, then $f(x)$, where f is defined above, has no value—whatever the values of $g_1(x)$ and $g_2(x)$.

For example, the following program does not necessarily compute f as defined:

$$W := g_1(X); \text{ IF } W = 0 \text{ THEN } [Y := g_2(X)] \text{ ELSE } [Y := g_3(X)]$$

(The portion $W := g_1(X)$ is an abbreviation for a program that computes the function g_1 with respect to X, W; similarly, for $Y := g_2(X)$ and $Y := g_3(X)$. We assume that these programs compute without changing the value of X.)

Indeed, let f_1 be the function computed by this program with respect to the variable sequence X, Y. In the event that g_1, g_2, and g_3 are total functions, f is the same as f_1. But if not, then f and f_1 may differ. To continue the example in which $g_3(x)$ has no value, $g_1(x) = 0$ and $g_2(x) = 19$, we trace through the program and see that, since the machine never gets into that part of the program where it is called upon to compute $g_3(x)$, $f_1(x)$ does have a value, namely 19.

Exercises 4.5.5

1. Carry through the construction of Section 4.5.1 (explicit definition) where the explicit definition is

$$f(x_1, x_2) = g_1(0, g_2(2, x_1, x_2), g_3(g_1(x_2, x_1, x_1)))$$

but where everything else is generally the same (e.g., P_1 computes g_1 with respect to W11, W12, W13, W14).

2. Suppose that g_1 and g_2 are two-argument total functions; P_1 computes g_1 with respect to the variable sequence W11, W12, W13; and P_2 computes g_2 with respect to the variable sequence W21, W22, W23. Suppose that P_1 and P_2 are DO-TIMES programs and f is defined by the primitive recursion

$$\begin{cases} f(x, y, 0) = g_1(g_2(x, y), y) \\ f(x, y, S(z)) = g_1(f(x, y, z), g_2(y, x)) \end{cases}$$

Construct a DO-TIMES program for computing f with respect to the variable sequence X, Y, Z, U, using P_1 and P_2. Make explicit any assumptions you make about variables occurring in P_1 and P_2.

3. Consider the following definition (which is distinct from, although it has a resemblance to, primitive recursion):

$$\begin{cases} f(0) = 17 \\ f(1) = 9 \\ f(S(S(x))) = h(f(x), f(S(x))) \end{cases}$$

Assuming that P_1 is a DO-TIMES program computing the total function h, make appropriate assumptions about the variables of P_1, and using P_1 write a DO-TIMES program P that computes f.

4. Let $f(x)$ be the smallest nonnegative integer z such that, for some $w \leq z + x$, $g(w, z) = 0$. Assume that g is a total function, but f may be a partial function. Assuming that P_1 is a WHILE-language program that computes g, make appropriate assumptions about the variables of P_1, and using P_1 write a WHILE-language program that computes f.

4.6 FORMAL COMPUTATIONS

In a rather natural way, we can compute the value of a function by writing a sequence of equations, beginning with the equations defining the function and ending with an evaluation. In this section we present formal rules for such computations and discuss their significance.

4.6.1 The Rules of Computation

We begin with a sample computation of $+(2, 1)$:

(1)	$+(x, 0) = x$	given
(2)	$+(x, S(y)) = S(+(x, y))$	given
(3)	$+(2, 0) = 2$	from (1)
(4)	$+(2, S(y)) = S(+(2, y))$	from (2)
(5)	$+(2, S(0)) = S(+(2, 0))$	from (4)

(6) $+(2, S(0)) = S(2)$ from (5) and (3)

(7) $S(2) = 3$

(8) $+(2, S(0)) = 3$ from (6) and (7)

(9) $S(0) = 1$

(10) $+(2, 1) = 3$ from (8) and (9)

Lines (1) and (2) are given as the defining equations of the function $+$. Line (3) is the result of substituting the numeral 2 for the variable in line (1). Lines (4) and (5) are also results of such substitutions.

Line (6) results from line (5) by replacing $+(2, 0)$ by its numerical value 2, justified by line (3). Lines (8) and (10) are obtained similarly.

Lines (7) and (9) cannot be justified by reference to other lines, since there is no definition of the function S.

Definition: An *evaluation* is an equation without variables whose left side consists of a function symbol followed by numeral arguments, and whose right side is a numeral.

Examples of evaluations are lines (3), (7), (9), and (10).

We now formalize the rules of computation.

Rule of uniform substitution: From an equation containing one or more variables, we may derive the equation that results by substituting some fixed numeral for *every* occurrence of one of these variables in the original equation.

For example, lines (3), (4), and (5) arc so obtained. Note that, although line (4) is obtained from (2) by substitution of 2 for the variable x, neither of the following two equations may be obtained from (2) by substitution:

$$+(2, S(y)) = S(+(x, y))$$

$$+(2, S(y)) = S(+(4, y))$$

Rule of evaluation replacement: Let $L = R$ be an evaluation. We may derive from an equation E and from $L = R$ the equation that results by replacing one occurrence of L by R in E.

Lines (6), (8), and (10) are obtained by evaluation replacement. Note that it is necessary to use this rule three times to obtain line (10) from line (5).

Another example: From the evaluation $h(2) = 1$ and from the equation

$$f(4) = g(h(2), h(2), h(2))$$

we may derive the equation

$$f(4) = g(1, h(2), h(2))$$

by the rule of evaluation replacement. By three applications of this rule we can derive the equation

$$f(4) = g(1, 1, 1)$$

It is not difficult to justify the rule of evaluation replacement. Once we have proved, for example, that $h(2) = 1$, we should be able to interchange $h(2)$ and the numeral 1 freely. The rule could be made more liberal, by allowing more than one replacement in a single step, by allowing replacement even when the equation $L = R$ is not evaluation, and so on, but such liberalization is not needed.

The rule of uniform substitution is justified by our understanding that when we write a defining equation with n variables, we declare the equation to be true for every ordered n-tuple of nonnegative integers. For example, when we write $+(x, S(y)) = S(+(x, y))$, we mean that whatever numbers the variables x and y denote, the equation is true. Therefore, we may substitute whatever numeral we like for either variable, and then later make an independent choice of a numeral to be substituted for the other variable.

But each substitution must be uniform, since in any equation all occurrences of the variable x must at any time denote the same number. And so, although we can make an arbitrary choice of substitution, once we have chosen we must make the same substitution for every occurrence of the variable in the equation.

We assume all S-evaluations, (i.e., all correct evaluations of the successor function) without further justification. Examples are lines (7) and (9) of the foregoing computation. Note that there is a slight problem in mechanically verifying the correctness of an S-evaluation, for example,

$$S(999976947999999) = 999976948000000$$

In allowing all S-evaluations without acknowledging the computational effort needed to establish them, we acknowledge that we are not getting all the way back to fundamentals with our formalism. Almost all the way, but not all the way. (This remark applies also to the foundational programming languages.)

(In much of the literature in the theory of computability, the decimal number system is not used formally. Instead, all numerals are constructed from the symbol 0 and the symbol S. $S(0)$ is then the numeral denoting 1, $S(S(0))$ the numeral denoting 2, $S(S(S(0)))$ the numeral denoting 3, and so on. This system of numerals, although clumsy, has the theoretical advantage that S-evaluations are unnecessary.)

Our formal rules do not apply to equations containing the mu symbol. But as we shall see, they apply very well to equations that are explicit definitions and primitive recursions.

4.6.2 *Formal Computations Defined*

Definition: A *derivation* from a set Φ of given equations is a finite sequence of equations such that each equation in the sequence either is one of the equations of Φ, is a correct S-evaluation, or follows from preceding lines in the sequence by means of the rule of uniform substitution or the rule of evaluation replacement. Any line in this derivation (in particular, the last line) is said to be *derivable* from the set Φ.

Definition: A *formal computation* is a derivation of an evaluation $L = R$ from a set Φ of given equations. In this case we say that the derivation of $L = R$ from Φ is a *formal computation* of L from Φ.

For example, let Φ be the set

$$\{\dot{-}(x, 0) = x,\ \dot{-}(x, S(y)) = P(\dot{-}(x, y)), P(0) = 0, P(S(x)) = x\}$$

The following is a formal computation of $\dot{-}(3, 1)$ from Φ. We give each equation a line number and a justification which, strictly speaking, is not part of the formal computation as defined.

(1) $\dot{-}(x, 0) = x$	given
(2) $\dot{-}(x, S(y)) = P(\dot{-}(x, y))$	given
(3) $P(S(x)) = x$	given
(4) $\dot{-}(3, S(y)) = P(\dot{-}(3, y))$	(2), substitution
(5) $\dot{-}(3, S(0)) = P(\dot{-}(3, 0))$	(4), substitution
(6) $\dot{-}(3, 0) = 3$	(1), substitution
(7) $\dot{-}(3, S(0)) = P(3)$	(5), (6), replacement
(8) $S(0) = 1$	S-evaluation
(9) $\dot{-}(3, 1) = P(3)$	(7), (8), replacement
(10) $P(S(2)) = 2$	(3), substitution
(11) $S(2) = 3$	S-evaluation
(12) $P(3) = 2$	(10), (11), replacement
(13) $\dot{-}(3, 1) = 2$	(9), (12), replacement

Definition: An n-argument function represented by a function symbol Q is *equationally defined* by a set Φ of equations if, for every n-tuple of numerals $(i_1, \ldots, i_n)$, no two distinct evaluations

$$Q(i_1, \ldots, i_n) = j$$
$$Q(i_1, \ldots, i_n) = k$$

(i.e., where $j \neq k$) are derivable from Φ. [If, for every n-tuple exactly one evaluation of $Q(i_1, \ldots, i_n) = j$ is derivable, then the function is total: otherwise, it is partial.] The set Φ is called a *defining set of equations* for the function.

For example, the total function $\dot{-}$ is equationally defined by the set of four given equations in the example just given. All four equations are necessary, including the two for P.

We shall see that primitive recursion, explicit definition, and mu recursion can be converted into equational definitions.

We note that the function defined by a set of equations may be one that is previously known to us. As in the case with other formal definitions in this chapter, we can therefore ask whether or not the function is defined correctly. This will be our procedure in the next section.

4.6.3 Some Helpful Propositions

We now make some general assertions about equational definability, rigorous proofs for which are beyond the scope of this text. (See Kleene [1952], pp. 262–276.)

> PROPOSITION 4.6.1: Let $\phi_1, \ldots, \phi_m$ be a sequence of functions such that ϕ_1 is the successor function and each ϕ_i, $i \geq 2$, is defined from preceding functions in the list by explicit definition or primitive recursion; then the function ϕ_m is total and is equationally defined by the set consisting of all these definitions.

This proposition, whose proof is left as an exercise, should be plausible to anyone who has read the earlier sections of this chapter. The following proposition is not as straightforward, because formal computations do not apply to mu recursions.

> PROPOSITION 4.6.2: If a function is defined by a mu recursion from equationally defined total function, then it is equationally definable (see Exercise 8 of Section 4.7).

> PROPOSITION 4.6.3: If a function is equationally definable, then there is a procedure to compute the function (which is an algorithm if the function is total).

The difficulty in proving this proposition is in showing that there exists a procedure to produce a formal computation, given that it exists. Note that the rules of formal computation are not commands, but merely permission-granting imperatives (see Section AIII.5). One can easily write a nondeterministic procedure to compute the function. As pointed out in Section 1.1.5, a nondeterministic procedure can be converted into a deterministic procedure (i.e., a procedure), although the technique is beyond the scope of this book.

1. From the set of four given equations consisting of the definitions of P and $\div$, write a formal computation of $\div(3, 3)$.

2. Estimate the number of equations in a formal computation of $\div(120, 50)$.

3. What is the number of equations in a formal computation of $\div(i_1, i_2)$ as a function of i_1 and i_2?

4. Follow the instructions of Exercise 3 for $*(i_1, i_2)$, where the given set of equations is

$$\{+(x, 0) = x, +(x, S(y)) = S(+(x, y)), *(x, 0) = 0, *(x, S(y)) = +(*(x, y), x)\}$$

5. From the set of three equations defining AP in Section 4.3.4, write a formal computation of AP(2, 1).

6. Prove Proposition 4.6.1.

7. (*Difficult*) Prove Proposition 4.6.3.

GENERAL EQUATIONAL DEFINITIONS 4.7

In this section we look at some equational definitions that are not explicit definitions or primitive recursions. Although equational definitions are interesting, we shall not make any use of this section in our theoretical development.

Some Previously Defined Functions 4.7.1

We noted that primitive recursions and explicit definitions are all examples of equational definitions. However, the set of defining equations for a function defined by either of these two schemes must include, besides the equation or equations of that definition, the defining equations of the functions occurring in that definition.

For example, the set of equations defining exponentiation has six equations; two for the equations defining exponentiation in terms of $*$, two for the equations defining $*$ in terms of $+$, and two for the definition of $+$.

General equational definitions, which we shall focus on in this section, can be thought of as generalizations of explicit definitions and primitive recursions. Consider now a new equational definition of the function ABD (absolute difference, listed in Section 4.2.4):

$$\begin{cases} \text{ABD}(x, 0) = x \\ \text{ABD}(Sx, Sy) = \text{ABD}(x, y) \\ \text{ABD}(x, y) = \text{ABD}(y, x) \end{cases}$$

From these three equations $ABD(i_1, i_2)$ is formally computable for any numerals i_1 and i_2. This definition, which is neither an explicit definition nor a primitive recursion, has the advantage that it requires no given function other than S.

The function MAX (also listed in Section 4.2.4) has an alternative general equational definition:

$$\left\{ \begin{array}{l} MAX(x, 0) = x \\ MAX(0, y) = y \\ MAX(Sx, Sy) = S(MAX(x, y)) \end{array} \right.$$

Section 4.3 contains two interesting equational definitions of functions that cannot be defined by primitive recursions and explicit definitions. One is the set of three equations defining the Ackermann–Péter function AP. The other is the set of equations defining A, Ackermann's function, which is a total of nine equations: the four equations defining $+$ and $*$, and the five listed for A itself.

A function that we have encountered before (Sections 3.5.1 and 4.4.3, Example 5) is the partial minus function f, where

$$f(x, y) \left\{ \begin{array}{ll} = x - y & \text{if } x \geqq y \\ \text{has no value} & \text{if } x < y \end{array} \right.$$

An equational definition of f is

$$\left\{ \begin{array}{l} f(x, 0) = x \\ f(S(x), S(y)) = f(x, y) \end{array} \right.$$

Note that for $i_1 < i_2$ there is no formal computation of $f(i_1, i_2)$ (although a rigorous proof of this fact is difficult).

4.7.2 New Examples

To simplify things, we shall use the functions in the list in Section 4.2.4 without rewriting the defining equations for these, since they can be obtained from the text of Section 4.2. Some of these new examples will be definitions of functions that were defined before in other ways. We shall in the course of discussion make certain assertions whose proofs will be left as exercises. We write SV and Si for $S(V)$ and $S(i)$, respectively, for any variable V and numeral i.

EXAMPLE 1. The 91 function. An intriguing general equational definition is the following:

$$\left\{ \begin{array}{ll} (1) & f(x + 101) = x + 91 \\ (2) & f(\dot{-}(100, x)) = f(f(\dot{-}(100, x) + 11)) \end{array} \right.$$

These two equations are presented in this way so that uniform substitution of any numeral is possible for any variable. The more usual way to render these equations would be by a definition by cases:

$$\begin{cases} (1') \ f(x) = x - 10 & \text{for } x \geq 101 \\ (2') \ f(x) = f(f(x + 11)) & \text{for } x \leq 100 \end{cases}$$

Note that (1) and (1') are equivalent since in (1) only arguments equal to 101 or more are possible, whatever numeral is substituted for x. Equations (2) and (2') are equivalent, since in (2) the expression $\dot{-}(100, x)$ may be at most 100.

Does this set define a function? If so, what is the function? Neither question has an immediate answer (unless you have seen this definition before). It is easy to derive an evaluation of $f(i)$ for any numeral $i \geq 101$ from the first equation. In particular, $f(101) = 91$ is derivable, by substituting 0 for x in (1). Then we can evaluate $f(100)$ by substituting 0 for x in (2):

$$f(100) = f(f(111)) = f(101) = 91$$

Then substituting 1 for x in (2) we get

$$f(99) = f(f(110)) = f(100) = 91$$

Indeed, $f(i) = 91$ is derivable for each numeral $i \leq 100$. (The proof is left to the reader.) Furthermore, no inconsistent values are derivable, so that the two equations (together with defining equations for $+$, $\dot{-}$, etc.) are a general equational definition of the function which in ordinary mathematical writing would be explained as follows:

$$\begin{cases} f(x) = 91 & \text{for } 0 \leq x \leq 100 \\ f(x) = x - 10 & \text{for } x > 100 \end{cases}$$

These two equations can be converted into the following general equational definition:

$$\begin{cases} f(x + 101) = x + 91 \\ f(\dot{-}(100, x)) = 91 \end{cases}$$

It is clear now that the original set of defining equations is a mere puzzle, since there exists a more straightforward definition. Nevertheless, it is still an interesting illustration of a general equational definition.

EXAMPLE 2. From the set of two equations

$$\begin{cases} f(x, 0) = S(f(x, 1)) \\ f(x, Sy) = f(Sx, y) \end{cases}$$

no evaluations of the function f can be derived. (A rigorous proof of this assertion is difficult. We leave it to the reader to justify it intuitively.) So these equations define the null partial function (i.e., the function f having no value for any set of arguments).

Furthermore, no set of equations of which this set is a subset defines a total function f over the nonnegative integers, which can be proved as follows. Suppose that there is such a total function. From the two equations we can infer

$$f(x, 0) = S(f(Sx, 0))$$

Thus, for all x and z,

$$f(x, 0) = f(x + z, 0) + z$$

Taking $x = 0$, we get

$$f(0, 0) = f(z, 0) + z$$

for all z. If $f(0, 0) = i$, then, by this equation, $f(i + 1, 0)$ cannot be a nonnegative integer.

We are inclined to say that these two equations together are nonsensical. At any rate, it is difficult to see how they could serve any useful purpose.

EXAMPLE 3. The Fibonacci numbers are the numbers $1, 2, 3, 5, 8, 13,$ $21, \ldots$; each number in the sequence beyond the second is the sum of the two preceding numbers. The sequence is formed by the values of the function FIB which is readily given by a general equational definition:

$$\left\{ \begin{array}{l} \text{FIB}(0) = 1 \\ \text{FIB}(1) = 2 \\ \text{FIB}(SSx) = \text{FIB}(x) + \text{FIB}(Sx) \end{array} \right.$$

This definition is rather straightforward. FIB can be defined by primitive recursion, and by mu recursion, but only with the use of advanced techniques.

EXAMPLE 4. The partial function of mathematical division over the nonnegative integers can be equationally defined by

$$f_1(Sx^*y, Sx) = y$$

$f_1(i_1, i_2)$ has an evaluation if and only if $i_2 \neq 0$ and i_1 is an integral multiple of i_2. However, this definition does not directly express a procedure for computing f_1, whereas the definition by mu recursion of the same function f_1 of Section 4.4.1 does.

4.7.3 *Equational Definitions and Algorithms*

EXAMPLE 5. The Euclidean algorithm yields an equational definition of the function that it computes, which illustrates how close to an algorithm an equational definition can be. For convenience, let $\text{EUC}(x, 0) = x$, $\text{EUC}(0, y) = y$, and $\text{EUC}(x, y) =$ the greatest common divisor of x and y if x and y are both positive. We get an equational definition of EUC from the subtraction version of the Euclidean algorithm as follows:

$$\left\{ \begin{array}{l} \text{EUC}(x, 0) = x \\ \text{EUC}(0, Sy) = Sy \\ \text{EUC}(Sx, Sy) = \text{EUC}(\text{MIN}(Sx, Sy), \text{ABD}(Sx, Sy)) \end{array} \right.$$

Recall that the version of the algorithm presented in Section 1.2.2 produced a sequence $x_1, x_2, x_3, \ldots$, of which x_1 and x_2 were the inputs. All the numbers in this sequence turn up in the computation of $\text{EUC}(x_1, x_2)$ by the equations given above.

The remainder version of the algorithm can also be given as a general equational definition:

$$\begin{cases} \text{EUC}(x, 0) = x \\ \text{EUC}(0, Sy) = Sy \\ \text{EUC}(Sx, Sy) = \text{EUC}(\text{MIN}(Sx, Sy), \text{REM}(\text{MAX}(Sx, Sy), \text{MIN}(Sx, Sy))) \end{cases}$$

EXAMPLE 6. Note that $\frac{23}{44} = 0.522727272727\ldots$ Let $f(x)$ be the digit in the xth place to the right of the decimal point in this ultimately periodic expansion; take $f(0) = 0$. Then the function f can be formally defined as follows:

$$\begin{cases} f(0) = 0 \\ f(1) = 5 \\ f(2) = 2 \\ f(2x + 3) = 2 \\ f(2x + 4) = 7 \end{cases}$$

Note why we must write $2x + 3$ and $2x + 4$; it must be possible to substitute any numeral for x, including zero: the smallest value that $2x + 3$ and $2x + 4$ can take on are 3 and 4, respectively, which is exactly what is required. This same technique can be used for any ultimately periodic function over the non-negative integers: A function f is *ultimately periodic* if there exists an m and a $p \geq 1$ such that for all $i \geq m, f(i) = f(i + p)$. Although an ultimately periodic function can be defined by an explicit definition, the general equational definition is more direct; even though it requires $m + p$ equations, those equations are quite simple.

Definitive Equations 4.7.4

In some cases a general equational definition suggests a computational procedure, and in some cases it does not. Example 4 does not suggest a computational procedure, and the reason seems to be that the equation defining f_1 has on its left side a rather complicated expression as an argument. It would seem natural to exclude such expressions from the argument places on the left side of an equation.

Definition: A *definitive equation* is an equation (1) whose left side begins with a function symbol other than S and, except for that, has no occurrences of any function symbols other than S; and (2) whose right side has no variable that does not occur on its left side.

All the equations in Examples 2, 3, and 5 are definitive equations. The equations defining Ackermann's function, and the set of equations defining the Ackermann–Péter function in Section 4.3, consist of definitive equations. All equations in explicit definitions and primitive recursions are definitive equations. But the two equations of Example 1, the single equation of Example 4, and the fourth and fifth equations of Example 6 are not definitive equations.

Now the first equation of Example 1 can be replaced by a definitive equation with 101 S's; the former seems like a convenient abbreviation for the latter. The second equation needs to be replaced by 101 definitive equations, one for each $f(i)$, $0 \leq i \leq 100$. Clearly, the second equation in the form that was given is a great convenience. Also, the fourth and fifth equations of Example 6 are quite convenient, since they distinguish between the odd- and even-valued arguments greater than 2. Thus we see that in restricting ourselves to definitive equations we are foresaking some rather convenient practices. Nevertheless, there is a theoretical purpose in focusing on those general equational definitions that have only definitive equations.

We now make another restriction on the set of defining equations.

Definition: A *numerical substitution instance* of a definitive equation is the result of making a uniform substitution for each variable occurring on the left side (so that no variables remain) and then making all replacements by S-evaluations that can be made (so that the result is an equation whose left side consists of a function symbol followed by arguments that are all numerals).

Definition: Two definitive equations are *apparently inconsistent* if there exist numerical substitution instances of these with a common left side.

For example, the two equations

$$f(x, Sy) = h(Sx, Sy)$$
$$f(Sx, y) = h(SSx, y)$$

are apparently inconsistent, since we can substitute 1 for x and 0 for y in the first equation, substitute 0 for x and 1 for y in the second equation, and then make S-evaluations, resulting in two numerical substitution instances with a common left side $f(1, 1)$. In this example the apparent inconsistency is not a real inconsistency but a redundancy, since both substitution instances are the same [i.e., $f(1, 1) = h(2, 1)$]. On the other hand, the two equations

$$f(x, 0) = 17$$
$$f(x, y) = h(x, Sy)$$

have, respectively, the two numerical substitution instances

$$f(0, 0) = 17$$
$$f(0, 0) = h(0, 1)$$

This apparent inconsistency may be a real inconsistency (i.e., may lead to contrary valuations), depending on the function h.

Definition: A set of equations is *apparently inconsistent* if there are two equations in the set that are apparently inconsistent. Otherwise, the set is *apparently consistent*.

For example, the set defining MAX in Section 4.7.1 is apparently inconsistent by virtue of the first two equations:

$$MAX(x, 0) = x$$
$$MAX(0, y) = y$$

However, the whole set is rendered apparently consistent by changing the second equation to

$$MAX(0, Sy) = Sy$$

All sets of equations in Examples 3 and 5 are apparently consistent sets. The set of equations of Example 2 is apparently consistent, although in a sense it is absurd (as we have observed). Primitive recursions are always apparently consistent sets of equations. So are the sets of equations defining Ackermann's function and the Ackermann–Péter function.

There are two advantages of having a function defined by an apparently consistent set of equations. First, with such a set, a procedure for computing the function is virtually given by the set of equations. Thus, suppose that one wishes to evaluate $f(i_1, \ldots, i_n)$, where $i_1, \ldots, i_n$ are given numerals. There is at most one equation having a substitution instance with $f(i_1, \ldots, i_n)$ on its left side. If there is none, that means that such an evaluation is impossible, and we can stop. Thus whenever we wish an evaluation, there is never an indecision about which of the equations in the set to apply. (Sometimes this procedure fails to terminate, e.g., when it is applied to the equations of Example 2.)

The second advantage of an apparently consistent set Φ of defining equations is that contradictory valuations cannot be derived from Φ. That is, there do not exist a function symbol Q and numerals $i_1, \ldots, i_n, k, k'$, where $k \neq k'$, such that both

$$Q(i_1, \ldots, i_n) = k$$
$$Q(i_1, \ldots, i_n) = k'$$

are derivable from Φ. (A rigorous proof of this plausible fact is not given.)

Thus, in general, one can write down an absurd set of definitive equations that is apparently consistent (e.g., Example 2). But the worst effect that the absurdity can have is that no evaluations are derivable.

It is possible to develop a great deal of the theory of computability by means of general equational definitions. It seems more convenient to follow virtually all the authors of books on the subject in recent years and develop the theory instead in terms of mu recursion. We have taken a brief excursus into equational definability mostly because of the fact that it is a natural generalization of primitive-recursive definitions, and because it has offered us some extra insights into functions and procedures for computing functions.

4.7.5 Exercises

The student is asked to prove certain things in spite of the fact that the text has avoided certain rigorous proofs. In general, it is feasible to prove that something can be formally computed, but very difficult to prove rigorously that something cannot be formally computed. Therefore, we suggest that in doing these exercises, the student accept plausible assertions of the latter kind without rigorous proof [e.g., that $+(2, 2) = 5$ is not derivable from the equations defining $+$].

1. Prove in Example 1 of Section 4.7.2 that, for each $i \leq 100$, $f(i) = 91$ is derivable from the first set of equations.

2. Consider the equation

$$f(x) = S(f(Sx))$$

Prove that no set of equations containing this one defines a total one-argument function f (see Example 2 of Section 4.7.2).

3. Consider the set

$$\begin{cases} g(x, x + Sy) = 0 \\ g(x, 0) = 0 \\ g(x + Sy, Sy) = S(g(x, Sy)) \end{cases}$$

Prove that this set of equations (together with the two equations defining plus) defines a total function g. What well known function is g?

4. Consider the set

$$\begin{cases} h(x, 0) = x \\ h(x + Sy, Sy) = h(x, Sy) \\ h(x, x + Sy) = x \end{cases}$$

Prove that this set of equations (with the two for plus) defines a total function h. What well-known function is h?

5. Let $g(x, y)$ be the greatest common divisor of x and y if x and y are both positive; $g(x, y)$ has no value otherwise. Give a general equational definition of g. Use the functions listed in Section 4.2.4 as given functions.

6. Consider the general equational definition of the one-argument function f in terms of the total one-argument function g (whose exact nature is not specified) and the quotient function QU:

$$\begin{cases} f(0) = 3 \\ f(S(x)) = g(f(QU(S(x), 2))) \end{cases}$$

Prove that f is a total function. Prove that if g is equationally definable, then so is f.

7. (*Difficult*) Define the function f of Exercise 6 in terms of g and the functions listed in Section 4.2.4 by means of explicit definition, primitive recursion, mu recursion, or a combination thereof.

8. Suppose that Φ is a set of equations defining a total function f of two arguments. Suppose that $g(x) = (\mu y)[f(x, y) = 0]$, and that the function symbols g and h do not appear in Φ. Prove that if $\Phi' = \Phi \cup \alpha$, where α is the set of three equations

$$\begin{cases} h(0, x, y) = y \\ h(Sz, x, y) = h(f(x, Sy), x, Sy) \\ \quad g(x) = h(f(x, 0), x, 0) \end{cases}$$

then Φ' equationally defines g. What is the function h, intuitively? (Note that formal computations with mu expressions are not involved here, since Φ and therefore Φ' have no mu expressions. This exercise constitutes a proof of Proposition 6.2 of Section 4.6.3.)

9. (*Difficult and completely impractical*) Consider the set of equations:

$$\begin{cases} f(0, 0, z) = Sz \\ f(0, Sy, 0) = f(0, y, 1) \\ f(0, Sy, Sz) = f(0, y, f(0, Sy, z)) \\ f(Sx, 0, z) = f(x, 0, f(x, 0, z)) \\ f(Sx, Sy, 0) = f(x, f(Sx, y, 0), 0) \\ f(Sx, Sy, Sz) = f(x, f(Sx, y, f(x, Sy, Sz)), f(Sx, Sy, z)) \end{cases}$$

Prove that for every ordered triple of numerals (i_1, i_2, i_3), an evaluation for $f(i_1, i_2, i_3)$ can be derived by uniform substitution and evaluation replacement. (It thus follows that this set of equations defines a total function f. Compare Exercise 1 of Section 4.3. The equations of this exercise constitute a multiple recursion; see Péter [1967].)

THE CLASS OF PRIMITIVE-RECURSIVE 4.8
FUNCTIONS

In this section we focus on a certain proper subclass of the class of all total computable functions, namely the class of functions that are definable entirely by means of explicit definition and primitive recursion. Since, of the two, primitive recursion is the more powerful method of generating new functions, the class is named for it rather than for explicit definition. We shall also make some remarks about the class of all computable functions.

Importance of the Class 4.8.1

Definition: The *class of primitive-recursive functions* is the class of all functions that can be defined by a sequence of explicit definitions and primitive recursions from the successor function. More precisely, a function f is in this class if there is a sequence of functions $g_1, g_2, \ldots, g_s$ such that g_1 is the successor function, g_s is f itself, and for each i, $2 \leq i \leq s$, g_i is definable from functions preceding it in the sequence by means of explicit definition or primitive recursion. In this case, the function f is called a *primitive-recursive function*.

The importance of this class rests on several things. The first is the fact that explicit definition and primitive recursion are types of definition that are easy to comprehend and easy to work with. Once we know how a function is defined in these terms, we have an algorithm to compute the function, given only that we have algorithms for the functions in terms of which it is defined. This point, already apparent when we introduced these types of function definitions in Sections 4.1.1 and 4.1.2, was reinforced by our constructions of programs for them in Section 4.5.1 and 4.5.2.

The second reason why the class of primitive-recursive functions is important is that every computable function can be defined in a rather simple manner from two primitive-recursive functions by a mu recursion and then an explicit definition. More precisely, for any such function f of n arguments ($n \geq 1$), there exists a one-argument function g and an $(n + 1)$-argument function h, both in the class of primitive-recursive functions, such that

$$f(x_1, \ldots, x_n) = g((\mu z)[h(x_1, \ldots, x_n, z) = 0])$$

(The proof can be found in virtually any advanced text in the theory of computability. A sketch of the proof is given in Chapter 5.)

The fact that a computable function can be given by a series of definitions in which mu recursion is used only once is significant in the theory of computability. For mu recursion is a bit more unmanageable than either explicit definition or primitive recursion, since it is subject to the possibility of not yielding function values for certain argument sets.

Thus, although the class of primitive-recursive functions does not contain all the computable functions, it brings us within easy reach of all of them. In fairness, this reason for the importance of the class is not compelling. There are simpler subclasses, e.g., the class of *elementary functions*, that also have this property. Although it is not possible at this point to offer an intelligible definition of this class, suffice it to say that the class of elementary functions includes successor, addition, and multiplication, but not exponentiation or any ϕ_i for $i \geq 3$. (See Brainerd and Landweber [1974], p. 269, or Kleene [1952], pp. 284–287.)

A third reason that the class of primitive-recursive functions is important is that it is identical to the class of functions computable by an interesting class of programs, the DO-TIMES programs of Section 3.7. Recall that such a program is guaranteed to halt, and, indeed, the number of times the machine goes through any loop in such a program equals the value of the variable that appears in the command between the DO and the TIMES.

We pointed out in Section 4.5.2 that any function defined by explicit definition and primitive recursion ultimately from the successor function is computable by a DO-TIMES program. These programs are studied in the literature under the term "loop programs." The proof that a function is computed by a loop program if and only if it is a primitive-recursive function (an important result due to A. R. Meyer and D. M. Ritchie in 1967) can be found in Engeler [1973], pp. 137–142, or in Brainerd and Landweber [1974], pp. 53–54. This result is another good reason for considering the class of primitive-recursive functions to be an important subclass of computable functions.

More Facts About the Class 4.8.2

The class of primitive-recursive functions includes, of course, all the functions listed in Section 4.2.4, all those explicitly mentioned in the exercises of Section 4.2, and all the functions ϕ_i defined in Section 4.3. However, Ackermann's function A, which summarizes all the ϕ_i functions, and the Ackermann–Péter function AP are not primitive-recursive functions. The proof of this negative proposition is beyond this book, but many advanced texts have a proof for the Ackermann–Péter function (e.g., Hermes [1969], pp. 82–88, and Brainerd and Landweber [1974], pp. 252–264). The general technique is to show that if we define

$$f(x) = AP(x, x)$$

then the one-argument function f majorizes every one-argument primitive-recursive function, [i.e., for every one-argument primitive-recursive function g, $f(x) > g(x)$ for all but finitely many x]. Thinking of it another way, f increases faster than any primitive-recursive function, so it cannot be primitive-recursive. Since f is defined explicitly from AP, AP cannot be primitive-recursive. This proof technique goes back to Ackermann [1928].

The family of functions ϕ_i gives us a rather precise feeling for how extensive the class of primitive-recursive functions is: All the functions in the family are in the class, but each of the two functions that we know that summarize all functions in the family are outside the class.

Many functions are primitive-recursive functions even though the definitions we have given for them here do not suggest that they are. For example, the function FIB for the Fibonacci sequence is primitive-recursive, although the conversion of the definition of Example 3 of Section 4.7.2 to a primitive-recursive definition requires an advanced technique. The original definition of FIB is an example of an interesting class of equational definitions:

Definition: A one-argument function f is defined from given functions h, $g_1, \ldots, g_m$ by a *course-of-values recursion* if

$$\begin{cases} f(0) = j \\ f(S(x)) = h(f(g_1(S(x))), f(g_2(S(x))), \ldots, f(g_m(S(x)))) \end{cases}$$

where j is a numeral, provided that, for all x and for each i, $g_i(S(x)) < S(x)$. [In other words, $f(S(x))$ is defined in terms of selected values taken from the entire sequence of preceding values $f(0), \ldots, f(x)$.]

(This definition is easily extended to functions with more than one argument, but for the present informal discussion this simpler restricted definition serves just as well.)

PROPOSITION 4.8.1: A function defined from primitive-recursive functions by a course-of-values recursion is a primitive-recursive function.

Proposition 4.8.1 is proved in many advanced texts on the theory of computability. The course-of-values recursion that defines the function FIB is as follows:

$$\begin{cases} \text{FIB}(0) = 1 \\ \text{FIB}(S(x)) = +(\text{FIB}(P(P(S(x)))), \text{FIB}(P(S(x)))) \end{cases}$$

Here, $m = 2$, $g_1(S(x)) = P(P(S(x)))$, g_2 is the function P, and h is the function $+$.

One technique for proving Proposition 4.8.1 involves the function f_1, where

$$f_1(x) = 2^{f(0)} * 3^{f(1)} * \ldots * \text{PRIME}(x)^{f(x)}$$

PRIME(x) being the xth prime in order of magnitude, counting 2 as the zeroth prime. The technique, in outline, is to define f_1 by a primitive recursion from $h, g_1, \ldots, g_m$, and then to define f in terms of f_1. With this remark, the proof (Exercise 4) of Proposition 4.8.1 is within the grasp of anyone who has completed the more difficult exercises of Section 4.2.

There are other theorems stating in effect that certain powerful ways of defining functions turn out to be reducible to primitive recursion and explicit definition, which are quite useful. We cannot describe them all here, but one of them is interesting because of its resemblance to mu recursion.

Definition: An $(n + 1)$-argument function f is obtained by *bounded minimization* from an $(n + 1)$-argument function h ($n \geq 0$) if f satisfies the following: If there is a $z \leq x_{n+1}$ such that $h(x_1, \ldots, x_n, z) = 0$, then $f(x_1, \ldots, x_n, x_{n+1}) = (\mu z)[h(x_1, \ldots, x_n, z) = 0]$; but if there is no such z, then $f(x_1, \ldots, x_n, x_{n+1}) = 0$.

PROPOSITION 4.8.2: If h is a primitive-recursive function and f is obtained from h by bounded minimization, then f is a primitive-recursive function (see Exercise 5).

We are justified in believing that all functions that will ever arise in practical algorithmic computation will be in the class of primitive-recursive functions.

On the other hand, not all primitive-recursive functions are practically computable; a clear counterexample is the function ϕ_5, discussed in Section 4.3. Some complexity theorists feel that ϕ_3 (exponentiation), as well as ϕ_4 and ϕ_5, is not practically computable. Although it may be difficult to draw the precise line between practically computable functions and those that are not, it seems clear that the class of functions that are practically and algorithmically computable is some proper subclass of the class of primitive-recursive functions.

In Chapters 3 and 4 we have been dealing exclusively with nonnegative integers. As we saw in Chapter 1, many important algorithms deal not with numbers at all but with other kinds of objects, such as graphs, expressions from a language, and many other such things. Most computations done with such objects consist of a sequence of steps that are quite simple. In Chapter 5 we shall show that such computations can be coded as computations with nonnegative integers. Operations on graphs, and linguistic expressions, thus go over as numerical functions.

All the simple operations on graphs and linguistic expressions go over as primitive-recursive functions—in fact, primitive-recursive functions of a rather restricted variety, the elementary functions that we mentioned above. However, the operations that consist of long sequences of such steps do not always go over as primitive-recursive functions, and generally require mu recursions, as we shall see in Chapter 5.

The Class of Computable Functions   4.8.3

We pass on now from the class of primitive-recursive functions to the class of all computable functions, both total and partial. This class can now be characterized in four different ways, in terms of what has been discussed in Chapters 2 to 4.

The first characterization is in terms of Turing machines: A function is *Turing-computable* if it is possible to construct a Turing machine that computes it.

Second, a function is *program-computable* if it is possible to write a program that computes it, either in the GOTO language or the WHILE language. Since a program in one of these languages can be rewritten in the other, and since this interchangeability is shared with many other programming languages, the choice of programming language is not too important here.

Third, a function is in the class of mu-recursive functions, or, more simply, it is *mu-recursive*, if it can be defined in a sequence of steps from the successor function by means of explicit definition, primitive recursion, and mu recursion.

Fourth, a function is *equationally definable* (or *general-recursive*) if it can be equationally defined in the formalism of functional expressions (see Section 4.6.2).

The concept of computability is not a precise mathematical concept, as we have discussed in Chapter 1 and as we shall dwell upon in Chapter 5, since it has no reference to a single formalism, but to all possible procedures. Each of these four definitions is, however, a mathematically precise concept because it refers to a mathematically precise language—the class of Turing machines, the foundational programming languages, or the formalism of functional expressions. It turns out that these four definitions are equivalent; all four classes can be proved to be mathematically the same, although the equivalence is not proved in this book. The proofs can be found in the assortment of advanced computability texts listed in the bibliography.

All these proofs involve an application of a certain idea: They all involve the mu operator, in one way or another, and the notion that a computation is a long sequence of simple steps. The mu operator is involved because one talks of the smallest i such that the ith step has a certain configuration, such as a halt or a function evaluation. This is the idea behind the proof that a function satisfying any of the other characterizations is in the class of mu-recursive functions. The first such proof was given by Kleene [1936]; all proofs since then are merely a new application of this technique, which is used in Chapter 5.

(In passing, we note that the definition of the class of mu-recursive functions can be simplified to exclude reference to definition by primitive recursion. One does not get very far from the successor function by means of explicit definition and mu recursion (see Exercise 3). However, if one includes a few other functions in the list of given functions, one does get the following equivalent definition: A function is in the class of mu-recursive functions if it can be defined in a series of steps from the successor function S, addition, floored subtraction, and multiplication, by means of explicit definition and mu recursion. In trying to prove the equivalence of these two definitions, the major hurdle is to prove that the latter class is closed under primitive recursion. The difficult, but interesting proof can be found in essence in Davis [1958], pp. 41–50.)

4.8.4 Closing Remarks for Chapter 4

In this rather elementary exposition of what is sometimes called "recursive arithmetic," we have seen how to define functions by means of the definition schemes. This has been a sort of practical pursuit: once we have defined a function by these means, it is a simple matter to write a program for it, although the resulting program is not necessarily an efficient one.

Our work with recursive arithmetic has already permitted us to make some broad observations about the class of computable functions. In Chapters 5 and 6 we shall be directly concerned with achieving the objective that we announced in Chapter 1: to determine what can be computed and what cannot be computed. In Chapter 5 we argue that any nonnumerical algorithm can be coded as an algorithm for computing a function over the nonnegative integers, and that any such function is mu-recursive (and hence also Turing-computable, program-computable, and equationally definable). Then in Chapter 6 we prove that certain specific functions are not computable.

1. (a) Let f be an $(n + 1)$-argument function that is obtained by bounded minimization from the $(n + 1)$-argument total function h. Suppose that you have a program in the WHILE language that computes h; from this construct a WHILE-language program for f. Prove that your program for f halts for all possible sets of arguments. (b) Revise your construction so that if the program computing h is a DO-TIMES program, the result is a DO-TIMES program.

2. The same as part (a) of Exercise 1 for the GOTO language.

3. (*Difficult*) Consider the smallest class of functions (partial and total) that contains the successor function and is closed under explicit definition and mu recursion. (a) Prove: If f is an n-argument total function in this class then, for some $i \leq n$ and one-argument function f_1, $f(x_1, \ldots, x_n) = f_1(x_i)$. (b) Prove: For every one-argument *total* function f in this class, there is a constant j such that either $f(x) = j$ or $f(x) = x + j$. (Recall that a function defined by explicit definition is partial if there is a partial function occurring on the right side with variable arguments; and that a partial function may not be used in a mu recursion.)

4. (*Difficult*) Prove Proposition 4.8.1. (*Hint:* Review Exercises 34 to 36 of Section 4.2 and follow the discussion following the statement of Proposition 4.8.1.)

5. (*Difficult*) Prove Proposition 4.8.2. (*Hint:* Review Exercise 44 of Section 4.2.)

5 Gödel Numbering and Church's Thesis

We turn back now to the general concept of algorithm as we were discussing it in Chapter 1, seeking to justify what we have done since then in terms of this general notion. We shall present an argument for a proposition that is beyond mathematical proof: namely, that for every algorithm there is a mu-recursive function over the nonnegative integers whose computation effectively does the work of the algorithm. In particular, if the algorithm computes a function over the nonnegative integers, that function is a mu-recursive function.

This proposition (in part) is known as Church's thesis, since it was first formulated in general form by Alonzo Church. Our argument for it, taken from an important proof by S. C. Kleene, rests on a technique of assigning nonnegative integers to discrete structures developed by Kurt Gödel.

5.1 GÖDEL NUMBERING

After a preliminary discussion, we show in this section how Gödel numbers can be assigned to discrete mathematical objects, including multidimensional structures.

5.1.1 Prospectus

Perhaps the most famous and most important of the several deep theorems about mathematical logic proved by Kurt Gödel was his incompleteness theorem (Gödel [1931]): for any sound logical axiomatic system that is sufficiently rich to contain the theory of numbers, there must be number-theoretic statements that can be neither proved nor disproved in the system. Gödel's theorem is one of the most significant discoveries made in the twentieth century, since it places a limit on the efficacy of mathematical reasoning itself.

Although most of the ideas of the proof are well beyond the scope of this book (Rosser [1939] is an informal exposition), there are some important points of contact. For example, one of Gödel's key lemmas says, in effect, that all primitive-recursive functions are expressible (in a sense that we need not go into) in the formal theory of numbers.

Another aspect of Gödel's proof is quite relevant to our present concern. Gödel developed a technique of showing that the formal concept of proof in a logical system could be described by primitive-recursive functions. His technique consisted of assigning numbers to logical formulas and to proofs in such a way that he could define a primitive-recursive function B, where $B(x, y) = 0$ if x is the Gödel number of a proof of the formula whose Gödel number is y, and $B(x, y) = 1$ otherwise.

Formal systems of mathematical logic are not our concern, but computational systems are. What we intend to indicate is that Gödel numbers can always be assigned to a computational system so that (1) no matter what the subject matter is of any procedure, we are always justified in regarding the procedure as if it computed a function (partial or total) over the nonnegative integers; and (2) the function is in the class of mu-recursive functions (see Section 4.8.3). It follows from (2) that a function over the nonnegative integers is computable if and only if it is a mu-recursive function, which is known as Church's thesis. (More properly speaking, this is one of several formulations of Church's thesis, which are all mathematically equivalent. The thesis gets its name from Church [1936a].)

In Section 5.3 our argument for (1) and (2) will not be a mathematical proof, but a plausibility argument based on our work on Gödel numbering. In Section 5.2 we show how Gödel numbers can be assigned to one computational system. We hope this demonstration will make plausible to the reader that Gödel numbers could be assigned to any computational system.

Only after some work at a more advanced level will the reader be able to feel the full force of the argument for Church's thesis. But be warned that no matter how advanced you get, you will never find a mathematical *proof* of Church's thesis, because it relates an intuitive nonformal concept to a formal one. The strong feeling you may get that Gödel numbers can always be assigned to every computational system is at best an empirical generalization, like the laws of physics and the other empirical sciences.

Finite Sequences of Positive Integers 5.1.2

The first class of objects to which we shall assign Gödel numbers is the class of finite sequences of positive integers. Recall the function PRIME of Chapter 4, where PRIME(i) is the ith prime in order of magnitude, counting 2 as the zeroth prime, 3 as the first, 5 as the second, and so on.

Definition: The Gödel number of the finite sequence of positive integers

$$i_1, i_2, \ldots, i_n$$

is

$$2^{i_1} * 3^{i_2} * \ldots * \text{PRIME}(n - 1)^{i_n}$$

For example, the sequence 3, 1, 2, 1 has the Gödel number $2^3 * 3^1 * 5^2 * 7^1$ $= 4200$.

We observe several consequences of this definition. First, Gödel numbers get quite large even when the terms of the sequences are small. The sequence

$$1, 1, 1, 1, 1, 1, 1, 1, 1$$

for example, has the Gödel number 223,092,870. We shall be interested in longer sequences whose terms are larger. Fortunately, we shall not have to compute these numbers out. Our purpose in showing that Gödel numbers can be assigned to various mathematical structures is not to offer a new way of computing with these structures. Rather, it is to show that concepts such as primitive-recursive function and mu-recursive function have significance not only in the domain of the nonnegative integers but in these other domains as well.

Second, no two distinct finite sequences have the same Gödel number. This fact is a consequence of the fundamental theorem of arithmetic: a positive integer can be decomposed in only one way, up to order, as a product of primes. Thus if $2^{i_1} * \ldots * \text{PRIME}(m - 1)^{i_m} = 2^{j_1} * \ldots * \text{PRIME}(n - 1)^{j_n}$, where the i's and j's are nonnegative integers with $i_m \neq 0 \neq j_n$, then $m = n, i_1 = j_1, i_2 = j_2, \ldots$, and $i_m = j_n$.

Third, a sequence having only one term i_1 has the Gödel number 2^{i_1}. The null sequence (i.e., the sequence with zero terms) has the Gödel number 1. Clearly, no nonnull sequence of positive integers has the Gödel number 1.

Fourth, zero and many positive integers are not Gödel numbers of finite sequences of positive integers. For example, $10 = 2^1 * 3^0 * 5^1$ is not, because 10 is divisible by 5 but not by 3. A positive integer g is a Gödel number if and only if the following holds: for all m and n, if $m < n$ and g is divisible by $\text{PRIME}(n)$ then g is divisible by $\text{PRIME}(m)$.

Thus, although all finite sequences have Gödel numbers, and no two have the same Gödel number, there are infinitely many positive integers that are not used as Gödel numbers in our scheme. Thus Gödel numbering is a one-to-one mapping (i.e., an injection) of the set of finite sequences of positive integers into the set of positive integers.

Given a sequence of positive integers, one can effectively compute the Gödel number of that sequence. In Chapter 4 we observed that the function PRIME is effectively computable. (It is, in fact, in the class of primitive-recursive functions.) Thus, given a sequence $i_1, \ldots, i_m$, we can compute $\text{PRIME}(0)^{i_1}, \ldots, \text{PRIME}(m - 1)^{i_m}$, and then multiply to get the Gödel number. The big practical obstacle is the size of the number itself.

Going the other way is slightly more involved, but is also effective. Given a positive integer g that we think may be a Gödel number of a sequence, we first express g as a product of powers of distinct primes. This can be done by dividing by 2 as many times as possible, then dividing by 3 as many times as possible, and so on. When we have obtained this prime decomposition of g, we can then tell whether g is the Gödel number of a sequence of positive integers by noticing whether every prime up to a certain prime PRIME$(n - 1)$ does divide g, and no prime greater than PRIME$(n - 1)$ divides g. If so, then the exponents of the primes in order up to the exponent of PRIME$(n - 1)$ are, respectively, the positive integers in the sequence whose Gödel number is g. If not (i.e., if there is a prime dividing g greater than another that does not divide g), then g is not the Gödel number of a sequence.

For example, take $g = 112,200$. We find that we can divide by 2, 3, and 5, and in fact,

$$112,200 = 2^3 * 3^1 * 5^2 * 187$$

We know that 187 is not divisible by 2, 3, or 5, since we have divided by these three primes as much as possible. We then try to divide 187 by 7 and find that we cannot do so (without remainder). At this point we see that g is not divisible by 7, but is divisible by some prime greater than 7, from which we can conclude that g is not the Gödel number of any sequence of positive integers. (As a matter of fact, it turns out that $187 = 11 * 17$, so that

$$112,200 = 2^3 * 3^1 * 5^2 * 11^1 * 17^1$$

which is the prime decomposition of g, in this example. However, this extra piece of information is unnecessary in establishing that g is not a Gödel number.)

For another example, take $g = 16,516,500$; we find that

$$g = 2^2 * 3^1 * 5^3 * 7^1 * 11^2 * 13^1$$

Since g is divisible by all the primes up to $13 = $ PRIME(5), it is a Gödel number. Its sequence is

$$2, 1, 3, 1, 2, 1$$

In summary, given a finite sequence of positive integers, we can effectively find its Gödel number. And given a positive integer g we can effectively tell whether or not g is the Gödel number of a sequence of positive integers, and if so obtain the sequence.

Gödel Numbers of Strings, etc.   5.1.3

It is now an easy matter to find a method of assigning Gödel numbers to any written piece of English text. First, assign a positive integer to every distinguishable character including blanks, small letters, capital letters, and each punctuation sign. One possible way is as follows: blank, 1; small a through z, 2 through 27; capital A through Z, 28 through 53; period, 54; comma, 55; and so on. The Gödel number of any piece of text is simply the Gödel number of the corresponding sequence of integers. For example, consider the sentence:

$$\text{If so, return.}$$

Its Gödel number is

$$2^{36} * 3^7 * 5^1 * 7^{20} * 11^{16} * 13^{55} * 17^1 * 19^{19} * 23^6 * 29^{21} * 31^{22} * 37^{19} * 41^{15} * 43^{54}$$

The impossible magnitude need not disturb us, since we shall never need to compute out such numbers.

In this way every piece of text (English or other than English) made up from the alphabet and punctuation has a Gödel number. There are several small items that we have not discussed, such as the line break, paragraphing, and paging. These things are easily taken care of, and it does not seem to be worthwhile to go into them here.

More generally, we have here a method of assigning Gödel numbers to strings over any alphabet: Assign positive integers to the characters in the alphabet in any way at all, as long as different characters have different positive integers. The Gödel number of any string is then the Gödel number of the corresponding sequence of integers.

5.1.4 Gödel Numbers of Graphs

We shall attempt to show that Gödel numbers can be assigned to the objects of any algorithmic computation. Since a mathematical proof of this assertion is impossible, we must stake our claim on some well-chosen examples. In the preceding subsection, we assigned Gödel numbers to strings, and we now show how Gödel numbers can be assigned to a rather unlikely class of objects— graphs.

Recall the definition of (undirected) *graph* from Section 1.2.3. The procedure of assigning to a graph a suitable Gödel number begins with an assignment of a distinct prime number to each node of the graph. This assignment is made arbitrarily. We then note that once we have the information about how many nodes there are and which nodes are connected to which by edges, we have complete information about the graph. Supposing the nodes have been numbered $p_0, \ldots, p_n$, we take a Gödel number of the graph to be the number

$$p_0^{k_0} * p_1^{k_1} * \ldots * p_n^{k_n},$$

where, for each i, k_i is the product of all those $p_j^{x_j}$ such that the node numbered p_i is connected by x_j edges to the node numbered p_j; thus $k_i = 1$ if the node numbered p_i is not connected to any other node.

For example, Fig. 5.1.1 is a graph in which the assignment of primes to the nodes is shown. The Gödel number of this graph is

$$2^{3^{2*5*7}} * 3^{2^2} * 5^{2*7} * 7^{2*5} * 11^1 = 2^{315} * 3^4 * 5^{14} * 7^{10} * 11$$

(There are variations on this way of assigning Gödel numbers to graphs, to be more economical, to accommodate labeled graphs, to accommodate directed graphs, and so on.)

We note that from the Gödel number of a graph one and only one graph with that number can be obtained *up to isomorphism*. That is, if two graphs have the same Gödel number, then the graphs are *isomorphic* (i.e., there is a one-to-one correspondence between the nodes of one graph and the nodes of the other such that two nodes in one graph are connected by the same number of edges as the corresponding two nodes in the other). For example, the graph of Fig. 5.1.2 is isomorphic to the graph of Fig. 5.1.1; the correspondence is shown by the assignment of primes to the nodes. By this assignment, Figs. 5.1.1 and 5.1.2 have the same Gödel number.

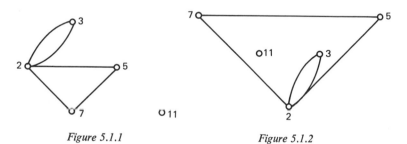

Figure 5.1.1   Figure 5.1.2

Although there is only one graph (up to isomorphism) having a given Gödel number, a given graph has in general several Gödel numbers, each coming from a different assignment of prime numbers to the nodes. For example, the graph of Fig. 5.1.3 is the same as the graph of Fig. 5.1.1, but its nodes are assigned different primes and its Gödel number is

$$3^{5^{2*23*37}} * 5^{3^2} * 23^{3*37} * 37^{3*23} * 47$$

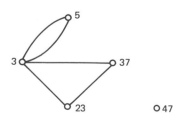

Figure 5.1.3

Not all positive integers are Gödel numbers of graphs. For example, $2^3 * 3^{35} * 5^9$ fails to be for three reasons: (1) the exponent of 5 indicates that there are two edges connecting nodes 5 and 3, whereas the exponent of 3 indicates there is only one such edge; (2) the exponent of 2 indicates that nodes 2 and 3 are connected, but the exponent of 3 indicates they are not; and (3) the exponent of 3 is divisible by 7, indicating that there is a node to which the prime 7 has been assigned, but 7 is not a factor of the number itself.

By virtue of this Gödel numbering, questions about graphs can be rephrased as questions about numbers. For example, consider the question: "Is there a path in a graph of length three (three edges) from the node numbered p_i to the node numbered p_j?" This question is clearly equivalent to the following question about the Gödel number g of the graph: "Do there exist primes p_h and p_k that are divisors of g, where no two of p_i, p_h, p_k, p_j are the same, and such that p_i, p_h, and p_k are, respectively, divisors of the exponents of p_h, p_k, and p_j?" (For example, there is a path in Fig. 5.1.1 from node 3 to node 5 of length 3, namely a path through nodes 2 and 7. In the Gödel number, 3, 2, and 7 are, respectively, divisors of the exponents of 2, 7, and 5.)

The question about a path of unspecified length from one node to another can be rendered as a more complicated number-theoretic question about the Gödel number of a graph. We shall not work out the details.

(This question is almost the same as the question answered by the labyrinth algorithm of Section 1.2.3. However, in our present thinking about algorithms, we are assuming no restraint on computing power, whereas in Section 1.2.4 we were allowing for the possibility that the labyrinth might be too large for the person walking through to learn completely.)

5.1.5   Gödel Numbers and Data Structures

A Gödel number for a graph is in effect a data-structuring technique. It is a solution to a problem of how to put data that are structured in a certain way into a computer that is structured in a contrary way. The remarkable thing is that an entire graph, however large, as long as it is finite, can be stored as a single positive integer. Indeed, as we hope the reader will appreciate from this example, any finite discrete structure can be stored as a single positive integer.

However, there is certainly no practical computing situation in which Gödel numbering is usable for structuring data. This statement is perhaps obvious, but it is helpful to state two reasons why it is so. First, the Gödel numbers of reasonably sized structures are of far larger magnitude than are the integer limits of any practical computer. Second, even if this were not the case, the time to do the arithmetic operations corresponding to structural operations would be much more than the time it would take to carry through the respective structural operations in practical data structuring.

It will be recalled that some Gödel numbers were given in this section as a product-of-powers expression and never multiplied out, simply because the number was too large. One can look at such an expression and see the graph, provided only that one has sufficient familiarity with the rather simple scheme for assigning numbers to graphs. If the numbers were multiplied out, however, the numeral in decimal form would not be as revealing. The same is true for machines: A computer that could handle an expression for a number in product-of-powers form could carry through the numerical operations corresponding to structural operations much more expeditiously.

We see, therefore, that the expression of the Gödel number in product-of-powers form is far closer to a practical structuring than is the decimal numeral. This remark and this entire subsection is an aside, since our present concern is not with the practical problems of data structuring. In the next section we continue our theoretical pursuit.

GÖDEL NUMBERS OF PROGRAMS 5.2

In this section we show how Gödel numbers can be assigned to programs in the GOTO language, and how a function computed by such a program can be expressed in terms of these Gödel numbers. We thereby complete a sketch of a proof that all functions computable in the GOTO language are in the class of mu-recursive functions (Theorem 5.2.1). The full proof of this theorem is beyond the scope of this text.

The manner of carrying through this proof is not peculiar to the GOTO language. Indeed, Gödel numbers can be assigned in any known computational system and the same construction carried through. Thus the demonstration carried through for the GOTO language in this section has a broader significance, which we hope the reader will catch.

The Gödel Number of a GOTO Program 5.2.1

A program is a string over the alphabet of its programming language. Thus one could assign Gödel numbers to programs in the way suggested in Section 5.1.3. However, there is a simpler way that will turn out to be more convenient for technical considerations.

Definition: A *program in special form* is a program of the GOTO language all of whose commands are labeled, where the labels are, in order, L1, L2, etc., and whose variables are, for some $n \geqq 1$, X1, X2, ... XΔ_n. (Δ_n is the GOTO-language numeral denoting the positive integer n.)

Thus a program in special form is, for some $m \geqq 1$,

$$L1: \alpha_1 ; L2: \alpha_2 ; \ldots ; L\Delta_m: \alpha_m$$

where $\alpha_1, \ldots, \alpha_m$ are unlabeled commands containing no variables other than X1, X2, ...

Clearly, every program in the GOTO language that is not in special form can be rewritten so that it is, simply by systematically adding and modifying the labels and modifying the variables. For convenience, we shall assign Gödel numbers only to programs in special form.

We begin by assigning the positive integers 1 through 7, respectively, to the command types of the GOTO language as follows: 1, variable assignment command; 2, numerical assignment command; 3, increment command; 4, decrement command; 5, unconditional transfer command; 6, conditional transfer command; and 7, the halt command.

We then assign Gödel numbers to each unlabeled command as follows.

Unlabeled command	*Gödel number*
$X\Delta_i := X\Delta_j$	$2^1 * 3^i * 5^j$
$X\Delta_i := \Delta_j$	$2^2 * 3^i * 5^j$
$INCR(X\Delta_i)$	$2^3 * 3^i$
$DECR(X\Delta_i)$	$2^4 * 3^i$
$GOTO\ L\Delta_j$	$2^5 * 5^j$
$IF\ X\Delta_i = 0\ GOTO\ L\Delta_j$	$2^6 * 3^i * 5^j$
$HALT$	2^7

Thus given the Gödel number g of an unlabeled command, the exponent of 2 in the prime factorization tells us the type of the command; the exponents of 3 and 5 tell us which labels, variables, or numerals occur in the appropriate places.

The following are some examples of commands and their Gödel numbers:

X1: = 3	$2^2 * 3^1 * 5^3 = 1500$
X1: = 0	$2^2 * 3^1 * 5^0 = 12$
X2: = X1	$2^1 * 3^2 * 5^1 = 90$
IF X1 = 0 GOTO L2	$2^6 * 3^1 * 5^2 = 4800$
GOTO L10	$2^5 * 5^{10} = 312{,}500{,}000$

Certain positive integers are not Gödel numbers of any unlabeled commands: for example, any integers divisible by a prime other than 2, 3 or 5; any odd integer; any integer divisible by 2^8; any integer of the form $2^1 * 3^i * 5^j$, where i or j is 0; any integer of the form $2^3 * 3^i * 5^j$ for $j \geq 1$; and so on.

Definition: The *Gödel number* of a program in special form

$$L1: \alpha_1;\ L2: \alpha_2;\ \ldots;\ L\Delta_m: \alpha_m$$

where $i_1, \ldots, i_m$ are the Gödel numbers of the unlabeled commands $\alpha_1, \ldots, \alpha_m$, respectively, is the Gödel number of the sequence $i_1, i_2, \ldots, i_m$, that is,

$$2^{i_1} * 3^{i_2} * \ldots * \text{PRIME}(m-1)^{i_m}$$

The Gödel Number of a Computation   5.2.2

Recall the discussion in Section 3.2 of how the machine computes a program in the GOTO language. During each time cycle, the machine is executing one command of the program. At the beginning of the time cycle, each variable has a value, and at most one of them will be changed during that time cycle.

Definition: The *total configuration* of the machine at any time cycle of its execution of a program P in special form, with m commands and n variables $X1, \ldots, X\Delta_n$, is the vector

$$\langle p, j, i_1, \ldots, i_n \rangle$$

where (1) p is the Gödel number of P; (2) $L\Delta_j$ is the label of the command to be executed during the time cycle ($j \leq m$); and (3) $i_1, \ldots, i_n$ are the values of the variables $X1, \ldots, X\Delta_n$, respectively, at the beginning of the time cycle.

The important fact about the total configuration of a time cycle in the execution of a program is that it gives us all the information about that moment of execution relevant to future execution. We see that this is so when we note the following fact: Given the total configuration at any time cycle in which a halt has not occurred, the total configuration of the next time cycle is determined, without regard to the past history of the computation. (Compare the concept of "total configuration" of a Turing machine in Section 2.1.2.) Furthermore, this determination is mechanical and quite simple in principle. We seek now to examine it in terms of Gödel numbers.

It is convenient to assign a single Gödel number to a total configuration. The technique used in Section 5.1.2 for finite sequences of positive integers does not apply directly because variables may have the value zero.

Definition: The *Godel number* of the total configuration $\langle p, j, i_1, \ldots, i_n \rangle$ is

$$2^p * 3^j * 5^{i_1+1} * \ldots * \text{PRIME}(n+1)^{i_n+1}$$

Now suppose that a program with n variables, $X1, \ldots, X\Delta_n$, is run with these set at the values $i_1, \ldots, i_n$, respectively, at the beginning. Put g_0 equal to the Gödel number of the sequence

$$p, 1, i_1 + 1, \ldots, i_n + 1$$

where p is the Gödel number of the program. Then g_0 is the Gödel number of the total configuration of the machine at the beginning, which we shall call here the zeroth time cycle of the computation.

From g_0, the Gödel number g_1 of the total configuration of the first time cycle is determined. More generally, there is a simple effective determination of each g_{i+1} from g_i [the Gödel numbers of the total configurations of the $(i + 1)$st and the ith time cycle, respectively] provided that there has not been a halt at or before the ith time cycle.

But since g_i and g_{i+1} are nonnegative integers, we can think of this relationship as a numerical function. Indeed, let us define a function NEXT so that $\text{NEXT}(g_i) = g_{i+1}$. More precisely, $\text{NEXT}(w)$ is defined for all nonnegative integers w as follows. If w is the Gödel number of a total configuration in which a halt is not to occur during that time cycle, then $\text{NEXT}(w)$ is the Gödel number of the total configuration of the next time cycle; otherwise, $\text{NEXT}(w) = 0$. Thus $\text{NEXT}(w) = 0$ if either w is not the Gödel number of a total configuration or it is the Gödel number of a total configuration in which the command to be executed during the time cycle is a halt. Thus NEXT is a total function.

Using techniques found in advanced texts on the theory of computability, one can readily show that NEXT is in the class of primitive-recursive functions. The reader who is not familiar with these techniques is asked to accept this important fact on faith.

5.2.3   The Function Computed by a Program

Suppose that a program in special form computes a certain function of k arguments with respect to the variable sequence

$$\text{X1, X2, } \ldots \text{, X}\Delta_k \text{, X}\Delta_{k+1}$$

Assume that the program has n variables for $n \geq k + 1$. In this subsection we describe how we can express this function in terms of p, the Gödel number of the program, the function NEXT, and other functions that we shall take note of.

We begin by defining a function TC, where $\text{TC}(w, i)$ is the Gödel number of the total configuration (if any) that occurs i time cycles after the total configuration whose Gödel number is w:

$$\begin{cases} \text{TC}(w, 0) = w \\ \text{TC}(w, i + 1) = \text{NEXT}(\text{TC}(w, i)) \end{cases}$$

This primitive-recursive definition shows that if NEXT is in the class of primitive-recursive functions, then TC is also in this class.

Note that if w is not the Gödel number of a total configuration, then $\text{TC}(w, i) = 0$ for $i \geq 1$. And if w is the Gödel number of a total configuration leading to a halt j time cycles later, for some $j < i$, then also $\text{TC}(w, i) = 0$.

We also consider the one-argument function HALT such that (1) HALT(w) = 0 if w is the Gödel number of a total configuration in which a halt command is to be executed, and (2) HALT(w) = 1 otherwise. We again ask the reader to take on faith that this function is in the class of primitive-recursive functions.

We must now define functions TIME and FINAL that are not total functions:

$$\text{TIME}(w) = (\mu i)[\text{HALT}(\text{TC}(w, i)) = 0]$$
$$\text{FINAL}(w) = \text{TC}(w, \text{TIME}(w))$$

If w is the Gödel number of a total configuration C_w from which the machine eventually comes to a halt, this halt will occur TIME(w) time cycles later. The final configuration (i.e., the total configuration when the halt occurs) has the Gödel number FINAL(w). In particular, if C_w is a total configuration in which a halt command is to be executed, then TIME(w) = 0 and FINAL(w) = w. On the other hand, if the machine never halts from C_w, then TIME(w) and FINAL(w) have no values. Finally, if w is not the Gödel number of a total configuration, then TIME(w) and FINAL(w) have no values.

For each value of $k > 0$, we define the function INIT$_k$ with $k + 1$ arguments: INIT$_k(p, h_1, \ldots, h_k) = 0$ if p is not the Gödel number of a program in special form. If p is the Gödel number of a program in special form whose variables are X1, $\ldots$, XΔ_n, INIT$_k(p, h_1, \ldots, h_k)$ is the Gödel number of the sequence $p, 1, h_1 + 1, \ldots, h_n + 1$, taking $h_{k+1} = \ldots = h_n = 0$ in the event that $n > k$. [Note that if $n < k$, then $h_{n+1}, \ldots, h_k$ will have no bearing on the value of INIT$_k(p, h_1, \ldots, h_k)$. We are not interested in cases where $n < k$; but in order that INIT$_k$ be in the class of primitive recursive functions, it must be total.]

Suppose now that we have a program in special form whose Gödel number is p, whose variables are X1, $\ldots$, XΔ_n, of which X1, $\ldots$, XΔ_k ($k < n$) are the input variables. If the variables X1, $\ldots$, XΔ_n are set initially to $h_1, \ldots, h_k$, $0, \ldots, 0$, respectively, then INIT$_k(p, h_1, \ldots, h_k)$ is the Gödel number of the initial total configuration of a computation for that program.

The reader who has done the more difficult exercises of Section 4.2 may be capable of proving that the functions INIT$_k$ are in the class of primitive-recursive functions.

[For the sake of definiteness in assigning Gödel numbers, we are setting all variables other than the input variables to zero at the beginning of a computation (i.e., the variables X$\Delta_{k+1}, \ldots$, XΔ_n). This may appear to contradict our stipulation in Chapter 3 that variables other than input variables can be set to any values at all without spoiling the correctness of the computation. Actually, there is nothing wrong in our reasoning here, because we are continuing under the assumption that a program does compute a certain function. Since it computes that function correctly for any initial setting of X$\Delta_{k+1}, \ldots$, XΔ_n, it certainly computes it correctly when these variables are initially set to zero.]

We need the two-argument function VAL where, if w is the Gödel number of a total configuration, $\text{VAL}(i, w)$ is the value of the variable $X\Delta_i$ in that total configuration; if $i = 0$ or if there is no variable $X\Delta_i$ in the program or if w is not the Gödel number of a total configuration, then $\text{VAL}(i, w) = 0$. Thus VAL is a total function.

If the program is run with $X1, \ldots, X\Delta_k$ initially set to $h_1, \ldots, h_k$, respectively, and all other variables set to zero, and if the machine halts eventually, then the value of the variable $X\Delta_{k+1}$ gives us the value of the function $\phi(h_1, \ldots, h_k)$ computed by the program. If it does not halt, then $\phi(h_1, \ldots, h_k)$ has no value. Thus if p is the Gödel number of this program, then the following is true, for all $h_1, \ldots, h_k$:

$$\phi(h_1, \ldots, h_k) = \text{VAL}(k + 1, \text{FINAL}(\text{INIT}_k(p, h_1, \ldots, h_k)))$$

It follows that ϕ is in the class of mu-recursive functions.

What we have done in this section so far amounts to a sketch of a proof via Gödel numbering of the following:

THEOREM 5.2.1: Every function computed by a program in the GOTO language is in the class of mu-recursive functions.

Furthermore, this proof would become complete with the detailed proof that the functions NEXT, HALT, INIT_k, and VAL are in the class of primitive-recursive functions. (The functions TC, TIME, and FINAL were defined formally in terms of these.) We shall not fill in these gaps here, hoping that the reader who is disturbed by them will be stimulated thereby to gain a more advanced understanding of the theory of computability, at which point he or she could straightforwardly prove these functions to be primitive recursive.

The proof that similar functions for Turing machines are primitive recursive can be found in Hermes ([1969], pp. 103–107).

5.2.4 A Universal GOTO Program

Define the two-argument function UF_1 as follows:

$$\text{UF}_1(p, x) = \text{VAL}(2, \text{FINAL}(\text{INIT}_1(p, x)))$$

From the last equation of Section 5.2.3, if p is the Gödel number of a program in special form that computes a function of one argument with respect to the variable sequence $X1, X2$, then $\text{UF}_1(p, x)$ is the value (if any) of this function for the argument x. If p is the Gödel number of a program in which the variable $X2$ does not occur, then $\text{UF}_1(p, x) = 0$, provided that $\text{FINAL}(\text{INIT}_1(p, x))$ has a value. $\text{UF}_1(p, x)$ has no value if $\text{FINAL}(\text{INIT}_1(p, x))$ has no value, that is, if either p is not the Gödel number of a program or the configuration whose Gödel number is $\text{INIT}_1(p, x)$ does not lead to a halt. Finally, if p is the Gödel number of a program with several variables that can be considered input variables (their initial setting influences the value of the output X2), then $UF_1(p, x)$ is the value (if any) of this function for $X1 = x$ and all other arguments equal to zero.

We see then that for all values of p, $UF_1(p, x)$ with p fixed is a one-argument function of x. Furthermore, for every one-argument function ϕ computable in the GOTO language, partial or total, there is a p such that $\phi(x) = UF_1(p, x)$. We call UF_1 the *universal function* for one-argument functions computable in the GOTO language.

Furthermore, the function UF_1 is given as an explicit definition in functions which, as mentioned without proof in Section 5.2.3, are in the class of mu-recursive functions. So there is a program UP_1 in the GOTO language that computes UF_1; let us assume that it does so with respect to the variable sequence X1, X2, X3.

The program UP_1 is thus a universal program in the GOTO language for all programs in this language that compute a one-argument function. If P is any such program in special form, one could use UP_1 to compute P by setting X1 equal to the Gödel number of P. (If P is not in special form, it is easy to rewrite it in special form.)

Similarly, for any $k > 1$, there exists a universal program UP_k for all programs in the GOTO language that compute k-argument functions. We get this by first defining

$$UF_k(p, x_1, \ldots, x_k) = VAL(k + 1, FINAL(INIT_k(p, x_1, \ldots, x_k)))$$

The function UF_k is in the class of mu-recursive functions, so there must be a program UP_k in the GOTO language that computes it with respect to the variable sequence $X1, \ldots, X\Delta_{k+2}$. UP_k is a universal program for k-argument functions: For any program P in special form computing a k-argument function, UP_k can be used to compute that function by setting X1 equal to the Gödel number of P.

These universal programs are useful in the advanced theory. They represent an analog to Turing's universal Turing machine, which we looked at in Section 2.2.

Because Gödel numbers are too large to deal with practically, the universal programs UP_1, UP_2, . . . are not practical in any sense. Leaving this point aside, we find it interesting to investigate how these programs work in simulating other programs. We see, from how the UF functions are defined, that the program is simulated time cycle by time cycle. At each new time cycle of the simulated execution, the universal program knows what command of the simulated program is to be executed and what the value of each simulated variable is. It then (possibly) modifies one of these variables and decides what the next command is to be. Of course, it takes many time cycles for the universal program to simulate one time cycle.

Indeed, these universal programs are very much like interpreters. This is clearer if we imagine that we had gone through assigning Gödel numbers to another programming language Q and defined universal functions for them. Let us call these new functions UFQ_1, UFQ_2, and so on. Then if we had written in the GOTO language programs UPQ_1, UPQ_2, and so on, to compute, respectively, UFQ_1, UFQ_2, and so on, we would have programs in the GOTO language that would simulate the language Q. They would, in effect, be interpreters written in the GOTO language for programs of Q.

5.3 THE ARGUMENT FOR CHURCH'S THESIS

In this section we draw upon what we have done in the last two sections and argue for two propositions.

> PROPOSITION 5.3.1: For every algorithm A there is a mu-recursive function f over the nonnegative integers (hence computable by the methods of Chapter 4) such that each question answered by A can be answered instead by effectively and readily transforming it into an argument for f whose corresponding value effectively and readily yields the answer.

The algorithm that converts the question for A to an argument for f, and the algorithm that converts the value of f to the answer that would have been produced by A, are easy algorithms even when the algorithm A and the function f are difficult, as measured, say, by execution time. This is the meaning of the word "readily."

> PROPOSITION 5.3.2: Every function over the nonnegative integers that has a procedure for its evaluation is in the class of mu-recursive functions.

Neither Proposition 5.3.1 nor Proposition 5.3.2 is subject to mathematical proof. It is Proposition 5.3.2 that is generally known as Church's thesis. Proposition 5.3.1 is also important, since it justifies our exclusive concern for the nonnegative integers in Chapters 3 and 4. Both propositions are argued for in this section on the basis of what has been asserted about Gödel numbering in Section 5.1 and 5.2.

5.3.1 The Argument

For the sake of the discussion that follows, we itemize the steps in our reasoning.

1. An algorithm must be capable of being written down.
2. As such it is a finite discrete expression in some language.

3. The execution of an algorithm occurs as a sequence of steps.

4. At each step there is a finite discrete structure known as the *total configuration*.

5. The total configuration before execution is the input, suitably prepared for execution, which can be done effectively. (In fact, it is a simple task to obtain the initial total configuration from the input.)

6. Each single step of the execution produces a change in the total configuration, deterministically and precisely, as prescribed by the algorithm. (This change is of bounded magnitude, although there is no bound on the magnitude of total configurations.)

7. The output, which is the answer to the question expressed by the input, is part of the terminal total configuration, as specified effectively by the algorithm. (In fact, it is a simple task to determine the output from the terminal total configuration.)

8. There exists a scheme for assigning positive integers (Gödel numbers) to each possible total configuration, and there exist functions NEXT and HALT in the class of primitive recursive functions satisfying the following conditions: (a) There is an algorithm to convert a given total configuration to its Gödel number. (b) There is an algorithm to obtain the total configuration from its Gödel number. (c) If g_1 is the Gödel number of a total configuration to which the algorithm is being applied, and g_2 is the Gödel number of the total configuration that results from the application of one step of the algorithm, then $\text{NEXT}(g_1) = g_2$. (d) $\text{HALT}(g) = 0$ if g is the Gödel number of a total configuration in which the algorithm calls for a termination, and $\text{HALT}(g) = 1$ otherwise.

(These functions NEXT and HALT are simpler than the functions NEXT and HALT of Section 5.2, which have as arguments the Gödel number of the program.)

9. If the form of the input to the algorithm is an n-tuple of nonnegative integers for some positive integer n, there is a primitive-recursive function INIT such that $\text{INIT}(x_1, \ldots, x_n)$ is the Gödel number of the input representing the n-tuple $(x_1, \ldots, x_n)$.

10. If the form of the output of the algorithm is a nonnegative integer, there is a primitive-recursive function VAL such that $\text{VAL}(g) = y$ holds whenever $\text{HALT}(g) = 0$ and y is the output given by the total configuration whose Gödel number is g.

11. Let the function TC be defined by the primitive recursion:

$$\begin{cases} \text{TC}(g, 0) = g \\ \text{TC}(g, t + 1) = \text{NEXT}(\text{TC}(g, t)) \end{cases}$$

If g is the Gödel number of a total configuration that occurs in the execution of an algorithm, after which the execution continues for at least t steps ($t \geq 1$), then $\text{TC}(g, t)$ is the Gödel number of the total configuration as it exists just after the tth step.

12. Consider the function FINAL, where FINAL(g) = TC(g, (μt)[HALT (TC(g, t)) = 0]). FINAL(g) is the Gödel number of the total configuration upon termination after beginning with a total configuration whose Gödel number is g. FINAL is in the class of mu-recursive functions. From its definition and the definitions of functions appearing therein, we can compute it by the methods of Chapter 4.

13. To complete the argument for Proposition 5.3.1, let A be a given algorithm. For any given input to A, the Gödel number g of the initial configuration corresponding to this input can be effectively obtained, by (4) and (8a). By (8b) and (7), the answer can be effectively obtained from FINAL(g). Thus taking f = FINAL, Proposition 5.3.1 follows.

14. For Proposition 5.3.2, if the algorithm is one for finding the values of an n-argument function ϕ on the nonnegative integers, then $\phi(x_1, \ldots, x_n)$ = VAL(FINAL(INIT($x_1, \ldots, x_n$))). Thus ϕ is in the class of mu-recursive functions since FINAL is mu-recursive and VAL and INIT are in the class of primitive-recursive functions.

5.3.2 Discussion

Items 1 through 7 of the argument of Section 5.3.1 follow from the very definition of *algorithm* and therefore cannot be disputed. Nevertheless, we should ask whether there might be something we could do to answer a class of questions that would not fall under this definition as we laid it down in Chapter 1.

One possible suggestion here might be an analog computer, whose storage is not discrete but continuous, violating item 4 of the argument. The question then is: Can an analog computer compute a function that cannot be computed by an algorithm?

The answer is that any real analog computer can give us answers only to a finite degree of approximation. Even the internal computations of the device are subject to this constraint. With this understood, we cannot say that a real analog computer offers us the benefits of continuous variation. Every wheel has a wobble, and every electric charge has some uncontrollable variation. However small these may be, they are enough to leave the device at the level of discrete variation, for all practical purposes. Furthermore, there is not even a theoretical hope of getting truly continuous variation, since contemporary physics seems to tell us that all matter and energy are discrete.

Item 8 has supporting evidence. Although Gödel numbers have not actually been assigned in all cases, they have been assigned and the corresponding functions defined in sufficient detail in enough cases to make it overwhelmingly clear that, for all algorithms known in our civilization at present, item 8 is true. Personally, I find it quite credible that item 8 is true of all possible algorithms.

Item 8 does not have the status of reasoned mathematical truth. Our confidence in it has the status of any empirical truth (i.e., a law or hypothesis that rests on observation and trust that the future will in some way resemble the past). All the laws of physics, and all the laws of any laboratory science, are in this category. The laws of mathematics are not, since they admit of the kind of proof that is independent of any particular observations about the world.

The reader who has not gone through Gödel numbering and the defining of the appropriate functions in detail has no reason to feel sure of item 8 for all algorithms. Conviction will come only when that reader picks up a suitable advanced text and goes through the whole process thoroughly.

Items 9 and 10 are credible if item 8 is credible. There is nothing new to discuss here. Items 11 to 14 are mathematical consequences of item 8, and hence not subject to any new dispute.

In summary, our argument for Church's thesis (and the companion Proposition 5.3.1) rests largely on the strong feeling based on experience that Gödel numbers can be assigned to all algorithmic formalisms, as stated in item 8, and in accord with items 9 and 10. On the other hand, most of the reasonable doubt a person might have about this argument is probably focused on items 8 to 10.

In this chapter we have attempted to lay the groundwork for items 8 to 10, by showing how Gödel numbers could be assigned to any systematic set of finite discrete structures. We have presented this assignment in detail for the GOTO language. In Chapter 2 we showed how a Turing machine's total configuration could be put into the form of a string of characters, to which Gödel numbers are easily assigned (as shown in Section 5.1.3).

However, the doubting person might refuse to admit the generalization to all algorithmic structures, pointing out that there might be algorithms whose total configurations are much more complicated than either of these two. As a matter of fact, such algorithms actually exist. We have attempted to suggest that Gödel numbers can be applied to these structures by showing in Section 5.1.4 how Gödel numbers could be assigned to graphs.

The existence of a method of assigning Gödel numbers to algorithmic structures is not all that items 8 to 10 assert. They also assert that this can be done in such a way that the functions NEXT, HALT, INIT, and VAL are in the class of primitive-recursive functions. We have done nothing in this book to bring conviction on this this point except to define the class of primitive-recursive functions in Chapter 4. Here the reader must study the more advanced literature merely to become able to acknowledge that our assertion is plausible.

Some have argued differently for Church's thesis. One widely advanced argument might be worded as follows:

Several mathematically precise formal languages have been put forth for expressing algorithms for functions over the nonnegative integers. (Turing machines, the two foundational programming languages, and the formalism of functional expressions are four such formal languages, but there are several others.) Each of these formalisms supplies us with a mathematically precise definition that constitutes an explication of the term "algorithmically computable function," which is not a mathematical concept. (Thus we have Turing-computable function, function computable in the GOTO language, function computable in the WHILE language, mu-recursive function, and others.)

Every known algorithm can be converted into each of these formalisms, and hence computes a function satisfying each of these definitions. Furthermore, we can prove mathematically that these definitions are all equivalent (i.e., that a function satisfies any one of them if and only if it satisfies each of the others).

The fact that several mathematical explications, of widely differing character, of the term "algorithmically computable function" turn out to be equivalent is strong evidence that all possible explications are equivalent to this term itself.

My personal inclination is that this argument is not as cogent as the argument that has been advanced in Section 5.3.1.

As a by-product of the argument of Section 5.3.1, we make one rather interesting observation. Any function ϕ over the nonnegative integers that has an algorithm can, by item 14, be put into the form $\phi(x_1, \ldots, x_n) = g((\mu y)[h(x_1, \ldots, x_n, y) = 0])$, where g and h are in the class of primitive-recursive functions. This form is called "Kleene normal form," since Kleene is the originator of the insight that forms the basis of the argument in Section 5.3.1 (Kleene [1936]). The significance is that in the sequence of steps by means of which ϕ is defined, using explicit definition, primitive recursion, and mu recursion, the scheme of mu recursion need be used at most once.

Unsolvable Problems 6

In Chapter 5 we argued specifically that the GOTO language is capable of expressing and executing all algorithms. We then inferred that the same is true of the WHILE language, the system of Turing machines, the formalism of functional expressions, and several formal computational schemes not described in this book.

In this chapter we demonstrate that certain problems are unsolvable (i.e., have no algorithms). Our proof (and, in fact, any proof) rests on Church's thesis. Since all the problems we consider are problems whose answers are "yes" and "no," in place of the term *unsolvable* we use the more specific term *undecidable* in most of this chapter.

We begin by proving the undecidability of the halting problem for the GOTO language (i.e., the problem of whether a given program halts for a given initial setting of its variables). The proof that this class of questions has no algorithm does not depend on the peculiar features of the GOTO language, but rests on the proposition that Church's thesis holds for it. Hence the proof is easily transferred to any other such language.

Although Church's thesis is required to establish that there is no decision procedure of any kind for the halting problem of GOTO-language programs, it is possible to establish without Church's thesis that there is no such decision procedure in the GOTO language itself (Section 6.1.2). We need Church's thesis because we wish to assert that there is no algorithm of any kind, even in unknown formalisms, for this halting problem. (Similarly, we can prove without Church's thesis that there is no decision procedure for any algorithmic language in that language itself.)

In Section 6.2 we go on to show that certain other problems are unsolvable. Perhaps the surprising thing is that several problems in other areas of mathematics, with no apparent relation to Turing machines or programs, can be proved undecidable by demonstrating how the halting problem can be reduced to each of them in turn.

6.1 THE HALTING PROBLEM

After proving that Church's thesis implies the undecidability of the halting problem for the GOTO language, we note that the halting problem for any known universal language (i.e., one in which all algorithms can be expressed) is undecidable.

6.1.1 Self-Convergence

Definition: A GOTO-language program P in special form (see Section 5.2.1) is *self-convergent* if the following is true: When P is run on the machine with the variable X1 set initially to the Gödel number of P and all other variables set initially to zero, then the machine eventually halts. If under these circumstances the machine never halts, then P is *self-divergent*.

Thus every program in special form is either self-convergent or self-divergent. The following lemma says, in effect, that there is no decision procedure for self-convergence in the GOTO language itself.

LEMMA 1: There is no program P_1 in special form that performs as follows: If P_1 is run with X1 initially set to the Gödel number g' of an arbitrary program P' in special form and all other variables initially set to zero, then P_1 eventually halts with X2 = 0 if P' is self-convergent, but with X2 = 1 if P' is self-divergent.

PROOF: Assume that such a P_1 exists, and assume it never halts by default (see Section 3.2.1). Construct a program P_2 from P_1 as follows: Let $L\Delta_n$ be a label not occurring in P_1. Change every "HALT" in P_1 to "GOTO $L\Delta_n$" and append the following:

$$; \ L\Delta_n: \ \text{IF} \ X2 = 0 \ \text{GOTO} \ L\Delta_n; \ \text{HALT}$$

Thus P_2 will run exactly like P_1, except that if P_1 halts with X2 = 0, then P_2 never halts. And so if P_2 is run with X1 set to the Gödel number of a program P' in special form and all other variables set to zero, the machine halts if and only if P' is self-divergent. Let us refer to this as the *performance description* of P_2.

We ask, is P_2 self-convergent or self-divergent? Let g_2 be the Gödel number of P_2.

Assume first that P_2 is self-convergent. This means that it halts when run with X1 set initially to g_2 and all other variables set initially to zero. Thus by the performance description of P_2, the program whose Gödel number is g_2 is self-divergent. That is, P_2 is self-divergent, which is a contradiction.

Assume now that P_2 is self-divergent. This means that it fails to halt when run with X1 set initially to g_2 and all other variables set initially to zero. Thus, by the performance description of P_2, the program whose Gödel number is g_2 is self-convergent. That is, P_2 is self-convergent; again a contradiction.

Now P_2 must be either self-convergent or self-divergent. But the assumption of either of these leads to contradiction. It follows that the original assumption in the proof must be at fault: There is no program P_1 that behaves in the way stated. ∎

COROLLARY: Church's thesis implies that the problem of whether a given program in the GOTO language in special form is self-convergent is undecidable.

PROOF: By Church's thesis, if there were an algorithm to tell whether a given program in the GOTO language is self-convergent, this algorithm could itself be converted into a program in the GOTO language (using Gödel numbers). Such a program could then easily be transformed into the P_1 of Lemma 1. ∎

Since Church's thesis is generally accepted, the proof of this corollary is the first proof, in effect, that a problem is unsolvable. In the next subsection, we extend this result to a more interesting problem.

Generalizing the Result *6.1.2*

Definition: The *halting problem* for a given algorithmic formalism is the problem of whether or not a given procedure of the formalism when executed with a given input eventually terminates.

THEOREM 6.1.1: Church's thesis implies that the halting problem for the GOTO language is undecidable.

PROOF: An algorithm to tell whether a given problem in the GOTO language halts for a given input could be used to tell whether a given program in the GOTO language in special form is self-convergent. Since the latter has no algorithm, the halting problem for the GOTO language has no algorithm either. ∎

This proof has a certain form that is used over and over again in the literature to establish the unsolvability of certain problems from the previously
established results about unsolvability. In this book it will be used twice more
in this section, and a few times in Section 6.2. In outline the proof is as follows:

1. From Q, R can be constructed.
2. But R does not exist (having already been proved to be impossible).
3. Hence Q does not exist.

In the proof of Theorem 6.1.1, Q is the algorithm mentioned in the statement of the theorem, and R is the algorithm mentioned in the corollary to the
lemma.

In each proof of this kind, it is step 1 that is the most difficult, depending
on the specific Q and R. In the proof of Theorem 6.1.1, the construction of
algorithm R from algorithm Q happens to be trivial (R's problem is a subprob-
lem of Q's problem). In many proofs of this kind, the construction of R is quite
involved.

Instead of proving Theorem 6.1.1, we could have proved a theorem to the
effect that no program in the GOTO language is an algorithm for the halting
problem for the GOTO language. Such a theorem would not have to mention
Church's thesis. The proof would have been a bit more difficult than the proof
of Theorem 6.1.1, proceeding from the assumption that such a program P exists
to the construction of a program P_1 satisfying Lemma 1.

Similarly, for any of the known formalisms for algorithms, it can be established without assuming Church's thesis that there is no decision procedure in
that formalism for the halting problem of GOTO-language programs; this result
follows from the demonstrable fact that any algorithm expressible in any of
those formalisms is translatable into the GOTO language. We need Church's
thesis in Theorem 6.1.1 (and in Theorem 6.1.2 which follows) because we wish
to assert that the problem has no algorithm of any kind whatsoever.

6.1.3   Other Formalisms

Definition: A formalism for algorithms is *universal* if all algorithms can
be stated and executed in that formalism. Such a formalism is *demonstrably
universal* if there exists an algorithm to express in that formalism any function
in the class of mu-recursive functions that is given as a sequence of explicit
definitions, primitive recursions and mu recursions from the successor function.

THEOREM 6.1.2:   Church's thesis implies that the halting problem for any
demonstrably universal formalism for algorithms is undecidable.

PROOF: Suppose that we had a decision procedure D for the halting problem for this formalism. From D we could construct the following decision procedure D' for the halting problem of the GOTO language:

Given a program and inputs, convert the program into special form and put

$$f(g, x_1, \ldots, x_k) = (\mu y)[\text{HALT}(\text{TC}(\text{INIT}_k(g, x_1, \ldots, x_k), y)) = 0]$$

(see Section 5.2.3), where g is the Gödel number of the program and $x_1, \ldots, x_k$ constitute the input. Express the function f in the formalism, and decide by D whether the procedure in the formalism for computing this f terminates for the input $g, x_1, \ldots, x_k$. If so, then the program in the GOTO language halts for the input; if not, not.

Since D' does not exist, D does not exist either. ∎

Because of their conceptual simplicity Turing machines are often singled out among the several universal models for theoretical arguments (which contrasts with their clumsiness in doing practical computations). We shall find it convenient to refer to the following theorem in Section 6.2.

THEOREM 6.1.3: Church's thesis implies that the halting problem for Turing machines is undecidable.

The proof of this theorem follows from the fact that the class of Turing machines constitutes a demonstrably universal formalism for algorithms. The latter is established by the constructive proof that all mu-recursive functions are computable by Turing machines, which can be found in many books (e.g., Davis [1958], Chap. II).

The phrase "the halting problem" is often used to refer to any problem covered by Theorem 6.1.2. Speaking loosely in this way, we can say that the proof of the undecidability of the halting problem is a significant achievement; the significance is clear once we reflect on how valuable such a decision procedure would be if we had it. In this respect, it is like our knowledge of the impossibility of a perpetual-motion machine, which is important because of the value that such a machine would have if it could be constructed.

Let it not be said, then, that the argument that the halting problem is undecidable is of *mere* theoretical significance. It reminds us of a very practical limitation.

The type of argument used to prove the undecidability of the halting problem (especially in the lemma of Section 6.1.1) is known as the *diagonal method.* Many important theorems of computability and other branches of mathematics are proved by this method. Because of their importance, some of these proofs are presented and compared in Appendix VI.

The unsolvability of the halting problem, an important fact in itself, also turns out to be fundamental in establishing the unsolvability of many problems. We now comment on these.

6.2 OTHER UNDECIDABILITY RESULTS

In two papers published in 1936, Alonzo Church formulated the thesis that was to bear his name, articulated the first undecidability result, and supplied the supporting mathematical considerations based on the work of Gödel and Kleene. The train of thought was, in a way, similar to the proof of the undecidability of the halting problem, although Turing machines were not considered.

Since then, many undecidability results have been proved, too many for us to enumerate here. All these results are relative to Church's thesis; anyone who had reason to doubt Church's thesis would have reason to doubt all these results. And the starting point for all these undecidability results is this work done in the 1930s by Church and others.

Many undecidability results can be proved from the undecidability of the halting problem for Turing machines. This fact in itself is remarkable in view of the varied subject matter of these results.

The purpose of this section is to exhibit some relatively simple proofs of undecidability, so as to give some idea of how research has proceeded. In the statements of these theorems in this section, we shall follow the practice in the general literature and omit the phrase "Church's thesis implies that . . . ." Strictly speaking, this phrase is necessary if we claim the proposition in each case as a mathematical theorem, since they all rest on Church's thesis and there is no way of proving this thesis itself as a mathematical theorem.

6.2.1 Halting from an All-Zero Input

As our first example of how undecidability results can lead to other undecidability results we prove:

THEOREM 6.2.1: There is no decision procedure to tell whether a given program in the GOTO language halts when run with all variables initially set to zero.

PROOF: Assume that there is such a decision procedure D. From D we construct the following decision procedure D' to tell whether a given program P in the GOTO language halts for any given input setting:

Assume without loss of generality that the variables of P are $X1, \ldots, X\Delta_n$. (Δ_n is the numeral in the GOTO language denoting n.) Let $i_1, \ldots, i_n$ be nonnegative integers representing a given input setting to these respective variables.

First, a program P_0 is constructed from P and $i_1, \ldots, i_n$, as follows:

$$X1 := \Delta_{i_1};$$
$$X2 := \Delta_{i_2};$$
$$\cdot$$
$$\cdot$$
$$\cdot$$
$$X\Delta_n := \Delta_{i_n};$$
$$P$$

Then, the decision procedure D is applied to the program P_0, telling us whether or not P_0 halts when all inputs are set to zero. If the answer is "yes," then P halts for the input setting $i_1, \ldots, i_n$. If the answer is "no," then P fails to halt for this input setting.

Thus the assumption of the existence of D implies the existence of D', a decision procedure for the general halting problem of the GOTO language, which is impossible by Theorem 6.1.1. Hence D does not exist. ∎

We commented in Section 6.1.2 about the general form used in the proof of Theorem 6.1.1 from the Corollary of the Lemma. Note how that format is used in the proof just concluded: D' is constructed from D, whence D is demonstrated to be impossible since D' is impossible. The construction of D' from D is the major part of the proof.

For the sake of further work in this section, let us give a more detailed sketch of this type of proof. A problem P_1 is known to be undecidable, and from this knowledge a problem P_2 is proved to be undecidable. The proof consists of an algorithm (or "construction") C for converting an instance x of P_1 into an instance $C(x)$ of P_2 such that $C(x)$ has the answer "yes" if and only if x has the answer "yes." The proof that the construction C has this property completes the proof that P_2 is undecidable. The logic behind the proof is that if there were a decision procedure for P_2, there would be a decision procedure for P_1 (constructible via C); the latter is impossible because it has already been proved that P_1 is undecidable. (For the sake of simplifying our discussion, we shall omit some obvious variations of this form of proof.)

When a proof proceeds in this way, one often says that P_1 is *reduced* to P_2. Thus a problem is proved to be undecidable by reducing a problem, already known to be undecidable, to it. The reduction is the construction method C.

Such constructions are often quite imaginative. As such, they make it possible to prove undecidability results in subject areas that might appear initially to be quite unlikely. The fact is, undecidability results (and more generally, unsolvability results) turn up by now in practically every mathematical theory, which is a reflection of the resourcefulness of mathematicians and logicians in translating problems in one subject area into problems of another. We shall do something to illustrate this process in Section 6.2.3 and beyond.

6.2.2 The Undecidability of Totality

In this subsection we prove (assuming Church's thesis) that there is no decision procedure to tell whether a given program computes a total function, and that there is none to tell whether the function defined by mu recursion from a given primitive-recursive function is total. We have commented on these results in Chapters 3 and 4.

THEOREM 6.2.2: There is no decision procedure to tell whether the function computed by a given program in the GOTO language with respect to a given sequence of variables is total.

PROOF: Assume that there is such a decision procedure D. From D a decision procedure D' to tell whether a given program halts for a given input setting is constructed as follows.

Let P be a given program with n variables. Assume without loss of generality that these variables are $X1, \ldots, X\Delta_n$. (Thus the variables Y and Z do not appear in P.) Let $i_1, \ldots, i_n$ be nonnegative integers. We wish to determine whether or not P halts when run with its variables $X1, \ldots, X\Delta_n$ initially set at $i_1, \ldots, i_n$.

Write the program P_0 as follows:

$$X1 := \Delta_{i_1};$$
$$X2 := \Delta_{i_2};$$
$$\cdot$$
$$\cdot$$
$$\cdot$$
$$X\Delta_n := \Delta_{i_n};$$
$$Z := Y;$$
$$P$$

Notice that if P halts when $X1, \ldots, X\Delta_n$ are set initially to $i_1, \ldots, i_n$, respectively, the program P_0 computes the identity function with respect to the variable sequence Y, Z. If P does not halt for this initial setting, then P_0 computes the empty function (i.e., the function that has no value for any argument) with respect to that variable sequence.

The decision procedure D is applied to the program P_0 for the variable sequence Y, Z, telling us whether the function computed by P_0 with respect to that sequence is total. If the answer is "no," it can only be because P fails to halt for this input setting.

If D is a decision procedure for totality, then D' as constructed is a decision procedure for the halting problem. Since D' does not exist (by Theorem 6.1.1), D cannot exist. ∎

The proof of the following theorem about mu recursions depends on Theorem 6.2.2 and some unproved assertions that were made in Section 5.2 in connection with the Gödel numbering of GOTO-language programs.

THEOREM 6.2.3: There is no decision procedure to tell, for a given $k \geq 1$ and for a given $(k + 1)$-argument function in the class of primitive-recursive functions, whether the k-argument function defined from it by mu recursion is total.

PROOF: We show that if we had such a decision procedure we could construct a decision procedure to tell whether an arbitrary program in the GOTO language computes a total function. Suppose that such a program with k inputs is given. This program is readily converted into a program P in special form with Gödel number g.

Recall from Section 5.2.3 that if ϕ is the function computed by this program with respect to the variable sequence $X1, \ldots, X\Delta_{k+1}$, then

$$\phi(h_1, \ldots, h_k) = \text{VAL}(k + 1, \text{FINAL}(\text{INIT}_k(g, h_1, \ldots, h_k)))$$

Replacing "FINAL" according to the definitions in Section 5.2.3 of "FINAL" and "TIME," we get

(1) $\phi(h_1, \ldots, h_k) = \text{VAL}(k + 1, \text{TC}(\text{INIT}_k(g, h_1, \ldots, h_k),$
$$(\mu i)[\text{HALT}(\text{TC}(\text{INIT}_k(g, h_1, \ldots, h_k), i)) = 0]))$$

As mentioned in Section 5.2, the functions VAL, TC, INIT_k, and HALT are all primitive-recursive functions. Hence the function ψ, where

$$\psi(h_1, \ldots, h_k, i) = \text{HALT}(\text{TC}(\text{INIT}_k(g, h_1, \ldots, h_k), i))$$

is a primitive-recursive function. Putting

$$\chi(h_1, \ldots, h_k) = (\mu i)[\psi(h_1, \ldots, h_k, i) = 0]$$

we note that χ is defined by mu recursion from a primitive-recursive function. But by substitution in (1) we get

$$\phi(h_1, \ldots, h_k) = \text{VAL}(k + 1, \text{TC}(\text{INIT}_k(g, h_1, \ldots, h_k), \chi(h_1, \ldots, h_k)))$$

Since all primitive-recursive functions are total, it follows that ϕ is total if and only if χ is total.

Thus if we had a decision procedure for telling whether a definition by mu recursion from a given primitive-recursive function yields a total function, we would have a decision procedure to tell whether a given program in the GOTO language computes a total function with respect to a given variable sequence, contrary to Theorem 6.2.2. ∎

6.2.3 Turing Machines and Semi-Thue Systems

We proceed with a demonstration of how an undecidability result in one mathematical theory can be used to prove an undecidability result in an apparently unrelated theory. As we remarked, such a proof usually begins with a one-to-one mapping (injection) of items in the first theory into items in the second theory.

In Section 2.2.3 we showed how the total configuration of a Turing machine could be coded as a string of characters. The alphabet used included the characters of the machine alphabet and also characters representing the states. In this subsection we shall modify that coding so as to map the subject matter of Turing machines into the subject matter of semi-Thue systems, which will be the beginning of a proof in Section 6.2.4 of an unsolvability result about semi-Thue systems.

Definition: A *semi-Thue system* over an alphabet Σ consists of a set of productions

$$U_1 \longrightarrow V_1$$
$$U_2 \longrightarrow V_2$$
$$\cdot$$
$$\cdot$$
$$\cdot$$
$$U_n \longrightarrow V_n$$

where each U_i and each V_i is a string of any length (possibly zero) over Σ. A string W is, by this system, *transformable in one step* into a string X if, for some i, $W = Z_0 U_i Z_1$ and $X = Z_0 V_i Z_1$, where Z_0, Z_1 are strings of any length (possibly zero). A string W is *transformable* by the system into a string X if there exists a sequence $W_1, W_2, \ldots, W_m, m \geq 1$, where $W_1 = W, W_m = X$ and, for each $i \leq m - 1$, W_i is transformable into W_{i+1} in one step.

An example of a semi-Thue system over the alphabet $\{b, c, d\}$ is

$$bd \longrightarrow db$$
$$cd \longrightarrow dc$$
$$bc \longrightarrow d$$
$$cb \longrightarrow d$$

The string *bbccdbd* is transformed into *ddddb* as follows:

$$bbccdbd$$
$$bdcdbd$$
$$dbcdbd$$
$$dddbd$$
$$ddddb$$

(Note that any string W over the alphabet $\{b, c, d\}$ can be transformed by this particular system into a string of one of two forms: $d^i b^j$ or $d^i c^j$, where $i \geq 0$ and $j \geq 0$.)

The term "semi-Thue system" refers to the logician Axel Thue. The systems studied by Thue about 1914 were less general in that if U_t could be rewritten as V_t, then V_t could also be rewritten as U_t. (We shall deal with these as semi-groups in Section 6.2.5.) The ideas for this present material that will occupy us through Section 6.2.6 come originally from Post [1947]. Semi-Thue systems are sometimes called "Post-production systems."

Semi-Thue systems bear some resemblance to the context-free languages of Chapter 7. It turns out that the former are powerful enough to be a computational model, whereas the latter are more restricted.

In the next subsection the transformation problem for semi-Thue systems is proved undecidable, using Theorem 6.1.3 (the undecidability of the halting problem for Turing machines). We now present a simulation theorem, which will be used in proving the unsolvability result.

THEOREM 6.2.4: Given a Turing machine T, a semi-Thue system S that *simulates* T can be constructed; that is, there is a one-to-one mapping (injection) ϕ of the set of total configurations C of T into the set of strings of S such that the total configuration C_1 is immediately followed by C_2 if and only if $\phi(C_1)$ is transformable by S into $\phi(C_2)$ in one step.

PROOF: Let $q_1, \ldots, q_m$ be the states of T and let $\{a_1, \ldots, a_n\}$ be its machine alphabet other than the blank. At the beginning of any time cycle, the machine is in a certain state scanning a square of tape, and the tape has symbols on finitely many squares; recall that all this constitutes the total configuration of that time cycle (see Section 2.1.2). The set $\Sigma = \{q_1, \ldots, q_m, a_0, a_1, \ldots, a_n, \rlap{/}c, \$\}$ (with $m + n +$ three distinct characters) will be the total alphabet of our semi-Thue system S; the character a_0 of S will be used to represent a blank square of the Turing machine when we require a written symbol for it.

Suppose that, at the beginning of a time cycle, there are r squares of the tape that are either nonblank or have been scanned then or previously by the reading head. Suppose also that at that time the pth of these squares from the left is the square scanned, and that the machine is in state q_k. For each j, the jth square from the left has the symbol a_{i_j}. We map this total configuration C to the string

$$\phi(C) = \textcent a_{i_1} \ldots a_{i_p} q_k a_{i_{p+1}} \ldots a_{i_r} \$$$

Here the $\textcent$ means that all the squares to the left are blank and have not yet been scanned, and the $\$$ means that all the squares to the right are blank and have not yet been scanned. (Note the similarity and differences between this representation of total configurations and the representation of Section 2.2.3.)

We then write productions for the semi-Thue system from the quintuples of the Turing machine (see Section 2.2.2). Suppose that

$$(a_w, q_x, a_y, R, q_z)$$

is a quintuple. For this we take $n + 2$ productions in the system:

$$a_w q_x a_j \longrightarrow a_y a_j q_z$$

for each j, $0 \leq j \leq n$, and

$$a_w q_x \$ \longrightarrow a_y a_0 q_z \$$$

For any quintuple of the form

$$(a_w, q_x, a_y, L, q_z)$$

we take the $n + 2$ productions:

$$a_j a_w q_x \longrightarrow a_j q_z a_y$$

for each j, $0 \leq j \leq n$, and

$$\textcent a_w q_x \longrightarrow \textcent a_0 q_z a_y$$

For any quintuple of the form

$$(a_w, q_x, a_y, C, q_z)$$

("C" means no move on the tape) we take just one production:

$$a_w q_x \longrightarrow a_y q_z$$

The construction of the semi-Thue system S is now complete. That it satisfies the requirements of the theorem should be clear. ∎

THEOREM 6.2.5:   There is no decision procedure to tell whether a given string is transformable into another given string in a given semi-Thue system.

Before beginning the proof, we make an observation. The proof seeks to demonstrate that the halting problem for Turing machines could be solved if we had a decision procedure for the transformation problem for semi-Thue systems. In order to carry through this demonstration, we show how to construct, for any Turing machine T, a semi-Thue system S' such that a decision procedure for the transformation problem for S' would give us a decision procedure for the halting problem for T.

However, we cannot put S' equal to the S of Theorem 6.2.4, as it is. The trouble with S is that there are infinitely many strings of S that correspond to the infinitely many possible halting configurations of T (i.e., all configurations with T in some state q_x scanning a square containing some a_w, where T has no quintuple beginning with a_w, q_x). In the proof this system S will be augmented to form another system, S'.

PROOF: Assume there is a decision procedure for the transformation problem of semi-Thue systems. Let T be a Turing machine, and let S be the semi-Thue system constructed in the proof of Theorem 6.2.4. Take S' to be the semi-Thue system with the same alphabet, whose productions are those of S together with all productions of the form

$$a_j a_w q_x a_k \longrightarrow a_w q_x$$
$$\cancel{c} a_w q_x a_k \longrightarrow \cancel{c} a_w q_x$$
$$a_j a_w q_x \$ \longrightarrow a_w q_x \$$$
$$\cancel{c} a_w q_x \$ \longrightarrow \cancel{c} \$$$

where no quintuple of T begins with a_w, q_x.

Note that by these new productions, we can transform any string representing a halting configuration into the string $\cancel{c}\$$. But we cannot do this in S' to a string representing a nonhalting configuration.

Since all the productions of S are also productions of S', by Theorem 6.2.4 any total configuration C leads to a halting configuration C_h if and only if $\phi(C)$ is transformable to $\phi(C_h)$. It follows that, for any total configuration C, T eventually halts from C if and only if $\phi(C)$ is transformable in S' to $\cancel{c}\$$.

Thus we have shown that the halting problem for Turing machines is reducible to the transformation problem for semi-Thue systems. It follows from Theorem 6.1.3 that there is no decision procedure for the transformation problem of semi-Thue systems. ▮

6.2.5 Semigroups

We now extend the result of the preceding section to show that a problem in abstract algebra is unsolvable.

Definition: A *semigroup* is an algebraic system $(S, *)$ where S is a set of elements and $*$ is an associative operator over S [which means that $x * (y * z) = (x * y) * z$ for all $x, y, z \in S$]. The set S itself is called a semigroup when the operator $*$ is understood. The operator sign $*$ is often omitted, $x * y$ being written as xy. (Occasionally, another operator sign is used such as $+$.)

Thus in any semigroup S, if $x, y \in S$, then $xy \in S$; and for $x, y, z \in S$, $x(yz) = (xy)z$, which is conveniently written as xyz.

The concept of semigroup has a simple definition, and hence has great generality. The concept has wide usage, both in pure and applied mathematics.

Definition: A set of *generators* for a semigroup S is a subset $(a_1, \ldots, a_m)$ of S such that every element of S can be expressed as a finite product of elements from this subset.

For example, the set of all positive integers under multiplication is a semigroup. A set G of generators for this semigroup is the subset consisting of 1 and all the primes. There is no finite set of generators.

Another example is the semigroup $(I, +)$, where I is the set of all integers and $+$ is addition. A set of two semigroup generators suffices here, namely $\{-1, +1\}$.

[Some readers may note that $(I, +)$ is also a group. The concept of group is more specific than the concept of semigroup, requiring an identity element and an inverse for every element. All groups are semigroups, but many important semigroups are not groups, such as the set of positive integers under multiplication.

According to the definition in group theory, $(I, +)$ has a singleton set of generators $\{+1\}$. This set, however, is not a set of generators for $(I, +)$ as a semigroup. The discrepancy is due to the fact that in group theory the operation of taking an inverse is allowed in the process of generation, as well as product. Thus -1 can be generated from $+1$ in the additive group of integers, but not in the additive semigroup of integers.]

Given a semigroup and a set of generators, each element equals a certain product of generators. Such a product requires no parentheses because of the associative law, and can be thought of as a string over the alphabet whose letters are names for the generators. Each semigroup element is represented by one or more strings.

An example of two strings denoting the same element in the multiplicative semigroup of the positive integers is 2 * 3 and 3 * 2 .We thus write 2 * 3 = 3 * 2. By virtue of the fact that this semigroup is commutative, there are many such equalities. A semigroup in which no two distinct strings denote the same element is called *free*.

Definition: A *finitely presented semigroup* is one having a finite set of generators, and a finite set of equations (sometimes called *relations*) in the generators. The list of generators and equations is called the *presentation*. An equation $T_1 = T_2$ (where each T_i is a product of the generators) is true in the semigroup if and only if there is a sequence $P_1, P_2, \ldots, P_n$ (called a *derivation*) such that P_1 is T_1, P_n is T_2, and for each i, $1 \leq i \leq n - 1$, there are products R_1, R_2, R_3, and R_4, where P_i is $R_1 R_2 R_3$, P_{i+1} is $R_1 R_4 R_3$, and $R_2 = R_4$ or $R_4 = R_2$ is one of the equations of the presentation.

Products of generators are often called *words*. The term *word* is synonymous with the term *string*; in this usage, the string is over an alphabet, each character of which denotes a generator. It can be proved (using techniques well known in abstract algebra) that, given a presentation, there is one and only one finitely presented semigroup, up to isomorphism, having that presentation.

For example, let S be the semigroup with the generator set $\{g_1, g_2, g_3\}$ and with the following equations:

$$g_2 g_1 = g_1 g_2$$
$$g_3 g_2 = g_2 g_2 g_3$$
$$g_3 g_1 = g_1$$

We can derive the equation $g_1 g_2 g_2 = g_1 g_2$ as follows:

$$g_1 g_2 g_2 =$$
$$g_2 g_1 g_2 =$$
$$g_2 g_2 g_1 =$$
$$g_2 g_2 g_3 g_1 =$$
$$g_3 g_2 g_1 =$$
$$g_3 g_1 g_2 =$$
$$g_1 g_2$$

6.2.6 An Undecidable Word Problem

Definition: The *word problem for semigroups* is the class of questions: Does a given product of generators equal another given product of generators in a given finitely presented semigroup?

The proof of the equality of two products in a semigroup is similar to the transformation of a string to another string in a semi-Thue system. The difference is that one can go only one way using a production of a semi-Thue system, whereas one can use the equation of a semigroup presentation in both directions. Thus the equation $g_2 g_1 = g_1 g_2$ in the semigroup presentation gives us the power of two productions in a semi-Thue system, namely $g_2 g_1 \longrightarrow g_1 g_2$ and $g_1 g_2 \longrightarrow g_2 g_1$.

A finitely presented semigroup can be regarded as a special case of a semi-Thue system, one in which if W_1 is transformable in one step to W_2, then W_2 is transformable in one step to W_1. Thus the word problem for semigroups is a special case of the transformation problem of semi-Thue systems, which is undecidable by Theorem 6.2.5. We cannot immediately infer from this alone that the word problem for semigroups is undecidable. It is possible that a class of questions has no algorithm but a subclass of that class does have an algorithm. Drawing this inference will require a bit more effort.

THEOREM 6.2.6: The word problem for semigroups is undecidable.

PROOF: Assuming that there is a decision procedure for the word problem for semigroups, we construct a decision procedure to tell whether a given Turing machine T halts for a given input.

From T construct the semi-Thue system as in the proof of Theorem 6.2.4; then replace each arrow by an equality sign. The result is a finitely presented semigroup.

The following lemma shows that the question of the halting of the Turing machine reduces to the question of equality in the semigroup. Since the halting problem for Turing machines is undecidable (Theorem 6.1.3), the proof of Lemma 2 will conclude the proof of Theorem 6.2.6.

LEMMA 2: If W is the string representing a given initial configuration, the equation $W = \rlap{/}{c}\$$ is derivable from the semigroup equations if and only if T halts from that configuration.

PROOF (see Kleene [1952], pp. 383–386): If T halts from the given configuration, then there exists a transformation in the semi-Thue system of W into $\rlap{/}{c}\$$, which constitutes a derivation of $W = \rlap{/}{c}\$$ in the semigroup.

Now assume (for the more difficult part of the proof) that $W = \rlap{/}{c}\$$ has a derivation in the semigroup. Let $W_1 = W_2 = \ldots = W_{s+1}$ be the derivation, where W_1 is W and W_{s+1} is $\text{¢\$}$. We may assume that W_{s+1} is the only occurrence of the string $\text{¢\$}$; otherwise, the derivation could be shortened. The string W_1, since it represents a configuration, begins with ¢, ends with \$, has no other occurrence of ¢ or \$, and has exactly one of the state characters (q_j, for some j). By examining the productions of the semi-Thue system, we see that the same must be true of each of $W_1, \ldots, W_s$, since none of these is $\text{¢\$}$.

For each i, $1 \leq i \leq s$, let us say the ith step is *forward* if W_i is transformable to W_{i+1} in one step by the semi-Thue system; otherwise, say the ith step is *backward*. Note that if the ith step is backward, then W_{i+1} is transformable by the semi-Thue system to W_i in one step.

Now if all s steps are forward, then the sequence $W_1, \ldots, W_{s+1}$ is a transformation in the semi-Thue system and (by the proof of Theorem 6.2.4) the Turing machine halts from W. If not all steps are forward, let the ith step be the last backward step. Now i cannot be s, for one can derive nothing in the semi-Thue system from $\text{¢\$}$. Hence W_{i+1} is transformable in one step in the semi-Thue system into both W_i and W_{i+2} (since the $(i + 1)$st step is forward).

An examination of the construction of the semi-Thue system shows that, since the Turing machine T is deterministic, no string with a single state character is transformable in one step in two distinct ways. Thus W_i is identical to W_{i+2}. It follows that there is a shorter derivation of $W = \text{¢\$}$, namely

$$W_1 = \ldots = W_i = W_{i+3} = \ldots = W_{q+1}$$

which has only $s - 2$ steps.

Therefore, any derivation of $W = \text{¢\$}$ with some backward steps can be shortened. This implies that a derivation of $W = \text{¢\$}$ of shortest length must be such that all its steps are forward. That is, it must correspond to a transformation in the semi-Thue system, proving that T halts from the given configuration. ∎

Et Cetera 6.2.7

We have seen how undecidability results can be proved about formal linguistic systems and about abstract algebraic theories. The proof in each case turns on a precise characterization of the action of a Turing machine in another subject matter.

We should point out that the proofs that we have given are quite easy, compared to other proofs establishing similar results. For example, proving that the word problem for groups is undecidable was far more difficult. The proof (given independently by W. W. Boone and P. S. Novikoff) did not come until 1954, ten years after the relatively easy proof that the word problem for semigroups is undecidable (given independently by Post and A. A. Markov).

(In group theory one has more to work with in proving equations from a given set of basic equations than in semigroup theory, namely, the ability to take inverses. For this reason, the word problem for groups—Are two given distinct products equal in a given finitely presented group?—turns out to be quite different from the word problem for semigroups.)

An unsolvable problem that has turned out to be quite important in computer science is Post's correspondence problem, which is: Given two lists of length k of strings over an alphabet Σ,

$$U_1, U_2, \ldots, U_k$$
$$V_1, V_2, \ldots, V_k$$

does there exist a sequence of positive integers $x_1, x_2, \ldots, x_p, p \geq 1$ and each $x_j \leq k$, such that the string $U_{x_1} U_{x_2} \ldots U_{x_p}$ equals the string $V_{x_1} V_{x_2} \ldots V_{x_p}$? From the unsolvability of this problem many problems about context-free grammars are proved to be unsolvable: for example, the problem of whether the languages of two given context-free grammars are equal. (See, e.g., Chapter XIV of Hopcroft and Ullman [1969].)

In 1900 David Hilbert posed a number of unsolved mathematical problems which he thought especially suitable for mathematical research. The tenth problem in his list was that of finding a decision procedure to tell whether a diophantine equation has a solution. Such an equation is of the form

$$P(x_1, \ldots, x_n) = 0$$

where P is a polynomial in the integer unknowns $x_1, \ldots, x_n$ with integer coefficients.

At the time Hilbert posed this problem, mathematicians did not consider the possibility of proving it unsolvable. Nevertheless, when undecidability results began to appear in the 1930s and early 1940s, many competent people began to suspect that the problem was unsolvable. Much work was done, but it was not until 1972 that the proof of the undecidability of Hilbert's tenth problem was completed by Y. Matiyacevič (see Davis [1973]).

This closes our brief account of unsolvability results. We hope that the reader has gained from it the beginning of an understanding of how such results are proved.

Context-Free Grammars for Formal Languages

7

Although we have used several formal languages in previous chapters, we have presented their syntax informally. In this chapter we introduce a certain kind of formalized grammar, the context-free grammar, for setting forth the syntax of formal languages. (A special form of context-free grammar, namely, the Backus–Naur form, is often used in presenting the syntax of practical programming languages.)

The usefulness of formal grammars is related to the need to have ways of computing with the syntax of languages, in compiling for example. These matters are discussed in Chapter 8; the present chapter simply presents the model and investigates how context-free grammars can be designed for various formal languages. The last chapter will study a special but quite useful kind of context-free grammar, the *regular grammar*.

Thus, the last three chapters of this book will have a somewhat different focus from previous chapters, where the study of algorithms caused us to look at certain formal languages for expressing algorithms. We now study formal grammars, so as to consider algorithms dealing with the syntax of the algorithmic language itself.

AN EXAMPLE AND THE DEFINITION 7.1

In this section we consider a simplified version of the formalism of functional expressions as an example, gradually build a context-free grammar for this language, and at the end give a general definition of the term *context-free grammar*.

7.1.1 The Concept

Recall the formalism of functional expressions as it was introduced in Section 4.1. Let us simplify things by assuming that there are only two function symbols, S and $+$, and only three number variables, x, y, and z. Also for simplicity, let us assume that numerals are given in the binary number system rather than in decimal. We first enumerate all the characters of this simplified formalism: S, $+$, x, y, z, 0, 1, (,), $=$, and the comma.

Recall that the first syntactic category that we introduced for this formalism was the category of *numeral*. In binary, a numeral is either 0 or any string of 0's and 1's beginning with a 1. We introduce the letter N to stand for this syntactic category; this letter will then be part of what will be called the *nonterminal vocabulary* of the context-free grammar.

We also introduce *productions* to generate all the binary numerals. These productions are as follows:

$$
\begin{array}{ll}
(1)\ N \longrightarrow 0 & (5)\ A \longrightarrow 1A \\
(2)\ N \longrightarrow 1 & (6)\ A \longrightarrow 0 \\
(3)\ N \longrightarrow 1A & (7)\ A \longrightarrow 1 \\
(4)\ A \longrightarrow 0A &
\end{array}
$$

Two symbols here that we have not talked about so far are the arrow and the letter A. The arrow means "may be rewritten as" in the process of string generation, which will be explained shortly; productions are sometimes called "rewriting rules." The letter A is another symbol of the nonterminal vocabulary. Unlike the letter N, however, it does not stand for a syntactic category, but is simply an auxiliary symbol.

Numerals are generated by means of these productions from the letter N; that is, beginning with the string that is simply the letter N by itself, we successively copy each string rewriting the nonterminal occurring in that string by means of one of the productions. For example, the numeral 1011 is obtained as follows:

$$N$$

$$1A$$

$$10A$$

$$101A$$

$$1011$$

The productions used were, respectively, (3), (4), (5), and (7). A sequence of strings so obtained is called a *derivation* from N. Since a derivation is usually written in this way, we call each string in the sequence a *line* in the derivation. The numerals are precisely those strings without nonterminals that are the last lines of such derivations. For this reason, the characters of the language are called *terminals*; the set of nonterminals and the set of terminals are disjoint.

A binary numeral that has more than a single digit may not begin with a zero. For example, 01101 cannot be derived from N, since there is no production $N \longrightarrow 0A$. As a matter of fact, this is the reason the nonterminal A is needed in the grammar; if numerals could begin with 0, a simpler set of productions without A would suffice for deriving numerals from N, namely, $N \longrightarrow 0$, $N \longrightarrow 1$, $N \longrightarrow 0N$, and $N \longrightarrow 1N$.

We go on to introduce other nonterminals and other productions to get the other syntactic categories of the formalism. The next is the syntactic category of number variable. Letting V be the nonterminal standing for this category, we need only three simple productions for the simplified formalism:

$$V \longrightarrow x \qquad V \longrightarrow y \qquad V \longrightarrow z$$

We could introduce a nonterminal standing for the syntactic category of function symbol. However, it turns out convenient not to treat this syntactic category in this manner.

It will be recalled that the syntactic category of functional expression was the most difficult one to explain. By forsaking the concept of level, we can now characterize this syntactic category, represented by E, quite simply:

$$E \longrightarrow +(E, E) \qquad E \longrightarrow N$$
$$E \longrightarrow S(E) \qquad E \longrightarrow V$$

With these productions, we can generate all functional expressions in our simplified formalism. For example, the functional expression $+(+(S(x), 11), S(0))$ can be generated as follows:

$$E$$
$$+(E, E)$$
$$+(+(E, E), E)$$
$$+(+(S(E), E), E)$$
$$+(+(S(V), E), E)$$
$$+(+(S(x), E), E)$$
$$+(+(S(x), N), E)$$
$$+(+(S(x), 1A), E)$$
$$+(+(S(x), 11), E)$$
$$+(+(S(x), 11), S(E))$$
$$+(+(S(x), 11), S(N))$$
$$+(+(S(x), 11), S(0))$$

The final syntactic category, *equation*, represented by Q, requires only one production:

$$Q \longrightarrow E = E$$

The equation $10 = S(1)$ is derived as follows:

$$Q$$
$$E = E$$
$$N = E$$
$$1A = E$$
$$10 = E$$
$$10 = S(E)$$
$$10 = S(N)$$
$$10 = S(1)$$

[The equation $10 = S(1)$ is true. With equal ease we could derive the false equation $10 = S(0)$. It is not the function of grammar to distinguish between truth and falsity, which are semantic concepts.]

The last two derivations exhibit a more general feature that previous examples did not have. The second line of each has two nonterminals, only one of which, namely the first, is replaced in the third line. We must restate the conditions under which one line follows from another in a derivation: A string is obtained from another string if any one occurrence of a nonterminal is rewritten according to one of the productions and everything else remains the same.

7.1.2 Derivations and Derivation Trees

The foregoing derivation from E of the functional expression $+(+(S(x), 11), S(0))$ is rather clumsy to write out and difficult to read. The reason is that when any nonterminal is rewritten by one of the productions the remainder of the line must be repeated.

We can avoid this useless repetition by adopting a new style: We indicate how each nonterminal is rewritten by a sequence of lines connecting the nonterminal to the characters that replace it; then the remainder of the line need not be repeated. In so doing we have the beginning of what we shall call a *derivation tree* in place of a derivation. For example, consider Fig. 7.1.1, which contains the first four lines of a derivation and the corresponding start of a derivation tree.

Some terminology is needed for discussing such trees. The place where each nonterminal or terminal character is written is a *node*; the character is the *label*

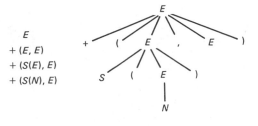

Figure 7.1.1

of the node. The lines connecting nodes are edges. The top node is the *root*, and the nodes that are not connected by edges beneath are *leaves*. (These trees are a generalization of the binary trees of Section AV.3. The terms described informally here will be defined formally in Section 7.1.4.)

The root of the tree of Fig. 7.1.1 corresponds to the first line of the derivation, *E*. The fourth line can be read by reading the leaves of the tree from left to right (which may take some effort, depending on how the tree is drawn). A derivation and corresponding derivation tree for the string $+(S(101), +(x, 1))$ is given in Fig. 7.1.2.

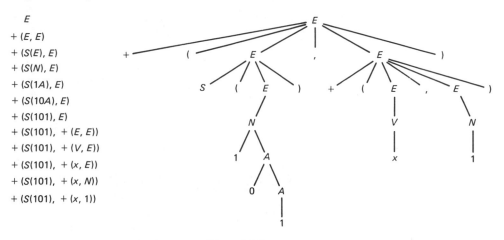

Figure 7.1.2

To verify that a tree is a derivation tree, the following must be verified for every nonleaf node: if Q is the label of that node and $R_1, R_2, \ldots, R_p$ are the labels of the nodes beneath, in order from left to right, then $Q \to R_1 R_2 \ldots R_p$ must be a production of the grammar. For example, if Fig. 7.1.3 is part of a derivation tree, then $Q \to R_1 R_2 R_3 R_4$ must be a production of the grammar.

It will often be convenient to use derivation trees rather than derivations. It should be noted that, for every derivation, a derivation tree is determined. Usually only one derivation tree for a string can be obtained from a derivation

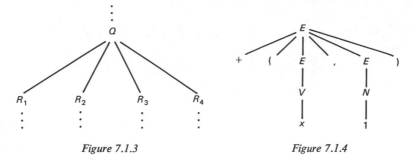

Figure 7.1.3   *Figure 7.1.4*

of that string. However, there are generally several derivations that correspond to a single derivation tree. For when a line has two or more nonterminals in it, the tree tells exactly how each of these is to be rewritten, but it does not specify in what order the various nonterminals are rewritten. From the derivation tree of Fig. 7.1.4, the first two lines of the derivation are determined:

$$E$$
$$+(E, E)$$

but the third line can be either $+(V, E)$ or $+(E, N)$. Each of these can be followed by either of two lines, and so on, so that several derivations are possible (in this case, six).

When several derivations are possible from a single derivation tree, for many purposes the manner in which the derivations differ from one another is not significant. Thus, for many purposes, derivation trees will be more interesting to us.

7.1.3 *Nonterminals Versus Syntactic Categories*

In constructing the context-free grammar for the simplified formalism of functional expressions, we have adopted the procedure of introducing nonterminals for some of the syntactic categories, and then writing productions that could generate strings in each of them. In general, the productions for a syntactic category involve nonterminals standing for other syntactic categories: For example, the productions for Q (equation) involve E (functional expression); and those for E involve N and V (numeral and variable).

As we have seen, in the process of using the syntactic categories to form a context-free grammar for a language, we may end up with a set of nonterminals that does not correspond in a one-to-one manner with the syntactic categories. In fact, we shall find ourselves no longer concerned with the various syntactic categories of a language. Rather we shall focus on one of the syntactic categories as the most important, or chief category, select a nonterminal for it, and then choose other nonterminals pragmatically, whether or not these correspond to syntactic categories.

In the simplified formalism of functional expressions, we take the syntactic category of equation as the chief category of the grammar. Thus we attach a singular importance to the nonterminal symbol Q, since derivations from Q give us the set of equations. We shall let all derivations begin with Q, which will be called the *start symbol* of the grammar. (In most of this chapter and the chapters beyond, we shall use S as the start symbol, following a well-established custom. We cannot do that here, of course, since the letter S has another usage.)

We shall henceforth use the term "derivation" to mean derivation from the start symbol unless some other nonterminal is specifically mentioned. Similarly, "derivation tree" will mean a derivation tree whose root has the start symbol as a label, unless another label is expressly indicated for the root of the tree.

Thus we have simplified our problem of constructing a grammar for a language to the problem of specifying the most important of its syntactic categories. Indeed, this brings us to a second meaning for the word "language."

Definition: A *language* (in the second sense) is a set of strings over some finite character set.

The first sense of the term "language" is the informal sense that has been used in this book up to now, and in Appendix III; no explicit definition was ever given. The biggest difference between the two senses is that the first sense includes semantics (and possibly pragmatics—see Section A.III.5), whereas the second sense includes only syntax.

It can be argued that the second sense of the term "language" does embrace all the essential syntactic considerations of what, all along, we have been calling a "language." If, for example, we know exactly which strings are equations, we know all we need to know about the syntax of the formalism of functional expressions. Perhaps this is also true of the written form of natural languages: If we know exactly which strings of characters are English sentences (taking *sentence* as the chief category), we know all we need to know about the syntax of the written English language. Similarly, the syntax of a programming language is characterized completely by its set of programs.

We shall not debate this contention here, with regard to formal languages or natural languages. We shall simply acknowledge a second meaning for the word "language," taking note of the fact that this second meaning is well entrenched in much of the technical literature.

The Definition 7.1.4

It is helpful to take a summary look at the grammar we have constructed for the simplified formalism of functional expressions:

1. The terminal alphabet: $S, +, x, y, z, 0, 1, (,), =$ and the comma.
2. The nonterminal alphabet: $N, A, V, E,$ and Q.
3. The start symbol: Q.

4. The productions:

$$
\begin{array}{ll}
N \longrightarrow 0 & V \longrightarrow y \\
N \longrightarrow 1 & V \longrightarrow z \\
N \longrightarrow 1A & E \longrightarrow +(E, E) \\
A \longrightarrow 0A & E \longrightarrow S(E) \\
A \longrightarrow 1A & E \longrightarrow N \\
A \longrightarrow 0 & E \longrightarrow V \\
A \longrightarrow 1 & Q \longrightarrow E = E \\
V \longrightarrow x &
\end{array}
$$

We can now formulate the concept in general terms.

Definition: A *context-free grammar* consists of (1) a set of characters known as the *terminal alphabet*; (2) a set of characters disjoint from the first, known as the *nonterminal alphabet*; (3) a designated character from the second set, known as the *start symbol*; and (4) a set of *productions*, each of which must consist of a nonterminal followed by an arrow pointing rightward followed by a string of characters from the *total alphabet* (i.e., the union of the terminal and nonterminal alphabets).

The notion of *string*, discussed in Section AIII.2, is assumed in this definition. Note that a single character is a string whose length is one. The string of zero length is called the *null string* and is symbolized by the lowercase Greek lambda.

A production of a context-free grammar may have lambda as its right side, for example,

$$
A \longrightarrow \lambda
$$

If a line is rewritten according to this production, the A is not really rewritten at all, but simply deleted. For the symbol λ is not a character from the terminal or nonterminal alphabet, but a special symbol denoting the null string. Such productions will be called lambda productions, and will prove quite useful in context-free grammars when they are introduced in Sections 7.4 and 7.5. (Many books use the lowercase Greek epsilon for the null string. That symbol denotes set membership in this book.)

We now recapitulate definitions given informally in Sections 7.1.1 to 7.1.3.

Definition: A *derivation* in a context-free grammar is a finite sequence of strings, the first of which is the start symbol, and in which each subsequent string is obtained by copying the preceding string, rewriting one occurrence of a nonterminal according to one of the productions. The last string of a derivation is called the *derived string* of the derivation. Each string in the sequence is called a *line* (after the manner of listing the strings in the derivation).

(In many books, a line of a derivation is called a "sentential form.")

In order to give a clear definition of the term *derivation tree*, we must begin by defining a concept that is a generalization of *binary tree* (Section AV.3).

Recursive Definition of *rooted tree*: A single node (with no edges) is a *rooted tree*, of which the node is both *root* and *leaf*. For $m \geq 1$, if $T_1, \ldots, T_m$ are rooted trees, no two of which have parts in common, the result of taking a new node N and connecting it by m edges to the roots of $T_1, \ldots, T_m$, respectively, is a *rooted tree*. The *root* of the new tree is N, and its *leaves* are the leaves of $T_1, \ldots, T_m$. (Nothing is a *rooted tree* unless its being so follows from this definition.)

Definition: A *derivation tree* in a context-free grammar is a rooted tree each of whose nodes is labeled with a character from the total alphabet so that (1) the root has the start symbol as a label; and (2) for each node N of the tree, if N is connected by edges to nodes below, the label of N is a nonterminal, say B, and the labels of the nodes below spell out, left to right, the right side of a production whose left side is B. A node that is not connected by an edge to any node below is called a *leaf* of the tree. The string spelled out by the labels of the leaves in order, from left to right, is the *derived string* of the tree; the latter is a derivation tree *of* this string. (A slight modification of this definition, for lambda productions, will be made implicitly in Section 7.4.1.)

In most derivation trees that we shall consider, the leaves are labeled with terminal characters. Note that *left* and *right* play an important role in the definition.

In the example of the grammar for the simplified formalism of functional expressions, note that the terminal alphabet is the set of characters that may occur in the formalism itself. The nonterminal symbols, on the other hand, are not part of this formalism, although they play an important structural role in the grammar for the formalism. This distinction will hold for all context-free grammars.

Definition: The *language* of a context-free grammar is the set of all strings over the terminal alphabet that are derivable from the start symbol. If G is a context-free grammar, then we denote by L(G) the language of G. Two grammars are *equivalent* if they have the same language.

Further Discussion 7.1.5

Context-free grammars are only one of several varieties of formal grammars, but they appear to be the best for formal languages. Formal grammars are an innovation more recent than formal languages. In the middle 1950s, Noam

Chomsky sought to investigate some mathematically precise models for grammars for natural languages. His main concern was to advance the study of the structural aspect of natural languages. He put forth for discussion (see Chomsky [1956]) three models of grammars: *finite-state grammars, phrase-structure grammars*, and *transformational grammars*. We shall be in a better position to explain finite-state grammars in Chapter 9. A transformational grammar for, say, the English language is a grammar based on rules for rewriting a sentence either as a single sentence that is in some way simpler, or as several sentences that are each simpler. Many linguists (Chomsky included) believe that transformational grammars offer the most in the way of understanding of natural languages. However, such grammars seem to have little or no utility in connection with formal languages, and will not be mentioned again in this book, even though they do have some significance in computer science. In studying formal languages, and formal grammars for them, we shall find ourselves departing from the most fruitful aspects of the study of natural languages and their grammars. (For further clarification, the early book Chomsky [1957] is helpful.)

Chomsky divided his second class, the class of phrase-structure grammars, into the context-free grammars and the context-sensitive grammars. His context-free grammars were essentially as we have defined them, and were seen to be inadequate for natural languages. The term *context-free* has to do with the kind of production allowed in the grammar: The nonterminal that forms the left side of a context-free production can be rewritten as the right side of the production in any string in which the nonterminal occurs, regardless of context. A *context-sensitive production* is one in which that kind of replacement could be made only if the context were as specified, and in which the length of the right side is no shorter than the length of the left side (the significance of this last condition, that of being noncontracting, is discussed in Section 7.4.2). An example of a context-sensitive production might be

$$bBQ \longrightarrow bddBcQ$$

This would mean that B can be rewritten as $ddBc$, but only if there is a b immediately to the left and a Q immediately to the right. A grammar, all of whose productions are either context-free or context-sensitive, and none of whose productions is a lambda production (see Section 7.4.1), is known as a *context-sensitive grammar*.

The term "context-free language" is used to mean the language of a context-free grammar. This term sometimes causes confusion, since it suggests a language in which the meaning of any entity in the language is independent of context. It is perfectly possible for the syntax of a language to be given by a context-free grammar, and yet for the semantics of the language to be such that the meaning of some things depend on context. An example is the *name* in the GOTO language of Chapter 3. Whether the name is a variable or label depends on the context; but the GOTO language has a context-free grammar, as will be shown in Section 7.2.

The manner of listing the productions of a context-free grammar given in this section is not always suitable. It is somewhat bothersome, in some grammars, to have to write all the separate productions with the same left side, repeating the nonterminal and the arrow so many times. Thus instead of writing the four productions

$$A \longrightarrow 0A$$
$$A \longrightarrow 1A$$
$$A \longrightarrow 0$$
$$A \longrightarrow 1$$

we shall on most occasions write the equivalent in one line:

$$A \longrightarrow 0A \,|\, 1A \,|\, 0 \,|\, 1$$

It should be clear that the vertical line here, like the arrow, is not part of the language but only part of the grammar. Generally, this device will enable us to present grammars more succinctly, especially grammars with large numbers of productions. The set of productions for the grammar for the simplified formalism of functional expressions is thus made more concise:

$$Q \longrightarrow E = E$$
$$N \longrightarrow 0 \,|\, 1 \,|\, 1A$$
$$A \longrightarrow 0A \,|\, 1A \,|\, 0 \,|\, 1$$
$$V \longrightarrow x \,|\, y \,|\, z$$
$$E \longrightarrow +(E, E) \,|\, S(E) \,|\, N \,|\, V$$

This form of presentation is similar to Backus–Naur form, named after John Backus and Peter Naur, who invented it to describe ALGOL 60.

GRAMMARS FOR SOME 7.2
SIGNIFICANT LANGUAGES

In this section we give context-free grammars for some of the formal languages in earlier chapters, and for some other meaningful formal languages. We shall not present a grammar for a practical programming language; it would be several pages long, which does not seem worthwhile for our purposes (see Cleaveland and Uzgalis [1977]).

7.2.1 The Full Formalism of Functional Expressions

We simplified this formalism in the preceding section for the sake of getting a simple context-free grammar. It is interesting at this point to see what a grammar for the full formalism looks like. However, in view of our desire for a language of strings (see Section AIII.2), there is one aspect of the formalism that creates an obstacle; the subscripts add a sort of two dimensionality to the language, which is therefore not a language of true strings.

One way to handle this problem is to bring all subscripted indices up to the line, writing

$$f\,101(x20, y3) = 41$$

rather than

$$f_{101}(x_{20}, y_3) = 41$$

Since the subscripting of indices is not necessary to remove ambiguities, this solution is acceptable and we use it here. Note, however, that we have lost something in visual clarity in giving up subscripts. [An alternative approach would be to add corners $\langle$ and $\rangle$ to the alphabet and enclose each index in corners. The sample equation would then become

$$f\langle 101 \rangle (x\langle 20 \rangle, y\langle 3 \rangle) = 41.]$$

The grammar that we present here must be a fixed grammar, with a fixed alphabet and a fixed set of productions. We thus encounter another difficulty in the fact that the formalism of functional expressions is growing steadily with the acquisition of new function constants. Some of these are special symbols such as $+$, $*$, and so on, whereas others are composed from capital letters from the Roman alphabet. Every time a new function constant is added, a new production must be added to the grammar, and if the function constant is a new special symbol, it must be added to the terminal alphabet.

Thus for our present purpose we shall have to "freeze" the formalism to a fixed and finite set of functions. Arbitrarily, we shall take it as it was at the end of Section 4.2; functions introduced in the exercises of that section, or in the text of later sections, are not included. We shall assume that this frozen formalism has two-argument, three-argument, and four-argument $+$, $*$, MAX. and MIN, but does not have any of these functions for five or more arguments. For convenience, we assume that all capital Roman letters are permanently part of the terminal alphabet.

1. Terminals: 0, 1, 2, 3, 4, 5, 6, 7, 8, 9, x, y, z, f, g, h, all Roman capital letters, (,), the comma, $+$, $*$, $\uparrow$, $\div$, $=$. (Thus there are 50 terminals.)

2. Nonterminals: δ, υ, α, β, η, γ, and θ.

3. The start symbol θ.

4. The productions

$$v \longrightarrow 0\,|\,\delta\,|\,\delta\alpha$$

$$\delta \longrightarrow 1\,|\,2\,|\,3\,|\,4\,|\,5\,|\,6\,|\,7\,|\,8\,|\,9$$

$$\alpha \longrightarrow 0\alpha\,|\,\delta\alpha\,|\,0\,|\,\delta$$

$$\beta \longrightarrow x\,|\,y\,|\,z\,|\,xv\,|\,yv\,|\,zv$$

$$\eta \longrightarrow \beta\,|\,v\,|\,f(\gamma)\,|\,g(\gamma)\,|\,h(\gamma)\,|\,fv(\gamma)\,|\,gv(\gamma)\,|\,hv(\gamma)$$

$$\cdot\eta \longrightarrow S(\eta)\,|\,+(\eta, \eta)\,|\,+(\eta, \eta, \eta)\,|\,+(\eta, \eta, \eta, \eta)$$

$$\eta \longrightarrow *(\eta, \eta)\,|\,*(\eta, \eta, \eta,)\,|\,*(\eta, \eta, \eta, \eta)$$

$$\eta \longrightarrow \uparrow(\eta, \eta)\,|\,P(\eta)\,|\,\dot{-}(\eta, \eta)\,|\,\text{ABD}(\eta, \eta)\,|\,Z(\eta)$$

$$\eta \longrightarrow \text{MAX}(\eta, \eta)\,|\,\text{MAX}(\eta, \eta, \eta)\,|\,\text{MAX}(\eta, \eta, \eta, \eta)$$

$$\eta \longrightarrow \text{MIN}(\eta, \eta)\,|\,\text{MIN}(\eta, \eta, \eta)\,|\,\text{MIN}(\eta, \eta, \eta, \eta)$$

$$\eta \longrightarrow \text{SG}(\eta)\,|\,\text{ISG}(\eta)\,|\,\text{REM}(\eta, \eta)\,|\,\text{QU}(\eta, \eta)$$

$$\eta \longrightarrow \text{GT}(\eta, \eta)\,|\,\text{GE}(\eta, \eta)\,|\,\text{EQ}(\eta, \eta)$$

$$\gamma \longrightarrow \eta, \gamma\,|\,\eta$$

$$\theta \longrightarrow \eta = \eta$$

The syntactic category of numeral is represented by v (with the aid of δ and α). The syntactic categories of number variable, functional expression and equation are represented by β, η, and θ, respectively. There are many productions for η, because each new definition of a functional constant requires a new production.

Note that γ generates the set of all finite sequences of functional expressions, separating the terms of each sequence by commas. We could modify this grammar so that $+$, $*$, MAX, and MIN may have any number of arguments greater than or equal to two. We would simply replace the 12 productions for these four functions by the four productions $\eta \rightarrow +(\eta, \gamma)\,|\,*(\eta, \gamma)\,|\,\text{MAX}(\eta, \gamma)\,|$ MIN(η, γ). However, although this revision would be in accord with the concept of context-free grammar, it would generate a language that would be contrary to the spirit of the formalism of functional expressions as we conceived it in Chapter 4, since it would imply infinitely many acts of definition.

This grammar serves only to set forth which strings of characters are equations. It is not concerned with the restrictions on explicit definitions and primitive recursions, even though these restrictions were expressed syntactically in Chapter 4. Thus a grammar may not embody all the interesting syntactic considerations of a language, only those necessary to make clear which strings are in its most important syntactic category (i.e., in the "language," in the second sense of that term defined in Section 7.1.3).

This is a large grammar. Fortunately, the problems of interest to us in our work with formal grammars allow us to consider examples that are much simpler.

7.2.2 PTG&E

This language is from Section AIII.3. Its grammar is as follows:

1. Terminals: $/, +, *, (,), >, =$.
2. Nonterminals: N, E, S.
3. Start symbol: S.
4. Productions:

$$N \longrightarrow /N\,|\,/$$
$$E \longrightarrow (E) + (E)\,|\,(E)*(E)\,|\,N$$
$$S \longrightarrow E = E\,|\,E > E$$

Each of the nonterminals represents a syntactic category: N, *numeral*; E, *expression*; S, *sentence*. But the syntactic categories of *operator* and *relation* have no nonterminals.

7.2.3 The GOTO Language

Our context-free grammar is fairly straightforward. We shall let v represent *numeral*, β *name*, γ *unlabeled command*, μ *labeled* command, and π *program*. δ, α, ζ, and η are auxiliary nonterminals used with v and β. Thus each of the five syntactic categories of the language as used in Chapter 3 is represented by a nonterminal, and there are four auxiliary nonterminals.

1. Terminals: All the capital letters of the Roman alphabet, all the decimal digits, colon, semicolon, equal sign, left parenthesis, and right parenthesis.
2. Nonterminals: $\delta, v, \alpha, \beta, \zeta, \eta, \gamma, \mu, \pi$.
3. Start symbol: π.
4. The productions are the productions for δ, v, and α as given in the formal grammar for the full formalism of functional expressions (Section 7.2.1), and the following. To avoid tedium, we use here an ellipsis to indicate a production for each letter of the alphabet.

$$\zeta \longrightarrow A\,|\ldots|\,Z$$
$$\beta \longrightarrow \zeta\,|\,\zeta\eta$$
$$\eta \longrightarrow 0\eta\,|\,\delta\eta\,|\,\zeta\eta\,|\,0\,|\,\delta\,|\,\zeta$$
$$\gamma \longrightarrow \beta := \beta\,|\,\beta := v\,|\,\text{INCR}(\beta)\,|\,\text{DECR}(\beta)$$
$$\gamma \longrightarrow \text{GOTO } \beta\,|\,\text{IF } \beta = 0 \text{ GOTO } \beta\,|\,\text{HALT}$$
$$\mu \longrightarrow \beta : \gamma$$
$$\pi \longrightarrow \gamma\,|\,\mu\,|\,\gamma\,; \pi\,|\,\mu\,; \pi$$

It should be noted that the programs derived in this grammar are not necessarily *proper programs* in the sense of Section 3.2.2. For example, the following is in the language of the grammar:

$$Z: \text{GOTO } Z; \; Z: \text{DECR(X)}$$

It would seem to be desirable to have a context-free grammar whose language is the set of all proper programs. It is possible to prove, however, using advanced theory, that there is no such context-free grammar, even though proper programs were characterized syntactically in Section 3.2.2.

For the details of how context-free grammars are used in practical programming-language definitions (beyond the scope of this text) see, for example, Chapter 2 of Cleaveland and Uzgalis [1977]. For techniques going beyond context-free grammars, see the later (and more difficult) chapters of that book.

Propositional Calculus with Parentheses 7.2.4

The logic of propositions is a simple part of logic, and offers us the advantage of a rather simple syntax. We shall in this and the next two subsections give grammars for three versions of the propositional calculus. In each of the three grammars only three operators will be included: *and*, *or*, and *not*, represented by & (ampersand), $\lor$ (wedge), and $\sim$ (tilde), respectively. Propositional variables will be $p, q, r, p', q', r', p'', q'', r''$, and so on. Thus there is provision for infinitely many variables using only the four symbols $p, q, r,$ and $'$.

The first version uses *infix* notation (binary operators are between their operands). Unambiguity is assured by using parentheses to group any strings that are joined by an operator. Our grammar G-IN is then as follows:

1. Terminals: &, $\lor$, $\sim$, $p, q, r,$ $',$ (,).
2. Nonterminals: S, A.
3. Start symbol: S.
4. Productions:

$$S \longrightarrow (S)\&(S) \,|\, (S)\lor(S) \,|\, \sim(S) \,|\, A$$
$$A \longrightarrow A' \,|\, p \,|\, q \,|\, r$$

We can think of this formal language as having two syntactic categories, variable and formula (sometimes called "well-formed formula," or "wff"). These correspond exactly to the nonterminals A and S, respectively. All variables are formulas, as indicated by the production $S \longrightarrow A$.

The language of G-IN is the set of all fully parenthesized propositional formulas made up from "and," "or," and "not." Some examples are as follows, derivations or derivations trees for which are easily constructed:

$$((p')\&(p))\lor(r'')$$

$$\sim((p)\lor(q'))$$

$$r''''''$$

In practice, when we use the propositional calculus, we do not write all the parentheses, and we omit the ampersand sign for "and." As a matter of fact, there is an orderly convention regulating the omission of parentheses, which tells clearly how they could be restored to get a fully parenthesized formula. The first convention is that in a conjunction of three or more conjuncts the grouping is from the left; similarly for disjunction. Thus the following formulas on the left are converted into the fully parenthesized formulas on the right:

$$pqr \qquad\qquad ((p)\&(q))\&(r)$$

$$p\lor q\lor r \qquad\qquad ((p)\lor(q))\lor(r)$$

Second, when conjunction, disjunction, and negation or any two of these come together without parentheses, parentheses for negation are put in first, then parentheses for conjunction, then parentheses for disjunction. So, for example, parentheses are replaced as follows:

$$\sim pq \qquad\qquad (\sim(p))\&(q)$$

$$p\lor qr \qquad\qquad (p)\lor((q)\&(r))$$

$$\sim p\lor r \qquad\qquad (\sim(p))\lor(r)$$

To give some more examples:

$$\sim p\sim q' \qquad\qquad (\sim(p))\&(\sim(q'))$$

$$\sim(p'\sim q) \qquad\qquad \sim((p')\&(\sim(q)))$$

$$\sim(pp')\lor\sim qq' \qquad\qquad (\sim((p)\&(p')))\lor((\sim(q))\&(q'))$$

$$\sim\sim p \qquad\qquad \sim(\sim(p))$$

$$\sim(\sim p\lor q) \qquad\qquad \sim((\sim(p))\lor(q))$$

$$\sim\sim p\lor q \qquad\qquad (\sim(\sim(p)))\lor(q)$$

Given these firm conventions, we can analyze the language of partially parenthesized propositional calculus in a formal manner, by bringing in some new syntactic categories: conjunction (C), disjunction (D), and negation (N). A *negation* is any well-formed formula beginning with $\sim$. A *conjunction* is a formula consisting of two or more formulas concatenated (which we can think of as joined by ampersand signs which are then deleted). And a *disjunction* is a formula consisting of two or more formulas joined by wedges. We shall use C, D, N as nonterminals in the grammar.

A *conjunct* or *disjunct* is any one of the formulas joined in a conjunction or disjunction, respectively. Let K and J be nonterminals standing for conjunct and disjunct, respectively. The grammar will have productions such that the set of all strings derivable from K is the set of formulas that could be conjuncts, and from J the set of strings that could be disjuncts.

The context-free grammar G-PP for the partially parenthesized propositional calculus is thus:

1. Terminal symbols: $\lor$, $\sim$, $p, q, r,$ ', (,).
2. Nonterminals: S, A, N, C, K, D, J.
3. Start symbol: S.
4. Productions:

$$S \longrightarrow A \mid N \mid C \mid D$$
$$A \longrightarrow A' \mid p \mid q \mid r$$
$$N \longrightarrow \sim N \mid \sim A \mid \sim(C) \mid \sim(D) \quad \text{negation}$$
$$C \longrightarrow CK \mid KK \quad \text{conjunction}$$
$$K \longrightarrow A \mid N \mid (D) \quad \text{conjunct expression}$$
$$D \longrightarrow D\lor J \mid J\lor J \quad \text{disjunction}$$
$$J \longrightarrow C \mid N \mid A \quad \text{disjunct exp}$$

Parenthesis-Free Propositional Calculus 7.2.5

Some things always surprise people when they first hear about them. Such is the fact that the propositional calculus (and other similar languages) can be rendered unambiguously without using parentheses at all. How is this possible? How is it possible to write $(p\lor q)r$ to distinguish it from $p\lor(qr)$ without using parentheses? The discovery was made by the Polish logician Jan Lukaciewicz in the 1920s that by placing each operator sign in front of its two arguments instead of between them, parentheses are not needed to avoid ambiguity.

If we write $\&pq$ instead of $p\&q$, and $\lor pq$ instead of $p\lor q$, we are using what is called "prefix notation" instead of what is called "infix notation." Then $(p\lor q)r$, which is really $(p\lor q)\&r$, is rendered as $\&\lor pqr$. And $p\lor qr$, which is really $p\lor(q\&r)$, is rendered as $\lor p\&qr$.

In Section 8.4 we prove that formulas in prefix notation are unambiguous. Here we offer a sample demonstration of how parentheses can be restored, which will suggest they can be restored in only one way. For example, suppose that we have the formula

$$\&\lor\&\lor pqr\&pqr$$

Looking at the last (i.e., rightmost) ampersand, we ask: What are its two arguments? They must be the p and the q immediately following. Similarly, the second wedge must have the p and the q immediately following it as its arguments. Putting in parentheses to indicate what we have decided so far, we get

$$\& \vee \&(\vee pq)r(\&pq)r$$

The second ampersand must have the parenthesized expression and the r immediately following it as its arguments. We thus get

$$\& \vee (\&(\vee pq)r)(\&pq)r$$

The next observation is that the remaining wedge must have the two outermost parenthesized expressions as its arguments:

$$\&(\vee (\&(\vee pq)r)(\&pq))r$$

We then see exactly what the arguments are for the remaining ampersand. This formula is translated into the partially parenthesized propositional calculus and fully parenthesized propositional calculus, respectively, as follows:

$$((p\vee q)r \vee pq)r$$

$$((((p)\vee(q))\&(r))\vee((p)\&(q)))\&(r)$$

To give another example, $\sim \&p''\sim q$ is translated into $\sim(p''\sim q)$ and $\sim((p'')\&(\sim(q)))$.

In the general case, we start with the rightmost operator, and place parentheses around it and its one or two arguments, which must be one or two variables immediately following it. We proceed from right to left. Each time we select the rightmost operator that has not yet been treated, find its one or two arguments (which are uniquely determined) and place parentheses around the operator and the one or two arguments.

Once we get used to this notation, we get to be able to see the grouping without putting in the parentheses, at least in modest-sized formulas.

A context-free grammar G-PRE for the propositional calculus in prefix notation is easy to give:

1. Terminals: $\&$, $\vee$, $\sim$, $p, q, r,\ '$.
2. Nonterminals: S, A.
3. Start symbol: S.
4. Productions:

$$S \longrightarrow \&SS\,|\vee SS\,|\sim S\,|A$$

$$A \longrightarrow A'\,|\,p\,|\,q\,|\,r$$

Two sample derivation trees in G-PRE are shown in Fig. 7.2.1, for $\& \vee \& \vee pqr\&pqr$ and $\sim \&p''\sim q$.

There is another version of parenthesis-free notation, which uses suffix notation rather than prefix notation. Writing all the operators after their argu-

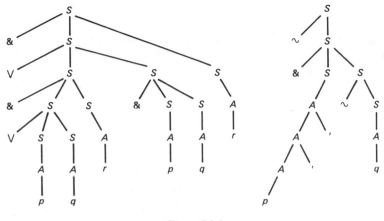

Figure 7.2.1

ments serves just as well as prefix notation for the purpose of avoiding ambiguities. *p*&*q* is rendered as *pq*&, *p*∨*q* is rendered as *pq*∨, and ∼*p* is rendered as
p∼. The formulas *pq*∨*r*&*pq*&∨*r*& and *p″q*∼&∼ in this notation are equivalent to the two formulas discussed above [i.e., ((*p*∨*q*)*r*∨*pq*)*r* and ∼(*p″*∼*q*) in
partially parenthesized form]. If strings are processed from left to right, then
suffix notation has a computational advantage over prefix notation, which will
be explained in Chapter 8.

The grammar (G-SUF) for parenthesis-free propositional calculus in suffix
notation is given as follows:

$$S \longrightarrow SS\& \,|\, SS\lor \,|\, S\sim \,|\, A$$
$$A \longrightarrow A' \,|\, p \,|\, q \,|\, r$$

Derivation trees for the formulas mentioned are given in Fig. 7.2.2.

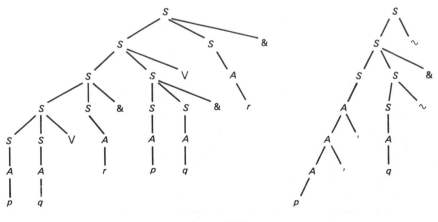

Figure 7.2.2

7.2.6 Exercises

Except for Exercise 1, these are all exercises for designing context-free grammars for significant languages and are *more difficult* than most of the exercises for designing grammars at the end of Section 7.3.

1. Construct derivation trees for the following strings in G-PP (Section 7.2.4);

$$\sim \sim p$$

$$\sim p \sim q'$$

$$\sim (pp') \vee \sim qq'$$

2. Write a context-free grammar for logical expressions in the arrow function $\downarrow$, in which variables are p, q, r, and these followed by primes, and in which both parentheses and square brackets are used for grouping. The rule is that parentheses are always used around an expression E when E is combined with another expression, unless E begins and ends with parentheses, in which case brackets are used, or unless E is a variable, in which case neither parentheses nor brackets are used. Two examples of such logical expressions are:

$$[(p \downarrow (p \downarrow (q \downarrow r))) \downarrow (r \downarrow (p \downarrow p))] \downarrow q$$

$$([(p \downarrow q) \downarrow (p \downarrow p')] \downarrow [(p \downarrow p') \downarrow (r \downarrow p')]) \downarrow q$$

(The logical expression $p \downarrow q$ means "neither p nor q," although this piece of semantic information is not needed for the exercise.)

3. Write a context-free grammar whose language is the set of well-formed formulas (wffs) of the following system of the predicate calculus. Propositional variables are p, q, r, and these followed by primes. Individual variables are x, y, z, and these followed by primes. Predicate variables are F, G, H, and these followed by primes. The wffs are as follows: (1) a propositional variable standing alone is a wff; (2) a predicate variable followed by open parenthesis followed by one or more individual variables, separated by commas if there are more than one, followed by close parenthesis is a wff; (3) if Γ is wff, then $\sim \Gamma$ is a wff; (4) if Γ_1 and Γ_2 are wffs, then $[\Gamma_1 \supset \Gamma_2]$ is a wff; and (5) if Γ is a wff and Δ is an individual variable, then $(\forall \Delta)\Gamma$ is a wff. An example of a wff is

$$[(\forall x)[p \supset F(x)] \supset (\forall y) \sim (\forall z) \sim [\sim F(y) \supset H(y, z)]]$$

(The style is that of Church [1956].)

4. Write a context-free grammar whose language is the set of all dates for the years 1900 through 1999, given in the form: October 24, 1905 (*Note:* There was no February 29 in 1900, but there was in 1904 and, after that, every 4 years through 1996.)

5. Write a context-free grammar for the polynomials in x of degree less than or equal to two with integral coefficients (e.g., $-16x^2 + x + 9, 30x^2 + 7, 17x^2 - 4x$, $8x, -7, 10, 0$). (*Note:* Although 0 is a polynomial, the numeral 0 does not appear in any other polynomial. A coefficient of 1 is always suppressed, as is an initial plus sign. The powers of x must occur in descending order, each power occurring at most once. Render x^2 as $x \uparrow 2 \uparrow$.)

6. Write a context-free grammar whose language is the set of all bubble equations, to be defined as the equations of the following formalism. A variable is either x, y, or z, or else one of these followed by any number of primes. A *bubble expression* is defined as follows: (1) a variable is a bubble expression; (2) If Γ_1, Γ_2 are bubble expressions, then $(\Gamma_1 \circ \Gamma_2)$ is a bubble expression. A bubble equation is defined as a string consisting of a bubble expression with its outer parentheses, if any, deleted, followed by the equal sign $=$, followed by a bubble expression with its outer parentheses, if any, deleted. Two sample bubble equations:

$$(x \circ y) \circ z = (x \circ x) \circ (y \circ y)$$

$$x = (z \circ (z \circ z)) \circ z$$

7. Write a context-free grammar for the set of strings that are assignment statements of FORTRAN beginning with "X =", in which no functions (such as "SQRT") occur. Disregard any length restrictions on such statements. Do not include the blank space in the alphabet of characters, and disregard card-column restrictions. (*Suggestion:* Consult a programming manual.)

8. Formulate a problem similar to Exercise 7 for some other high-level programming language and solve it (with a suitable programming manual).

GRAMMARS FOR GIVEN SETS 7.3 OF STRINGS

We have seen that context-free grammars for important languages get quite large. For this reason, we shall in most of this book confine ourselves to problems of considering context-free grammars for sets of strings that are not themselves significant formal languages. Designing grammars for such sets can be quite challenging, as we shall see in this section.

Subgrammars as Subgoals 7.3.1

An example of a subgoal was the design in Section 7.1.1 of a set of productions for generating numerals in the simplified formalism of functional expressions. In effect we constructed a subgrammar whose start symbol is N and whose language is the set of all binary numerals. The terminal alphabet of the subgrammar is $\{0, 1\}$ and the productions are all the productions of the larger grammar in which no nonterminal other than N or A occurs, namely, the following:

$$N \longrightarrow 0 \mid 1 \mid 1A$$
$$A \longrightarrow 0A \mid 1A \mid 0 \mid 1$$

We go on to consider other sets of strings that might conceivably be subproblems in the construction of larger grammars. For convenience, we shall in this section (and indeed through most of the remainder of this book) adopt the convention that the nonterminals of a context-free grammar are capital letters from the Roman alphabet. We also stipulate that terminal symbols are lower-case Roman letters from the beginning of the alphabet (unless there is some special reason to use other characters), and the start symbol is S. These conventions save us the trouble of announcing each time what the terminals, nonterminals, and start symbol are; grammars will be presented simply by listing their productions.

EXAMPLE 1. Suppose that we wish to construct a context-free grammar whose language is the set of all nonnull strings over the alphabet $\{b, c, d\}$ in which b is not immediately followed by c (in other words, the set of all nonnull strings of which bc is not a substring). One thing about context-free productions is that, loosely speaking, they can provide for something to happen but cannot be used in a direct way to prevent something from happening. We therefore ask: If b cannot be followed by c, what are the remaining possibilities? The answer is that each b that occurs must either be at the right end of the string, or else be immediately followed by d or another b.

We construct a grammar that generates the strings from left to right. The nonterminals are S and E, and the productions are

$$(1)(2)(3) \quad S \longrightarrow bE \,|\, cS \,|\, dS$$
$$(4)(5)(6) \quad S \longrightarrow b \,|\, c \,|\, d$$
$$(7)(8) \quad\;\; E \longrightarrow bE \,|\, dS$$
$$(9)(10) \quad\; E \longrightarrow b \,|\, d$$

Let us now prove that we have indeed solved the problem we began with. Let σ be the set of nonnull strings over $\{b, c, d\}$ in which b is never immediately followed by c, and let G be the grammar we have constructed. We must prove that (I) $\sigma \subseteq L(G)$ and (II) $L(G) \subseteq \sigma$. To prove (I) we must prove that any string in σ is derivable in the grammar G. To prove (II) we must prove that any string over the terminal alphabet that is derivable in G is a string of σ. We emphasize that both of these require proof.

PROOF OF (I): Let $x_1 x_2 \ldots x_n$ be a string in σ; thus, for any i, if $x_i = b$, then $x_{i+1} \neq c$. We construct a derivation tree for $x_1 x_2 \ldots x_n$ as shown in Fig. 7.3.1.

For each $i \leq n - 1$, if $x_i = b$, then $Y_i = E$, but if $x_i = c$ or d, then $Y_i = S$. We must prove that this tree is a derivation tree according to the grammar G.

To this end, we note that for $1 \leq i \leq n - 2$, if $Y_i = S$, then the nodes x_{i+1} and Y_{i+1} are in accord with productions (1), (2), or (3). If $Y_i = E$, then $x_i = b$ and $x_{i+1} \neq c$, so the nodes x_{i+1}, Y_{i+1} are in accord with productions (7) or (8). If $Y_{n-1} = S$, then the single node underneath (i.e., x_n) is in accord with

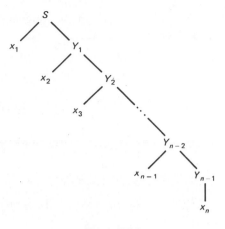

Figure 7.3.1

productions (4), (5), or (6). Finally, if $Y_{n-1} = E$, then $x_n \neq c$ and that node is in accord with productions (9) or (10). ∎

PROOF OF (II): We must prove that any string derivable in the grammar has no c immediately following a b. This is clear because a terminal string must be derived from left to right; any b that is generated is never generated with an S, and S is the only one of the two nonterminals that can generate c as the next terminal letter of the string. ∎

In most of the examples that follow, we shall omit a proof of the correctness of the constructed grammar.

Further Examples 7.3.2

EXAMPLE 2. The set of nonnull strings over the terminal alphabet $\{b, c\}$ having an even number of b's. (*Note:* Since zero is an even number, any string that has no b's at all is included.) We again use the style of left-to-right string generation. Our nonterminals are S and D, and our productions are

$$S \longrightarrow cS \,|\, bD \,|\, c \qquad D \longrightarrow cD \,|\, bS \,|\, b$$

The key idea is that, in generating a string from left to right, an S means that an even number (possibly zero) of b's have appeared so far to the left, while a D means an odd number of b's.

EXAMPLE 3. The set of nonnull strings over the terminal alphabet $\{(,), b\}$, in which the parentheses, if they occur at all, are mated in the ordinary sense, and in which the *b*'s occur freely. To understand this problem, it is important to understand which strings are not to be in the language of the constructed grammar. Some examples of excluded strings are

$$)b($$

$$(bb(b)$$

$$()())b$$

$$b)(b)$$

Our grammar has just one nonterminal *S*, the start symbol. The productions are

$$S \longrightarrow SS\,|\,(S)\,|\,()\,|\,b$$

Figure 7.3.2 is a sample derivation tree in this grammar for the string *b(b(b))*.

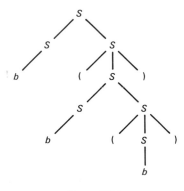

Figure 7.3.2

Note that these productions do not, in general, generate the terminal symbols in a derived word from left to right. It turns out that the nature of the given set of strings makes this style impossible, since a left parenthesis may be mated to a right parenthesis that is quite far away. (The technique of carrying through a rigorous proof of impossibility is shown in Chapter 9.)

This grammar and its language will occupy our attention in Chapter 8.

EXAMPLE 4. The set of nonnull strings over the alphabet {*b, c*} that read the same backward as forward, in other words, the set of palindromes over the alphabet {*b, c*}. A grammar for this set has the productions

$$(1)(2) \qquad S \longrightarrow bSb\,|\,cSc$$

$$(3)(4)(5)(6) \quad S \longrightarrow bb\,|\,cc\,|\,b\,|\,c$$

It is easy to see that any string derivable in this grammar reads the same forward as backward, and that any palindrome over {*b, c*} is derivable in the grammar. Note that if the palindrome has odd length, then the derivation must end with prodution (5) or (6); but if it has even length, it must end with (3) or (4).

EXAMPLE 5. The set σ of nonnull strings over the terminal alphabet $\{b, c\}$ having as many b's as c's. A grammar G for this set has the productions

$$(1)(2)(3)(4)(5) \qquad S \longrightarrow bSc \,|\, cSb \,|\, SS \,|\, bc \,|\, cb$$

It is quite clear that $L(G) \subseteq \sigma$. We now give a detailed proof that $\sigma \subseteq L(G)$.

LEMMA: If a nonnull string W has as many b's as c's, begins with b and ends with b, then $W = W_1 W_2$, where W_1 and W_2 are each nonnull strings having as many b's as c's; similarly, if W begins with c and ends with c.

PROOF: Assume that $W = x_1 x_2 \ldots x_p$, where each x_i is either b or c, $x_1 = b$ and $x_p = b$. Define $f(i)$ for $0 \leq i \leq p$: $f(0) = 0$; and, for $i > 0, f(i)$ is the number of c's minus the number of b's in the substring $x_1 x_2 \ldots x_i$. Thus $f(1) = -1, f(p) = 0$ (since W has as many b's as c's), and $f(p - 1) = +1$ (since $x_p = b$). For each i, $f(i)$ and $f(i + 1)$ differ by one; since $f(1)$ is negative and $f(p - 1)$ is positive, there must be a value of i between such that $f(i) = 0$. Thus, if we take $W_1 = x_1 x_2 \ldots x_i$ and $W_2 = x_{i+1} \ldots x_p$, W_1 and W_2 each has as many b's as c's. ∎

We now complete the proof that $\sigma \subseteq L(G)$ by showing, with the aid of Lemma 1, that all positive-length strings with as many b's as c's are derivable from productions (1) through (5).

PROOF: If W is such a string, it has even length; let its length be $2q$. Our proof is a course-of-values induction on q. (See Appendix V.)

Basis: $q = 1$. Then $W = cb$ or bc and is derivable by production (4) or production (5).

Assume as an inductive hypothesis that $q > 1$ and all strings of length less than $2q$ with as many b's as c's are derivable by means of the five productions. Let W be of length $2q$ with as many b's as c's.

Case 1. W begins and ends with b. Then by the lemma, $W = W_1 W_2$, where both W_1 and W_2 are nonnull strings with as many b's as c's. Both W_1 and W_2 have length less than $2q$. By inductive hypothesis, therefore, W_1 and W_2 are derivable from S. We can therefore construct a derivation of W by first using production (3) getting SS, deriving W_1 from the first S and then W_2 from the second S.

Case 2. W begins and ends with c. Similar to case 1.

Case 3. W begins with b but ends with c. Then $W = bW'c$ and, since W has as many b's as c's, W' has as many b's as c's. W' being of length less than $2q$ is derivable from S. A derivation of W beginning with production (1) is thus possible.

Case 4. W begins with c, ends with b. Similar to Case 3, using production (2) in place of production (1). ∎

We thus see that we sometimes need to use some ingenuity to construct a context-free grammar for a given set of strings; even when a rather simple grammar suffices, the proof that it does suffice may be somewhat involved. Fortunately, most examples that we shall deal with do not require such a detailed proof.

This example should be compared with Example 3, in which the parentheses had to be mated. If there are as many b's as c's, then in a certain sense the b's and c's are mated. However, in the present example, the b and the c can come in either order, whereas the "(" must precede the ")" to which it is mated.

7.3.3 Formulas for Certain Strings

EXAMPLE 6. The set of strings over the alphabet $\{b, c, d, e\}$ that are of the form

$$b^m c^n d^n e^m$$

where m and n are integers ≥ 1. Such a string has all its b's preceding all its c's, which precede all its d's, which precede all its e's; there are as many b's as e's and as many c's as d's, and at least one of each.

The grammar for this set is readily given:

$$(1)(2) \quad S \longrightarrow bSe \mid bJe$$

$$(3)(4) \quad J \longrightarrow cJd \mid cd$$

Note that, given integers m and n, one can apply a recipe (i.e., a simple algorithm) for deriving $b^m c^n d^n e^m$ in this grammar: one applies production (1) $m - 1$ times, then production (2) once, then production (3) $n - 1$ times, and finally production (4) once.

We have a convenient set-theoretic notation for this set of strings:

$$\{b^m c^n d^n e^m \mid m, n \geq 1\}$$

We shall use this sort of notation where possible in the statement of problems like this.

EXAMPLE 7. The set $\{b^m c^{2m} d e^n f^n \mid m, n \geq 1\}$. A grammar for this set has the productions

$$(1) \quad S \longrightarrow JdK$$

$$(2)(3) \quad J \longrightarrow bJcc \,|\, bcc$$

$$(4)(5) \quad K \longrightarrow eKf \,|\, ef$$

We now expand the set-theoretic notation we have been using for languages whose (terminal) alphabet consists exclusively of lowercase letters from the beginning of the Roman alphabet. We use lowercase letters from the middle of the alphabet to represent nonnegative integers (letters i through q). b^m means a string of exactly m b's. $(bc)^m$ means a string of exactly m bc's concatenated. (The parentheses are metasymbols here and are not part of the terminal alphabet.) Thus $(bc)^3$ is the string $bcbcbc$, while bc^3 is the string $bccc$.

The notation b^* means a string consisting of zero or more b's: thus $\{(b^*c)^m(b^*d)^m \,|\, m \geq 1\}$ is the set of strings W such that, for some $m \geq 1$, $W = U_1 U_2 \ldots U_m V_1 V_2 \ldots V_m$, where each U_i is one of the strings c, bc, bbc, and so on, and each V_i is one of the strings d, bd, bbd, and so on. For example, one string in this set is $bbcbccbbbbbbddbd$ ($m = 3$).

EXAMPLE 8. $\{b^m c^n d^n e^m f^p (gh^*)^p \,|\, m \geq 2, n \geq 0, p \geq 1\}$. A grammar for this set has the productions

$$(1) \qquad S \longrightarrow JK$$

$$(2)(3)(4) \quad J \longrightarrow bJe \,|\, bbee \,|\, bbLee$$

$$(5)(6) \qquad L \longrightarrow cLd \,|\, cd$$

$$(7)(8) \qquad K \longrightarrow fKQ \,|\, fQ$$

$$(9)(10) \quad Q \longrightarrow Qh \,|\, g$$

Note that, by using production (9) and (10), one can generate from Q any of the strings g, gh, ghh, and so on, which are those designated by the notation gh^*. In generating a string in this language, (3) or (4) is used, depending on whether or not the value of n in the formula is zero.

We are sure that any string in the given language can be derived by means of the constructed grammar. It is also important to convince ourselves that any terminal string over the terminal alphabet that is derivable is in the set; in other words, that no string outside the set can be derived. We omit a rigorous proof of this fact and note only that, by virtue of production (3), m cannot be less than 2, and by virtue of production (8), p cannot be less than 1.

EXAMPLE 9. $\{b^m c^n \,|\, 1 \leq n \leq m \leq 2n\}$. One grammar G for this set has the four productions

$$(1)(2)(3)(4) \quad S \longrightarrow bSc \,|\, bbSc \,|\, bc \,|\, bbc$$

PROOF THAT $L(G) \subseteq \{b^m c^n | 1 \leq n \leq m \leq 2n\}$:   We prove something more, that the number of b's in any line of a derivation is between the number of c's and twice the number of c's. The proof is by simple mathematical induction on i, where i is the number of the line in the derivation.

For $i = 1$, the line must be S, which has zero b's and zero c's, and the proposition is true for it. Now assume that the proposition is true for i, the ith line being $b^m S c^n$, where $n \leq m \leq 2n$. For the $(i + 1)$st line there are four cases, depending on which production is used.

Case 1. Production (1) is used. Then the $(i + 1)$st line is $b^{m+1} S c^{n+1}$. Since $n \leq m, n + 1 \leq m + 1$. And since $m \leq 2n, m + 1 < 2(n + 1)$. Thus $(n + 1) \leq m + 1 \leq 2(n + 1)$.

Case 2. Production (2) is used. Then the $(i + 1)$st line is $b^{m+2} S c^{n+1}$. It is again easy to verify that $n + 1 \leq m + 2 \leq 2(n + 1)$.

Cases 3 and 4 [productions (3) and (4)] are similar to cases 1 and 2, respectively. ▎

EXAMPLE 10. A grammar for the set

$$\{b^{m+p} c d^{m+n} e f^{n+p} | m, n, p \geq 0\}$$

has the productions

$$(1)(2) \quad S \longrightarrow bSf \,|\, GH$$
$$(3)(4) \quad G \longrightarrow bGd \,|\, c$$
$$(5)(6) \quad H \longrightarrow dHf \,|\, e$$

7.3.4 Exercises

Group I

Give a formula (see Section 7.3.3) for the language of each of the following grammars:

1. $S \longrightarrow bbSe \,|\, H$
   $H \longrightarrow cHdd \,|\, cd$

2. $S \longrightarrow HSK \,|\, HK$
   $H \longrightarrow bH \,|\, c$
   $K \longrightarrow Ke \,|\, dd$

3. $S \longrightarrow HSKK \,|\, HK$
   $H \longrightarrow bH \,|\, c$
   $K \longrightarrow Ke \,|\, d$

4. $S \longrightarrow bSe \,|\, HK$
   $H \longrightarrow cHd \,|\, cd$
   $K \longrightarrow dKe \,|\, de$

5. $S \longrightarrow bSc \,|\, bScc \,|\, bSccc \,|\, bc$

Group II

In each exercise, give a context-free grammar for the set of strings described. Exclude the null string from consideration.

6. $\{b^{m+n}c^md^n \mid m \geq 0; n \geq 1\}$

7. $\{b^{m+n}c^md^n \mid m \geq 1; n \geq 0\}$

8. $\{b^{m+n}c^pd^{m+p}e^{2n} \mid m \geq 1; n \geq 2; p \geq 3\}$

9. $\{(bc)^{m+n}(dc)^nb^{p+m}c^p \mid m, n, p \geq 1\}$

10. $\{b^{3m}c^{2m+2n}b^{3n+1} \mid m, n \geq 0\}$

11. $\{(d*c)^m(c*d)^m \mid m \geq 2\}$

12. $\{(d*b)^mc(b*d)^m \mid m \geq 0\}$

13. $\{c*b^{2m}c(c*d)^m \mid m \geq 0\}$

14. $\{b^m(c*d)^{2n}c*e^m \mid m, n \geq 1\}$

15. $\{b^mc^nd^p \mid m, n \geq 1; p = |m - n|\}$

16. $\{b^mc^n \mid 2 \leq 2n \leq m \leq 3n\}$

17. The set of nonnull strings over the alphabet $\{b, c, d\}$ in which all the b's (if any) precede all the c's and d's, and all the c's (if any) precede all the d's (if any).

18. The set of strings over the alphabet $\{b, c\}$ that end in b, and in which b occurs an even number of times.

19. The set of strings of odd length over the alphabet $\{b, c\}$.

20. The set of nonnull strings over the alphabet $\{b, c\}$ in which the number of b's is divisible by three (possibly zero).

21. The set of strings over the alphabet $\{b, c, d\}$ in which (1) there is exactly one b somewhere, and (2) there is exactly one c somewhere. (There are any number of d's, possibly zero, anywhere.)

22. The set of nonnull strings over the alphabet $\{b, c, d\}$ in which each b (if any) and each c (if any) that occurs has at least one d to its immediate left and has at least one d to its immediate right (e.g., *ddd* and *dcdbdd* are in this set).

23. The set of nonnull strings over the alphabet $\{b, c\}$ of which *ccc* is not a substring.

24. The set of nonnull strings over the alphabet $\{b, c, d\}$ in which c does not occur any place to the right of any b.

25. The set of nonnull strings over the alphabet $\{b, c\}$ of which neither *bb* nor *cc* is a substring.

26. The set of nonnull strings over the alphabet $\{b, c, d\}$ of which neither *bd* nor *dc* nor *cb* is a substring.

27. The set of strings over the alphabet $\{b, c\}$ in which the substring *bcc* occurs at least three times.

28. The set of strings over the alphabet $\{b, c\}$ in which the number of b's is one more than the number of c's.

The remaining problems are probably *more difficult* than those above.

29. The set of nonnull strings over the alphabet $\{b, c, d\}$ in which (1) c is always immediately preceded by b, (2) d is always immediately preceded by b and (3) the substring *bc* occurs as many times (possibly zero) as the substring *bd* (e.g., *bbb* and *bcbbdb* are in this set).

30. The set of nonnull strings over the alphabet $\{b, c\}$ that do not read the same backward as forward, in other words, the set of nonpalindromes over the alphabet $\{b, c\}$.

31. The set of nonnull strings over the alphabet $\{b, (,)\}$ in which (1) the parentheses (if they occur at all) are mated, but (2) three close parentheses never come together. (*b* occurs freely.)

32. The set of nonnull strings over the alphabet $\{b, c, d\}$ in which (1) either there are fewer than two *b*'s or else every pair of *b*'s has at least one occurrence of *c* somewhere between, and (2) either there are fewer than two *c*'s or else each pair of *c*'s has at least one occurrence of *b* somewhere between.

33. The set of strings over the alphabet $\{b, c\}$ that begin with *b*, end with *b*, and have between any two *b*'s an even number of *c*'s (e.g., the strings *b*, *bb*, and *bccccbb* are in the set).

34. The set of strings over the alphabet $\{b, c, d, e\}$ in which (1) all *b*'s precede all *c*'s and *d*'s, (2) all *e*'s follow all *c*'s and *d*'s, (3) there are as many *b*'s as *e*'s and at least one of each, and (4) there are an even number of *d*'s and at least two. (The *c*'s and *d*'s can occur in any order among themselves.)

35. (*Very difficult*) The set of nonnull strings over the alphabet $\{b, c\}$ in which the number of *b*'s is three times the number of *c*'s.

36. (*Very difficult*) $\{b^i c^j \mid i > 0; \frac{2}{3} \leqq j/i \leqq \frac{3}{2}\}$.

Group III

37. In each of Examples 1 through 10, a set σ of strings was defined and a grammar G was constructed so that $L(G) = \sigma$. This fact was not always proved. Prove it for Examples 2 and 7.

38. Prove that $L(G) \subseteq \sigma$ for Example 6. (The converse was proved in the text.)

39. Prove $L(G) = \sigma$ for Example 10. Prove that $\sigma \subseteq L(G)$ for Example 9.

40. Find a nonnull string with an equal number of *b*'s and *c*'s that is not in the language of the following grammar:

$$S \longrightarrow bcS \mid cbS \mid bSc \mid cSb \mid Sbc \mid Scb \mid bc \mid cb$$

41. Prove that every string in the language of the following grammar has twice as many *b*'s as *c*'s:

$$S \longrightarrow SS \mid cMM \mid McM \mid MMc$$
$$M \longrightarrow bS \mid SbS \mid Sb \mid b$$

(*Hint:* Prove first that in any derived line the number of *M*'s plus the number of *b*'s is twice the number of *c*'s.)

42. (*Difficult*) Prove that all nonnull strings over $\{b, c\}$ having twice as many *b*'s as *c*'s are in the language of the grammar of Exercise 41. (*Hint:* Prove both of the following propositions simultaneously by induction on the length of the string W: (1) If W has twice as many *b*'s as *c*'s, W is derivable from S. (2) If W has one more than twice as many b's as c's, W is derivable from M. The proof technique used in Example 5 can be adapted.)

43. (*Very difficult*) Prove that for any three integers m_1, m_2, and n, where $0 \leqq m_1 \leqq m_2$ and $0 < n$, there exists a context-free grammar whose language is

$$\left\{ b^i c^j \,\middle|\, i > 0; \frac{m_1}{n} \leqq \frac{j}{i} \leqq \frac{m_2}{n} \right\}$$

Use without proof the following arithmetic lemma: If $i \geqq 2n$ and $m_1/n \leqq j/i \leqq m_2/n$, then either

$$\frac{m_1}{n} \leqq \frac{j - m_1}{i - n} \leqq \frac{m_2}{n} \qquad \text{or} \qquad \frac{m_1}{n} \leqq \frac{j - m_2}{i - n} \leqq \frac{m_2}{n}$$

(Then one can derive $b^i S c^j$ either from $b^{i-n} S c^{j-m_1}$ using the production $S \longrightarrow b^n S c^{m_1}$, or else from $b^{i-n} S c^{j-m_2}$ using the production $S \longrightarrow b^n S c^{m_2}$.)

THE NULL STRING 7.4
AND LAMBDA PRODUCTIONS

The null string (λ) was mentioned briefly in Section 7.1.4, but no use has been made of it until now. We see how useful it is to have included the null string in our concept of string when we consider the operation of *concatenation*, namely, the joining of two strings. If we concatenate the string $bccb$ and the string cb (in order), we get the string $bccbcb$. If we concatenate $bccb$ with c, we get $bccbc$. Finally, if we concatenate $bccb$ with λ, we get $bccb$. Concatenating the null string to another string is like adding zero to another number: the operation seems trivial at first, but including it as a possibility leads to convenience and the power of generality in our thinking.

The null string must not be confused with the empty set. The set of strings $\{cb, c, \lambda\}$ has three members, the set $\{\lambda\}$ has just one member, and the empty set has no members at all, not even the null string. The null string is just as much a string as any other string.

In this section we introduce lambda productions, and show their utility in context-free grammars. In the next section we see that we can for most purposes get rid of lambda productions from a context-free grammar, at the possible expense of enlarging the set of productions.

Lambda Productions 7.4.1

Suppose that we wish to construct a context-free grammar for the set

$$\{b^m c^m h d^n e^n h f^p g^p \mid m, n, p \geqq 0\}$$

It would be convenient to have the production

$$S \longrightarrow Bh\,Dh\,F$$

the idea being that B, D, and F shall be capable of generating strings of the form $b^m c^m$, $d^n e^n$, and $f^p g^p$, respectively.

Let us focus on B for the moment. Since B must generate λ (i.e., $b^m c^m$, for $m = 0$) we would like the production

$$B \longrightarrow \lambda$$

To get $b^m c^m$, for $m > 0$, we then want

$$B \longrightarrow bBc$$

These are all the B productions that are needed.

Similarly for D and F. The complete set of productions of our grammar is thus

(1)	$S \longrightarrow BhDhF$	(4)(5)	$D \longrightarrow dDe \mid \lambda$
(2)(3)	$B \longrightarrow bBc \mid \lambda$	(6)(7)	$F \longrightarrow fFg \mid \lambda$

The shortest string in the language is hh, where $m = n = p = 0$. A derivation tree for this string in the grammar is Fig. 7.4.1. In reading the leaves of the tree to get the terminal string derived, we skip λ's when they occur. Since "λ" is in neither the terminal nor the nonterminal alphabet, this practice of labeling a node λ departs from the definition of Section 7.1.4. Figure 7.4.2 is a derivation tree for the string $bbbccchhffgg$ ($m = 3, n = 0, p = 2$).

It is interesting to see what we would have to do to write a context-free

Figure 7.4.1

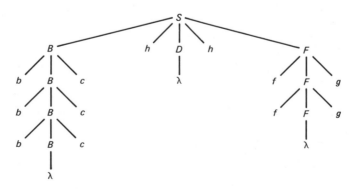

Figure 7.4.2

grammar for this language without lambda productions. We would then have to use the productions

$$(3') \quad B \longrightarrow bc \qquad (5') \quad D \longrightarrow de \qquad (7') \quad F \longrightarrow fg$$

instead of (3), (5), and (7), respectively, of the old grammar. However, the productions (1), (2), (3'), (4), (5'), (6), and (7') could not generate any string

$$b^m c^m h d^n e^n h f^p g^p$$

in which $m = 0$ or $p = 0$ or $n = 0$. To get these possibilities, we must introduce seven new variations on production (1), which are (8) through (14) in the following complete set of productions for the new grammar:

$$(1) \qquad S \longrightarrow BhDhF \qquad (4)(5') \quad D \longrightarrow dDe \,|\, de$$
$$(2)(3') \quad B \longrightarrow bBc \,|\, bc \qquad (6)(7') \quad F \longrightarrow fFg \,|\, fg$$
$$(8)–(14) \quad S \longrightarrow hDhF \,|\, BhhF \,|\, BhDh \,|\, Bhh \,|\, hDh \,|\, hhF \,|\, hh$$

We see that if we wish to do without lambda productions, we need twice as many productions in this example. Generally, lambda productions are quite convenient.

Consider now a slight variation of the language just considered:

$$\{b^m c^m d^n e^n f^p g^p \,|\, m, n, p \geq 0\}$$

A grammar for this language is a trivial variation of the original grammar: $(1'')\ S \rightarrow BDF$; (2) to (7) as above. Note that λ is in this language ($m = n = p = 0$), Fig. 7.4.3 being its derivation tree.

Figure 7.4.3

There is no way of converting this grammar into an *equivalent* grammar (i.e., one with the same language) without lambda productions, since no such grammar has a derivation of the null string.

As a final example, consider the set of all strings over the alphabet $\{b, c\}$, including the null string, having an even number of b's (see Example 2 of Section 7.3). A grammar for this language has four productions:

$$S \longrightarrow cS \,|\, bD \,|\, \lambda$$
$$D \longrightarrow cD \,|\, bS$$

7.4.2 Noncontracting Productions

Context-free grammars without lambda productions have an important property that grammars with lambda productions do not have. A context-free production other than a lambda production is *noncontracting*; that is, the right side is no shorter than the left side. Thus, in any derivation in a context-free grammar without lambda productions, a line is never shorter than the line from which it follows. Any grammar with this property is called a *noncontracting grammar*. (This term applies to all the context-sensitive grammars, which we discussed in passing in Section 7.1.5.)

We shall use the concept of noncontracting productions to prove that there is a decision procedure to tell whether or not a given string is derivable in a given context-free grammar. The proof will be complete at the end of Section 7.5. Meanwhile, we prove:

THEOREM 7.4.1: There is a decision procedure to tell whether a given string is derivable in a given context-free grammar without lambda productions.

PROOF: We note first that for a given grammar and a given positive integer d, there is an effective way of listing all the strings over the total alphabet that are derivable in d or fewer lines. First, there is only one string derivable in a derivation of length one, the string which is the start symbol itself. A string is derivable in a derivation of length two if and only if it is the right side of a production whose left side is the start symbol.

Now suppose that we have listed, for some integer i, all the lines that are derivable in a derivation of length i. We can proceed to make a list of the strings derivable in a derivation of length $i + 1$ by examining each string in the previous list and each production and then writing down every string that follows immediately from one of the strings using one of the productions. Both the total alphabet and the set of productions of a given grammar are finite; hence, if there are finitely many strings derivable by a derivation of length i, there are finitely many strings derivable in a derivation of length $i + 1$, so we can write them all down. Thus by mathematical induction on i, and taking $d = i$, we can say that, for any d, there is an effective way of writing down all the strings derivable in a derivation of length d or less. (Note that this result holds whether or not there are lambda productions.)

Next we note that if there is a derivation of a string in a grammar, then there is a loop-free derivation of that same string. A *loop* in a derivation is simply a repeated string together with all the lines between the first and second occurrences of that string. If $L_1, \ldots, L_i, \ldots, L_j, \ldots, L_d$ is a derivation of the string L_d, with L_j exactly the same as L_i, then we can delete all the lines $L_{i+1}, \ldots, L_j$; the result of the deletion

$$L_1, \ldots, L_i, L_{j+1}, \ldots, L_d$$

is still a derivation of L_d. In this way all loops in a derivation can be deleted. Thus any derivable string is derivable by a loop-free derivation. (Again, this result holds for any grammar, whether or not there are lambda productions.)

Let G be a given context-free grammar without lambda productions. All the productions of G are then noncontracting. Let p be the sum of the number of nonterminals and the number of terminals. We note that the number of strings (derivable or not) of length i over the total alphabet of G is p^i. Thus if we have a loop-free derivation whose last line is a string of length e, then the length of the derivation is at most

$$q = \sum_{i=1}^{e} p^i$$

Now suppose that we are given a string W of length e over the terminal alphabet of G and are asked: Is W in the language of G? We can answer the question effectively as follows. We enumerate all the strings derivable in derivations of length less than and equal to q. If W is in the list, then it is in the language of the grammar; but if not, then not. ∎

With the knowledge that the advanced theory of context-free languages offers, the efficiency of this decision procedure can be vastly improved (see Ullman [1973] pp. 183ff.).

We note that this proof that a context-free grammar without lambda productions has a recursive language depends on the fact that such a grammar has noncontracting productions, but in no other way makes use of the fact that the productions are context-free productions. The proof therefore goes over to the more general class of noncontracting grammars.

Exercises 7.4.3

Give a context-free grammar for the set of strings mentioned in each exercise. Use lambda productions where convenient. Be careful of the membership or nonmembership of the null string itself in the language of your grammar. Exercises 1 through 13 will be quite simple for those who have mastered the examples and exercises of Section 7.3.

1. $\{b^m c^m d^n e^n \mid m, n \geq 0\}$

2. $\{b^m c^{m+n} d^n \mid m, n \geq 0\}$

3. $\{(bc)^{m+n}(dc)^n b^{p+m} c^p \mid m, n, p \geq 0\}$

4. $\{b^{3m} c^{2m+2n} b^{3n+1} \mid m, n \geq 0\}$

5. $\{b^m c^{2m} d e^n f^n \mid m, n \geq 0\}$

6. $\{b^m c^n d^n e^m f^p (gh^*)^p \mid m \geq 2; n, p \geq 0\}$

7. $\{b^m c^n \mid 0 \leq n \leq m \leq 2n\}$ (see Example 9 of Section 7.3).

8. The set of strings over the alphabet $\{b, c, d\}$ of which bc is not a substring (see Example 1 of Section 7.3).

9. The set of strings over $\{b, c\}$ in which the number of b's is divisible by 3 (see Exercise 20 of Section 7.3).

10. The set of strings over $\{b, c\}$ having as many b's as c's (cf. Example 5 of Section 7.3).

11. The set of strings over the alphabet $\{b, c, d, e\}$ of the form $W_1 W_2 W_3 W_4$, where W_1 is a nonnull string of b's, W_2 a string (possibly null) of c's, W_3 a string (possibly null) of d's, and W_4 a string (possibly null) of e's.

12. The set of strings over $\{b, c\}$ that have between any two b's an even number of c's. (In particular, the strings bb and $bccccbbccc$ are in the set, as are any strings with no occurrence of b or just one occurrence.)

13. The set of strings over $\{(,), [,], b\}$ in which (1) the parentheses if they occur are mated, (2) brackets if they occur are mated, (3) the b's occur freely, and (4) each) that occurs is immediately followed by [and each [that occurs is immediately preceded by). (In particular, λ itself is in this set. Note that parentheses and brackets are *not* mated in ()[()][], and hence this string is not to be in the language of your grammar.)

14. $\{b^m c^n d^p \mid m, n, p \geqq 0$ and either $m \neq n$ or $n \neq p\}$. (The only strings of the form $b^m c^n d^p$ that are excluded from this language are those for which $m = n = p$.)

15. (*Difficult*) Prove that the language of the following grammar is the set of all strings over the alphabet $\{b, c\}$ with twice as many b's as c's (including the null string):

$$S \longrightarrow SbSbScS \mid SbScSbS \mid ScSbSbS \mid \lambda$$

(See Example 5 and Exercises 41 and 42 of Section 7.3.)

16. (*Very difficult.* Recall Example 5 and Exercises 41 and 42 of Section 7.3.) Prove that, for any two positive integers m and n, there exists a context-free grammar whose language is the set of all strings (including λ) over the alphabet $\{b, c\}$ in which the ratio of the number of occurrences of b to the number of occurrences of c is m/n. (*Hint:* let the nonterminals be $N_{-p}, N_{-p+1}, \ldots, N_q$, where N_0 is the start symbol and where, for each i, a string over the terminal alphabet is to be derivable from N_i if and only if m times the number of c's minus n times the number of b's equals i. Thus, in Exercise 41 of Section 7.3, $m = 2, n = 1, S = N_0$, and $M = N_{-1}$. Judiciously select p and q to minimize the length of your proof.)

7.5 THE DISPENSABILITY OF LAMBDA PRODUCTIONS

It turns out that lambda productions do not affect the important computational properties of context-free grammars. We now present an algorithm for converting a context-free grammar with lambda productions into a context-free grammar with the same, or almost the same, language. (The new language will not have λ even if the original language does.) Because of this algorithm, we shall be able to extend the decision procedure of Theorem 7.4.1 to context-free grammars with lambda productions.

The grammar that results from the algorithm is quite close in its parsing properties to the original grammar: derivation trees in the two grammars for the same terminal strings will be quite similar.

For many purposes, it is convenient to have context-free grammars with lambda productions (they generally have fewer productions), and for many other purposes it is convenient to have context-free grammars without lambda productions. It is therefore worthwhile to know that, given a grammar with lambda productions, we can readily construct a grammar without lambda productions that is close to it in important respects.

Lambda-Yielding Nonterminals 7.5.1

We say that a nonterminal in a context-free grammar *yields* λ if one can derive λ from that nonterminal, either directly (in case there is a lambda production with that nonterminal on the left) or indirectly.

The method to determine which nonterminals are lambda-yielding is simple. All one needs is a list of all the productions and a writing implement to place check marks in certain places on this list.

First, every nonterminal that is the left side of a lambda production yields lambda. So, one puts a check mark above each occurrence of each of these nonterminals in all the productions, left sides and right sides. Next one looks for an unchecked nonterminal on the left side of a production whose right side consists exclusively of checked nonterminals. This nonterminal is then checked in all its occurrences (since we have determined that it yields lambda). We repeat this step as often as possible; we stop only after we see that there is no production remaining whose left side is unchecked and whose right side consists exclusively of checked nonterminals. It should then be clear that a nonterminal of the grammar yields lambda if and only if it has been checked.

We illustrate this method with a simple grammar:

$$
\begin{array}{llll}
(1) & S \longrightarrow eSe & (5) & D \longrightarrow BDh \\
(2) & S \longrightarrow CD & (6) & D \longrightarrow \lambda \\
(3) & C \longrightarrow fCg & (7) & B \longrightarrow hB \\
(4) & C \longrightarrow \lambda & (8) & B \longrightarrow f
\end{array}
$$

The two nonterminals C and D, which do have lambda productions, are checked in their every occurrence. Then we notice that production (2) has an unchecked nonterminal on its left, but that its right side consists exclusively of checked nonterminals, whereupon S is checked in every occurrence. Since no more checking is possible, we conclude that S, C, and D yield lambda in this grammar, but B does not.

7.5.2 Constructing G_1 and G_2

Let G_0 be a grammar with lambda productions, to be converted into one without lambda productions. Our algorithm for the conversion consists of three steps. The first step is the procedure described in Section 7.5.1 for determining which of the nonterminals of G_0 yield lambda. The second step is the construction of a grammer G_1 from G_0, and the third step is the construction of G_2, which will have the desired properties.

We begin the second step of the algorithm by considering in turn each production of G_0 with one or more occurrences of lambda-yielding nonterminals on the right side. Suppose that such a production is

$$B \longrightarrow \ldots C_1 \ldots C_2 \ldots \ldots \ldots C_p \ldots$$

where $C_1, C_2, \ldots, C_p$ (not necessarily distinct) are all the occurrences of lambda-yielding nonterminals on the right side. We add to the list each production that can be formed by picking a nonempty subset of $\{C_1, C_2, \ldots, C_p\}$ and deleting just those occurrences that are members of the subset. At most $2^p - 1$ new productions will result.

For example, suppose that one of the productions of G_0 is

$$B \longrightarrow \overset{\checkmark}{C}Eb\overset{\checkmark\checkmark}{C}D$$

and suppose that C and D yield lambda but E does not (as shown by the checks from step 1). Then the seven ($= 2^3 - 1$) productions added are

$$B \longrightarrow EbCD \,|\, CEbD \,|\, CEbC \,|\, CEb \,|\, EbC \,|\, EbD \,|\, Eb$$

Since this must be done for every production of G_0 having lambda-yielding nonterminals on the right side, G_1 may have many more productions that G_0.

It is to be noted that G_1 will have a lambda production for each lambda-yielding nonterminal. To see this, suppose that H is a lambda-yielding nonterminal and $H \longrightarrow \lambda$ is not a production of G_0. Then in step 1, H must have been checked because it is the left side of a production of G_0 whose right side consists exclusively of checked nonterminals. Suppose, for example, that production is

$$H \longrightarrow \overset{\checkmark\checkmark}{C}B$$

where C and B are lambda-yielding. Then the three productions added are

$$H \longrightarrow C \,|\, B \,|\, \lambda$$

The last production results from $H \longrightarrow CB$ by deleting the set $\{C, B\}$.

Note also that G_1 has precisely the same terminals, nonterminals, and start symbol as G_0. It has all the productions of G_0 and, in general, others besides.

The construction of G_2 from G_1 is simple. G_2 has the same terminals, nonterminals, and start symbol of G_1 (and hence of G_0). The set of productions of G_2 is the set of all the productions of G_1 that are not lambda productions. Thus G_2 has, in general, productions that G_0 does not have, but lacks its lambda productions.

An Example 7.5.3

Let G_0 be the grammar considered in Section 7.5.1. We determined that the nonterminals S, C, and D are lambda-yielding and B is not. Since the start symbol S is lambda yielding, $\lambda \in L(G_0)$.

The grammar G_1 is then

(1)(1a)	$S \longrightarrow eSe \mid ee$	(5)(5a)	$D \longrightarrow B\check{D}h \mid Bh$
(2)(2a)(2b)(2c)	$S \longrightarrow CD \mid D \mid C \mid \lambda$	(6)	$D \longrightarrow \lambda$
(3)(3a)	$C \longrightarrow fCg \mid fg$	(7)	$B \longrightarrow hB$
(4)	$C \longrightarrow \lambda$	(8)	$B \longrightarrow f$

Note that the new production (1a) comes from the old production (1); (2a), (2b), and (2c) come from (2); and so on.

Finally, G_2 is the grammar whose productions are those of G_1 that are not lambda productions.

It is interesting to look at derivation trees of the string *effggfhfhhe* in G_0 and in G_2 (Fig. 7.5.1), and the same for the string *eeee* (Fig. 7.5.2). An asterisk in these figures indicates a place where the tree in G_0 differs from the

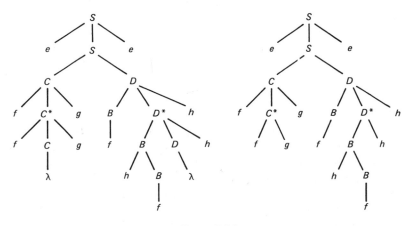

Figure 7.5.1

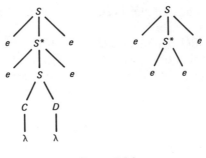

Figure 7.5.2

tree in G_2 because further down a lambda production is used in the G_0 tree. The parts of the corresponding trees above the asterisks are the same.

We can generalize from these examples and say that the derivation trees in the grammars G_0 and G_2 are very much alike. The only difference is in the vicinity of nodes to which a lambda production is applied in G_0. In constructing the corresponding tree in G_2, we simply arrange that a node for a nonterminal that is to yield λ never appears. The production in G_0 that produced that non-terminal (or, in some cases, a production that produced another nonterminal that in turn produced it, etc.) is replaced by a new production in which that nonterminal is omitted. This replacement is in accord with the constructive proof below of Theorem 5.1, via the lemmas.

7.5.4 The Equivalence of G_0 and G_1

We shall prove that $L(G_2) = L(G_0) - \{\lambda\}$. Note that if $\lambda \notin L(G_0)$, then this equation tells us that $L(G_2) = L(G_0)$. But if $\lambda \in L(G_0)$, the equation tells us that $\lambda \notin L(G_2)$ and, apart from λ, $L(G_2)$ has the same members as $L(G_0)$. In either case, the equation says that a nonnull word is derivable in G_2 if and only if it is derivable in G_0.

In carrying through this proof, we shall use capital letters from the end of the Roman alphabet (U, V, W, X, Y, Z) to designate strings of symbols over the total alphabet of the grammar; these are not symbols of the grammar.

LEMMA 2: $L(G_0) = L(G_1)$.

PROOF: Since every production of G_0 is a production of G_1, every deriva-tion in G_0 is a derivation in G_1. So $L(G_0) \subseteq L(G_1)$.

To prove that $L(G_1) \subseteq L(G_0)$, we prove that any string over the total alphabet derivable in G_1 is derivable in G_0. The proof is by mathematical induc-tion on the length (i.e., the number of lines) of the derivation.

Note for the basis of the induction that the start symbol is the only string derivable in a derivation of length 1, in both G_0 and G_1.

As an inductive hypothesis, assume that every string that is the ith line of a derivation in G_1 is derivable in G_0. Let W be line $i + 1$ in a derivation in G_1. Our proof is complete if we can show that W is derivable in G_0.

Let W' be the ith line in this derivation. By the inductive hypothesis W' is derivable in G_0. If the production used to get W from W' is a production of G_0, then W is derivable in G_0. But, if not, W is obtained from W' by a production of G_1 not in G_0, which must have been formed from a production of G_0 by deleting some of the lambda-yielding nonterminals on the right side. Suppose that the production of G_0 is

$$B \longrightarrow X_1 C_1 X_2 C_2 \ldots X_p C_p X_{p+1}$$

and the production of G_1 is

$$B \longrightarrow X_1 X_2 \ldots X_p X_{p+1}$$

where $C_1, \ldots, C_p$ are lambda-yielding nonterminals of G_0.

Then W' is of the form $U_1 B U_2$ and W is of the form $U_1 X_1 X_2 \ldots X_p X_{p+1} U_2$. Since W' is derivable in G_0, $U_1 X_1 C_1 X_2 C_2 \ldots X_p C_p X_{p+1} U_2$ is derivable in G_0. Each C_i yields lambda in G_0, so it follows that W is also derivable in G_0. ∎

Justifying the Algorithm 7.5.5

We must go on now to establish the relationship (discussed above) between G_1 and G_2. The key is Lemma 3, which implies that lambda productions can be dispensed with in deriving nonnull strings in G_1.

LEMMA 3: If there is a derivation in G_1 of a nonnull terminal string W using lambda productions, then there is a shorter derivation in G_1 of W.

PROOF: Suppose that the lambda production $C \rightarrow \lambda$ is applied to the ith line $X_1 C X_2$, yielding $X_1 X_2$ as line $(i + 1)$ (see Fig. 7.5.3) in a derivation whose length is n. Since the last line of the derivation is nonnull, $X_1 X_2$ is nonnull. Therefore, either X_1 or X_2, or both, are nonnull. Thus $i > 1$, and C must have come from some application of some production, say $B \rightarrow U_1 C U_2$, to the jth line for some $j < i$. Let $V_1 B V_2$ and $V_1 U_1 C U_2 V_2$ be the jth and $(j + 1)$st lines, respectively. [The number $j + 1$ may or may not equal i. Even if not, we are assuming that, whatever happens between the $(j + 1)$st and the ith line, no productions are applied to this C.]

By the nature of the way G_1 is constructed, C must have been a lambda-yielding nonterminal of G_0; and, since $B \rightarrow U_1 C U_2$ is a production of G_1, $B \rightarrow U_1 U_2$ is a production of G_1.

Hence, a new derivation of W of length $n - 1$ can be constructed as follows (see Fig. 7.5.3). Let the first j lines be exactly the same as in the old deriva-

	Old derivation	New derivation
	.	.
	.	.
	.	.
Line j	$V_1 B V_2$	$V_1 B V_2$
Line $j + 1$	$V_1 U_1 C U_2 V_2$	$V_1 U_1 U_2 V_2$
	.	.
	.	.
	.	.
Line i	$X_1 C X_2$	$X_1 X_2$
Line $i + 1$	$X_1 X_2$	.
	.	.
	.	W
	.	
	W	

Figure 7.5.3

tion. For $j + 1 \leq h \leq i$, let the hth line of the new derivation be like the hth line of the old derivation except for the deletion of the noted occurrence of C. For $i < h \leq n - 1$, the hth line is the same as the $(h + 1)$st line of the old derivation.

Clearly, the length of the new derivation is shorter than the old derivation. But we must verify that it is a derivation (i.e., that each line after the first follows by one of the productions of G_1). The lines up to the jth line are all right, as are the lines after the ith line. The $(j + 1)$st line, $V_1 U_1 U_2 V_2$, follows from the jth line by the production $B \longrightarrow U_1 U_2$. For any $h, j + 2 \leq h \leq i$ (if any), the hth line follows from the $(h - 1)$st line exactly as the $(h + 1)$st line followed from the hth line in the old derivation, since the occurrence of C is not involved.   ∎

LEMMA 4: $L(G_2) = L(G_1) - \{\lambda\}$.

PROOF: Since all the productions of G_2 are productions of G_1, $L(G_2) \subseteq L(G_1)$. Furthermore, since $\lambda \notin L(G_2)$, $L(G_2) \subseteq L(G_1) - \{\lambda\}$.

Now let $W \in L(G_1) - \{\lambda\}$. Where Δ is a shortest derivation in G_1 of W, no lines in Δ follow by lambda productions. (If Δ had lambda productions, Lemma 3 tells us it could not be a shortest derivation.) Since G_2 differs from G_1 only in the absence of λ productions, Δ is a derivation in G_2 and $W \in L(G_2)$. Hence $L(G_1) - \{\lambda\} \subseteq L(G_2)$.   ∎

THEOREM 7.5.1:   Where G_2 results from the application of the above algorithm to the context-free grammar G_0, G_2 has no lambda productions and $L(G_2) = L(G_0) - \{\lambda\}$.

The proof is immediate from Lemmas 2 and 4.

As the example in Section 7.5.3 suggests, the grammar G_2 that results from an application of the algorithm to a given grammar G_0 is intimately related to G_0 in a way that the statement of Theorem 7.5.1 does not say. The two grammars have the same terminals, the same nonterminals, and the same start symbol. Moreover, all the productions of G_0 other than the lambda productions are productions of G_2. The productions of G_2 that are not in G_0 are there simply so that lambda productions can be dispensed with. For these reasons, derivations and derivation trees in one grammar are quite similar to the derivations and derivation trees in the other.

In fact, the proof of Theorem 7.5.1 goes over to a proof of a more general proposition about G_0 and G_2. Let $NND_0(A)$ and $NND_2(A)$ be, respectively, the set of all nonnull strings over the terminal alphabet derivable from the nonterminal A in G_0 and in G_2, respectively.

THEOREM 7.5.2: If G_2 is constructed from G_0 by the algorithm and A is any nonterminal of G_0 and G_2, then $NND_0(A) = NND_2(A)$.

The proof is by analogy from Theorem 7.5.1.

We can say more than what Theorem 7.5.2 says, namely that derivation trees in G_2 are quite similar to those of G_0. In other terms, G_2 and G_0 have similar parsing properties, as exemplified by Figs. 7.5.1 and 7.5.2.

What is the significance of the algorithm? At first one is inclined to say that it enables us to get rid of lambda productions from a grammar in cases where we are not interested in deriving the null string. It may be important to be able to do this in some circumstances, but it should be recalled that lambda productions are quite helpful in writing down context-free grammars for certain sets of strings. In many circumstances, we shall not want to get rid of them.

As a matter of fact, the existence of this simple algorithm (certainly feasible by means of a simple computer program) tells us that we can feel secure in our use of lambda productions, because we know we could get rid of them if we should want to. For example, we shall see that lambda productions will not be used in our model of the parsing automaton in Chapter 8.

Finally, we are able to generalize our decision procedure of the preceding section.

THEOREM 7.5.3: There is a decision procedure to tell whether a given string is derivable in a given context-free grammar (with or without lambda productions).

PROOF: Let G_0 be a context-free grammar and W a string. If $W = \lambda$, then the method of Section 7.5.1 enables us to determine if W is derivable. If $W \neq \lambda$, convert G_0 to G_2 (if necessary) by the method of Section 7.5.2 and use the decision procedure of Theorem 7.4.1 to determine if W is derivable in G_2. ∎

7.5.7 Exercises

1. Construct G_1 and G_2 where G_0 is

$$S \longrightarrow bEf \qquad\qquad K \longrightarrow cKd \,|\, \lambda$$
$$E \longrightarrow bEc \,|\, GGc \qquad L \longrightarrow dLe \,|\, \lambda$$
$$G \longrightarrow b \,|\, KL$$

2. Construct G_1 and G_2 where G_0 is

$$S \longrightarrow eSe \,|\, GH \qquad H \longrightarrow JHd \,|\, \lambda$$
$$G \longrightarrow cGb \,|\, \lambda \qquad\quad J \longrightarrow bJ \,|\, f$$

3. Find a context-free grammar with six productions (including lambda productions) equivalent to the following grammar:

$$S \longrightarrow b \,|\, bHF \,|\, bH \,|\, bF \qquad F \longrightarrow dFe \,|\, de \,|\, G$$
$$H \longrightarrow bHc \,|\, bc \qquad\qquad\quad G \longrightarrow dG \,|\, d$$

(*Hint:* A grammar with seven productions is easy. To get it down to six, an extra trick is needed.)

4. In general, the grammar G_2 constructed by the algorithm of this section has more productions than G_0. Prove that, for any positive integer p, there exists a context-free grammar G_0 with three productions, but where the corresponding G_2 as constructed by the algorithm has more than p productions.

5. Let G be a context-free grammar without lambda productions. Describe in general terms how to convert G into an equivalent context-free grammar without lambda productions and without any production whose right side consists of a single nonterminal. (*Hint:* Make sure that your algorithm takes care of the case in which G has the productions $A \longrightarrow B$, $B \longrightarrow C$, and $C \longrightarrow A$; and also the case of a grammar in which G has the productions $A \longrightarrow B$ and $B \longrightarrow C$ but no other productions of this kind. The solution to this exercise can be found in the literature; for example, in Hopcroft and Ullman [1979], pp. 91–92.)

6. Given two grammars:

G: (1) $S \longrightarrow EFG$ G′: (1′) $S \longrightarrow EQ$
    (3)(4) $E \longrightarrow bEc \,|\, \lambda$ (2′) $Q \longrightarrow FG$
    (5)(6) $F \longrightarrow cFd \,|\, \lambda$ (3)–(8) as in G
    (7)(8) $G \longrightarrow dGb \,|\, \lambda$

Give an algorithm for converting a derivation in G′ of a terminal string into a derivation in G of the same terminal string.

7. G: (1)(2)(3) $S \longrightarrow bSc \,|\, bc \,|\, bSSc$

   G′: (4) $S \longrightarrow bJ$
       (5)(6)(7) $J \longrightarrow bJc \,|\, c \,|\, bJbJc$

(a) Give an algorithm for converting a derivation in G of a terminal string into a derivation in G′ of the same terminal string. (b) Give an algorithm for converting a derivation in G′ of a terminal string into a derivation in G.

Parsing   8

The question of the meaning of linguistic occurrences in any language is a semantic question, but the syntactic operation of parsing a string of a formal language, as an aid in determining its meaning, is often done without reference to semantics at all. Since our syntax is set forth by a context-free grammar, the parsing of a string is a matter of constructing a derivation tree of the string in that grammar.

If any string has two distinct (i.e., nonisomorphic) derivation trees, the grammar is ambiguous, which is generally an undesirable feature of the syntax of a formal language. We now study various techniques of avoiding ambiguities, together with various methods of parsing. The chapter ends with a study of a parsing automaton, giving us a machine-efficient style of parsing with many applications.

AMBIGUITY IN FORMAL LANGUAGES 8.1

After some informal discussion of parsing and ambiguity, this section presents the definitions of *isomorphic derivation trees* and *ambiguity*.

Eighth-Grade Parsing 8.1.1

One of the tasks a grade-school student of English grammar had to do years ago (and perhaps in some schools today) was to diagram English sentences. For example, in one system of diagramming, the sentence "He sees the yellow ball" is diagrammed as in Fig. 8.1.1, showing that "He" is the subject of the

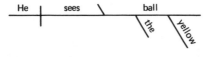

Figure 8.1.1

verb "sees," whose object is the word "ball." The words "the" and "yellow" are
modifiers of the word "ball," as shown by the slanting lines.

The process of constructing such a diagram is one way of parsing the
sentence. Generally, to parse a sentence is to determine the structural relationships between its parts.

One cannot parse sentences of natural languages without taking meaning
and context into consideration. In diagramming the sentences, (1) "She walked
into the room with the piano," and (2) "She walked into the room with the
idea," one must take note of a profound difference in the two "with" phrases
(Fig. 8.1.2). In sentence (1) the phrase "with the piano" modifies the noun

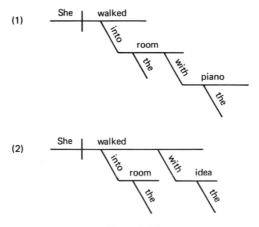

Figure 8.1.2

"room," whereas in sentence (2) the phrase "with the idea" modifies the verb
"walked." We know this must be so because of general knowledge: People do
not walk with pianos, and rooms do not have ideas.

If we were assigned to diagram the sentence "She walked into the room with
the lamp," we would have to acknowledge that the sentence is ambiguous, and
could be diagrammed either like sentence (1) or like sentence (2). Since people
can walk with lamps, and rooms do have lamps, we cannot tell which of the two
meanings the sentence has without information about the context of the sentence.

We have just come upon an important property of natural languages:
The meaning of a sentence depends on a knowledge of context. Sometimes an
ambiguity cannot be resolved even with a knowledge of the complete text
from which the sentence is taken. Ultimately, such ambiguities are resolvable
only by querying the author of the sentence.

Ambiguities are inevitable in natural languages because of the wide variety of purposes they serve, and because new words and phrases do not come into being fast enough for new things and situations to be talked about. There is reason to think that a natural language without ambiguities (if it could exist) would be too unwieldy to be of general service.

A formal language serves its purpose best if it is generally free of ambiguities. Any troublesome ambiguity we may find in it is the result of faulty design. Part of the objective of this chapter is to continue our study of language design to avoid, or otherwise deal with, ambiguities.

Lexical and Structural Ambiguities 8.1.2

Ambiguity is fundamentally a semantic concept. An ambiguous phrase or sentence refers in two different ways to the world outside. The kind of ambiguity that is easiest to understand is *lexical ambiguity*, when a symbol or an expression of the kind that is supposed to denote something actually denotes at least two different things. Natural languages are full of these. The word "plant," for example, can denote vegetation growing from the ground and can denote a factory. Only by a proper use and understanding of contexts can we function with the many lexical ambiguities in a natural language.

In formal languages, such ambiguities are not widespread. We would not tolerate using the same symbol both for the digit 2 and for the plus sign. Nevertheless, formal languages do have lexical ambiguities; for example, the minus sign in common mathematical notation. When we write "$5 - 3 = 2$" and "$-3 = (-1) * 3$," the sign $-$ in the first equation denotes binary subtraction, and in the second equation unary negation. This practice is widespread even in formal programming languages, where it sometimes causes momentary confusion but is on the whole quite useful because of the connection in meaning ($-x$ being ideally synonymous with $0 - x$).

An ambiguity of this kind, in which a symbol or expression has two different meanings, but where there is a significant relationship between the two meanings, is sometimes called a *systematic ambiguity*. We should think of it as a technique to be exploited in language design. The deliberate use of this technique was made in Chapter 4, where the function symbols $+$, $*$, MIN, and MAX could each denote functions of any number of arguments. It is used often in programming languages, where it is called *overloading* an operator symbol.

Since the number of ideas that we have to accommodate in a formal language is relatively small, it is easy to guard against the troublesome kind of lexical ambiguities and avoid them. We now turn our attention to another deeper kind, the structural ambiguities.

Generally, the meaning of an expression depends on the meanings of the symbols that are its parts; but it also depends on the parsing of the expression. When an expression can be parsed in two different ways, the expression can have two different meanings, even if there are no lexical ambiguities involved. Such a situation is called a *structural ambiguity*.

Above we gave an example of a structural ambiguity in English: "She walked into the room with the lamp." In natural languages structural ambiguities are as common as lexical ambiguities.

It is important to be able to design formal languages to be free of structural ambiguities. One type of problem in this chapter will be to modify a given structurally ambiguous formal language (sometimes by modifying only the grammar, leaving the language as it was) so as to make it unambiguous.

Structural ambiguity, like lexical ambiguity, is fundamentally semantic, since it concerns meaning. However, since the ambiguity is a matter of parsing, and parsing is generally considered to be a syntactic operation (generally one can parse without regard to meaning), structural ambiguity is sometimes called *syntactic ambiguity*. Lexical ambiguity is sometimes called *semantic ambiguity*.

From here on we shall use the term *ambiguity* to mean structural ambiguity, and proceed more technically.

8.1.3   The Derivation Tree As a Parse

If the syntax of a formal language is given formally as a context-free grammar, then we can regard a derivation tree as a parsing of a derived string of the language. For example, recall the context-free grammar from Section 7.2.5 for the parenthesis-free propositional calculus in prefix notation:

$$G\text{-PRE:}\quad S \longrightarrow \&SS\,|\,\bigvee SS\,|\sim S\,|\,A$$
$$A \longrightarrow A'\,|\,p\,|\,q\,|\,r$$

Consider the string $\&\bigvee p \sim qr$. Its derivation tree in G-PRE (Fig. 8.1.3) tells us that p and $\sim q$ are joined by the wedge to become a formula that is joined by the ampersand to the r.

The derivation tree gives the information needed for the structural meaning of the string. If the derivation were used for this purpose, the structure would be more difficult to see. Furthermore, the derivation obscures the important fact

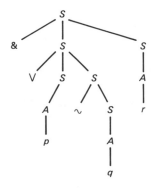

Figure 8.1.3

that, if two nonterminals appear in a line, what happens to one of these in later lines by the productions is completely independent of what happens to the other. In the derivation, one of these will be replaced before the other, yet from the point of view of the structural meaning, it does not matter which of them gets replaced first.

We find that all relationships shown in the derivation tree are relevant to the structural meaning of the derived string, and conversely that the derivation tree reveals the structural meaning completely. For this reason, and because of its graphic simplicity, we are justified in regarding a derivation tree as a parse of its derived string.

Isomorphism of Derivation Trees   8.1.4

If a string has several distinct derivation trees, it must have that many distinct structural meanings, and must therefore be structurally ambiguous. But we must be careful what we mean by "distinct" here. Figure 8.1.4 shows two

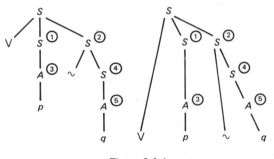

Figure 8.1.4

drawings of what we regard as the same derivation tree. The important relationships between terminal symbols and nonterminal symbols are exactly the same, in spite of the different appearance. We now formalize the relationship between these two trees.

Definition: Two derivation trees are *isomorphic* if there is a one-to-one correspondence between the nodes of one tree and the nodes of the other, such that (1) corresponding nodes have the same labels; and (2) for every node N_0 in the first tree, if N_0 is connected to exactly p nodes below it ($0 \leq p$), which are in order from left to right $N_1, \ldots, N_p$, then the node N_0' in the second tree corresponding to N_0 is connected to exactly p nodes beneath it; if these are, in order from left to right, $N_1', \ldots, N_p'$, then, for each i, $1 \leq i \leq p$, N_i' corresponds to N_i in the first tree.

As a consequence of this definition, if two trees are isomorphic, the two roots must be corresponding nodes. Also, the leaves of one tree correspond, in order from left to right, to the leaves of the other. The correspondence of the nodes in the two derivation trees in Fig. 8.1.4 is shown, apart from the root and the leaves, by the circled numerals.

Definition: A context-free grammar is *ambiguous* if there exists a string in the language of the grammar that has (at least) two nonisomorphic derivation trees, each with the start symbol at the root. We say that this string is an *ambiguous string* for the grammar.

An example of an ambiguous grammar is the following:

$$S \longrightarrow bS \,|\, Sb \,|\, c$$

An ambiguous string is *bcb*, two nonisomorphic derivation trees for which are shown in Fig. 8.1.5.

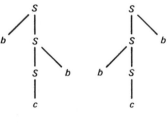

Figure 8.1.5

It is important to see why the two trees in this figure are not isomorphic. If they were isomorphic, the two root nodes would have to correspond. Then the two nodes beneath each would have to correspond. But the node labeled *b* is to the left of the node labeled *S* in one tree, and the node labeled *b* is to the right of the node labeled *S* in the other tree. Thus there is no way to let the nodes correspond to take care of both parts (1) and (2) of the definition.

The reader may have seen other definitions of "isomorphic" before. All the uses of this word in various mathematical theories are related, but there are significant differences. Two objects are isomorphic if (1) they are made up in a one-to-one manner from corresponding parts; and (2) the relationship between the parts of one object and the relationship between the corresponding parts of the other object are exactly the same, in those aspects that are of concern in the theory at hand.

A tree is a variety of graph, as studied in graph theory. It should be noted, however, that the concept of isomorphism that we have just introduced is not the same as the most common concept of isomorphism in graph theory, which generally makes no reference to left and right. Since our considerations are linguistic, we must explicitly recognize the left-to-right order in which some nodes occur in the tree.

According to this definition, a grammar, not a language, is said to be ambiguous; it is the manner of specifying the syntax that is faulty. We shall see that in some cases a language (i.e., set of strings) can have two different grammars, one of which is ambiguous, the other not. (Later, we shall define "inherently ambiguous language" as a language any grammar for which is ambiguous.)

DESIGNING UNAMBIGUOUS 8.2 FORMAL LANGUAGES

In this section we consider two ways of making an ambiguous formal grammar unambiguous. One is to modify the language in some way or other (e.g., adding parentheses, or permuting the order in which characters occur in strings). The other is to change the grammar without modifying the language. In the course of this investigation, we also see how operator precedence is related to the problem of resolving ambiguities.

The Utility of Parentheses 8.2.1

Suppose that someone comes forth with the following grammar intended to generate the formulas of the propositional calculus, in infix notation but without parentheses:

$$\text{G-SIMP:} \quad S \longrightarrow S\&S \mid S \vee S \mid \sim S \mid A$$
$$A \longrightarrow A' \mid p \mid q \mid r$$

That this grammar is ambiguous is proved in Fig. 8.2.1, which shows two nonisomorphic derivation trees for the string $p\&q \vee r$.

Note that the two derivation trees for this string represent two distinct structural meanings that we wish to be expressible in the propositional calculus. Thus we can say that the person who designed the grammar has done an inade-

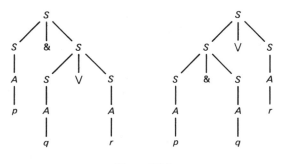

Figure 8.2.1

quate job. A basic revision is necessary, so that the two distinct structures are represented by two distinct strings.

The problem is to bring this language into usable form by removing all ambiguities. The obvious solution is to introduce parentheses in the appropriate way, thus coming back to the grammar G-IN of Section 7.2.4. We emphasize that, in doing things in this way, we are modifying not only the grammar, but also the set of derivable strings; they now have parentheses whereas they did not before.

Parentheses are just one pair of symbols among many for accomplishing an important purpose in formal languages. Other common sets of symbols serving the same purpose are brackets and braces. In some programming languages (ALGOL 60, for example) the words "**begin**" and "**end**" act as parentheses. In this chapter we shall talk almost exclusively of parentheses, with the understanding that the essential linguistic properties apply to these other pairs of symbols as well

It is interesting to see the need for parentheses that arose in the design of a programming language. Two statement forms of ALGOL 60 were the "**if** . . . **then**" and the "**if** . . . **then** . . . **else**" as, for example, in the two statements

$$\text{if } X = 0 \text{ then } Y := 0$$
$$\text{if } X = 0 \text{ then } Y := 0 \text{ else } Y := 1$$

These statements could be compounded, in which case there had to be a prohibition against allowing "**if**" to follow a "**then**" immediately. For example, if one were permitted to write

$$\text{if } X = 0 \text{ then if } W = 0 \text{ then } Y := 0 \text{ else } Y := 1$$

a serious ambiguity would result, since it could not be determined which of the two occurrences of "**if**" the "**else**" belonged to. In case $X \neq 0$, a crucial difference in execution turns on this ambiguity: Under the interpretation that the "**else**" belongs to the first "**if**" Y should be set equal to 1; but under the interpretation that the "**else**" belongs to the second "**if**" no change in Y should result.

The possibility of such ambiguity was prevented by the requirement that a program never have "**then**" followed immediately by "**if**." Parentheses would have to be used in the form of "**begin** . . . **end**" with "**begin**" placed between "**then**" and "**if**." Thus a programmer would have to write, in place of the ambiguous piece above, one of the following:

$$\text{if } X = 0 \text{ then begin if } W = 0 \text{ then } Y := 0 \text{ end else } Y := 1$$
$$\text{if } X = 0 \text{ then begin if } W = 0 \text{ then } Y := 0 \text{ else } Y := 1 \text{ end}$$

In the first of these the "**else**" belongs to the first "**if**"; in the second the "**else**" belongs to the second "**if**." Although there was a general prohibition of following "**then**" by "**if**" there was no prohibition of following "**else**" by "**if**" since that practice did not lead to ambiguity. For example, the following was allowed:

if X = 0 **then** Y := 0 **else if** W = 0 **then** Y := 1 **else** Y := 2

If parentheses are acceptable, they are always a sure way of doing away with ambiguities. They are not always the best way; for many purposes parenthesis-free notation is possible and superior. Many formal languages use several species of parentheses. ALGOL 60, for example, uses parentheses in algebraic expressions, while using "**begin** . . . **end**" in compound statements. The use of brackets, braces, and parentheses simultaneously in order to gain clarity in large algebraic formulas is well known.

The power of parentheses to prevent ambiguities is investigated mathematically in Section 8.3.

Unambiguous Grammars for Fixed 8.2.2
Languages

Up to now we have been considering the problem of designing languages so that they have unambiguous grammars. It was all right to modify the language (add parentheses, for example) as long as the modification did not interfere with the function that the language was to serve.

We now consider the problem of finding an unambiguous grammar for a given language without modifying the language. The language might have been given originally by an ambiguous grammar, which now requires modification.

For example, suppose that we wish to alter G-SIMP (p. 235) to form a new unambiguous grammar with the same language. We must be mindful that the new grammar cannot have all the derivation trees that G-SIMP has. In fact, a feasible approach is to arrange, for every ambiguous string in the language of G-SIMP, that the new grammar have exactly one of the several derivation trees that G-SIMP has of that string. In other words, the problem is thought of as making, for each ambiguous string in the language, a selection of exactly one structural meaning among the several structural meanings it has in G-SIMP. One solution is the following:

$$G\text{-SIMPU-1:} \quad S \longrightarrow A\&S \mid A \bigvee S \mid \sim S \mid A$$
$$A \longrightarrow A' \mid p \mid q \mid r$$

We defer proving that G-SIMPU-1 is unambiguous and equivalent to G-SIMP. Meanwhile we note that $p\&q \bigvee r$ has only one parsing in G-SIMPU-1, namely the derivation tree of Fig. 8.2.2.

Another solution is the following:

$$\text{G-SIMPU-2:} \quad S \longrightarrow D \vee S \,|\, D$$
$$D \longrightarrow C \& D \,|\, C$$
$$C \longrightarrow \,\sim C \,|\, A$$
$$A \longrightarrow A' \,|\, p \,|\, q \,|\, r$$

Figure 8.2.3 is the derivation tree for $p \& q \vee r$ in G-SIMPU-2.

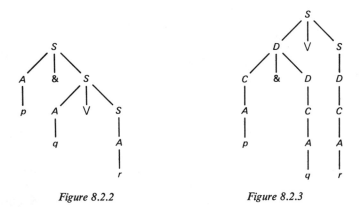

Figure 8.2.2   *Figure 8.2.3*

We shall be concerned with this method of removing ambiguities from grammars in Section 8.2.5. It is not as useful for dealing with a complete formal language with a prescribed purpose as with a sublanguage where the set of strings itself is prescribed.

8.2.3 Precedence of Operators

We now approach the problem of ambiguity from a different point of view. In many languages certain symbols or strings of symbols denote objects (let us call these *object strings*), while other symbols (and, in rarer occasions, strings of symbols) denote operators. Objects might be numbers, sets, and so on, but in the propositional calculus they are propositions. The operator symbols of the propositional calculus are the &, the $\vee$, and the $\sim$. Generally, the operator symbols are capable of joining two strings that denote objects to form a larger string that denotes an object. Clearly, one must understand the semantics of a language to decide what the object strings and operator symbols of the language are. But once they have been singled out, we can deal with this notion in a syntactic way, which we now do.

When we look at a string in the language, we may at first be unable to tell which object strings are joined to which other object strings to form larger object strings. In such languages, this problem is often the crux of parsing.

One principle is that an object string cannot be the operand of more than one operator sign. In the string $p \& q \lor r$, with or without parentheses, the q cannot be operated on by both the $\&$ and the $\lor$. If it is joined by $\&$, then it is the new string "$p \& q$" that is then joined by the $\lor$, not q itself.

Definition: An *operator grammar* is a context-free grammar in which (1) one or more nonterminals are specified as *object* nonterminals, (2) one or more terminals are specified as *operator symbols*, and (3) each production that contains an operator symbol contains only one occurrence of that operator symbol and no occurrence of any other, has as its left side an object nonterminal, and has at least one object nonterminal on its right side.

Definition: Given a derivation tree in an operator grammar of a terminal string from the start symbol: Of two occurrences of operator signs in the string, one has *precedence* over the other if the former is part of the object string that is joined by the latter. (Alternatively, one has *precedence* over the other if there is an upward path in the derivation tree from the former to the node just above the latter.)

The word "precedence" has been used for this concept quite naturally: If one operator has precedence over another, it operates on its operands *before* the second operator operates on its operands, because one of the latter operands has the former operator as a part. If neither of two operators has precedence over the other, it does not matter which operates first, since neither produces an object that is an operand, or part of an operand, of the other.

We note that the crux of the ambiguity of $p \& q \lor r$ in G-SIMP of Section 8.2.1 is the question of which of the two operator signs has precedence. The two distinct unambiguous grammers of Section 8.2.2, G-SIMPU-1 and G-SIMPU-2, decided this question differently, as can be noted by comparing the derivation trees of Figs. 8.2.2 and 8.2.3.

Operator Precedence and Parsing *8.2.4*

It is not always easy to figure out the precedence of operators; fortunately, practical parsing algorithms do not demand that we first determine operator precedence before we begin to parse. However, when we are faced with the problem of devising the algorithm itself for parsing an operator grammar, we do well to take the time to study the general conditions of operator precedence.

It is worthwhile, therefore, to look at operator grammars and ask: Under what conditions does one operator occurrence have precedence over another? The answer to this question for G-SIMPU-1 is easy: One operator sign has precedence over another if and only if the former is to the right of the latter.

The precedence rule for G-SIMPU-2 is more involved. To begin, we assign a *priority* of 3 to the tilde, 2 to the ampersand, and 1 to the wedge. Now let O_1 and O_2 be two occurrences of operator signs in a string, where O_1 is to the left of O_2, and let $p(O_1)$ and $p(O_2)$ be their priorities. Then O_2 has *precedence* over O_1 if and only if $p(O_2) \geqq p(O_1)$ and, for any occurrence O_3 of an operator sign between O_2 and O_1, $p(O_3) \geqq p(O_1)$. O_1 has precedence over O_2 if and only if $p(O_1) > p(O_2)$ and, for any O_3 between O_1 and O_2, $p(O_3) > p(O_2)$.

Thus an operator sign has precedence over possibly many operator signs to its left: namely, over any such sign of lower or equal priority where there is no operator between of priority lower than both. And it has precedence to the right over at most two operator signs: the first one O' of lower priority (if any), and the first one to the right of O' of lower priority than O' (if any).

In spite of the complication in this formulation, we can decide on a parsing order which comes out to be less complicated. One way to parse a string in the language of G-SIMPU-2 is to parse all the tildes in the order of their occurrence from right to left, then all the ampersands from right to left, then all the wedges from right to left. A second way would be to parse all operator signs from right to left, with the exception that the parsing of an operator sign must be delayed until all operator signs to its left up to (but not including) the first sign to its left of equal or smaller priority have been parsed. Various points of this discussion are illustrated in the parsing of the string

$$p \lor \sim q \& \sim \sim r \& p' \lor \sim p \lor r$$

which is shown in Fig. 8.2.4.

One curious thing is that, whatever parsing method is selected, a right-to-left order is favored (see Exercise 2). Apart from this feature, the precedence rule

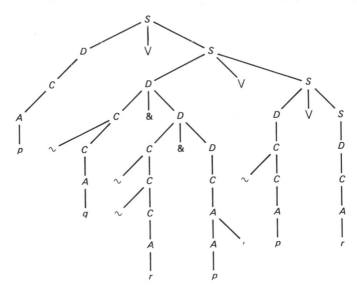

Figure 8.2.4

for G-SIMPU-2 is quite similar in some aspects to precedence rules of many practical languages.

The precedence rule for the fully parenthesized propositional calculus G-IN (Section 7.2.4) is quite simple. Let us say that a parenthesis and its mate are *associated* with an operator sign if the operator sign occurs either just before the left parenthesis or just after the right parenthesis. Then one operator sign has precedence over a second operator sign if and only if the former is within a pair of parentheses associated with the latter. (The matter of mating of parentheses is discussed in detail in Section 8.3.)

Most user-oriented scientific programming languages use partially parenthesized algebraic expressions. Programming manuals invariably give some precedence rules to show how algebraic expressions are parsed at points where there are no parentheses. The manuals do not discuss the parsing problem as such, but simply the order in which the computer computes the quantities corresponding to the subexpressions. But this amounts to the same problem as parsing, in dealing with algebraic expressions (see Exercise 3).

Examples for Finding Equivalent 8.2.5 Unambiguous Grammars

We return now to the problem we introduced in Section 8.2.2. We shall consider several ambiguous grammars, and in each case we shall try to find an unambiguous grammar exactly equivalent to it. By studying this type of problem, we shall gain insight into the various kinds of ambiguity that can arise, and how to avoid them.

EXAMPLE 1. The grammar

$$S \longrightarrow bS \,|\, Sb \,|\, c$$

was shown in Fig. 8.1.5 to be ambiguous. To remove the ambiguity we must regulate the order in which the b's are generated. Our solution generates all the b's to the left of c before it generates any of the b's to the right:

$$S \longrightarrow bS \,|\, A$$
$$A \longrightarrow Ab \,|\, c$$

Two more solutions are as follows:

$$\begin{cases} S \longrightarrow bS \,|\, c \,|\, cA \\ A \longrightarrow bA \,|\, b \end{cases} \qquad \begin{cases} S \longrightarrow AcA \\ A \longrightarrow bA \,|\, \lambda \end{cases}$$

EXAMPLE 2.

$$S \longrightarrow bS \,|\, cS \,|\, D$$
$$D \longrightarrow bD \,|\, cD \,|\, \lambda$$

Figure 8.2.5 shows that the string b is ambiguous. More generally, any nonnull string over the alphabet of $\{b, c\}$ is ambiguous, since the D yields only b's and

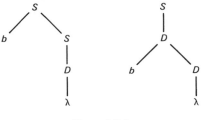

Figure 8.2.5

c's that S by itself could have yielded. A solution is to get rid of D:

$$S \longrightarrow bS \,|\, cS \,|\, \lambda$$

EXAMPLE 3.

$$S \longrightarrow bS \,|\, cS \,|\, bbS \,|\, \lambda$$

We leave it to the reader to show that the string bb is ambiguous. The solution is to eliminate the production $S \rightarrow bbS$ (because the effect of this production can be obtained by two applications of the production $S \rightarrow bS$):

$$S \longrightarrow bS \,|\, cS \,|\, \lambda$$

EXAMPLE 4.

$$S \longrightarrow B \,|\, D$$
$$B \longrightarrow bBc \,|\, \lambda$$
$$D \longrightarrow dDe \,|\, \lambda$$

The only ambiguous string is λ (Fig. 8.2.6). A solution is quite easy:

$$S \longrightarrow B \,|\, D \,|\, \lambda$$
$$B \longrightarrow bBc \,|\, bc$$
$$D \longrightarrow dDe \,|\, de$$

$$
\begin{array}{ccc}
S & & S \\
| & & | \\
B & & D \\
| & & | \\
\lambda & & \lambda
\end{array}
$$

Figure 8.2.6

EXAMPLE 5.

$$S \longrightarrow SS \,|\, (S) \,|\, b \,|\, \lambda$$

(This grammar is a variation of Example 3 of Section 7.3.) It is the first production $S \rightarrow SS$ that makes for ambiguity here, as Fig. 8.2.7 shows. It is easy to

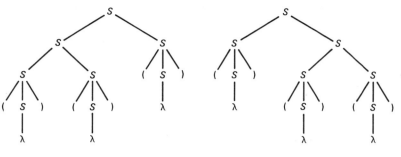

Figure 8.2.7

see that, in any grammar with this production, if some terminal string can be derived from S, then the grammer is ambiguous.

Our solution is

$$S \longrightarrow bS \,|\, (S)S \,|\, \lambda$$

The derivation tree in this grammar for the string ( )( )( ) is Fig. 8.2.8. A little experimentation shows that there is no nonisomorphic derivation tree for this

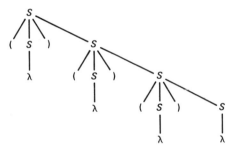

Figure 8.2.8

string. That the second grammar is unambiguous and equivalent to the first will be provable at the end of the next section (Exercise 1).

EXAMPLE 6.

$$S \longrightarrow DcD$$

$$D \longrightarrow bD \,|\, cD \,|\, \lambda$$

The language of this grammar is the set of strings over $\{b, c\}$ with at least one c. Any string with two or more c's in it is ambiguous, since any of these c's could be the c that results from the production $S \rightarrow DcD$. To remove such ambiguities we can simply arrange it so that (arbitrarily) the leftmost c is always so derived:

$$S \longrightarrow BcD$$

$$D \longrightarrow bD \,|\, cD \,|\, \lambda$$

$$B \longrightarrow bB \,|\, \lambda$$

An alternative solution, in which strings are derived in left-to-right fashion, is

$$S \longrightarrow bS \,|\, cE$$
$$E \longrightarrow cE \,|\, bE \,|\, \lambda$$

8.2.6 More Examples

EXAMPLE 7.

$$S \longrightarrow EF$$
$$E \longrightarrow bE \,|\, cE \,|\, \lambda$$
$$F \longrightarrow cF \,|\, dF \,|\, \lambda$$

The language of this grammar is $\{W \,|\, W = W_1 W_2, W_1 \in \{b, c\}^*, W_2 \in \{c, d\}^*\}$ (i.e., the set of strings over $\{b, c, d\}$ in which no d is anywhere to the left of any b). Ambiguity comes about because in some cases W_1 (derived from E) and W_2 (derived from F) can vary for a given W (e.g., in the string bcd, we could take $W_1 = b$, $W_2 = cd$, or we could take $W_1 = bc$, $W_2 = d$).

To remove the ambiguities, we can decide that W_2 shall begin with the leftmost d, and that $W_2 = \lambda$ if there are no d's. Our solution (where now W_2 is derivable from dF in case $W_2 \neq \lambda$) is as follows:

$$S \longrightarrow E \,|\, EdF$$
$$E \longrightarrow bE \,|\, cE \,|\, \lambda$$
$$F \longrightarrow cF \,|\, dF \,|\, \lambda$$

Finally, this grammar can be converted into an unambiguous grammar with left-to-right derivations:

$$S \longrightarrow bS \,|\, cS \,|\, \lambda \,|\, dF$$
$$F \longrightarrow cF \,|\, dF \,|\, \lambda$$

EXAMPLE 8. (See Example 9 of Section 7.3.).

$$S \longrightarrow bSc \,|\, bbSc \,|\, \lambda$$

Figure 8.2.9 shows the string $bbbcc$ is ambiguous in this grammar. Generally, the trouble is that a production in which two b's are generated can be applied before or after a production in which a single b is generated. In the following

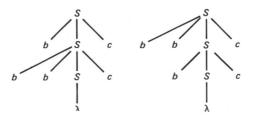

Figure 8.2.9

solution, it is impossible to apply a production yielding a single b after a production yielding two b's:

$$S \longrightarrow bSc \,|\, D$$

$$D \longrightarrow bbDc \,|\, \lambda$$

EXAMPLE 9.

$$S \longrightarrow bS \,|\, E$$

$$E \longrightarrow Ed \,|\, F$$

$$F \longrightarrow bFd \,|\, \lambda$$

One solution is simply to remove the last two productions and convert the production $E \to F$ to $E \to \lambda$. But suppose that another constraint is put on the solution, that is, that the production $F \to bFd$ be kept, and that in the unambiguous grammar, as many b's and d's be matched by this production as possible. Then a convenient solution is

$$S \longrightarrow bQ \,|\, Rd \,|\, F$$

$$Q \longrightarrow bQ \,|\, F$$

$$R \longrightarrow Rd \,|\, F$$

$$F \longrightarrow bFd \,|\, \lambda$$

Note that the three productions with S are used, respectively, in three disjoint cases: case I, there are more b's than d's; case II, there are more d's than b's; and case III, there are as many b's as d's.

EXAMPLE 10. Not every ambiguous context-free grammar has an unambiguous equivalent. Figure 8.2.10 demonstrates that the string bbccdd

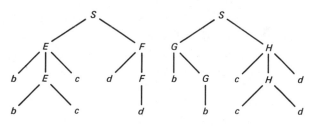

Figure 8.2.10

is ambiguous (and indeed indicates that all strings of the form $b^i c^i d^i$ are also) in the following grammar:

$$S \longrightarrow ED \,|\, BF$$

$$E \longrightarrow bEc \,|\, bc$$

$$D \longrightarrow Dd \,|\, d$$

$$B \longrightarrow Bb \,|\, b$$

$$F \longrightarrow cFd \,|\, cd$$

The language is $\{b^m c^m dd^* \,|\, m \geqq 1\} \cup \{bb^* c^n d^n \,|\, n \geqq 1\}$.

It can be shown that every grammar equivalent to this grammar has ambiguous strings of the form $a^i b^i c^i$. (The proof can be found in Ginsburg [1966], Chap. Six; Salomaa [1973], p. 205; etc.) Such a language is called *inherently ambiguous*.

It has been proved that there is no decision procedure to tell whether a grammar is ambiguous, and none to tell whether its language is inherently ambiguous (see, e.g., Hopcroft and Ullman [1979], pp. 200, 206).

A question that a reader might naturally ask after reading this subsection and trying the group of exercises soon to follow is: Does there exist a procedure to convert an ambiguous context-free grammar that is not inherently ambiguous into an equivalent unambiguous context-free grammar? It is known that no such algorithm exists (which is clearly implied by a result proved in Schmidt and Szymanski [1977]). It would appear that if we are challenged repeatedly with the task of converting an ambiguous grammar into an unambiguous one, we must be prepared to face each grammar as an individual problem, with no guarantee that problems we have solved in the past will be helpful.

8.2.7 Exercises

    1. For the unambiguous grammar

$$S \longrightarrow S + P \,|\, P$$
$$P \longrightarrow P*V \,|\, V$$
$$V \longrightarrow V' \,|\, x \,|\, y \,|\, z$$

when does an occurrence of * have precedence over another *? When does a + have precedence over another +? When does a * have precedence over a +? Your answers must be in terms of conditions that can be observed in any string of the language of the grammar, without reference to the derivation tree.

    2. The grammar G-SIMPU-2 favors right-to-left parsing. Construct an alternative unambiguous grammar for the same language for which the following parsing order will work: Parse all the tildes from left to right, then parse all the ampersands from left to right, then parse all the wedges from left to right.

    3. Recall G-PP, the incompletely parenthesized propositional calculus of Section 7.2.4. For the sake of having an explicit operator symbol for conjunction, we write the following variant of that grammar:

$$S \longrightarrow A \,|\, N \,|\, C \,|\, D$$
$$A \longrightarrow A' \,|\, p \,|\, q \,|\, r$$
$$N \longrightarrow {\sim}N \,|\, {\sim}A \,|\, {\sim}(C) \,|\, {\sim}(D)$$
$$C \longrightarrow C\&K \,|\, K\&K$$
$$K \longrightarrow A \,|\, N \,|\, (D)$$
$$D \longrightarrow D \vee J \,|\, J \vee J$$
$$J \longrightarrow C \,|\, N \,|\, A$$

The operator symbols are $\sim$, &, and $\vee$ and the object nonterminals are all the nonterminals. Under what conditions will an occurrence of the conjunction operator in a string in the language of this grammar have precedence over an occurrence of the disjunction operator; under what conditions will the latter operator have precedence over the former, and under what conditions will neither have precedence over the other? [*Hint:* To get started, consider the sample string $p\&q\&(p'\&q'\vee r)\&r'$. Then choose other sample strings judiciously.] The same question for two occurrences of the conjunction operator. [Begin with the same sample string.] The same question for an occurrence of the conjunction operator and an occurrence of the negation operator. [Begin with the sample string $\sim p\&\sim(q\&r)$.]

4. Prove that in G-SUF (i.e., the parenthesis-free propositional calculus in suffix notation, Section 7.2.5) no operator occurrence has precedence over an operator occurrence to its left. Show by examples that an operator occurrence sometimes has and sometimes does not have precedence over an operator occurrence to its right.

5. Give unambiguous grammars for Exercises 21, 27, and 32 of Section 7.3.

6. Give an unambiguous grammar for Exercise 30 of Section 7.3.

In each of the following, (1) show the grammar is ambiguous with two non-isomorphic derivation trees for the same string, and (2) find an equivalent unambiguous grammar. In part (2) some care must be taken to verify in each exercise that the grammar that results is *both* unambiguous and equivalent to the original grammar. These exercises are arranged roughly in order of increasing difficulty.

7. $S \longrightarrow bSE \mid \lambda$
$E \longrightarrow bE \mid b$

8. $S \longrightarrow ScScS \mid b$

9. $S \longrightarrow bSc \mid bSd \mid bS \mid \lambda$

10. $S \longrightarrow bS \mid Sd \mid bd \mid SS$

11. $S \longrightarrow cS \mid cSb \mid Q$
$Q \longrightarrow cQc \mid c$

12. $S \longrightarrow QSR \mid \lambda$
$Q \longrightarrow bbQ \mid bb$
$R \longrightarrow ccR \mid cc$

13. $S \longrightarrow bSE \mid \lambda$
$E \longrightarrow cE \mid c$

14. $S \longrightarrow EFEF$
$E \longrightarrow bE \mid cE \mid \lambda$
$F \longrightarrow cF \mid dF \mid \lambda$

15. $S \longrightarrow bS \mid bE$
$E \longrightarrow Ed \mid Fd$
$F \longrightarrow bFd \mid bddd$

16. $S \longrightarrow eS \mid eA \mid bd$
$A \longrightarrow bA \mid bd \mid c$

17. $S \longrightarrow bS \mid cS \mid bbE \mid ccE$
$E \longrightarrow bE \mid cE \mid \lambda$

18. $S \longrightarrow A \mid QR$
$A \longrightarrow bAd \mid B$
$B \longrightarrow bBc \mid \lambda$
$Q \longrightarrow bQc \mid \lambda$
$R \longrightarrow cRd \mid \lambda$

19. $S \longrightarrow bSd \mid dS \mid Sb \mid c$

20. $S \longrightarrow dSbc \mid dSb \mid dSc \mid \lambda$

21. $S \longrightarrow QR \mid c$
$Q \longrightarrow dQ \mid d$
$R \longrightarrow bR \mid S$

22. $S \longrightarrow ccD \mid bbS \mid b$
$D \longrightarrow cD \mid cS$

23. $S \longrightarrow cS \mid bA \mid b$
$A \longrightarrow bA \mid bD$
$D \longrightarrow cD \mid cS$

24. $S \longrightarrow bbbS \mid bbbbS \mid bbb \mid bbbb$.

The three remaining exercises are all *quite difficult*.

25. $S \longrightarrow bSd \mid MNP$
     $M \longrightarrow bMc \mid bc$
     $N \longrightarrow cN \mid c$
     $P \longrightarrow cPd \mid cd$

26. $S \longrightarrow bS \mid Sd \mid EF$
     $E \longrightarrow bEc \mid bc$
     $F \longrightarrow cFd \mid cd$

27. $S \longrightarrow bSe \mid PQR$
     $P \longrightarrow bPc \mid \lambda$
     $Q \longrightarrow cQd \mid \lambda$
     $R \longrightarrow dRe \mid \lambda$

8.3 THE UNAMBIGUITY OF GRAMMARS WITH PARENTHESES

Everyone who has studied high-school algebra appreciates how parentheses function to resolve ambiguities. In this section we make a detailed study of the way parentheses work, and go on to a proof of the unambiguity of the grammar G-IN and a parsing method for strings in its language.

8.3.1 Mating Operations

Parentheses are used for grouping: The left parenthesis and the right parenthesis that is its mate serve to demarcate the beginning and end of a functional unit in a string. In this way, the pair of parentheses is similar in its purpose to the frame of a picture, which indicates that the things inside relate to one another, and (perhaps with minor exceptions) only the picture as a whole relates to what is outside. Parentheses, however, involve difficulties in that many pairs of parentheses occur in an expression, often one pair inside another, with no graphic connection between a parenthesis and its mate.

The mating of parentheses is an important part of the parsing of strings that have them, so we proceed to analyze this matter in detail. The definitions and theorems in this subsection may seem so obvious to the reader that he or she may even wonder why we have bothered to write them down. Nevertheless, a rigorous analysis of parentheses will contribute to an understanding of the entire question of ambiguity.

Let us suppose that we have a string and that we can, once we have determined that two parentheses are mates, indicate the mating with a mark of some sort.

Definition: A *proper mating operation* on a string (some of whose parentheses may already be mated) mates an unmated left parenthesis with an unmated right parenthesis which is somewhere to its right with no unmated parentheses between. A *complete mating sequence* is a sequence of proper mating operations, starting with a string in which no parentheses are mated, and ending with the same string with parentheses so mated that no proper mating operation is possible to any unmated parentheses in the string.

For example, if parentheses are mated in the order shown in Fig. 8.3.1, the result is a complete mating sequence. The order shown is not the only order for a complete mating sequence. The first could have been the second and the second the first; the 7th, 9th, 6th, and 8th, respectively, could have been the 6th, 7th, 8th, and 9th, and so on. There are 66,528 possible complete mating sequences in this example, all of which end up with the same result, as we shall prove.

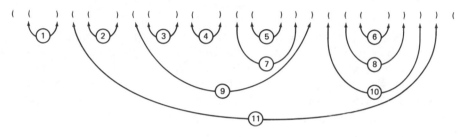

Figure 8.3.1

If, after a complete mating sequence of an arbitrary string, not all the parentheses are mated, then either these are all left parentheses, or these are all right parentheses (as in Fig. 8.3.1), or all the unmated left parentheses are to the right of all the unmated right parentheses. An example of the last possibility is the string) ( ) (( ) (, in which the first, fourth, and seventh parentheses will be unmated in any complete mating sequence.

These are all examples of strings with parentheses only. In useful languages characters other than parentheses also appear in strings; such characters can generally be ignored in mating parentheses.

In this section we confine our attention to languages with only one species of parentheses, shown as round parentheses. Our analysis could easily be extended to languages with several species. It is to be understood that in such a language a left parenthesis cannot be mated to a right parenthesis of another species, and that parentheses of the same species cannot be mated if there are any unmated parentheses, even of another species, between. For example, if round parentheses and brackets are used, then there is no way of mating in the string ([ )], although there is in [( )], ([ ]) and ( ) [ ].

Some Theorems About Mating 8.3.2

We prove now that the order in which parentheses are mated is immaterial.

Definition: Four distinct parentheses in a string are *cross-mated* if the first (in order from left to right) is mated to the third and the second to the fourth.

LEMMA 1: Cross-mating never results from a sequence of proper mating operations.

PROOF: If the first parenthesis of four is mated to the third, the second could not be subsequently mated to the fourth. On the other hand, if the second is mated to the fourth, the first could not subsequently be mated to the third. ▮

THEOREM 8.3.1: If two parentheses are mated as a result of one complete mating sequence, then they are mated as a result of any complete mating sequence.

PROOF: Suppose that we have a string and two complete mating sequences applied to the string. We must prove that every pair of parentheses mated by the first sequence is also mated by the second sequence. The proof is by a course-of-values induction on n, the length of the substring between the parentheses assumed to be mated as a result of the first complete mating sequence. Clearly, the theorem is true for $n = 0$; in this case the left parenthesis must immediately precede the right parenthesis and they will be mated in any complete mating sequence.

Assume now for a given n that the theorem is true for all pairs of parentheses mated in a given complete mating sequence, where the length of the string between the two is less than n. Let $(_1$ and $)_1$ be a pair of parentheses mated by the given complete mating sequence where the string as a whole is

$$W_1(_1 W_2)_1 W_3$$

and the length of W_2 is n. Each parenthesis in W_2 must be mated in the first complete mating sequence; otherwise, $(_1$ could not be mated to $)_1$. By Lemma 1, each such parenthesis is mated to a parenthesis also in W_2. But the length of the string between any two symbols in W_2 must be less than n, since n is the length of W_2. Therefore, by the inductive hypothesis, parentheses in W_2 mated in the first complete mating sequence must be mated in the second mating sequence. Since all parentheses between $(_1$ and $)_1$ are mated in the second complete mating sequence, $(_1$ and $)_1$ must be mated also. ▮

Definition: A parenthesis is *the mate* of another parenthesis in a string if the two are mated in any complete mating sequence of the string. (The use of the word "the" is justified by Theorem 8.3.1.)

COROLLARY: The parentheses $(_1$ and $)_1$ are mates in the string $(_1 W_2)_1$ if and only if they are mates in the string $W_1(_1 W_2)_1 W_3$.

In other words, whether parentheses are mated depends only on what occurs between them and not outside. The proof of the theorem is easily modified to accommodate the corollary.

THEOREM 8.3.2: If all parentheses of W_2 have mates in W_2, then any two parentheses in $W_1 W_3$ are mates if and only if they are mates in $W_1 W_2 W_3$.

PROOF: Begin a complete mating sequence of $W_1 W_2 W_3$ with the parentheses of W_2, not mating any of the parentheses of W_1 or W_3 until all those in W_2 are mated. Thereafter, a parenthesis of W_1 is mated to a parenthesis of W_3 in $W_1 W_2 W_3$ if and only if it is so mated in the string $W_1 W_3$. ∎

A complete set of mating operations is like a parsing of the string. For most languages in which parentheses are used, part of the job in parsing is finding the mates of parentheses, which actually makes the entire job easier. We shall go on to use what we have established about the mating of parentheses to prove that certain grammars for languages involving parentheses are unambiguous.

The Unambiguity of G–IN 8.3.3

We repeat from Section 7.2.4 the productions of G-IN:

$$(1)(2)(3)(4) \qquad S \longrightarrow (S)\&(S)\,|\,(S)\lor(S)\,|\sim(S)\,|\,A$$
$$(5)(6)(7)(8) \qquad A \longrightarrow A'\,|\,p\,|\,q\,|\,r$$

In order to prove this grammar unambiguous, we establish several lemmas, making use of what we have established about the mating of parentheses. Note that some of these lemmas involve derivations, others involve derivation trees.

LEMMA 2: All parentheses in a derived string are mated. Two mated parentheses in a derived string of a derivation came about from the same application of a production.

PROOF: By induction on i, we easily prove that for all i, Lemma 2 is true of the ith line in any derivation. The first line is S, in which there are no parentheses, so Lemma 2 is true vacuously for $i = 1$. Now assume that Lemma 2 is true of the ith line. If one of productions (4) to (8) is used to form the $(i + 1)$st line, there is no change in the parentheses.

Note that the parentheses in the right side of productions (1), (2), and (3) are mated. Thus if $W_1 S W_3$ is the ith line and $S \to W_2$ is the production used, then $W_1 W_2 W_3$ is the $(i + 1)$st line. By Theorem 8.3.2, since Lemma 2 is true of $W_1 S W_3$, it is also true of $W_1 W_3$, and therefore also of $W_1 W_2 W_3$. ∎

LEMMA 3: Every & and every $\lor$ in a derived string has a) to its immediate left and a (to its immediate right. Every $\sim$ has a (to its immediate right.

The proof is immediate from inspection of productions (1), (2), and (3), and the fact that terminal characters adjacent in any line in a derivation remain adjacent in all following lines.

LEMMA 4:   The following is true of every derivation tree in G-IN: Each &, or $\vee$, the) to its immediate left, its mate, the (to its immediate right, and its mate are all connected to the same S.

The proof is immediate from Lemmas 2 and 3. (Recall how a derivation tree is obtained from a derivation.)

LEMMA 5:   Every derivation in G-IN of a string W begins with the same production.

LEMMA 6:   In any two derivation trees for the same string, the S at the top is connected to exactly the same symbols in the derived string.

PROOF OF LEMMAS 5 AND 6:   (I) If production (1) is the first production used in any derivation, then (is the first character in W; its mate is immediately followed by &, then (, whose mate is at the right end of W. (II) If production (2) is first in any derivation, then the same is true as in (I), except that $\vee$ follows the mate of the opening parenthesis. (III) If production (3) is the first in any derivation, then the first two characters of W are $\sim$ and (, whose mate is at the right end of W. (IV) If production (4) is the first in any derivation, then the first character is p, q, or r, and all the other characters in W, if any, are primes.

Every derivation must begin with one of these four productions. By looking at possibilities (I) through (IV), we see that no two derivations of W can begin with different productions. ∎

THEOREM 8.3.3:   G-IN is unambiguous.

PROOF: Assume that G-IN is ambiguous, letting W be an ambiguous string of minimum length. Then two nonisomorphic derivation trees T and T' exist for W. Lemma 6 justifies the following breakdown into cases.

Case 1. The top of T and of T' are each of the form shown in Fig. 8.3.2, where $(_1$ and $)_1$ are mates in W, as are $(_2$ and $)_2$; W is of the form $(_1 W_1)_1 \&(_2 W_2)_2$.

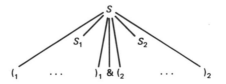

Figure 8.3.2

(Subscripts do not occur in the tree, and are put in here for identification purposes only.) The part of T, consisting of S_1, just those nodes of T beneath and connecting branches, constitutes a derivation tree T_1 for the string W_1. Similarly, T_2, the part of T under S_2, is a derivation tree for W_2. Similarly, T'_1, the part of T' under S_1, and T'_2, the part of T' under S_2, are derivation trees for W_1 and W_2, respectively.

Since W_1 and W_2 are each shorter than W, they are unambiguous and therefore T_1 must be isomorphic to T'_1 and T_2 isomorphic to T'_2. But then, if there is the one-to-one relationship between the nodes of T_1 and the nodes of T'_1 which constitutes an isomorphism, and also a one-to-one relationship between the nodes of T_2 and the nodes of T'_2, it is an easy matter to see that these two relations can be combined and extended to construct a one-to-one relationship between the nodes of T and the nodes of T' constituting an isomorphism of T and T', which is a contradiction.

Case 2. The top of T and T' are each as in Fig. 8.3.2, except that the & is replaced by the $\vee$. The proof is similar to that of case 1.

Case 3. The top of T and T' are each as in Fig. 8.3.3; W is of the form $\sim (W_1)$. Since W_1 is shorter than W, W_1 must be unambiguous. From here on the argument is the same as in case 1 (and indeed simpler, since there is only one subtree of T, and one of T', to consider).

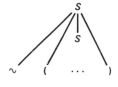

Figure 8.3.3

Case 4. None of the other three cases holds. Then any derivation of W cannot begin with productions (1), (2), or (3), so every derivation must begin with production (4). Since the remainder of the derivation can involve only productions (5), (6), (7), and (8), it is easy to see that W must be unambiguous.

∎

A Parsing Method for G–IN   8.3.4

Suppose that we have a string in the language and we wish to draw its derivation tree. Or, more generally, suppose we have a string that we think may be in the language, and we wish to decide whether it is or is not by ascertaining whether or not we can draw a tree.

Looking at the productions of G-IN, we see that there is an S between each pair of mated parentheses on the right sides of those productions in which parentheses are introduced. By Lemma 2, the portion of a string between any two mated parentheses must parse to an *S* if the string as a whole is to parse to an *S*.

This suggests that before parsing the string we should first mate all the parentheses. It turns out that this is not an optimal way to do things. It is much better to mate parentheses as part of the job of parsing.

We begin parsing a string by writing it at the bottom of a sheet of paper (or blackboard, etc.) as leaves of a tree to be constructed upward. We shall construct, or attempt to construct, the tree in an upward direction, thus doing a *bottom-up parse*.

Stage 1 begins by placing an *A* directly over each *p*, *q*, and *r*, using productions (6), (7), and (8). Then, for each *A* that is directly followed by a prime, a new *A* is placed over both of these [production (5)], repeating as often as there are primes. Finally, an *S* is placed over each topmost *A* [production (4)]. At the end of stage 1 (e.g., see Fig. 8.3.4a) each *p*, *q*, *r*, prime, and *A* have something on top of them, ultimately an *S*.

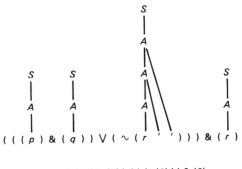

Top string (((*S*) & (*S*)) ∨ (∼(*S*))) & (*S*)

Figure 8.3.4a

Definition: The *top string* of a stage in the bottom-up parse (in which part of the derivation tree has been constructed) is the string of those characters that are the labels of the nodes at the top, from left to right (e.g., see Fig. 8.3.4a, b, and c).

At the end of stage 1, it may be that the whole string is parsed and stage 2 does not occur. If so, the string was a single variable without operators and without parentheses. If not, further construction involves only productions (1), (2), and (3), since *p*, *q*, *r*, prime, and *A* do not occur in the top string.

Stage 2 consists of the following step repeated as often as possible: Find in the top string a substring that is the right side of one of productions (1), (2), or (3). Place an *S* above these nodes and draw connecting branches (see Fig. 8.3.4b and c).

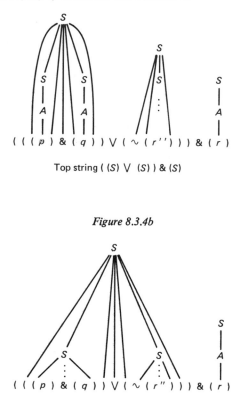

Top string (((S) $\vee$ (S)) & (S)

Figure 8.3.4b

Top string (S) & (S)

Figure 8.3.4c

In case we do not know if the original string is in the language, we simply follow the instructions until we see that we can no longer follow the instructions at some point. If the top string is anything other than just *S*, we can conclude that the original string is not in the language.

If all we are interested in is whether or not the string is in the language, and provided that we are not interested in having the completely drawn tree, we can get by with a piece of paper that is only large enough for the string being tested. We mark through any substring we find that parses to *S*. For example, the string of Fig. 8.3.4 would be treated as follows:

$$(((p)\&(q))\vee(\sim(r'')))\&(r)$$
$$(((-)\&(-))\vee(\sim(—)))\&(-)$$
$$((———)\vee(———))\&(-)$$
$$(————————)\&(-)$$

Something similar to this technique is carried through by the parsing automaton with arbitrary context-free grammars, as we shall see later in this chapter.

Let us note that we have been careful not to use the words *algorithm* or *procedure* in discussing the method of this subsection. Since we have not specified the order in which the steps of stage 1 or stage 2 are executed, our method is an incompletely specified algorithm (see Section 1.1.5).

When we discuss the parsing automaton, we shall have to decide on the order in which some things are done. Indeed, what we shall do (briefly speaking) is to mix up stages 1 and 2; at each step we shall (with one exception) work on the leftmost substring that has the right side of one of the productions. In this way we can do everything in one pass through the string from left to right.

8.3.5 Exercises

1. (a) Prove that G_2, below, is unambiguous. (b) Give a parsing method for it. (A difficult part of this task is to formulate in general where λ's are to be placed.) (c) Prove that G_1 and G_2 (from Example 5 of Section 8.2.5) are equivalent:

$$G_1: \quad S \longrightarrow SS \,|\, (S) \,|\, b \,|\, \lambda$$
$$G_2: \quad S \longrightarrow bS \,|\, (S)S \,|\, \lambda$$

2. Prove that the grammar G-PP of Section 7.2.4 (incompletely parenthesized propositional calculus) is unambiguous, and give a parsing method for it.

3. Construct an unambiguous grammar for Exercise 2 of Section 7.2, prove it is unambiguous, and give a parsing method for it.

4. Repeat Exercise 3 for Exercise 3 of Section 7.2.

8.4 THE UNAMBIGUITY OF OTHER GRAMMARS

In this section we demonstrate how ambiguities can be avoided by the use of parenthesis-free notation (sometimes called "Polish notation"). We prove the unambiguity of G-PRE, and discuss parsing methods for it and other similar grammars. We also investigate a class of grammars that have a property that makes for very easy, mistake-free bottom-up parsing: the class of the *perfectly univocal* grammars.

8.4.1 Unambiguity of G–PRE

In Section 7.2.5 we showed how parentheses could be restored in parenthesis-free notation. In effect, this was a parsing algorithm, which carried with it a strong suggestion that the grammar was unambiguous. We now give a rigorous proof that this is so for the grammar G-PRE (parenthesis-free propositional calculus in prefix notation):

$$(1)(2)(3)(4) \quad S \longrightarrow \&SS \,|\, \vee SS \,|\, \sim S \,|\, A$$
$$(5)(6)(7)(8) \quad A \longrightarrow A' \,|\, p \,|\, q \,|\, r$$

The proof of the unambiguity of G-PRE will be quite different in character from the proof of the unambiguity of G-IN, since no parentheses are involved. We begin by defining a numerical value for each string over the total alphabet, and proving that all derived strings have the same value.

Definition: If W is a string over the total alphabet of G-PRE, and i is a positive integer no greater than the length of W, then

$$f(i, W) = \begin{cases} -1 & \text{if the } i\text{th character from the left in } W \text{ is \& or } \vee \\ 0 & \text{if the } i\text{th character is } \sim \\ 1 & \text{if the } i\text{th character is } S, A, p, q, r, \text{ or prime} \\ & \text{and the } (i + 1)\text{st character is not prime} \\ 0 & \text{if the } i\text{th character is } S, A, p, q, r, \text{ or prime} \\ & \text{and the } (i + 1)\text{st character is prime} \end{cases}$$

$$f(W) = \sum_{i=1}^{n} f(i, W), \quad \text{where } n \text{ is the length of } W$$

We shall use these two functions to count from left to right on a string to see if the string has exactly the right number of operands, and in the right places, for the operators in the string. If a string has no operators, then it needs just one proposition variable. The $\sim$, which is a unary operator, does not change that; there is still the need for just one proposition variable, but this time as operand for the $\sim$. A binary operator creates a deficiency of 1; if a binary operator is inserted, the formula now needs one more proposition variable than it did before. This explains roughly the values given to $f(i, W)$.

The essence of the following proofs may be easier to grasp on first reading if the reader ignores production (5) and assumes that derived strings under consideration do not have the prime character. The parts of the proofs having to do with production (5) and the prime character may then simply be skipped over. Note that if W has no primes then $f(i, W) = 1$ whenever the ith character of W is S, A, p, q or r.

LEMMA 7: If W is a derived line of G-PRE, and X is the string that results when a production is applied to one of the nonterminals of W, then $f(X) = f(W)$.

PROOF: There are eight cases, depending on which production of G-PRE is used.

Case 1. $W = USY$, $X = U\&SSY$. Assume that the length of U is i. Then for $k \leqq i$ the kth character of X is the kth character of W. And for $k > i + 1$, the $(k + 2)$nd character of X is the kth character of W. The first character of Y cannot be prime, since W is a derived string. Hence $f(i + 1, W) = +1$, $f(i + 1, X) = -1$, $f(i + 2, X) = +1$, and $f(i + 3, X) = +1$. A simple computation then shows that $f(X) = f(W)$.

Cases 2 to 8 (the other seven productions) are all either similar to case 1 or simpler, and are omitted. ∎

LEMMA 8: If W is a string derived from S in G-PRE, then (I) $f(W) = 1$; and (II) if $W = Z_1 Z_2$ and Z_2 begins with a character other than prime, then $f(Z_1) < 1$.

(Intuitively, if W is a derived string, then W has the right number of operands for its operators; and if $W = Z_1 Z_2$, where Z_2 begins with a character other than prime, then Z_1 has a deficiency of operands.)

PROOF: Let $W_1, W_2, \ldots, W_n$ be a derivation in G-PRE. We prove by mathematical induction on j that for all $j \leqq n$, (I) and (II) of Lemma 8 are true of W_j. Since $W_1 = S$, (I) and (II) are clearly true of W_1.

Assume now that (I) and (II) are true of W_j. Lemma 7 tells us that (I) is true of W_{j+1}. To prove that (II) is true, there are eight cases according to which production is used to obtain W_{j+1} from W_j.

Case 1. $W_j = USY$, $W_{j+1} = U\&SSY$. Assume now that $W_{j+1} = Z_1 Z_2$, where Z_2 begins with a character other than prime. If Z_1 is part of U, or U itself, then $f(Z_1) < 1$, since (II) is true of W_j. If $Z_1 = U\&$ or $Z_1 = U\&S$, $f(Z_1) \leqq f(U) < 1$. If $Z_1 = U\&SSZ_3$, where $Y = Z_3 Z_2$, then, using Lemma 7, $f(Z_1) = f(USZ_3) < 1$, since (II) is true of W_j.

Cases 2 and 3 [productions (2) and (3)] are similar to Case 1.

Cases 4, 6, 7 and 8. The reasoning is straightforward where production (4), (6), (7), or (8) is used, and is left to the reader.

Case 5. $W_j = UAY$, $W_{j+1} = UA'Y$ [production (5)]. Y may or may not begin with prime. In either case the reasoning is straightforward and is left to the reader. ∎

LEMMA 9: If the leftmost character of a string in the language is &, $\vee$, or $\sim$, then the S at the top of any derivation tree in G-PRE of that string is directly connected to that leftmost character.

LEMMA 10: The leftmost character of a string in the language of G-PRE is not a prime.

We leave the easy proofs of these two lemmas to the reader.

THEOREM 8.4.1:   G-PRE is unambiguous.

PROOF: Assume that G-PRE is ambiguous, let W be an ambiguous string of minimal length, and let T and T_0 be two nonisomorphic derivation trees for W.

Case 1. The leftmost character of W is &. Then T and T_0 are as in Fig. 8.4.1. Suppose that $W = \&W_1W_2$, where W_1 is under S_1 and W_2 is under S_2 in T. Similarly, suppose that $W = \&W_{01}W_{02}$, where W_{01} is under S_{01} in T_0 and W_{02} is under S_{02} in T_0.

Figure 8.4.1

Suppose that W_1 is longer than W_{01}. Then $W_1 = W_{01}Y$, where $Y \neq \lambda$ and Y does not begin with a prime. Since W_1 is derivable from S, by Lemma 8, $f(W_1) = 1$ and $f(W_{01}) < 1$. But since W_{01} is derivable from S, by the same lemma, $f(W_{01}) = 1$, a contradiction. So W_{01} is not shorter than W_1. Similarly, W_1 cannot be shorter than W_{01}, so $W_1 = W_{01}$ and $W_2 = W_{02}$.

Since T is not isomorphic to T_0, it must be that either that part of T from S_1 to W_1 is not isomorphic to that part of T_0 from S_{02} to $W_{01} = W_1$ or else that that part of T from S_2 to W_2 is not isomorphic to that part of T_0 from S_{02} to $W_{02} = W_2$. Thus either W_1 or W_2 is an ambiguous string for G-PRE. But this contradicts the assumption that W is a shortest-length ambiguous string for G-PRE. ∎

A Parsing Method for G–PRE   8.4.2

We are aided by a rough discussion of parsing for G-PRE in Section 7.2.5, and by the more thorough discussion of the parsing for G-IN in Section 8.3.4. Accordingly, we can be brief.

We begin (as with G-IN) by writing the string to be parsed along the bottom of a sheet of paper, as the leaves of a tree to be constructed upward. Since productions (4) through (8) are exactly the same in G-PRE as in G-IN, stage 1 is exactly the same as before. If the string is in L(G-PRE), then at the end of stage 1, the characters in the top string are just S, &, $\vee$, and $\sim$ (e.g., see Fig. 8.4.2a). Therefore, the remainder of the construction involves only productions (1), (2), and (3).

Stage 2 consists of the following step repeated as often as possible. Find anywhere in the top string any of the patterns $\&SS$, $\vee SS$, or $\sim S$ [the right sides of productions (1), (2), and (3), respectively]; place an S above and draw

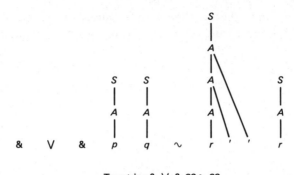

Top string & ∨ & SS ∼ SS

Figure 8.4.2a

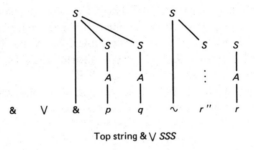

Top string & ∨ SSS

Figure 8.4.2b

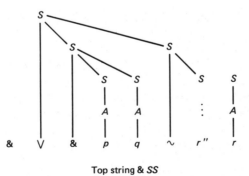

Top string & SS

Figure 8.4.2c

connecting branches to these characters. At the end of stage 2, the derivation tree is complete if the original string is in L(G-PRE) (e.g., see Fig. 8.4.2b and c).

If we start with a string whose membership in the language is uncertain, we follow this procedure as long as we can. If at the end the top string is S, we know that the original string is in the language and the construction that results is the derivation tree. If at the end the top string is not S and the step of stage 2 cannot be executed, then the original string is not in the language.

Parsing by the parsing automaton will proceed by mixing up stages 1 and 2, and by parsing (with one exception) as far to the left as possible on the top string, at each step.

Top-Down Parsing 8.4.3

We begin by introducing a variant of G-PRE:

$$\text{G-PRE}': \quad (1)\,(2)\,(3)\,(4) \quad S \longrightarrow \&SS \,|\, \vee SS \,|\, {\sim}S \,|\, A$$
$$(5')\,(6)\,(7)\,(8) \quad A \longrightarrow {}'A \,|\, p \,|\, q \,|\, r$$

The only difference is in production (5'); variable strings have their primes to the left of the p, q, or r instead of to the right. With this unconventional treatment of primes, we can use the prime in the same way we use the operator signs as a clue to parsing as we go from left to right in the string. A new parsing method results which is itself a proof of unambiguity.

We observe that all the productions of G-PRE' except (4) have a right side that begins with a terminal. In any derivation tree in this grammar, any application of production (4) must have just below it an application of one of the other productions.

A second observation is that each terminal in the grammar occurs exactly once on the right side of a production of the grammar, and is the leftmost character of the right side in which it occurs.

The parsing method we illustrate, which is well suited to G-PRE' and many grammars, is the *top-down method,* so called because the tree is constructed downward from the topmost node, making connections to the terminal string when possible. This time we find ourselves describing an actual algorithm, since there are no options.

We begin with the string written along the bottom of a large-enough sheet of paper, with an S at the top to be the root of the tree. We look at the first character in the string. If it is $\&$ or $\vee$, we connect the S with a branch to that character, placing two more S's between the root and the remainder of the string, and draw connecting branches from them to the root. If the first character is $\sim$, then we do the same, except that only one additional S is so placed. If the first character is prime, we place an A between the prime and the root with connecting branches, and place another A between the first A and the remainder of the string, with a connecting branch to the first A. Finally, if the first character is p, q, or r, we place an A between that character and the root with connecting branches. (In this last case, the job is complete after this first step. If there are any more characters, the string is not in the language.)

At this point we note that in all cases the tree is in accord with the productions, and there is a connection, direct or indirect, from the root to the first terminal in the string. Furthermore, the construction so far is inevitable; given the initial character, there is no other way the top of the tree could be constructed.

At any time during this construction, there is a portion of a derivation tree. All the nodes labeled with terminals are there, but just some of the nodes labeled with nonterminals. Let T be the leftmost terminal-labeled node that has no branch connecting upward and let N be the leftmost nonterminal-labeled node that has no branch connecting downward.

Case I.   If N is labeled S, then the next step of the construction is exactly as described in the first step, with N taking the place of the root and T taking the place of the first character of the string.

Case II.   If N is labeled A and T is labeled prime, then a connecting branch between T and N is drawn, and another A is placed between N and the remainder of the terminal string with a connecting branch to N.

Case III.   If N is labeled A and T is labeled p, q, or r, then a connecting branch is drawn between T and N.

The construction terminates when the construction step cannot be performed. At that point, if neither T nor N exists the string is in the language, and the result of the construction is a derivation tree. In all other cases, the string is not in the language.

THEOREM 8.4.2:   If a string W is in the language of G-PRE$'$, then a derivation tree for W results from the construction method just described. This tree is isomorphic to any derivation tree for W in G-PRE$'$.

The proof of this theorem is left as Exercise 36. The following is an obvious consequence:

COROLLARY: G-PRE$'$ is unambiguous.

We remark that with a small amount of complication, this parsing method could be adopted for G-PRE (Exercise 37).

It is significant that this top-down parsing method works on the terminal string from left to right. Grammars to which this method can be applied are thought to be desirable in systems programming. A class of grammars to which it can be applied is the class of *s-grammars*, studied in Chapter 8 of Lewis, Rosenkrantz, and Stearns [1976]: the grammars in which (1) the right side of each production begins with a terminal and has no other terminals, and (2) there do not exist two distinct productions having the same nonterminal on the left side and the same first character on the right side. [G-PRE' departs from this pattern only in production (4).] The parsing method that we have given for G-PRE' can be applied to any s-grammar, providing a proof of its unambiguity. However, the top-down parsing method is not considered in this book after this section.

Perfectly Univocal Grammars 8.4.4

Sometimes when we parse a string we may do a lot of work only to realize that what we have done cannot be completed to a tree; the only thing to do is either to start all over again or else go back to some previous stage in the construction. It is desirable to construct languages and grammars for them so that this process, known as *backtracking*, is never necessary; G-IN and G-PRE were constructed in this way.

We now examine a class of grammars for which backtracking during a bottom-up parse is not necessary. In fact, these grammars will have an even stronger property.

Recall the construction of a derivation tree by the bottom-up parse. At any stage, the part of the tree that has not yet been constructed is the part above the topstring for that stage. It is actually a derivation tree for the topstring, with nonterminals as labels for some of its leaves. The possibilities of drawing this tree given the topstring determine the remaining possibilities of parsing the original string.

Definition: A grammar is *univocal* if, for every production $A \rightarrow W$ and for every derived string over the total alphabet $X_1 W X_2$, in any derivation tree of $X_1 W X_2$, the leaves labeled with the W portion are connected immediately above to an A.

The significance of a univocal grammar is that, in doing a bottom-up parse of a string, whenever there is a substring of the top string that is the right side of a production, that substring may be parsed to a node labeled with the left side of that production, without looking at the other parts of the top string, and without fear of having to backtrack. All univocal grammars are thus unambiguous, although an unambiguous grammar need not be univocal.

It is difficult to tell whether a grammar is univocal. However, there is a stronger condition on a grammar that we can ascertain by checking the set of productions:

Definition: A grammar is *perfectly univocal* if (1) there are no two distinct productions whose right sides are of the forms $U_1 U_2$ and $U_2 U_3$, where $U_2 \neq \lambda$; (2) there are no two distinct productions whose right sides are of the forms

$U_1U_2U_3$ and U_2; and (3) there is no production whose right side can be written as both UV and XU for $U, V, X \neq \lambda$.

THEOREM 8.4.3: A perfectly univocal grammar is univocal.

The proof is left as Exercise 44.
We illustrate situations violating the definition of *perfectly univocal* grammar:

I. The pair of productions $A \rightarrow U_2$ and $B \dashrightarrow U_2$ would violate both (1) and (2) (with $U_1 = U_3 = \lambda$).

II. $A \rightarrow \lambda$, together with any other production, would violate (2) (taking $U_1 =$ the right side of the second production, and $U_2 = U_3 = \lambda$).

III. $A \rightarrow U_1U_2$ and $B \rightarrow U_2$, for $U_2 \neq \lambda$, violate (1) and (2).

IV. $A \rightarrow U_2U_3$ and $B \rightarrow U_2$, similarly.

V. The single production $A \rightarrow bcb$ violates (3) (taking $U = b$, $V = cb$, $X = bc$).

The grammar G-PRE is not perfectly univocal, although it almost has that property. The failure is due to the productions $S \rightarrow A$ and $A \rightarrow A'$. These two rules, it will be recalled, caused complication in the proof of unambiguity, and a minor difficulty in the parsing method; one had to refrain from parsing an A to an S until one verified that no prime followed.

G-PRE cannot be converted into a perfectly univocal grammar without changing its language. As long as p, p', p'', p''', and so on, are all to be variables, the parser knows the end of the variable string only when he sees beyond what he is to parse. To overcome this feature one could introduce an end-of-variable marker $\#$. Variables will then be $p\#, p'\#, p''\#, p'''\#$, and so on (and similarly for strings beginning in q and r).

We can then get a modified grammar that is perfectly univocal for a modification of L(G-PRE):

$$\text{G-PREM:} \quad S \longrightarrow \&SS \,|\, \lor SS \,|\, {\sim}S \,|\, A\#$$
$$A \longrightarrow A' \,|\, p \,|\, q \,|\, r$$

G-IN has the same difficulty that G-PRE has and another as well. It turns out that the method of placing parentheses is enough to make G-IN unambiguous but not enough to make it perfectly univocal. Note that $S \rightarrow (S)\&(S)$ and $S \rightarrow (S)\lor(S)$ each violates (3), and together they violate (1) of the definition. Thus, if one sees $\ldots (S)\&(S)\&(S) \ldots$, one could parse to $\ldots S\&(S) \ldots$ or to $\ldots (S)\&S \ldots$. (There is no harm in this possibility because this string could not be a substring of any string in the language.)

One method of converting G-IN into a perfectly univocal grammar is to

arrange for each production that introduces parentheses to have a right side
that begins with (, ends with), and has no other parentheses. We thus get:

$$\text{G-INM:} \quad S \longrightarrow (S\&S)\,|\,(S \lor S)\,|\,(\sim S)\,|\,A\#$$
$$A \longrightarrow A'\,|\,p\,|\,q\,|\,r$$

In this modification, variables are different and parentheses are placed differently.
E.g., the string $(p)\&(q)$ of L(G-IN) becomes $(p\#\&q\#)$ in L(G-INM).

A perfectly univocal grammar has an advantage in mechanical parsing, but
its language is apt to be clumsy for the user. What normal user of the language
of G-PREM or G-INM will not be irritated at having to write $p\#$ and $q'\#$
instead of p and q' as he would in the language of G-PRE or G-IN?

Exercises 8.4.5

Give a parsing method for the following unambiguous grammars. These exercises are
arranged very roughly in order of increasing difficulty for someone who has read all
of Sections 8.3 and 8.4.

1. (1)(2)(3)(4) $S \longrightarrow bES\,|\,cDS\,|\,bE\,|\,cD$
  (5)(6) $D \longrightarrow cD\,|\,b$
  (7)(8) $E \longrightarrow bE\,|\,c$

2. (1) $S \longrightarrow EQF$
  (2)(3) $E \longrightarrow bEc\,|\,bc$
  (4)(5) $Q \longrightarrow cQ\,|\,c$
  (6)(7) $F \longrightarrow cFd\,|\,cd$

3. (1)(2) $S \longrightarrow AcS\,|\,Ac$
  (3)(4) $A \longrightarrow bAb\,|\,c$

4. (1)(2) $S \longrightarrow ESF\,|\,EF$
  (3)(4) $E \longrightarrow Ec\,|\,b$
  (5)(6) $F \longrightarrow Fc\,|\,d$

5. (1) $S \longrightarrow EF$
  (2)(3)(4) $E \longrightarrow bE\,|\,cE\,|\,b$
  (5)(6)(7) $F \longrightarrow Fc\,|\,Fd\,|\,d$

6. (1) $S \longrightarrow EbbbF$
  (2)(3)(4)(5) $E \longrightarrow bE\,|\,cE\,|\,dE\,|\,\lambda$
  (6)(7)(8) $F \longrightarrow cF\,|\,dF\,|\,b$

7. (1)–(6) $S \longrightarrow bSb\,|\,cSc\,|\,bb\,|\,cc\,|\,b\,|\,c$

8. (1)(2)(3)(4) $S \longrightarrow bS\,|\,bcH\,|\,bcK\,|\,b$
  (5)(6) $H \longrightarrow ccH\,|\,cS$
  (7)(8) $K \longrightarrow ccK\,|\,S$

What simpler grammar with simpler parsing is equivalent to that of Exercise 8?

9. (1)(2) $S \longrightarrow bS\,|\,E$
  (3)(4)(5) $E \longrightarrow Ec\,|\,dSd\,|\,\lambda$

10. (1)(2)(3)(4) $S \longrightarrow bSd\,|\,cSd\,|\,\lambda\,|\,E$
  (5)(6) $E \longrightarrow bcEd\,|\,bcd$

11. (1)(2) $S \longrightarrow bSc\,|\,D$
  (3)(4) $D \longrightarrow bbDc\,|\,\lambda$

12. (1)(2)(3) $S \longrightarrow bSd\,|\,E\,|\,F$
  (4)(5) $E \longrightarrow bEc\,|\,bc$
  (6)(7) $F \longrightarrow cFd\,|\,\lambda$

13. (1)(2)(3) $S \longrightarrow (S)(S)\,|\,(S)\,|\,\lambda$

14. (1)–(4) $S \longrightarrow bS\,|\,cS\,|\,dE\,|\,\lambda$
  (5)–(8) $E \longrightarrow Ed\,|\,Ec\,|\,Fb\,|\,\lambda$
  (9)–(12) $F \longrightarrow bF\,|\,cF\,|\,dG\,|\,\lambda$
  (13)–(15) $G \longrightarrow Gc\,|\,Gd\,|\,\lambda$

What is the language of the grammar of Exercise 14?

15. (1)(2) $S \longrightarrow bSd \mid EF$
       (3)(4) $E \longrightarrow bEc \mid \lambda$
       (5)(6) $F \longrightarrow cFd \mid \lambda$

What is the language of this grammar? [*Suggestion:* Given $W = b^m c^n d^p$, determine numerically whether W can be derived, and if so how many times productions (1), (3), and (5), respectively, must be used.]

16. (*Difficult*)

$$(1)(2)   \quad S \longrightarrow AS \mid A$$

$$(3)(4)(5)   \quad A \longrightarrow cMM \mid PcM \mid PPc$$

$$(6)(7)   \quad M \longrightarrow cMMM \mid b$$

$$(8)(9)   \quad P \longrightarrow PPPc \mid b$$

(Read, but do not follow, the suggestion for Exercise 32.)

17–32. Prove that the grammars of Exercises 1 to 16, respectively, are unambiguous. [Suggestion for Exercise 32, which is considerably more difficult: Put $f(A) = f(S) = 0, f(c) = +2, f(P) = f(b) = f(M) = -1, f(W_1 W_2) = f(W_1) + f(W_2)$. (Compare the f of Section 8.4.1.) Prove successively the following lemmas: If W (a string over the total alphabet) is derivable from T (for any nonterminal T), then $f(W) = f(T)$. If $W_1 W_2$ is derivable from M and $W_2 \neq \lambda$, then $f(W_1) > -1$. If $W_1 W_2$ is derivable from P and $W_1 \neq \lambda$, then $f(W_2) > -1$. If $W_1 W_2$ is derivable from A and $W_1 \neq \lambda \neq W_2$, then $f(W_1) \neq 0 \neq f(W_2)$.]

33. (*Difficult*) Prove that the language of the grammar of Exercise 16 is the set of all nonnull strings over the alphabet $\{b, c\}$ with twice as many b's as c's. (Follow the suggestion of Exercise 32 and prove suitable converses to the lemmas.)

34. (*Abstract and difficult*) Prove that the following grammar is unambiguous and that its language is the set of all strings over $\{b, c\}$ having as many b's as c's:

$$(1)(2)(3)   \quad S \longrightarrow bES \mid cDS \mid \lambda$$

$$(4)(5)   \quad D \longrightarrow cDD \mid b$$

$$(6)(7)   \quad E \longrightarrow bEE \mid c$$

(Read the suggestion for Exercise 32.)

35. (Not difficult if you have done Exercises 32 to 34.) Construct a grammar and prove that it is unambiguous and that its language is the set of strings over $\{b, c\}$ having three times as many b's as c's.

The remaining exercises all concern perfectly univocal grammars, and other theoretical material.

36. Prove Theorem 8.4.2.

37. Give a top-down parsing method for G-PRE.

38. Which of the examples in Sections 7.3 and 7.4 are perfectly univocal grammars?

39. Of the unambiguous grammars given as examples in Section 8.2, which are perfectly univocal?

40. Give a perfectly univocal grammar equivalent to

$$S \longrightarrow bE$$
$$E \longrightarrow cE \,|\, c$$

41. Give a perfectly univocal grammar equivalent to

$$S \longrightarrow bS \,|\, cbKd$$
$$K \longrightarrow bK \,|\, \lambda$$

42. (*Difficult*) Give a perfectly univocal grammar equivalent to

$$S \longrightarrow dE$$
$$E \longrightarrow bE \,|\, cF$$
$$F \longrightarrow bF \,|\, cG$$
$$G \longrightarrow bG \,|\, cF \,|\, \lambda$$

43. (*Difficult*) Give a perfectly univocal grammar equivalent to

$$S \longrightarrow bS \,|\, cH$$
$$H \longrightarrow bH \,|\, cJ$$
$$J \longrightarrow bJ \,|\, cH \,|\, d$$

44. Prove Theorem 8.4.3. Disprove the converse by counterexample.

45. Prove that if a grammar has the following two properties, it is perfectly univocal: (1) no two productions have the same right side, and (2) the right side of every production begins with (, ends with), and has no other parentheses. (Grammars satisfying (2) are sometimes called *parenthesis grammars*. See Salomaa [1973], pp. 287ff.)

46. A proof that G-PRE′ (p. 261) is unambiguous can be modeled after the proof in Section 8.4.1 that G-PRE is unambiguous. The f function must be modified and can be simplified. What is it? In which other places (lemmas, their proofs, proof of Theorem 8.4.1) is the proof simplified?

47. (*Difficult*) Recall the construction of G_2 from G_0 in Section 7.5.2. Prove that if G_2 is ambiguous, then G_0 is ambiguous. (*Suggestion:* Reread Sections 7.5.4 to 7.5.6.)

48. Prove that the following grammar is unambiguous:

$$S \longrightarrow cScS \,|\, b$$

(*Hint:* Someone who has read all of this section may get a very short proof.)

A NONDETERMINISTIC PARSING 8.5
AUTOMATON

In the final three sections of this chapter, we consider an automaton that effectuates a bottom-up parse of a string in the language of a given context-free grammar, by making one pass over the string from left to right. This automaton uses the principle of the pushdown store; it writes (i.e., *pushes*) certain things in its store, and then later clears (or *pops*) these things. But if it pushes two things and later pops them, the order in which they are popped is the reverse of the order in which they were pushed. In other words, the first in is the last out.

8.5.1   Parsing in Practice

In our use of formal languages we do not draw derivation trees any more than we draw diagrams of sentences of the English that we read or write. If we understand the meaning of a string in any language, then in some way or other we must have done something mentally to parse the string or sentence. This mental act, whatever it is, is often quite an achievement, since syntactic structure involves many subtle points that we are able to perceive in an instant.

If we do not draw the tree or a parsing diagram of any kind, what do we do? Unfortunately, the study of this psychological problem would take us too far from our main concern. Let us redirect the question to the machine: What does a machine do in reading a string of a formal language to understand its meaning? We are about to offer a beginning of one answer to this question. It is tempting to speculate that an understanding of how the machine functions in this regard does throw light on how the human mind functions. Maybe so, but we have nothing more to say in this book about the problem of the mental understanding of linguistic meaning.

Perhaps the major task to be done by a machine today on strings of a formal language is to translate them into strings of another language, namely, the translation of a high-level programming language into machine code. There is another task that is often given to a machine; that is to give the machine a formula with certain numerical values for the variables and have the machine compute the value of the formula. These two operations on strings are accomplished by techniques that are quite similar. For both of these tasks the machine must respond to the structural meaning of the string it is processing.

It is clear from our study of context-free grammars that long strings are meaningful because they are decomposable into meaningful constituents, which are meaningful because they in turn can be decomposed into meaningful constituents, and so on until we reach the basic constituents. What the derivation tree shows us is exactly how all the constituents are related to one another. Somehow a machine (or, if you prefer, the machine's program) must deal with the structural meaning of strings without having at any time a completed drawing of the derivation tree. How is this possible? We shall attempt to answer this question by studying what we shall call a *parsing automaton*.

In these sections we shall be content for the most part to reveal the method of operation in the simplest possible task that we can think of, which is the task of ascertaining whether or not a given string is in the language of a given context-free grammar. Our automaton will try to construct this tree, and if it succeeds it will conclude that the string is in the language.

This automaton is capable of reading and writing a certain set of symbols, its *machine alphabet*, and is capable of handling any grammar without lambda productions whose alphabet is a subset of the machine alphabet, provided that the right side of none of its productions is longer than k characters. The positive integer k is a characteristic of the automaton. It does not matter what particular value k has; we assume that, whatever grammar we may wish to process, we can always get a suitable automaton whose k is greater than or equal to the length of the longest right side of a production.

The automaton has three tapes: a production tape, an input tape, and a parsing tape. At the beginning we manually write the start symbol and the productions of a grammar on the production tape and a string on the input tape. The parsing tape is cleared, which means that there is a single asterisk on one of its squares and all other squares are blank. The asterisk appears only once on the parsing tape and nowhere else. The machine can read it there, but cannot write it or erase it. It is therefore not regarded as part of the machine alphabet.

The automaton will read the input string once from left to right, consulting the production tape several times, and executing on the parsing tape a computation which is, in a way, a parsing of the input string. Since the parsing tape is a one-dimensional tape, it is impossible to draw a tree on it; the labels of the derivation tree are written, and are erased when they are no longer needed.

We need not concern ourselves with exactly how the production tape is organized. The input tape is divided into squares; the string to be tested is written one character per square, consecutively, from left to right. There is an input reading head, capable of reading exactly one square, and then moving itself one square to the right. Eventually, when the string has been completely read, the input head is reading a blank square. The input head does not write on or erase from the input tape, and it cannot move left on it. The automaton is therefore restricted to one pass over the input string from left to right.

The automaton has a parsing-tape reading and writing head which at any time scans k consecutive squares of the parsing tape. It can move right and left on the parsing tape, and it can write and erase. However, there are restrictions. Whenever it moves to the right, it writes on each new square that it scans. And whenever it moves to the left, it erases each square before leaving it. As a result, between the asterisk and the rightmost square scanned by the parsing-tape head there are no blanks; but all squares to the right are blanks. The parsing-tape head never writes on squares to the left of the asterisk, and never moves so its rightmost square is to the left of the asterisk; so we can think of the parsing tape as beginning at the asterisk and going off to the right.

At the beginning the input head is on the leftmost nonblank square of the input tape. The parsing-tape head is placed so that the rightmost square that it scans is the one with the asterisk. The automaton then begins its fully mechanical operation.

The interval of its operation consists of discrete time steps. The automaton may eventually halt and therefore have a last time step, or it may never halt, in which case there will be infinitely many time steps.

The automaton is *nondeterministic*. Let us suppose that there are p productions written on the production tape. It begins each time step by making a random choice of an integer between one and $p + 2$. We need not concern ourselves with how this choice is made or what if any probabilities are associated with each of the $p + 2$ possibilities. It is essential that we stipulate here that the automaton be capable of choosing any of the $p + 2$ integers, and that this choice not be influenced by any consideration. (This stipulation will be nullified in Section 8.6, when we make the automaton deterministic.)

If the integer chosen is $p + 1$, and if the input head is scanning a character, then the parsing-tape head moves one square to the right, and copies the character scanned by the input head on the new (i.e., rightmost) square in its scan. The input head then moves one square to the right. If the input head is scanning a blank square (because the input string has already been completely read), there is no operation during this time step and the automaton advances to the next time step.

If the integer chosen is $p + 2$, the automaton halts.

If the integer i is chosen, for $1 \leq i \leq p$, the automaton ascertains whether the right side of the ith production on the production tape appears right-justified in the scan of the parsing-tape head. If so, the automaton carries through a *simplification* of the parsing tape. That is, just these characters are erased from the parsing tape, the single character that is the left side of the ith production is written on the leftmost of these squares, and the parsing-tape head moves leftward if necessary so that the rightmost square scanned is the character it has just written. If the right side of the ith production does not appear right-justified in the scan of the pushdown head, no operation results and the automaton goes to the next time step.

If the automaton halts with the input head scanning a blank square (which means that the input string has been completely read) at a time when $*S$ appears right-justified to the parsing-tape head (assuming that S is the start symbol of the grammar as written on the production tape), the automaton *accepts* the string. If the automaton halts without accepting, we do not say that it "rejects" the string; since the automaton is nondeterministic, its failure to accept may just be the result of a wrong choice somewhere in its history. (Indeed, it seems rather unlikely in any given history that the automaton will ever make exactly the right sequence of choices for an acceptance. We shall return to this point.)

Thus there are two ways in which the automaton may fail to accept a string: It may halt without accepting, or it may go on forever without halting. We emphasize that the automaton does not halt when there is no operation (i.e., when the integer chosen is $p + 1$, but there is no character on the input to copy, or when the integer chosen is $i \leq p$, but the right side of the ith production is not right-justified on the parsing tape). It halts when and only when the integer chosen is $p + 2$.

The asterisk at the left end of the parsing tape is not necessary since a blank square could just as well signify the left end. We prefer the asterisk here for stylistic reasons. We could have included in our design a special symbol for the right end of the input tape, which we have chosen not to have, again for rather arbitrary stylistic reasons.

A Sample History 8.5.3

For definiteness we assume that $k = 3$, and we write the grammar whose productions are, in order,

$$S \longrightarrow Sc$$
$$S \longrightarrow bSc$$
$$S \longrightarrow bc$$

on the production tape. Thus $p = 3$.

We then write *bbcccc* on the input tape. Figure 8.5.1 is an example of a sequence of steps that could possibly ensue, ending in a halt and acceptance at time step 11.

This possible history of the automaton is most fortuitous. Not only does it end in an acceptance, but it does so without any waste motions (i.e., "no-operations"). A no-operation would have occurred, for example, if the number 1, 2, or 3 had been chosen in the first time step.

The following concept is important in analyzing the linguistic significance of the automaton's operations:

Definition: The *designated string* of a time step in the history of the parsing automaton is the string consisting of the concatenation of the contents of the parsing tape to the right of the asterisk at the end of that time step, with the unread portion of the input tape (including the square scanned by the input head) at the end of the time step.

The acceptance of the string *bbcccc* by the automaton corresponds to a derivation (and hence derivation tree) of the string in the grammar. To see this we form the sequence consisting of the input string followed by the designated strings of all the time steps in order. The sequence is written as follows, where a slash in each string indicates where the parsing-tape part of the string ends and the input part begins:

	/bbcccc	6	S/cc
1	b/bcccc	7	Sc/c
2	bb/cccc	8	S/c
3	bbc/ccc	9	Sc/
4	bS/ccc	10	S/
5	bSc/cc	11	S/

Time step	Number chosen	Input head and input tape at end of time step	Parsing tape at end of time step
Beginning		bbcccc ↑	*
1	4	bbcccc ↑	*b
2	4	bbcccc ↑	*bb
3	4	bbcccc ↑	*bbc
4	3	bbcccc ↑	*bS
5	4	bbcccc ↑	*bSc
6	2	bbcccc ↑	*S
7	4	bbcccc ↑	*Sc
8	1	bbcccc ↑	*S
9	4	bbcccc ↑	*Sc
10	1	bbcccc ↑	*S
11	5	bbcccc ↑	*S

Figure 8.5.1

We note that the designated string of any time step in which there is a copy or halt is exactly the same as the designated string of the previous time step. It is modified at a time step in which the parsing tape is simplified. Each simplification is a replacement of a substring which is the right side of a production by the left side of that production—exactly the reverse of the arrow.

Let us therefore write this sequence of strings in reverse order, omitting repetitions:

$$S$$
$$Sc$$
$$Scc$$
$$bSccc$$
$$bbcccc$$

This sequence is a derivation of the string *bbcccc* in the grammar, and the reason why should be clear from the discussion in the preceding paragraph.

We give another possible history of the automaton:

Time Step	Number Chosen	Designated String	
		/bbcccc	
1	2	/bbcccc	(no operation)
2	4	b/bcccc	
3	4	bb/cccc	
4	4	bbc/ccc	
5	1	bbc/ccc	(no operation)
6	3	bS/ccc	
7	4	bSc/cc	
8	1	bS/cc	
9	4	bSc/c	
10	1	bS/c	
11	4	bSc/	
12	1	bS/	
etc.			

The input string has been completely read and *bS* is on the parsing tape. It is clear that whatever happens from time step 13 onward, the automaton will never accept the string. The fatal point was time step 12, when the automaton chose number 1; had it chosen number 2, it would have been in position to accept the string.

There are many possible histories for the automaton processing the input string *bbcccc*. It could halt at the very first time step. It might go forever without a halt; this would mean an infinite number of time steps, with all no-operations beyond a certain point. It might go forever with the input completely read and **S* on the parsing tape, forever ready to accept and never accepting. It could just copy the whole input string and then halt without performing a single simplification of the parsing tape; and so on.

We are interested in this model not from the point of view of what it actually does, nor from the point of view of the sum total of all things it could do. Rather we are interested in what it can possibly do in the most favorable circumstances, which Theorem 8.5.3 (in Section 8.5.6) will characterize for us.

8.5.4 Possible Histories

When we run a program on a computer for selected inputs, generally there is only one sequence of actions that can possibly result, barring a malfunction. Digital computers do not usually make random choices; even when a program is run with "random numbers," the machine uses what are really pseudo-random numbers and the entire operation is deterministic.

Furthermore, the concepts of *algorithm* and *procedure* that we have been studying in this book are deterministic concepts: the action at each step of an algorithm or procedure must be precisely determined by what has occurred in the past.

Why have we suddenly turned to a nondeterministic automaton? The principal reason is that we can prove something interesting about the nondeterministic automaton, but we cannot prove anything nearly as interesting about any deterministic automaton related to it (namely, that a string on the input tape is accepted in some possible history of the automaton if and only if it is in the language of the grammar on the production tape).

We must admit right from the start that the nondeterministic automaton in itself has no practical significance. There will be no practical applications until we return in the next section to the principle of determinism.

8.5.5 Rightmost Derivations

It turns out that the intimate relationship between a history of the automaton and a derivation can be generalized to prove a fundamental theorem. To prepare ourselves for the proof, we must make a few observations about derivations and derivation trees.

In the remainder of Section 8.5 we make an assumption that amounts to a slight revision of the concept of derivation. We assume that it is understood which nonterminal of a line in a derivation is replaced according to a production to form the next line. This understanding is not always a consequence of the definition of "derivation" in 7.1.4; for example, if $A \rightarrow AB$ and $C \rightarrow BC$ are both productions of a grammar and AC, ABC are successive lines in a derivation, there is no conceptual determination of whether A is replaced by AB or C is replaced by BC. (This situation is rather rare; in most cases of interest to us, there can be only one nonterminal in a line of a derivation that is replaced to form the next line.)

Definition: A *rightmost derivation* is a derivation having the property that in each line except the last the rightmost nonterminal occurrence is replaced according to one of the productions to form the next line.

The derivation constructed from an accepting history of the automaton is always a rightmost derivation, as will be shown.

THEOREM 8.5.1: Every string in the language of a context-free grammar has a rightmost derivation in the grammar.

PROOF: Let W be a string in the language of a context-free grammar G and let T be a derivation tree for W in G. From T we construct a sequence $W_0, W_1, \ldots$, with each nonterminal in the derivation corresponding to a node in T, as follows: Let W_0 be the label of the root of T, namely the start symbol S. Assume that W_i has been determined, with each occurrence of a character in W_i corresponding to a node in T. If there is no nonterminal in W_i, then W_i is the last string in the sequence. If there is a nonterminal in W_i, then rewrite W_i as W_{i+1} by replacing the rightmost nonterminal occurrence by the characters, left to right, that are under the node corresponding to it in T. These characters correspond to the nodes in the derivation tree that they come from, while the other symbols in W_{i+1} correspond to the nodes in the same way they did in W_i.

Let W_n be the last string in the sequence. From our work in Section 7.1.2, we see that $W_0, W_1, \ldots, W_n$ is a derivation of $W = W_n$ in G. The construction method assures that it is a rightmost derivation. ∎

We illustrate Theorem 8.5.1 by a derivation of the string *bbccbcbc* in the grammar

$$S \longrightarrow PS \,|\, P$$

$$P \longrightarrow bPc \,|\, bc$$

The following is the rightmost derivation taken from the derivation tree of Fig. 8.5.2. (The brackets are there to illustrate the next definition.)

$$
\begin{aligned}
W_0 &= S & W_4 &= PP[bc] \\
W_1 &= [PS] & W_5 &= P[bc][bc] \\
W_2 &= P[PS] & W_6 &= [bPc][bc][bc] \\
W_3 &= PP[P] & W_7 &= b[bc]c[bc][bc]
\end{aligned}
$$

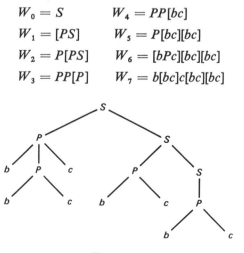

Figure 8.5.2

Definition: A *phrase* in a line of a derivation is an occurrence of a substring identical to the right side of a production that replaces a nonterminal occurrence in some preceding line of the derivation.

Thus if UAV and UXV are successive lines of a derivation, where $A \longrightarrow X$ is a production, then that occurrence of X is a phrase of the line UXV and of all subsequent lines before the first line in which some character in that occurrence of X is replaced by a new phrase.

In the previous example the phrases of each string in the derivation are enclosed in brackets. Note that W_0 does not have any phrases (since it does not come from a production). All the phrases in a line are phrases in the next line except that phrase, if any, that contains the nonterminal occurrence that is replaced. Note that the phrases in any line do not overlap.

THEOREM 8.5.2:   In any line beyond the first in a rightmost derivation, the new phrase in that line (i.e., the one that replaces a nonterminal occurrence in the immediately preceding line) is the leftmost phrase.

PROOF: Suppose that $W_0, W_1, \ldots, W_n$ is a rightmost derivation, and that the new phrase in W_{i+1} is not leftmost, where $0 \leq i \leq n - 1$. Thus $W_i = UX_1 YCV$, $W_{i+1} = UX_1 YX_2 V$, X_1 is a phrase of both W_i and W_{i+1}, C is a nonterminal, and $C \longrightarrow X_2$ is a production. Let W_j be the earliest line in which X_1 is a phrase. Then $1 \leq j \leq i$, $W_{j-1} = U_0 BV_0$, and $W_j = U_0 X_1 V_0$, where $B \longrightarrow X_1$ is a production. The derivation is thus as follows:

$$W_0 \;\; = S$$

$$\vdots$$

$$W_{j-1} = U_0 BV_0$$
$$W_j \;\; = U_0 X_1 V_0$$

$$\vdots$$

$$W_i \;\; = UX_1 YCV$$
$$W_{i+1} = UX_1 YX_2 V$$

$$\vdots$$

$$W_n$$

Since X_1 remains unchanged from W_j through W_i, the substring YCV is either equal to V_0 or derived from it. In either case, there must be at least one nonterminal in V_0: either C itself or another nonterminal from which a substring of YCV is derived. However, a nonterminal in V_0 occurs to the right of the B in W_{j-1} that is replaced by X_1 in W_j, which is contrary to the assumption that the derivation is a rightmost derivation. ∎

COROLLARY: In any line of a rightmost derivation, other than the first or the last, the rightmost nonterminal is either to the left of the leftmost phrase or is part of it.

PROOF: Consider the line W_i in the proof of the theorem. The proof shows that this line, with the rightmost nonterminal C to the right of the leftmost phrase X_1, is impossible in a rightmost derivation. Hence the rightmost nonterminal occurrence in any line must either be part of the leftmost phrase or to the left of it. ∎

The Main Theorem 8.5.6

THEOREM 8.5.3: The string on the input tape is accepted by the parsing automaton in some possible history if and only if the string is in the language of the grammar whose productions are written on the production tape.

PROOF: Assume (for the easy part) that the string W on the input tape is accepted in some history of the automaton, consisting of n time steps. Put $U_0 = \lambda$ and $W_0 = V_0 = W$. For each i, $1 \leq i \leq n$, put $U_i =$ the string on the parsing tape at the end of the ith time step, not including the asterisk, $V_i =$ the unread portion of the input tape (including the square scanned by the input head), and $W_i = U_iV_i$, the designated string of the ith time step (see the comments following the first example in Section 8.5.3). Clearly, $W_n = S$.

If the automaton copies, halts, or has a no-operation during the ith time step, then $W_i = W_{i-1}$. On the other hand, if the machine simplifies during the ith time step, then W_i results from W_{i-1} by taking a substring identical to the right side of one of the productions and replacing it by the left side of that production.

From these remarks it should be clear that if we write

$$W_n, W_{n-1}, \ldots, W_1, W_0$$

and then delete repetitions, we have a derivation of $W = W_0$ in the grammar on the production tape.

Assume now (for the difficult part of the proof) that the string W is in the language of the grammar on the production tape. By Theorem 8.5.1, there is a rightmost derivation

$$W_0, W_1, \ldots, W_n$$

of $W = W_n$. We shall complete the proof by actually constructing from this derivation a possible history of the automaton in which W is accepted.

For each i, $1 \leq i \leq n - 1$, let $W_i = U_iA_iV_i$, where A_i is the rightmost nonterminal of W_i.

The machine begins by copying as far as the leftmost phrase of $W = W_n$ onto the parsing tape (recall Theorem 8.5.2). It then replaces this phrase by A_{n-1}.

At this point, $*U_{n-1}A_{n-1}$ is on the parsing tape, and V_{n-1} is the uncopied portion of the input tape.

Assume now that we have constructed the history of the machine so that $*U_iA_i$ is on the parsing tape and V_i is the uncopied portion of the input tape. By the Corollary to Theorem 8.5.2, A_i in its designated occurrence, which is the rightmost nonterminal of W_i, is either to the left of the leftmost phrase of W_i or is part of it. Hence we have the machine copy (if necessary) so that all of this leftmost phrase and no more is on the parsing tape. Then we have the machine erase this phrase, replacing it with A_{i-1}, whereupon $*U_{i-1}A_{i-1}$ is on the parsing tape and V_{i-1} is the uncopied portion of the input tape.

Finally, when $i = 1$, the leftmost phrase of W_1 must be all of W_1, $*W_1$ is on the parsing tape, the whole input tape having been copied. W_1 is replaced by $S = W_0$, and the history of the machine is complete with a halt and an acceptance. ▮

As an example of the construction in the second part of this proof, we start with the derivation in Section 8.5.5 of the string *bbccbcbc* in the grammar

$$S \longrightarrow PS \,|\, P$$
$$P \longrightarrow bPc \,|\, bc$$

The accepting history for the string is shown in the sequence of designated strings, where the portion to the left of the slash is on the parsing tape, and the portion to the right is the unread portion of the input tape:

$$|bbccbcbc$$
$$b|bccbcbc$$
$$bb|ccbcbc$$
$$bbc|cbcbc$$
$$bP|cbcbc$$
$$bPc|bcbc$$
$$P|bcbc$$
$$Pb|cbc$$
$$Pbc|bc$$
$$PP|bc$$
$$PPb|c$$
$$PPbc|$$
$$PPP|$$
$$PPS|$$
$$PS|$$
$$S|$$

In this method of constructing an automaton history from a derivation of length $n + 1$ $(S = W_0, W_1, \ldots, W_n)$ of a string W_n of length e, $n + e + 1$ time steps will result, one to copy each character in W_n, one for a simplification corresponding to each line of the derivation beyond the first, and one for the halt.

1. Prove the converse of Theorem 8.5.2. That is, prove that if a derivation has the property that the new phrase in every line beyond the first is the leftmost phrase, then the derivation is a rightmost derivation.

2. A *loop* of nonterminals in a grammar is, for some $j \geq 1$, a subset $\{A_1, \ldots, A_j\}$ of the set of nonterminals such that $A_j \longrightarrow A_1$ is a production and, for each h, $1 \leq h < j$, $A_h \longrightarrow A_{h+1}$ is a production. (For $j = 1$ this means simply that $A_1 \longrightarrow A_1$ is a production.)

Prove that if a parsing automaton (in processing a finitely long input string) has an infinite history, then either the grammar on the production tape has a loop of nonterminals or there is a time in the history after which there is a no-operation at every time step.

3. Prove that every grammar with a loop of nonterminals can by a simple algorithm be converted into a simpler equivalent grammar without. (This exercise is simpler than Exercise 5 of Section 7.5.)

4. Assume the scan-3 parsing automaton has accepted an input string of length m with G-SUF on its production tape (suffix propositional calculus, Section 7.2.5). Prove that the number of characters on the parsing tape in addition to the asterisk was never more than $(m + 3)/2$. (This matter is discussed in Section 8.6.5.)

THE DETERMINISTIC PARSING 8.6 AUTOMATON

In this section we take the nondeterministic parsing automaton as we developed it in Section 8.5 and, without adding to the structure of the device, make it deterministic. In so doing, we become able to accommodate some, but not all, context-free grammars. In terms of our work in Sections 8.3 and 8.4, the working of each deterministic parsing automaton is an efficient bottom-up parsing algorithm that makes one pass over the string from left to right.

We emphasize that the nondeterministic parsing automaton has no practical significance. It would be absurd, for example, to think of its as a probabilistic automaton, in which there is one chance in $p + 2$ at each time step of it making any one of the choices. In the example just given (at the end of Section 8.5.6) $p = 4$, so the probability of any choice at any time step would be $\frac{1}{6}$. Since there are 16 time steps in the possible history we considered, it follows that there would be a probability of only

$$(\tfrac{1}{6})^{16} \cong 3.5*10^{-13}$$

that this history will occur.

A more appropriate question to ask is: What is the probability that the string will be accepted? That probability will be somewhat higher because variations are possible in the accepting history. (For example, if there is a no-operation, the the chance of accepting is not spoiled but simply delayed.) The things that could prevent an acceptance are a premature halt, a premature conversion of P to S, or a copy operation (if possible) beyond a point where a simplification should occur. The probability of acceptance in this example thus computes to $2.7*10^{-6}$, certainly no standard for satisfactory performance!

Another even more cogent consideration is that when the nondeterministic parsing automaton does not accept a string, there is nothing that we can conclude about the string. The only time that we can draw a conclusion is when we are lucky enough to get an acceptance.

8.6.1 D Functions

In making the automaton deterministic, we shall allow the automaton to decide which of the $p + 2$ choices to make on the basis of what it sees and what it has done, but without giving it any new sensing mechanism.

What does the parsing automaton see? Our strict answer is that it sees only (1) what is written on the production tape, (i.e., all the productions); (2) what the input head sees, which is only one square of the input tape containing the first uncopied character of the input string, or containing nothing at all if the entire input string has been copied; and (3) the k squares of the parsing tape in the scan of the parsing-tape head.

It has no other way of looking at the input tape, and no other way of looking at the parsing tape. It cannot know what is on any square of the input tape until the input head arrives there. And it cannot consult any square to the left of the parsing-tape head on the parsing tape without going back there, which necessitates erasing squares as it goes left.

The deterministic parsing automaton is like the nondeterministic parsing automaton, except that the choice of the integer between 1 and $p + 2$ is not random; rather, the chosen integer is a function of the single character viewed by the input head (including the possibility of blank) and the substring of length at most k viewed by the parsing-tape head (possibly including the asterisk). We shall call this function the D function, and write $i = D(\beta, X)$, where β is the content of the square scanned by the input head, X is the string observed by the parsing-tape head, and i is the integer chosen. Thus if $i = p + 1$, the automaton copies; if $i = p + 2$, it halts; and if $i \leq p$, the automaton simplifies according to the ith production. The value of β is either a character in the terminal alphabet or λ, the latter signifying that that square is blank and therefore that the entire input string has been copied.

If a halt occurs with the input head scanning a blank (the entire input string having been copied) and just $*S$ on the parsing tape, then the deterministic automaton, like the nondeterministic automaton, accepts the input string. Unlike the nondeterministic automaton, the deterministic automaton can reject the input string; it does so whenever a halt occurs with either the input head scanning a nonblank square or the parsing-tape head scanning something other than just $*S$. The justification for rejecting, which means that the automaton declares that the string is not in the language of the grammar, is that the input string could not have been processed in any other way; the string not only *is not* accepted, it *could not have been* accepted.

We stipulate that, for use by a scan-k automaton with a grammar with p productions, a D function be such that $D(\beta, X)$ is defined and equal to some positive integer $\leqq p + 2$, for $\beta = \lambda$ and for all β in the terminal alphabet in the grammar; and for all strings X of length k over the total alphabet and for all $X = *X_1$, where X_1 is a string of length $k - 1$ or less over the total alphabet.

We shall also stipulate that a D function be such that it never causes a no-operation. Thus the D function will never direct the automaton to copy if the input head is viewing a blank, or to direct the automaton to simplify by the ith production if the right side of the ith production does not appear right-justified to the parsing-tape head:

Definition: An *allowable D function* for the scan-k parsing automaton, with a context-free grammar on its production tape with p productions, is a D function D such that $D(\lambda, X) \neq p + 1$ for any X; and if $D(\beta, X) = i \leqq p$, then the right side of the ith production is a suffix of X (possibly X itself).

We continue to stipulate that the automaton always begins with a finitely long string on the input tape. Thus a deterministic automaton will eventually come to a halt for any allowable D function except for certain unusual grammars:

Definition: A *loop of nonterminals* in a context-free grammar is a subset of its nonterminals $\{A_1, \ldots, A_m\}$ such that $A_m \rightarrow A_1$ is a production and, for each i, $1 \leqq i \leqq m - 1$, $A_i \rightarrow A_{i+1}$ is a production ($m \geqq 1$).

THEOREM 8.6.1: A deterministic parsing automaton with a context-free grammar on its production tape with no loops of nonterminals, acting by any allowable D function and with any string on the input tape, will eventually halt.

The proof is left to the reader (see Exercise 2 of Section 8.5). A loop of nonterminals in a context-free grammar generally serves no purpose. Furthermore, such a grammar can easily be converted into one without a loop of nonterminals (Exercise 3 of Section 8.5).

Thus we can say that, in all interesting cases, the deterministic automaton when operating with an allowable D function will eventually halt, either accepting or rejecting the input string. If the D function is appropriately chosen for the grammar, rejection will mean that the string is not in its language.

8.6.2   The Functions $D_{p,k}$

Definition: Let X be any string over the total alphabet (except that X may possibly begin with an asterisk) of a grammar on the production tape with p productions, whose longest right side is no longer than k, and let β be λ or any terminal character of the grammar. Then

$$D_{p,k}(\beta, X) = i$$

where i is the smallest integer such that the right side of the ith production is a suffix of X; or if there is no such production, $i = p + 1$ if $\beta \neq \lambda$, and $i = p + 2$ if $\beta = \lambda$.

The automaton acting deterministically according to $D_{p,k}$ will always simplify the parsing tape if possible. If more than one production is applicable, it will simplify by the earliest of these on the list. If it cannot simplify and if there is a character viewed by the input head, it will copy that character. If it cannot simplify and if there is no character to copy, it will halt.

The order in which the productions are written on the production tape is important when the automaton acts according to $D_{p,k}$. For example, for the grammar considered in Section 8.5.3, we can write the following on the production tape:

$$S \longrightarrow bc$$
$$S \longrightarrow bSc$$
$$S \longrightarrow Sc$$

We leave it to the reader to verify that the deterministic parsing automaton will accept every string in the language of this grammar if it operates according to the function $D_{3,3}$. If the productions were written on the production tape in the order given in Section 8.5.3:

$$S \longrightarrow Sc$$
$$S \longrightarrow bSc$$
$$S \longrightarrow bc$$

then any string in the language of this grammar with two or more b's would be rejected by the automaton operating according to $D_{3,3}$. The key fact is that the automaton must not be allowed to simplify by the production $S \longrightarrow Sc$ when it can simplify by $S \longrightarrow bSc$; otherwise there may be an excess of b's on the parsing tape at the end.

The grammar we have been discussing is an ambiguous grammar, as shown in Fig. 8.6.1, and yet we have shown how the parsing automaton can process it deterministically. How is this possible? It so happens that, although all strings in the language of the grammar are parsed on the parsing tape and accepted, not all derivation trees of the grammar will be involved. For example, the automaton will never parse the string *bbccc* according to the derivation tree on the right in Fig. 8.6.1.

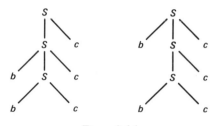

Figure 8.6.1

We have here another method of removing ambiguities from a given ambiguous context-free grammar. Rather than construct a new unambiguous grammar, we can sometimes get the deterministic parsing automaton to process the ambiguous grammar as it is. If so, then the automaton is, in effect, removing the ambiguities by establishing a priority among the productions.

Other Examples Using $D_{p,k}$ 8.6.3

Any univocal grammar with p productions, with right sides no longer than k, can be processed by the deterministic scan-k parsing automaton using $D_{p,k}$. Furthermore, for such grammars the priority among productions does not play a necessary role; the productions can be arranged in any order on the production tape. This follows from our definition of "univocal" (Section 8.4.4). Since all perfectly univocal grammars are univocal, this remark applies to them *a fortiori*.

The grammar G-PRE' of Section 8.4.3 (primes precede the p, q, or r in a variable string) is not univocal. We renumber its productions as follows:

$$(1)(2)(3)(4) \quad A \longrightarrow p \,|\, q \,|\, r \,|\, 'A$$
$$(5)(6)(7)(8) \quad S \longrightarrow A \,|\, \&SS \,|\, \vee SS \,|\, \sim S$$

Then the parsing automaton acting deterministically according to $D_{8,3}$ will accept all and only all the strings of the language.

It is critical that if $'A$ are the rightmost two characters on the parsing tape, the automaton should simplify by production (4) rather than (5). Other than this, the ordering of the productions does not matter.

Another example of an ambiguous grammar that can be processed deterministically, this time by $D_{4,3}$, is

$$S \longrightarrow SS\,|(S)|(\ )|b$$

The priority among the productions plays no role in this example, since there can never be a situation in which the automaton could simplify in two alternative ways. Nevertheless, it will never parse according to a derivation tree that has a part like Fig. 8.6.2a. This is because the first two S's will be combined when they appear on the parsing tape, and the parse will be according to Fig. 8.6.2b.

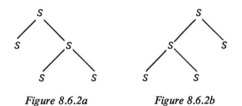

Figure 8.6.2a   *Figure 8.6.2b*

8.6.4 Using the Input Head

For G-PRE, G-IN, and G-SUF, a D function other than those in the $D_{p,k}$ class is needed.

$$
\begin{aligned}
\text{G-PRE:} \quad &(1)(2)(3)(4) \quad S \longrightarrow \&SS\,|\vee SS\,|\sim S\,|A \\
&(5)(6)(7)(8) \quad A \longrightarrow A'\,|\,p\,|\,q\,|\,r \\
\text{G-IN:} \quad &(1)(2)(3)(4) \quad S \longrightarrow (S)\&(S)\,|(S)\vee(S)\,|\sim(S)\,|A \\
&(5)(6)(7)(8) \quad A \longrightarrow A'\,|\,p\,|\,q\,|\,r \\
\text{G-SUF:} \quad &(1)(2)(3)(4) \quad S \longrightarrow SS\&\,|SS\vee\,|S\sim\,|A \\
&(5)(6)(7)(8) \quad A \longrightarrow A'\,|\,p\,|\,q\,|\,r
\end{aligned}
$$

We assume that $k = 7$ for all these grammars (although $k = 3$ is all that is needed for G-PRE and G-SUF). Then for all three grammars we can define $D_{\text{PC}}(\beta, X) = i$, where:

    I. If the right side of a production other than (4) is a suffix of X, then i = the number of that production.

    II. If the last letter of X is A and β is the prime, then $i = 9$.

    III. If the last letter of X is A and β is not the prime, then $i = 4$.

    IV. If I, II, and III are not applicable and $\beta \neq \lambda$, then $i = 9$.

    V. If I, II, and III are not applicable and $\beta = \lambda$, then $i = 10$.

Note that there can be no conflict by I of this definition with the grammars G-PRE, G-IN, or G-SUF: The parsing tape never has two or more alternatives for simplification according to the productions (1)–(3), (5)–(8).

We summarize verbally how the deterministic parsing automato vorks according to D_{PC}. At any time it simplifies if possible by one of the productions (1)–(3), (5)–(8). If not, and if the next input character is not a prime, it simplifies by production (4) if possible; but if the next character is a prime, it copies the prime. If it cannot simplify by any of the productions, it copies the next input character, if there is one, and halts if there is none.

The only complication in D_{PC} has to do with the need to forgo converting A to S if there are more primes. By all three grammars, a prime can be absorbed by an A but not by an S.

Another example shows another D function that makes critical use of what the input head sees:

$$(1)(2)(3) \quad S \longrightarrow bS \mid bSc \mid bc$$

The D function that works is defined as follows ($p = 3, k = 3$):

    I. $D(\beta, ybc) = 3$, for all β and y.
    II. $D(\beta, bSc) = 2$, for all β.
    III. $D(\lambda, ybS) = 1$, for all y.
    IV. $D(\beta, X) = 4$, for $\beta \neq \lambda$ and X not covered by I and II.
    V. $D(\lambda, X) = 5$, for X not covered by I, II, and III.

What makes this D function different from the others is that production (1) is not applied until after the input string has been completely copied. The strategic purpose is to absorb all the c's with matching b's before absorbing the b's that have no matching c's. In processing this ambiguous grammar by this D function, the deterministic automaton will not yield any parsing in which production (2) is used above production (1) in the derivation tree.

Efficiency of Suffix Notation **8.6.5**

Suppose that D_{PC} is used in processing the string $\&p\&p\&p\&p\&pp$ in G-PRE. We note that at a certain point

$$*\&S\&S\&S\&S\&S\&S$$

is on the parsing tape with the input head scanning the last character p of the input string. The p is then copied onto the parsing tape and then converted to an A, which is then converted to an S. Now the parsing tape will have

$$*\&S\&S\&S\&S\&SS$$

During the next five time steps the automaton repeatedly simplifies by production (1), until the parsing tape becomes *S and the automaton halts and accepts.

Thus, by the time the input string has been completely read, the parsing tape is as long as the input string. The automaton does much of its computing only after it has taken in the entire input. For many purposes it would be nice to intersperse simplifications and copy operations so that the automaton halts not too long after it has taken in its last input character, and the parsing tape accordingly does not get too long.

Interestingly, this phenomenon never occurs when the deterministic automaton processes strings for G-SUF using D_{PC}; in fact, if the input is a string in the language of G-SUF of length m, the number of characters on the parsing tape in addition to the asterisk is never more than $(m + 3)/2$. Thus when suffix notation is used, the parsing tape never gets longer than slightly more than half the length of the input string. (See Exercise 4 of Section 8.5.)

For example, if the input string is *ppppp&&&&&* ($m = 11$), then the parsing tape at its biggest will be *$SSSSSS\&$ [$7 = (m + 3)/2$ characters, in addition to the asterisk].

In many cases the parsing tape will remain much shorter. For example, if the input string is *pp&p&p&p&p&*, the parsing tape never has more than three characters.

8.6.6 Designing a Suitable Grammar

When we are given a set of strings, and wish to have the deterministic parsing automaton tell us whether strings are in this set or not, the first thing we must do is to find a suitable grammar: not just any grammar for the set will do.

For example, the deterministic automaton cannot handle the following grammar for the language $\{b(ccc)^*d\} \cup \{b(cc)^*e\}$:

$$
\begin{array}{ll}
(1)(2) & Q \longrightarrow b \,|\, Qccc \\
(3)(4) & R \longrightarrow b \,|\, Rcc \\
(5)(6) & S \longrightarrow Qd \,|\, Re
\end{array}
$$

The automaton would have to copy the leftmost b in the input string and convert it into either a Q by production (1) or to an R by production (3), depending on whether the last character of the input string (which could be arbitrarily long) is d or e. Since a parsing automaton cannot look ahead on the input string, and (being deterministic) must make a correct decision before copying another input character, it is impossible to design a D function for this grammar.

We must redesign the grammar. Since the d or e at the right end of the string determines whether it is a Q string or an R string, parsing should not begin until then. Accordingly, we get the following grammar:

$$(1)(2) \quad Q \longrightarrow d\,|\,cccQ$$

$$(3)(4) \quad R \longrightarrow e\,|\,ccR$$

$$(5)(6) \quad S \longrightarrow bQ\,|\,bR$$

The deterministic parsing automaton can process this grammar using the function $D_{6,4}$ of Section 8.6.2.

The last solution is somewhat undesirable since the entire input must be copied onto the parsing tape before any simplifications occur. We can construct another grammar without the distinction between Q strings and R strings, which will permit the automaton to keep simplifying between copy operations:

$$(1)(2) \qquad G \longrightarrow b\,|\,Gcccccc$$

$$(3)(4)(5)(6)(7) \quad S \longrightarrow Ge\,|\,Gd\,|\,Gcccd\,|\,Gcce\,|\,Gcccce$$

We leave it to the reader to verify that this is a grammar for the given language, and that the parsing automaton processes it with the function $D_{7,7}$.

A more involved, and perhaps more interesting, example is the set $\{UdVe\breve{U}\,|\,U, V \in \{b, c\}^*\} \cup \{UdVf\breve{V}\,|\,U, V \in \{b, c\}^*\}$. ($\breve{U}$ is the string U written backwards.) The given set is a union of two sets, and it is convenient to let the grammar consist of two parts, one to generate the first set and the other to generate the other set. Before we go any further in the design of the grammar, we should ask the crucial question: Given a string, when can the automaton "know" which of the two subsets it is in (assuming that it is in the whole set at all)? The answer is, only when it sees the e or the f. Our solution will be such that the automaton will do no simplifications until after it has copied the e or the f on the parsing tape; we arrange for this by writing the grammar in such a way that the only productions that have exclusively terminal characters on the right side are the productions in which e or f occur:

$$
\begin{array}{lll}
& (1)(2) & S \longrightarrow Q\,|\,R \\
\text{Part I} \left\{ \begin{array}{l} (3)(4)(5) \\ (6)(7)(8) \end{array} \right. & \begin{array}{l} E \longrightarrow e\,|\,bE\,|\,cE \\ Q \longrightarrow dE\,|\,bQb\,|\,cQc \end{array} \\
\text{Part II} \left\{ \begin{array}{l} (9)(10)(11) \\ (12)(13)(14) \end{array} \right. & \begin{array}{l} F \longrightarrow f\,|\,bFb\,|\,cFc \\ R \longrightarrow dF\,|\,bR\,|\,cR \end{array}
\end{array}
$$

Note that part I of the grammar is used to generate strings with e, and part II is used to generate strings with f. Production (3) or production (9) must be the first to be used by the automaton in simplifying any string.

The D function ($p = 14$, $k = 3$) is defined as follows:

I. If a suffix of X is the right side of the ith production, for $3 \leq i \leq 14$, then $D(\beta, X) = i$ for any β. [Note that there can be no conflict among productions (3) through (14).]

II. $D(\lambda, *Q) = 1$.

III. $D(\lambda, *R) = 2$.

IV. For $\beta \neq \lambda$, $D(\beta, X) = 15$, if I does not apply.

V. $D(\lambda, X) = 16$, if I, II, and III do not apply.

A final example illustrates the use of characters sensed by the parsing-tape head, other than those that are to be replaced by a simplification operation. Consider the language

$$\{bd^n e^n \,|\, n \geq 1\} \cup \{cd^n e^{2n} \,|\, n \geq 1\}$$

For this language we use a grammar especially designed for the deterministic parsing operation:

$$
\begin{array}{lll}
(1)(2) & S \longrightarrow bR \,|\, cQ \\
(3)(4) & R \longrightarrow dRe \,|\, de \\
(5)(6) & Q \longrightarrow FQee \,|\, Fee \\
(7) & F \longrightarrow d
\end{array}
$$

By this grammar d's are used directly in parsing strings that begin with b, but d's are converted to F's in parsing strings that begin with c. The parsing automaton converts d to F only if either c or F is to its immediate left on the pushdown tape. Thus $p = 7$, $k = 4$, and the D function is as follows:

I. $D(\beta, yzcd) = D(\beta, *cd) = D(\beta, yzFd) = 7$, for all β, y, and z.

II. $D(\beta, X) = i$, for $1 \leq i \leq 6$, if the right side of production (i) is a suffix of X.

III. $D(\beta, X) = 8$, for $\beta \neq \lambda$, in cases not covered by I and II.

IV. $D(\lambda, X) = 9$, in cases not covered by I and II.

8.6.7 Exercises

For Exercises 1 to 17, specify p, k, and a D function that will enable the parsing automaton to process the grammar deterministically. Renumber the productions if you wish. In those exercises given by reference, number the productions clearly. The exercises are arranged approximately in order of increasing difficulty.

$$
\begin{array}{lll}
\textbf{1.} \ (1) & S \longrightarrow Ae \\
\quad (2)(3) & A \longrightarrow Ae \,|\, e
\end{array}
\qquad
\begin{array}{lll}
\textbf{2.} \ (1) & S \longrightarrow EF \\
\quad (2)(3) & E \longrightarrow bEc \,|\, bc \\
\quad (4)(5) & F \longrightarrow cFd \,|\, cd
\end{array}
$$

3. (1)(2) $S \longrightarrow bSd \mid G$
(3)(4) $G \longrightarrow bGc \mid bc$

4. The grammar for the simplified formalism of functional expressions in Section 7.1.4.

5. (1)(2) $S \longrightarrow SAc \mid Ac$
(3)(4) $A \longrightarrow bAb \mid bcb$

6. (1)(2)(3) $S \longrightarrow bS \mid Se \mid cFd$
(4)(5) $F \longrightarrow cFd \mid cd$

7. (1)(2) $S \longrightarrow AS \mid AH$
(3)(4) $A \longrightarrow bAc \mid bc$
(5)(6) $H \longrightarrow bH \mid b$

8. (1)(2) $S \longrightarrow SE \mid E$
(3)(4)(5)(6) $E \longrightarrow bSc \mid dSe \mid bc \mid de$
(*Orientation:* Think of b, c, d, and e as
$($, $)$, $[$, and $]$, respectively.)

9. (1)(2) $S \longrightarrow SdF \mid F$
(3)(4)(5) $F \longrightarrow eFe \mid bFb \mid G$
(6)(7) $G \longrightarrow Gc \mid c$

10. (1)(2)(3) $S \longrightarrow bS \mid b \mid bG$
(4)(5) $G \longrightarrow bGb \mid Hd$
(6)(7) $H \longrightarrow cH \mid c$

11. (1)(2)(3) $S \longrightarrow bSc \mid ASA \mid d$
(4)(5) $A \longrightarrow eAf \mid f$

12. (1)(2) $S \longrightarrow DeS \mid Dee$
(3)(4) $D \longrightarrow cD \mid cA$
(5)(6) $A \longrightarrow cAb \mid cb$

13. The grammar G-SIMPU-1 of Section 8.2.2. Compare your answer with the discussion in Section 8.2.4 of precedence of operator occurrences in strings produced by the grammar.

14. The grammar G-SIMPU-2 Section 8.2.2. Compare your answer to the discussion in Section 8.2.4 of precedence for the grammar.

15. (1)(2)(3) $S \longrightarrow bSc \mid bGd \mid f$
(4)(5) $G \longrightarrow bGd \mid bSc$

16. The grammar for the GOTO language in Section 7.2.3 (with reference to Section 7.2.1).

17. (*Quite difficult*)

(1)(2) $S \longrightarrow GN \mid P$

(3)(4) $N \longrightarrow Hee \mid HNee$

(5)(6)(7) $G \longrightarrow cb \mid Gb \mid bG$

(8) $H \longrightarrow d$

(9)(10) $Q \longrightarrow dQe \mid de$

(11)(12) $P \longrightarrow bQ \mid bP$

18. (*Quite difficult and long*) The grammar G-PP partially parenthesized propositional calculus of Section 7.2.4. (*Hint:* Read the second half of Section 7.2.4. Use the examples to check your solution.)

In Exercises 19 to 23, find for the given language a grammar that the parsing automaton can process deterministically, number the productions, and specify the D function. These exercises are approximately in order of increasing difficulty.

19. $\{b^m c^{m+n+p} d^n \mid m, n \geq 1; p \geq 0\}$.

20. $\{b^{m+n} c^n d^{p+m} e^p \mid m, n, p \geq 1\}$.

21. The set of all nonnull strings over $\{b, c\}$ with an even number of c's. Find a solution in which there are never more than two characters on the parsing tape, besides the asterisk, at any time.

22. The set of all nonnull strings over $\{b, c, d\}$ in which there is no b anywhere to the right of any d. (*Note:* This set includes all strings without any b's, and all strings without any d's. See Example 7 of Section 8.2.6.)

23. $\{b^m c^n \mid 1 \leqq n \leqq 2m\}$.

24. (*Abstract and difficult*) Suppose that the deterministic parsing automaton uses the function $D_{5,3}$ with the grammar

$$(1)(2)(3)(4)(5) \quad S \longrightarrow bSc \mid cSb \mid SS \mid bc \mid cb$$

on its production tape. Prove that it will accept all and only all the nonnull strings over the alphabet $\{b, c\}$ with as many b's as c's (an alternative to the theoretical discussion of this grammar as Example 5 of Section 7.3.2).

25. (*Abstract and more difficult*) Suppose that the deterministic parsing automaton uses the function $D_{13,5}$ with the grammar

$$(1)(2)(3)(4) \qquad S \longrightarrow bSbSc \mid bbSc \mid bSbc \mid bbc$$

$$(5)(6)(7)(8) \qquad S \longrightarrow bScSb \mid bcSb \mid bScb \mid bcb$$

$$(9)(10)(11)(12) \quad S \longrightarrow cSbSb \mid cbSb \mid cSbb \mid cbb$$

$$(13) \qquad\qquad\quad S \longrightarrow SS$$

on its production tape. Prove that it will accept all and only all the nonnull strings over the alphabet $\{b, c\}$ with twice as many b's as c's. (*Hint:* First prove the following lemma: In any string over the alphabet $\{b, c, S\}$ with twice as many b's as c's, there is at least one substring that is the right side of one of the 13 productions of this grammar.)

8.7 SIMILAR AUTOMATA

We have mentioned that our parsing automaton works on the principle of the pushdown store. Its parsing tape is a pushdown stack, since it follows the last-in-first-out principle. Thus, what we accomplished in Section 8.5 was to reveal the important relationship between pushdown operations and context-free languages. And the accomplishment in Section 8.6 was the development of effective parsing techniques for some context-free languages using pushdown operations.

Our parsing automaton is not the most general of pushdown automata, and parsing is not the only useful thing that pushdown automata can do. In this section we informally contrast the parsing automaton with the more general pushdown model, and show how the parsing automaton itself can be adapted to perform tasks that go beyond the relatively simple one of parsing.

8.7.1 Limited Power of the Present Model

Our deterministic parsing automaton must make decisions on the basis of what it presently sees through its parsing-tape head and input head. Thus our automaton has no internal memory (i.e., no memory apart from the parsing tape).

In this respect it differs from the usual variety of pushdown automaton, which is allowed to have a finite-state memory.

An example in which such memory seems to be indispensable is the following grammar:

$$(1)(2)(3) \quad S \longrightarrow bS \,|\, bQ \,|\, cR$$

$$(4)(5) \quad Q \longrightarrow dQe \,|\, de$$

$$(6)(7) \quad R \longrightarrow bR \,|\, bN$$

$$(8)(9) \quad N \longrightarrow dNee \,|\, dee$$

The language of this grammar is $\{b^*bd^ie^i \,|\, i \geqq 1\} \cup \{b^*cb^*bd^ie^{2i} \,|\, i \geqq 1\}$. A string in this language, if it has no c, has as many e's as d's; but if it has a c, then it has twice as many e's as d's. A deterministic automaton should use production (5) if there is no c, but should use production (9) if there is. The most convenient way to arrange this is to have the automaton remember whether or not it has ever copied c, and make its decision accordingly. Such a decision, however, would not be according to a D function.

But unless we endow our automaton with memory, there seems to be no way of getting it to process this grammar deterministically. (There is, however, a more complex grammar for the same language that can be processed by our model of deterministic parsing automation; see Exercise 17 of Section 8.6.)

Consider the grammar

$$(1)(2) \quad S \longrightarrow bS \,|\, Accc$$

$$(3)(4) \quad A \longrightarrow bAc \,|\, bc$$

In processing this grammar the crucial question is when to defer a simplification by production (3) so as to copy two more c's for production (2). The answer is clear: when the two more c's to be copied are at the right end of the input string. Here is an example in which we would like to have the deterministic automaton make its decision by looking ahead on the input tape, namely to the square that is two squares to the right of the square viewed by the input head. If that square is blank, then we want the automaton to copy two more characters. Otherwise, we want the automaton to simplify by production (3).

Without such a look-ahead on the input tape, it is impossible for the deterministic parsing automaton to process this grammar. Many authors allow a look-ahead with a fixed limit, although for most pushdown operations this look-ahead is unnecessary. (It is easy to give an equivalent grammar that can be processed by our deterministic parsing automaton.)

In the literature there is a rather standard model of pushdown automaton (see, e.g., Ginsburg [1966], pp. 59ff., or Hopcroft and Ullman [1979], Chap.5). Although it does not allow look-ahead on the input tape (which is theoretically dispensable) it does have a finite-state memory in addition to its pushdown stack. The model is not explicitly formulated in terms of the notion of context-free grammar (it has no production tape on which productions are written), nor does it function according to any one particular parsing method. However, it is easy to prove that for any context-free language there is a pushdown automaton accepting all and only all the strings of the language. We shall not describe this model here in any detail.

8.7.2 Nondeterministic Languages

Just as there are context-free languages that are inherently ambiguous, there are context-free languages that are inherently nondeterministic: No matter what grammar we design for them, there is no way to process them by a deterministic parsing automaton. Even with the most liberal model of pushdown automaton in the literature, there is still no way. Such languages are called *nondeterministic languages*.

An example is the language of nonnull palindromes over the alphabet $\{b, c\}$ (the set of all nonnull strings that read the same backward as forward). A grammar for this language (from Example 4 of Section 7.3.2) is

$$(1)(2)(3)(4)(5)(6) \quad S \longrightarrow bSb \,|\, cSc \,|\, bb \,|\, cc \,|\, b \,|\, c$$

Note the impossibility of this grammar for the deterministic parsing automaton. There is no way for it to know which of productions (3), (4), (5), or (6) to apply or when to apply it. We know that the correct point for this first simplification is the halfway point in the input string. But there is no way to determine, given the inherent limitation on pushdown operations, where this midpoint is. If one could mark the midpoint with a special character on the input tape, the automaton could know. But then the solution would really be a change of the language, with an increased alphabet. It is known that no equivalent grammar will enable any model of deterministic pushdown automaton to work.

Another nondeterministic language is $\{b^m c^n \,|\, 1 \leqq m \leqq n \leqq 2m\}$. Let us focus on an unambiguous grammar for this language:

$$(1)(2)(3) \quad S \longrightarrow bSc \,|\, bc \,|\, D$$
$$(4)(5) \quad\quad D \longrightarrow bDcc \,|\, bcc$$

(see Example 8 of Section 8.2.6). The problem for the deterministic automaton here is whether to apply production (2) or production (5) for its first simplification; and, if it applies (5), when to apply (3) to convert the D to an S. To do this correctly it would have to use information about exactly how many c's there are ahead, which by the very nature of the deterministic parsing automaton, it cannot know. As in the case of palindromes, there is no grammar for this language that will permit the automaton to act deterministically. The same is true for the general pushdown model.

It is to be noted that the grammars given for both languages are unambiguous. In each case there is just one way of parsing a string in the language; in neither case can the parsing be done by a deterministic pushdown automaton. We see then that there are unambiguous nondeterministic languages.

Are there inherently ambiguous, deterministic languages? The answer is in the negative. We have seen how the deterministic parsing automaton can process ambiguous grammars. It turns out that whenever this is possible, there always is another equivalent unambiguous grammar (see Ginsburg [1966], p. 79).

In summary, no deterministic languages are inherently ambiguous, but there exist unambiguous languages that are not deterministic.

Recall again the inherently ambiguous language $\{b^m c^m dd^* \mid m \geq 1\} \cup \{bb^* c^n d^n \mid n \geq 1\}$ (Example 10 of Section 8.2.6) and a grammar for it:

$$
\begin{array}{ll}
(1)(2) & S \longrightarrow ED \mid BF \\
(3)(4) & E \longrightarrow bEc \mid bc \\
(5)(6) & D \longrightarrow Dd \mid d \\
(7)(8) & B \longrightarrow Bb \mid b \\
(9)(10) & F \longrightarrow cFd \mid cd
\end{array}
$$

There is no way for the deterministic parsing automaton to know whether to simplify by production (8) or keep copying b's until it gets its first c to simplify by production (4). For there is no way it can know whether the string is an ED string (as many b's as c's) or a BF string (as many c's as d's) without somehow counting before it begins. And there is no change of grammar or (deterministic) liberalization of the pushdown model that will improve things.

Formula Evaluation   8.7.3

Before ending this chapter, we show how the deterministic parsing automaton can be used to evaluate a formula, given values for its variables, and how it can be adapted to translate strings from one language to another. Both of these tasks involve semantics in one way or another, contrasting with the purely syntactic test of well-formedness.

The semantics of the propositional calculus has to do with the truth and falsity (i.e., truth values) of propositions. The truth value of an expression made up by an operator from operands depends on the truth values of the operands. Assuming that the reader is familiar with the manner in which the three operators $\&$, $\vee$, and $\sim$ determine truth values, we focus now on G-SUF. Letting 0 represent falsity and 1 represent truth, we can write these truth-value dependencies as if they were the productions of a context-free grammar. The complete set for

&, $\lor$, and $\sim$ are the following 10 operator evaluation productions:

(5) $0 \longrightarrow 00\&$ (9) $0 \longrightarrow 00\lor$ (13) $1 \longrightarrow 0\sim$

(6) $0 \longrightarrow 01\&$ (10) $1 \longrightarrow 01\lor$ (14) $0 \longrightarrow 1\sim$

(7) $0 \longrightarrow 10\&$ (11) $1 \longrightarrow 10\lor$

(8) $1 \longrightarrow 11\&$ (12) $1 \longrightarrow 11\lor$

Suppose that we wish to evaluate the expression $p''q\&p\sim pr'\lor\&\sim\lor$, where p'' is false, q is true, p is false, and r' is false. We write the string on the input tape. Then we write on the production tape:

(1) $0 \longrightarrow p''$ (3) $0 \longrightarrow p$

(2) $1 \longrightarrow q$ (4) $0 \longrightarrow r'$

followed by all 10 operator evaluation productions. Accordingly, we take $k = 3$ and $p = 14$. The parsing automaton operates deterministically by a variation on a familiar D function. That is, it simplifies by any production, unless the next uncopied input symbol is prime, in which case it copies. If it cannot simplify by any production, it copies if possible. If it cannot simplify and there is no character to copy, it halts.

Upon halting there are three possibilities of interest to us. If the parsing tape is *1 or *0, the expression is true or false, respectively. In all other cases, the original expression was not well formed. Thus we still have here our well-formedness test together with our evaluation procedure.

The history of the computation for the string we mentioned is, in abbreviated form, as follows (see Section 8.5.3):

Time Step	Number Chosen	Designated String at End of Time Step
Beginning		$/p''q\&p\sim pr'\lor\&\sim\lor$
1	15 (copy)	$p/''q\&\ldots$
3	15	$p''/q\&\ldots$
4	1	$0/q\&\ldots$
7	15	$01\&/p\sim pr'\lor\ldots$
8	6	$0/p\sim pr'\lor\ldots$
10	3	$00/\sim pr'\lor\ldots$
11	15	$00\sim/pr'\lor\ldots$
12	13	$01/pr'\lor\ldots$
18	15	$0100\lor/\&\sim\lor$
19	9	$010/\&\sim\lor$
20	15	$010\&/\sim\lor$
21	7	$00/\sim\lor$
22	15	$00\sim/\lor$
23	13	$01/\lor$
24	15	$01\lor/$
25	10	$1/$
26	16 (halt)	$1/$

Thus we see that formula evaluation is quite feasible by a parsing automaton. Suffix notation is most convenient, since a new computation (i.e., a simplification by means of an operator evaluation production) takes place when and only when a new operator sign has just appeared on the parsing tape. (This principle is exploited in some hand calculators.) But infix and prefix notation would work essentially the same way. The method is easily adapted to the multidigit numbers of arithmetic calculations; some modification of the basic concept is necessary, since these numbers cannot readily be regarded as nonterminals of a grammar. Much of the principle of pushdown organization remains the same, and such techniques are used frequently in programming practice.

Translation of Formal Languages   8.7.4

Translation is a rather complicated matter. In the domain of the natural languages, fully mechanical translation has never been achieved, and some say it never will. Fully mechanical translation from one formal language to another is often possible, but the matter is still complicated. The initial difficulty is stating precisely what is wanted as the translation into a second language of a given string in the first language. Inevitably, the relationship between these strings must also involve a relationship between parts of the first string and corresponding parts of the second. The various techniques of executing the translation are difficult to come by, and are well beyond the scope of this book.

We shall not begin to discuss the general problems of translation here, leaving the reader to more advanced books (e.g., Aho and Ullman [1972], Chap. 3; and Lewis, Rosenkrantz, and Stearns [1976]). We shall select a simple example that provides a smooth use of a slight variation of our parsing automaton. We shall have the automaton translate the formulas of prefix propositional calculus into suffix notation. The reader will be left without any competence to carry through another translation, unless he or she pursues other references.

Let us first make clear what we want to happen as a result of this translation. We want &pq to be translated to pq&, and not, for example, to qp&. More generally, if W is a string in the language of G-PRE, and $T(W)$ is the translation of W as a formula of the language of G-SUF, then we want: (I) $T(W) = W$ if W is a variable string. (II) $T(W) = T(U)T(X)$& if $W = \&UX$, where U and X are strings in the language of G-PRE. (III) Similarly for $\bigvee$. (IV) $T(W) = T(U)\sim$ if $W = \sim U$. Finally, let us say that we do not care what $T(W)$ is if W is not a string in the language of G-PRE.

The parsing automaton is now augmented by an output tape and an output writing head for writing the translation. Roughly speaking, as the automaton reads the input string (from left to right), it will place some symbols directly onto the output tape, and save other symbols on the parsing tape to be written later. Thus the string as it is written on the output tape will be the symbols from the input string, but in a different order. (In other examples, these symbols may be changed.)

The manner in which the automaton consults the production tape is radically different from before, there being productions for the output grammar as well as productions for the input grammar. In this account, we shall simplify our explanation by omitting reference to the production tape.

This augmented parsing automaton is a variety of what is sometimes called in the literature a "pushdown transducer."

8.7.5 A Sample Translation

Before explaining how the translation works for general input strings, let us consider the input string $\vee\, \& p'' \sim qr$. This string is to be translated into the output string $p''q \sim \& r \vee$, and it is helpful to look at the two derivation trees (Fig. 8.7.1), where subscripts on the S's show the correspondence between input and

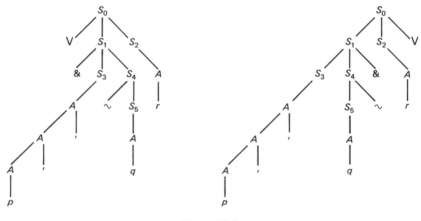

Figure 8.7.1

output. Note that the derivation tree in G-SUF is obtained from the derivation tree in G-PRE by the specifications we have laid down for the translation. In effect these stipulations are rules for converting one derivation tree to the other. The utility of the pushdown organization is to make it unnecessary to draw either tree.

We shall describe the writing of the characters of the two trees on the parsing tape. We shall put subscripts on these nonterminals, as the subscripts appear in the two trees, for the sake of revealing the important relationships. Of course, the automaton does not actually use subscripts at all, and we shall verify that it does not need them.

At the beginning the parsing tape contains $*S_0$.

The input string begins with $\vee$, so the last character in the output string will be $\vee$. Furthermore S_1 will be produced before S_2 is produced. Accordingly, the automaton reads $\vee$ and replaces S_0 on the parsing tape with $\vee S_2 S_1$, in recognition of the fact that as the parsing tape is emptied, the S_1 will come out first, then the S_2, then the $\vee$. [Actually, subscripts do not occur at all: The automaton reads $\vee$ from the input tape (advancing the input head), and replaces S on the production tape by $\vee SS$ in the first time step; the procedure will be able to determine which S is which.]

The automaton reads & and replaces S_1 on the parsing tape by $\&S_4S_3$, for similar reasons. The next character is p, which it knows to be the first character of a variable string. Thus S_3 must produce that variable string, which must be the beginning of the output string. For simplicity we shall not have the automaton deal with the nonterminal A. Thus the automaton erases S_3 from the parsing tape and copies p'' from the input tape onto the output tape. And so on.

The complete history of this translation is given in Fig. 8.7.2. The input

Input tape

$$\vee \quad \& \quad p \quad ' \quad ' \quad \sim \quad q \quad r$$

$$(1)\ (2)\ (3)\ (4)\ (5)\ (6)\ (7)\ (10)$$

Time step	Parsing tape at end of time step	Output tape at end of time step
beginning	$*S_0$	
1	$* \vee S_2 S_1$	
2	$* \vee S_2 \& S_4 S_3$	
3	$* \vee S_2 \& S_4$	p
4	$* \vee S_2 \& S_4$	p'
5	$* \vee S_2 \& S_4$	p''
6	$* \vee S_2 \& \sim S_6$	p''
7	$* \vee S_2 \& \sim$	$p''q$
8	$* \vee S_2 \&$	$p''q\sim$
9	$* \vee S_2$	$p''q\sim\&$
10	$* \vee$	$p''q\sim\&r$
11	$*$	$p''q\sim\&r \vee$
12 halt	$*$	$p''q\sim\&r \vee$

Figure 8.7.2

tape showing where the input head is at various points is at the top; a number under a character shows the time step when that character is read. The actual history is given in the table part of the figure.

Note that, at the end, the automaton is simply copying operator characters from the parsing tape to the output tape. The halt occurs when the input tape has been read and the parsing tape is empty except for the asterisk.

8.7.6 General Formulation

We now state the general rules governing the deterministic automaton in carrying through our translation, without making explicit reference to productions of G-PRE or G-SUF.

This translation involves, among other things, three kinds of copy operation, only one of which we have seen before. The first is copying a character from the input to the parsing tape, which is exactly as it was before. The second is copying a character from the input tape to the output tape. Here, the character viewed by the input head is written on the first blank square of the output tape, and the input head is moved one square to the right. The third is copying a character from the parsing tape to the output. Here, the rightmost character of the parsing tape is written on the first blank square of the output tape, that character is erased from the parsing tape, and the parsing-tape head is moved one square to the left.

At the beginning of the translation of a string W in the language of G-PRE to a string in the language of G-SUF, $*S$ is on the parsing tape, W is on the input tape, the input head is at the leftmost character, and the output tape is blank. The following govern each time step:

1. If the input head is viewing a prime, copy the prime onto the output tape.

2. If the input head is not viewing a prime, and if the rightmost character of the parsing tape is an operator symbol (&, $\vee$, or $\sim$), copy this character from the parsing tape to the output tape.

3. If the input head is viewing &, $\vee$, or $\sim$, and S is the rightmost character of the parsing tape, move the input head one square to the right and replace the S on the parsing tape by $\&SS$, $\vee SS$, or $\sim S$, respectively.

4. If the input head is viewing p, q, or r, and S is the rightmost character on the parsing tape, copy that character from the input tape to the output tape, and erase the S on the parsing tape (moving the parsing-tape head one square to the left).

5. If 1 to 4 do not apply, halt.

At the halt, if the parsing-tape head views the asterisk and no symbol to its right and the input head reads a blank square, the automaton knows that the input string has been completely read and that if it was a string in the language of G-PRE, the output string is its translation according to the specifications. Whatever the input string, the halt will always occur. If a halt occurs with at least one character to the right of the asterisk on the parsing tape or with the input head on a nonblank square, the automaton knows that the input string was not in the language of G-PRE. (In some cases it will translate a string that is not in the language of G-PRE as if it were: for example, $\&p\vee 'qr$ is translated as $p'qr \lor \&$. Modifications could have been made in our procedure to prevent this.)

In this translation example, we have used the parsing automaton in a manner radically different from its original conception in Section 8.5. Up to now, we have stressed its linguistic aspect, namely its relation to a context-free grammar for a test of well-formedness. This method of translation stresses the mechanical aspect (i.e., the last-in-first-out principle by means of which the parsing tape works). We thus provide for the later operators in the input string to appear in the output string before those operators that were earlier in the input string.

The common use of pushdown operations in tests of well-formedness, evaluation of formulas, translation, and other applications is significant. However, we could not claim to communicate this significance fully without delving more deeply into the general problem of formal-language translation, which we shall not do.

9 Regular Languages and Finite Automata

In this chapter we turn our attention to those grammars that generate strings in a left-to-right fashion. The languages of such grammars are called *regular languages*. We shall prove that a language is regular if and only if there is a read-only, finite-state device (i.e., a finite automaton) that accepts all and only all the strings in the language. In the course of this chapter, we offer several other representations of regular languages.

Although not all important languages are regular, it is worthwhile to know the various techniques of dealing with them, simply because the techniques themselves are so convenient to use.

9.1 REGULAR GRAMMARS AND TRANSITION GRAPHS

In this section we introduce regular grammars and transition graphs, two ways of representing regular languages. We then consider several examples of such languages, devising for each a transition graph.

9.1.1 Graphical Representation

Definition: A *regular grammar* is a context-free grammar each of whose productions has as its right side either:

1. A terminal character followed by a nonterminal,
2. A single terminal character, or
3. λ.

A language is *regular* if there is a regular grammar for it.

A example is taken from Section 7.3:

$$G_1: \quad S \longrightarrow cS \,|\, bD \,|\, c$$
$$D \longrightarrow cD \,|\, bS \,|\, b$$

$L(G_1)$ (i.e., the language of the grammar G_1) is the set of nonnull strings over $\{b, c\}$ having an even number of b's. The following grammar is also regular:

$$G_2: \quad S \longrightarrow cS \,|\, bD \,|\, \lambda$$
$$D \longrightarrow cD \,|\, bS$$

$L(G_2)$ is the set of all strings over $\{b, c\}$ (including λ) having an even number of b's.

Clearly, when a string is derived in a regular grammar, it is derived from left to right. Any parsing of the string from the bottom up, the manner studied in most of Sections 8.3 and 8.4, must go from right to left on the string. (A top-down parsing, exhibited in Section 8.4.3, will go from left to right.) All of this can be reversed by defining another type of grammar.

Definition: A context-free grammar is *reverse-regular* if the right side of each of its productions is either (2) or (3) in the definition of "regular grammar" or the following:

(1′)   a nonterminal character followed by a terminal.

The following is an example of a reverse-regular grammar:

$$G_2': \quad S \longrightarrow Sc \,|\, Db \,|\, \lambda$$
$$D \longrightarrow Dc \,|\, Sb$$

$L(G_2') = L(G_2)$, the set of all strings over $\{b, c\}$ with an even number of b's. We shall ignore reverse-regular grammars until Section 9.2.8.

Perhaps the most attractive feature of a regular grammar is that it can be put into the form of a directed graph representing each nonterminal as a node and each production as an arc. Figures 9.1.1 and 9.1.2 represent the grammars G_1 and G_2, respectively; the nodes are the circles and the arcs are the arrows. A string generated by a grammar is generated by a walk through the corresponding graph (see p. 59).

We explain precisely the relationship between the grammar G_1 and the graph of Fig. 9.1.1. The grammatical productions $S \rightarrow cS$, $S \rightarrow bD$, $S \rightarrow c$ correspond, respectively, to the arc labeled c looping on node S, the arc labeled b going from node S to node D, and the arc labeled c from node S to node E. Similarly for the other three productions, $D \rightarrow cD$, $D \rightarrow bS$, and $D \rightarrow b$, and

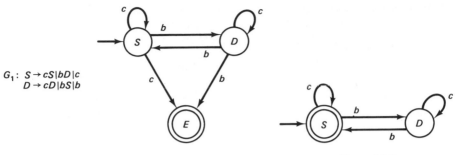

$G_1: S \rightarrow cS|bD|c$
$\quad\ D \rightarrow cD|bS|b$

Figure 9.1.1   *Figure 9.1.2*

the other three arcs. Corresponding to the grammatical derivation

$$S$$
$$cS$$
$$cbD$$
$$cbcD$$
$$cbcbS$$
$$cbcbc$$

we have the walk in Fig. 9.1.1 that touches nodes in the following order: S, S, D, D, S, E. The labels on the successive arcs traveled form the string $cbcbc$, which is the same string that is derived, the arcs corresponding exactly to the productions in the derivation.

Clearly then, a walk through the graph of Fig. 9.1.1 that begins at S and ends at the double circle E corresponds to a derivation in the grammar, and vice versa. The string derived is the string spelled out by the walk.

The same correspondence exists between the grammar G_2 and Fig. 9.1.2, although there is a slight difference. There is no arc in G_2 corresponding to the lambda production $S \longrightarrow \lambda$. Instead, the S node is represented as a double circle. Consider the following derivation in G_2:

$$S$$
$$cS$$
$$cbD$$
$$cbcD$$
$$cbcbS$$
$$cbcbcS$$
$$cbcbc$$

It corresponds to the walk in G_2 that touches nodes in the following order: S, S, D, D, S, S. The application of the lambda production $S \to \lambda$ in the derivation corresponds not to an arc but simply to the decision to end the walk at S.

There is a one-to-one correspondence between derivations in G_2 and walks in Fig. 9.1.2 that begin at S and end at S. The short unlabeled arrow pointing to S indicates that such walks should begin at S (as in Fig. 9.1.1) and the double circle indicates (as it did in Fig. 9.1.1) that walks should end there.

The empty string has the following derivation in G_2:

$$S$$

$$\lambda$$

The walk corresponding to this derivation that spells out lambda is the null walk beginning at S ending at S, without going along any arcs.

Transition Graphs 9.1.2

We now formalize the notions introduced in the previous subsection, building on definitions on p. 59.

Definition: A *transition graph* is a directed graph whose arcs have as labels characters from an alphabet, one of whose nodes is the *start node* and some subset of whose nodes are *accepting nodes*. (In the figures, the start node will have a short unlabeled arrow pointing to it, accepting nodes will be double circles, and nodes that are not accepting nodes will be single circles.)

We shall refer to a walk by its sequence of nodes, if there is no ambiguity in this designation. (If a graph has two or more arcs going from one node to another, a walk using any of these arcs will not be uniquely designated by its sequence of nodes.)

Definition: The string *spelled out* by the walk $N_0, A_1, N_1, \ldots, N_{n-1}, A_n, N_n$ in a transition graph is the string formed by the labels on the arcs $A_1, \ldots, A_n$, in order. The string spelled out by a null walk is the null string.

Definition: The *language* $L(G)$ of a transition graph G is the set of all strings spelled out by all walks from the start node to the accepting nodes. Two transition graphs, or a transition graph and a grammar, are *equivalent* if they have the same language.

THEOREM 9.1.1: For every regular grammar there is an equivalent transition graph (easily) constructible from it.

The general proof of this theorem should be clear from the two examples in Section 9.1.1. Moreover, the construction of the graph from the grammar is quite direct; in fact, we are justified in thinking of the graph so constructed as being the grammar itself in a different format.

THEOREM 9.1.2:   For every transition graph there is an equivalent regular grammar (easily) constructible from it.

PROOF: Select a set of nonterminals $\{B_1, \ldots, B_m\}$ for the grammar in one-to-one correspondence with the nodes of the graph, where the start symbol B_1 corresponds to the start node of the graph. The terminal alphabet of the grammar is the set of labels on the arcs.

The productions of the grammar are as follows. There is a production $B_i \longrightarrow cB_j$ if and only if there is an arc labeled c going from node B_i to node B_j in the graph. And there is a production $B_i \longrightarrow \lambda$ if and only if node B_i is an accepting node. (There are no productions whose right side is a single terminal character, by this construction.)

To complete the proof, it must be verified (1) that, for every walk in the graph from the start node to an accepting node, there is a derivation in the grammar of the string spelled out; and (2) that for every derivation of a terminal string, there is such a walk spelling out that string. We leave these two propositions to the reader; they are not difficult in view of the examples in Section 9.1.1. ∎

9.1.3 Some Examples

Most people who have experience with both prefer transition graphs to regular grammars, because they get a sense of the set of strings represented much more quickly by looking at the transition graph, provided the graph is not too complex. Consider the following:

EXAMPLE 1. The set of all strings over $\{b, c\}$ having three consecutive c's somewhere. A transition graph for this language is Fig. 9.1.3, and a regular grammar is as follows:

$$S \longrightarrow bS \,|\, cS \,|\, cD$$
$$D \longrightarrow cE$$
$$E \longrightarrow cF$$
$$F \longrightarrow bF \,|\, cF \,|\, \lambda$$

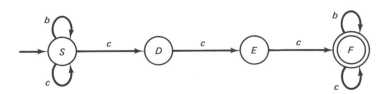

Figure 9.1.3

One can see almost immediately by looking at the graph that a string over $\{b, c\}$ is accepted if and only if it has three consecutive c's. One can get the corresponding insight from the grammar only with a bit more effort. The graph and the grammar are interchangeable, but the graph is easier for most people to read. The same is true whenever the language we are dealing with is not such as to require a very large graph. Since all our examples require transition graphs with fewer than ten nodes, we shall henceforth deal with transition graphs instead of regular grammars. Indeed, it is the fact that they can be represented by transition graphs (and other things that we shall introduce later) that makes regular languages a worthwhile topic of study.

EXAMPLE 2. The set of all nonnull strings over $\{b, c, d\}$ of which bc is not a substring. Fig. 9.1.4 is the transition graph constructed from the grammar given in Example 1 of Section 7.3.1 for this language. (Note the multiple

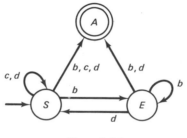

Figure 9.1.4

labels separated by commas on some of the arcs in Fig. 9.1.4. The loop arc on S labeled "c, d" is an abbreviation for two arcs, one labeled "c" the other labeled "d." Thus Fig. 9.1.4 is really an abbreviation for a transition graph with 10 arcs.)

EXAMPLE 3. The set of strings over $\{b, c, d\}$ in which each b that occurs (if any) is immediately followed by c has Fig. 9.1.5 as a transition graph. Note that the null string is accepted, correctly.

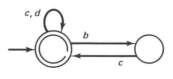

Figure 9.1.5

EXAMPLE 4. The set of all strings over $\{b, c, d\}$ that have bcd as a proper prefix and have bcd as a proper suffix is represented by Fig. 9.1.6. (The string bcd itself is *not* in this language since it is not a *proper* prefix or suffix of itself.)

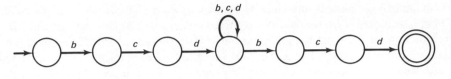

Figure 9.1.6

EXAMPLE 5. The set of strings over $\{b, c, d\}$ in which no d appears any-where to the left of any b is represented by Fig. 9.1.7. (In particular, any string without a b is in this set, as is any string without a d. *A fortiori*, λ is in the set.)

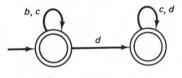

Figure 9.1.7

Figure 9.1.7 is the first transition graph we have considered with more than one accepting node. In this transition graph, the walk spelling out a string of the language may end at either of the two nodes.

EXAMPLE 6. The set of strings over $\{b, c, d\}$ in which there is an even number (possibly zero) of occurrences of the substring *bcd* is represented by Fig. 9.1.8.

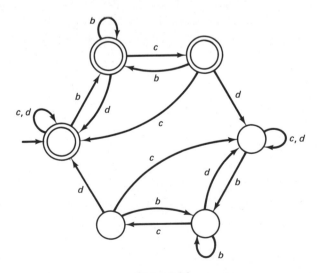

Figure 9.1.8

EXAMPLE 7. The set of all strings of the form $(bcd)^*$ is represented by Fig. 9.1.9.

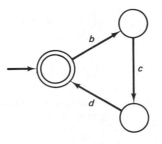

Figure 9.1.9

EXAMPLE 8. The set of all strings of the form $V_1 V_2 \ldots V_n$, $n \geq 0$, where each $V_i = bc$ or cb, is represented by Fig. 9.1.10. (Taking $n = 0$, we get λ.)

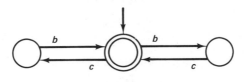

Figure 9.1.10

Exercises 9.1.4

In Exercises 1 to 22, draw a transition graph for each set. Exercises 18 to 22 are *more difficult* than those that precede.

1–10. The sets of Exercises 17 to 23, and 25 to 27, respectively, of Section 7.3.

11. The set of all strings over $\{b, c\}$ whose length is no greater than 5.

12. The set of all strings over $\{b, c\}$ whose length is at least 5.

13. The set of all strings over $\{b, c\}$ with length at least two, having an even number (possibly zero) of b's.

14. The set of strings over $\{b, c, d\}$ in which the number of occurrences of the substring bc is odd.

15. The set of strings over $\{b, c\}$ with an odd number of b's and with suffix ccc.

16. The set of strings over $\{b, c\}$ either with an odd number of b's or with suffix ccc. (In particular, both b and ccc are in this set.)

17. The set of strings over $\{b, c\}$ having both bb and cc as substrings. (In particular, $bbcc$, $ccbb$, $bbbcc$, and $bbccbb$ are in this set.)

18. The set of all strings over $\{b, c\}$ having ccc as suffix, but in which ccc does not occur elsewhere as a substring. (For example, ccc is in this set but $cccc$ is not.)

19, 20. The sets of Exercises 32 and 33, respectively, of Section 7.3.

21. The set of all strings over $\{b, c\}$ (1) ending in b, (2) having an occurrence of the substring bb, and (3) whose rightmost occurrence of bb is to the right of the rightmost occurrence of cc, if any.

22. The set of strings over $\{b, c, d\}$ beginning with b, ending with another b, and such that between any b and the next occurrence of b there are an odd number of c's and also an odd number of d's.

23. (*Abstract and difficult*) Show how to construct, for each $n \geq 1$, a transition graph whose language is the set of all strings over $\{b, c\}$ for which the following is true for each i, $1 \leq i \leq n$: b^i is a substring, and either c^i is not a substring or the rightmost occurrence of b^i is to the right of the rightmost occurrence of c^i. (For example, any string with the suffix b^n is in the set, as is $b^n c^{n-1} b^{n-1} c^{n-2} \ldots bbbccbbcb$, but b^{n-1} and $b^n c^n b^{n-1}$, as well as any string ending in c, are not. *Hint:* Exercise 21, which is this problem for $n = 2$, is not typical. Solve the problem for $n = 3$ and then for $n = 4$ before generalizing.)

24. Find a regular grammar equivalent to

$$S \longrightarrow bSb \,|\, FG$$
$$F \longrightarrow bF \,|\, bcb$$
$$G \longrightarrow Gb \,|\, c$$

25. (*Difficult*) Find a regular grammar equivalent to

$$S \longrightarrow Q \,|\, R$$
$$Q \longrightarrow bbQc \,|\, Qc \,|\, bb$$
$$R \longrightarrow bM \,|\, c$$
$$M \longrightarrow bRc \,|\, bR$$

26–30. Find a verbal phrase, in the spirit of the verbal phrases given in the examples and preceding exercise, for the sets of strings that are the languages of Figs. 9.1.11 through 9.1.15, respectively.

9.2 FINITE AUTOMATA

If we design a computing device to examine strings over an alphabet, it is important to understand (among other things) how much memory the device uses. In this chapter we focus on those devices that have a fixed upper bound on the amount of memory they use in examining strings that are arbitrarily long. The finite automaton, which is well studied in the literature, is the prototype of such devices.

Let us note first that other automata that we have looked at in this book do not have such a bound. The parsing automaton, for example, can augment its memory indefinitely by extending its parsing tape, even if the production tape has on it a fixed grammar. Turing machines and the idealized computer for computing programs also allow arbitrarily large memory.

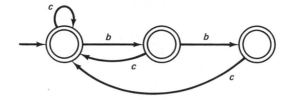

Figure 9.1.11

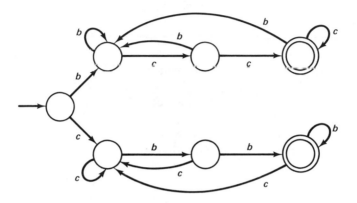

Figure 9.1.12

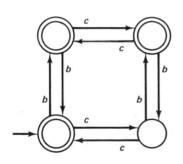

Figure 9.1.13

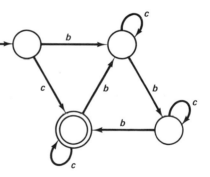

Figure 9.1.14

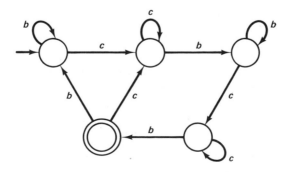

Figure 9.1.15

In this section we define "finite automaton," prove that a language is regular if and only if it is the language of a finite automaton, and prove several other theorems about such languages.

9.2.1 Definition

Like the deterministic parsing automaton, the finite automaton examines a string on its input tape in one pass from left to right, and at the end either *accepts* the string or *rejects* it. Unlike the parsing automaton, it has no parsing tape.

It has a finite set of states, one of which is called the *start state*. Some of these states are *accepting states*; those states that are not accepting states are *rejecting states*. Those characters that the automaton can read on the input tape comprise its *machine alphabet*.

A finite automaton has a *transition function* t where, for each of its states Q and for each character b in the machine alphabet, $t(Q, b)$ is a state. At the beginning of each time step the automaton is scanning one square of the input tape, in a certain state Q. If there is a character b on that square, during that time step the automaton makes the transition from state Q to state $t(Q, b)$ and goes right one square on the input tape, ready to begin its next time step. But if there is no character in the scanned square the automaton halts, making no transition to another state; there is then no next time step. (Thus it is a Turing machine that goes right only, neither writes nor erases, and halts on a blank square.)

We set the automaton to work by writing a string, one character per square, on the input tape, and by placing the input head on the leftmost nonblank square with the automaton in the start state. The automaton goes automatically according to its transition function. If at the halt it is in an accepting state, the string is *accepted*; otherwise, it is *rejected*. The *language* of the automaton is the set of all strings over the machine alphabet that are accepted.

In particular, the null string can be given to the automaton, and the automaton will halt at time step 1 in the initial state. So the null string is in the language of a finite automaton if and only if the start state is an accepting state.

The automaton is *deterministic*: Since there is only one thing it can do at each time step, there is only one possible history for any given input string.

9.2.2 The State Graph

As an example, we consider a finite automaton with three states S, Q, R and with machine alphabet $\{b, c\}$. The start state is S; Q is an accepting state and S and R are rejecting states. The transition function is as follows:

$$t(S, b) = t(Q, c) = S$$
$$t(S, c) = Q$$
$$t(Q, b) = t(R, b) = t(R, c) = R$$

An example of an accepted string is *bbccc*; the six states assumed in order are *S, S, S, Q, S, Q*. The string *cbbc* is rejected; the five states assumed in order are *S, Q, R, R, R*. The string *ccbcc* is also rejected; the six states assumed in order are *S, Q, S, S, Q, S*.

A finite automaton is conveniently presented as a transition graph rendering each state as a node. The example just considered is pictured in Fig. 9.2.1.

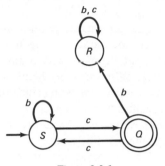

Figure 9.2.1

Note that *all* the information about the finite automaton is contained in Fig. 9.2.1: the states, the start state, the accepting states, the rejecting states, the machine alphabet, and the transition function. Henceforth, all our examples of finite automata will be given as transition graphs like Fig. 9.2.1.

Definition: A *state graph* is a transition graph for which there exists a finite automaton (1) whose states are represented as nodes of the graph, one by one; (2) whose transition function is precisely specified by the arcs and labels; (3) whose start state is the start node; and (4) whose accepting states are the accepting nodes.

Not every transition graph is a state graph. In fact, a transition graph is a state graph if and only if for every node and for every character in the alphabet of the graph there is exactly one arc leaving that node labeled with that character.

For example, of the 15 transition graphs shown in Section 9.1, Figs. 9.1.2, 9.1.8, and 9.1.12 through 9.1.15 are state graphs, whereas all the others are not. Figure 9.1.1 is not because there is no arc labeled *b* or *c* leaving the double-circled node *E*. Figure 9.1.3 is disqualified for three reasons, any one of which would be sufficient: (1) there are two arcs leaving node *S* labeled *c*; (2) there is no arc leaving *D* labeled *b*; and (3) there is no arc leaving *E* labeled *b*.

The Nondeterministic Finite Automaton 9.2.3

Transition graphs that do not represent finite automata are often called *nondeterministic state graphs,* and are said to represent *nondeterministic finite automata.*

A nondeterministic finite automaton is like the deterministic finite automaton in our description above except for its transition function, which is nondeterministic. That is, given a state Q and a character b, $t(Q, b) = \sigma$, where σ is now a subset of the set of states. If σ has more than one state as member, then at any time step in which this automaton begins in state Q scanning the character b, the automaton makes a transition into one of the states of σ during the time step, as it moves one square to the right. If σ has exactly one state as a member, the automaton makes a transition into that one state as it moves right, just like the deterministic finite automaton. Finally if σ is the empty set, the automaton halts without moving right, in state Q.

The nondeterministic finite automaton accepts an input string in the same way that its deterministic counterpart does, by halting on the blank square immediately following the input string. A halt in any other circumstance, however, is not a rejection: If it halts on a nonblank square, or if it halts in a nonaccepting state, it does not reject the string since there may be an alternative history in which the string would be accepted.

The *language* of the nondeterministic finite automaton is the set of all strings that are accepted by it in some possible history.

The nondeterministic finite automaton bears the same functional relationship to the deterministic finite automaton that the nondeterministic parsing automaton bears to the deterministic parsing automaton. Both nondeterministic automata are significant and useful theoretical constructs, but they are not physically realized as machines.

It should be clear that every transition graph can be interpreted as a nondeterministic finite automaton. Since every such automaton can be rendered as a transition graph, it follows that conceptually the nondeterministic finite automata can be identified with the transition graphs. Because deterministic finite automata are important, we shall be interested in converting a transition graph into a state graph.

Probabilistic finite automata have received attention in the literature. Such an automaton is one whose transition function t is a probability function: If Q and R are states and b is a character, then $t(Q, b, R)$ is the probability that the automaton in state Q scanning input character b will make a transition into state R. Interesting problems arise when we consider the probability that such an automaton will accept a given string. Unfortunately, we cannot consider these problems in this book. (See Salomaa [1969], pp. 73ff, or Paz [1971].)

9.2.4 Transition Graphs into State Graphs

We have seen that there are things that nondeterministic pushdown automata can do that deterministic pushdown automata cannot do. In contrast, every nondeterministic finite automaton can be converted by an algorithm into an equivalent deterministic finite automaton.

There are two versions of our algorithm to convert a transition graph into a state graph. The first version is more theoretically elucidating, while the second is more practical.

SUBSET ALGORITHM, FIRST VERSION: Given a transition graph with n nodes, let $\sigma_0, \sigma_1, \ldots, \sigma_{2^n-1}$ be all the subsets of the set of n nodes, where σ_0 is the empty set and σ_1 is the unit set of the start node. We construct a state graph with the same alphabet and with 2^n states $Q_0, Q_1, \ldots, Q_{2^n-1}$, as follows:

Q_1 is the start state. For each i, Q_i is an accepting state if and only if there is at least one accepting node in the set σ_i. For each character b in the alphabet of the transition graph, $t(Q_i, b) = Q_j$, where σ_j is the set of those nodes to which some arc labeled b comes from some node in the set σ_i.

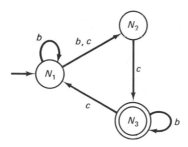

Figure 9.2.2

We give an example of this construction. Let Fig. 9.2.2 be the transition graph. Then put

$$\sigma_0 = \varnothing \quad \text{(empty set)} \qquad \sigma_4 = \{N_1, N_2\}$$
$$\sigma_1 = \{N_1\} \qquad\qquad\qquad \sigma_5 = \{N_1, N_3\}$$
$$\sigma_2 = \{N_2\} \qquad\qquad\qquad \sigma_6 = \{N_2, N_3\}$$
$$\sigma_3 = \{N_3\} \qquad\qquad\qquad \sigma_7 = \{N_1, N_2, N_3\}$$

The states of the constructed state graph will be $Q_0, Q_1, \ldots, Q_7$ corresponding to these σ's. Q_3, Q_5, Q_6, Q_7 will be the accepting nodes (corresponding to those σ's containing N_3, the only accepting node).

To see how we construct the transition function, consider first $t(Q_6, c)$. The set $\sigma_6 = \{N_2, N_3\}$, and the set of nodes to which an arc labeled c leads from N_2 or N_3 is $\{N_1, N_3\} = \sigma_5$. Hence $t(Q_6, c) = Q_5$.

To compute $t(Q_2, b)$, we note that $\sigma_2 = \{N_2\}$ and there is no arc labeled b from N_2. Hence the set of nodes to which such arcs lead is the empty set σ_0, and so $t(Q_2, b) = Q_0$.

The same reasoning also shows that $t(Q_0, b) = t(Q_0, c) = Q_0$.

We should also note how $t(Q_6, b)$ is computed. $\sigma_6 = \{N_2, N_3\}$. The only arc labeled b leading from either N_2 or N_3 is the arc looping on N_3. Since $\{N_3\} = \sigma_3$, $t(Q_6, b) = Q_3$.

The completed state graph is given in Fig. 9.2.3. To make the relationship with Fig. 9.2.2 clear, rather than labeling the states with the Q's, we label them

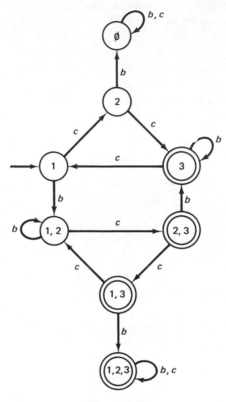

Figure 9.2.3

with the set of nodes of Fig. 9.2.2, in abbreviated notation. Thus the state Q_4 is labeled 1, 2 (an abbreviation for $\{N_1, N_2\}$). Q_0 is labeled $\varnothing$.

If we apply the string *cccbc* to the start state of Fig. 9.2.3, we end up in the state labeled 2, 3. This tells us that the set of nodes where we could have ended up in the transition graph of Fig. 9.2.2 is $\{N_2, N_3\}$.

The string *cb* applied to the start state of Fig. 9.2.3 ends up at the state labeled $\varnothing$, corresponding to the empty set of nodes. This means that there is no walk in the transition graph beginning at the initial node spelling out *cb*. The state labeled $\varnothing$ is a *dead state*: Once the machine gets there, it can never reach an accepting state, whatever happens thereafter. It is also a *trap state*: Once the machine gets there, it can never reach any other state.

THEOREM 9.2.1:   The application of the subset algorithm to a transition graph yields a state graph equivalent to it.

The proof should be clear from the discussion, and is left to the reader.

In most examples, the first version of the algorithm is unnecessarily awkward, because not all the subsets of the set of states are needed.

Consider, for example, the transition graph of Fig. 9.2.4. Since there are five nodes, there are 32 subsets. An examination shows that not all of these are needed in the state graph: the initial state corresponds to the unit set $\{N_1\}$; applying b (the only character in the alphabet) we get the set $\{N_1, N_2\}$; applying b again we get $\{N_1, N_2, N_3, N_4\}$; applying b again we get $\{N_1, N_2, N_3, N_4, N_5\}$; from any number of further applications of b we still get $\{N_1, N_2, N_3, N_4, N_5\}$. There is no way to get any other set, so the deterministic state graph equivalent to Fig. 9.2.4—shown in Fig. 9.2.5—needs only four states.

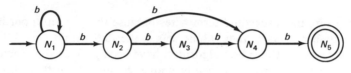

Figure 9.2.4

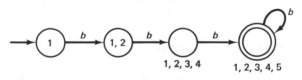

Figure 9.2.5

If we were to go through the construction of the first version of the algorithm, most of the 32 states would play no useful role in the state graph, since there would be no walk to them from the initial state.

In the vast majority of examples we meet in practice, a transition graph with n nodes has an equivalent state graph, where the number of states exceeds n but is far less than 2^n. For this reason, we modify the first version of the algorithm.

SUBSET ALGORITHM, SECOND VERSION: The notation is the same as in the first version. The construction begins with the single state Q_1, corresponding to the set $\sigma_1 = \{N_1\}$. We consider a character of the alphabet, and determine the set of nodes to which there is an arc labeled with that character from N_1. If σ_i is the set and $i \neq 1$, we add a new state Q_i and draw an arc from Q_1 to Q_i labeled with that character. If $i = 1$, which means there is only one arc leaving N_1 so labeled, a loop arc leading back to N_1, we draw a loop arc so labeled from Q_1 to Q_1.

We continue. At each stage in the construction of the state graph we look to see if there is an arc leaving each state labeled with each character of the alphabet. If there is, the nodes and arcs are complete. If there is a state Q_i with no arc labeled b (for some character b in the alphabet), we consult the transition graph and compute the set σ_j of all nodes to which there is an arc labeled b from some node of σ_i. If there is a state Q_j already in the state graph corresponding to the set σ_j, we draw an arc from Q_i to Q_j labeled b. If not, we add the state Q_j to the state graph and then draw the arc.

When the set of nodes and arcs are complete, we make each state in the constructed state graph an accepting state if and only if there is at least one accepting node in the set of nodes of the transition graph corresponding to that state.

We are sure this procedure terminates because there is an upper bound of 2^n on the number of states that will appear in the state graph.

Both versions of the subset algorithm have been presented as incompletely specified algorithms. Both are readily converted into algorithms proper, the second version being a bit more difficult to state, since new subsets bring in newer subsets in turn and there is an involved test to determine whether the set of nodes and arcs is complete.

9.2.6 An Example and a Theorem

Figures 9.2.4 and 9.2.5 constitute an example of how the second version of the subset algorithm works out. As another example, we begin with the transition graph of Fig. 9.2.6. Figure 9.2.7d is the result of the construction. Figure 9.2.7a is what the construction might look like after a few steps, and Fig. 9.2.7b results from Fig. 9.2.7a by drawing the arc from the node *SF* (representing the set {*S*, *F*}) labeled *b* to the node *SE*. Figure 9.2.7c results from Fig. 9.2.7b by drawing a new node *SG* and adding the arc to it labeled *c* from *SF*.

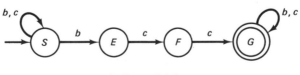

Figure 9.2.6

If the second version of the algorithm is applied to Fig. 9.2.2, then Fig. 9.2.3 will result with all eight states, representing all eight subsets. In this regard Fig. 9.2.2 is an unusual transition graph, because most often the number of states in the result is much less in the second version than in the first version of the subset algorithm.

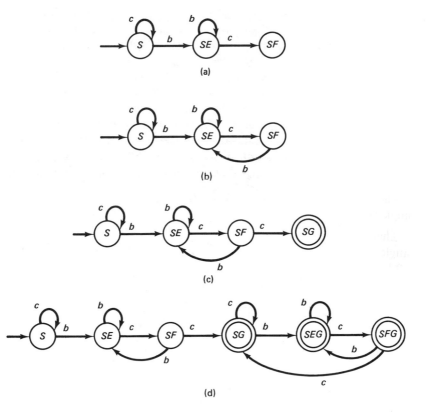

Figure 9.2.7

THEOREM 9.2.2: If the second version of the subset algorithm is applied to a transition graph, the result is a state graph equivalent to it.

The proof should be clear from the discussion and is left to the reader.

Simplification of State Graphs **9.2.7**

It is easy to see that the language of Fig. 9.2.6 is the set of all strings over the alphabet $\{b, c\}$ having at least one occurrence of a substring bcc. If a string W is in this set, WX is also in this set for any string X.

This fact is also apparent in the state graph. If W is in the language of Fig. 9.2.7d, the walk from S spelling out W must end either in SG, SEG, or SFG. The walk from S spelling out WX must then also end in one of these three states, since there is no way to get back to S, SE, or SF from SG, SEG, or SFG.

This fact allows us to simplify the state graph of Fig. 9.2.7d, by collapsing the states SG, SEG, and SFG down to a single state, as in Fig. 9.2.8.

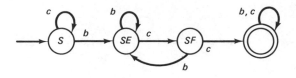

Figure 9.2.8

There are many state graphs in which several states can be collapsed into a single state, resulting in an equivalent simpler state graph. For example, Fig. 9.2.9 has four states and it is equivalent to Fig. 9.2.10, which has only two. The latter comes about by collapsing S and G together to form S', and collapsing F and H together to form F'.

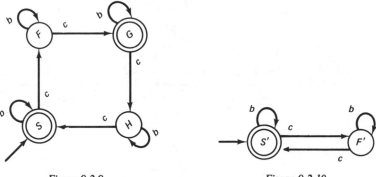

Figure 9.2.9   Figure 9.2.10

One can look at Fig. 9.2.9 and see these possibilities of collapsing if one notes that the language of the graph is the set of all strings with an even number of c's. A walk starting at S reaches an accepting state if the string spelled out has an even number of c's, and the same is true of a walk beginning with G. But a walk beginning at F or H, reaches an accepting state if the string spelled out has an odd number of c's. This shows that S and G can be collapsed, and that F and H can be collapsed.

The process of simplifying a state graph by collapsing states is known as the *reduction algorithm*; when applied to a state graph it yields the simplest possible equivalent state graph. (See Moore [1956] or Salomaa [1969], pp. 40ff.) We shall not discuss this algorithm further except to say that it is quite easy to apply. In some examples, like the two we have been discussing, simplification can be achieved by inspection.

A significant fact (proved in the advanced literature) is that two reduced equivalent state graphs are isomorphic, from which it follows that if we know we have a reduced state graph, we know that any other essentially different (i.e., nonisomorphic) state graph equivalent to it must be bigger, in the sense of having more states. In other words, for every finite automaton there is a unique (within isomorphism) finite automaton which is the simplest equivalent to it, namely *the* reduced automaton. And the reduced automaton can be obtained by a rather efficient algorithm.

These facts about the reduced finite automaton (or, equivalently, about the reduced state graph) are a part of what make regular languages so tractable among the context-free languages. For example, there is no known algorithm that finds from a given context-free grammar the simplest equivalent grammar; this seems to be true whatever reasonable definition one takes of "simplest" (e.g., smallest number of nonterminals, smallest number of productions, etc.). There are many important aspects of formal languages that cannot be handled by regular grammars. But when we find a chance to apply finite-automata theory in a computational problem about languages, we are well advised to do so.

Some Theorems 9.2.8

The proofs of the following are left as exercises, using what has already been established in this chapter. Reverse-regular grammars are considered now for the first time since the definition early in Section 9.1.1.

THEOREM 9.2.3: For any of the following there is an algorithm to obtain any of the other four equivalent to it:

1. Regular grammar
2. Reverse-regular grammar
3. Transition graph
4. State graph
5. Finite automaton

(Theorem 9.3.4 will enable us to add "restricted regular expression" to this list.)

COROLLARY: The following are equivalent for a language L:

1. L is regular.
2. L is the language of a transition graph.
3. L is the language of a state graph.
4. L is the language of a finite automaton.

(The corollary to Theorem 9.3.4 will add "restricted regular expression" and "general regular expression" to this list.)

THEOREM 9.2.4:   If L is a regular language, then $\check{L}$ (the set of all strings of L written backwards) is regular.

Indeed, one can easily write down a reverse-regular grammar for $\check{L}$ from a regular grammar for L.

THEOREM 9.2.5:   If L_1 and L_2 are regular languages, then $L_1 \cup L_2$ is regular.

THEOREM 9.2.6:   If L is a regular language over an alphabet Σ, then $\Sigma^* - L$ is regular. ($\Sigma^* - L$ is the set of all strings over Σ that are not in L.)

THEOREM 9.2.7:   If L_1 and L_2 are regular, so is $L_1 \cap L_2$.

These theorems suggest that finite automata and regular languages form a coherent theory. Indeed, the theory of finite automata is more coherent as a mathematical theory than the theory of context-free languages, although the applications of the latter are more important for computer science. Much of the well-known finite-automata theory (as much of context-free-language theory) is too advanced for this book.

We mentioned that the computational significance of finite automata is that they represent the kind of computation in which there is a fixed limit on the amount of memory used for an input of arbitrary length. There is, however, a variation on our model which seems as if it might be more powerful. Suppose that we allow the automaton to move left and right on the input tape (like the Turing machine), but still restrict the automaton against writing on the tape (unlike the Turing machine). We would still have a computation with a fixed limit on the amount of memory. Such an automaton is called a *two-way finite automaton*. A formal definition of this concept is not needed in this book. (See Hopcroft and Ullman 1979, pp. 36ff.) M. Rabin proved that the two-way finite automata are not more powerful than the one-way finite automata: For every two-way automaton there is an equivalent one-way automaton, of the kind satisfying our definition. (A constructive proof by J. C. Shepherdson can be found in Hopcroft and Ullman [1979].)

9.2.9   Exercises

1–9.   Convert Figs. 9.1.1, 9.1.3 to 9.1.7, and 9.1.9 to 9.1.11, respectively, into equivalent state graphs. (Some of these require only small modifications to become state graphs.)

10–13.   Construct a state graph equivalent to the transition graphs of Figs. 9.2.11 to 9.2.14, respectively. (*Hint:* In some of these, labor can be saved by first simplifying the transition graph.)

In Exercises 14 to 17, draw a state graph for the language indicated.

14.   The set of all strings over $\{b, c, d\}$ in which the sum of the number of b's plus twice the number of c's plus three times the number of d's is divisible by 6.

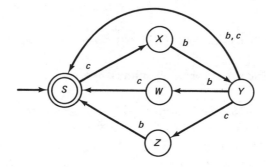

Figure 9.2.11

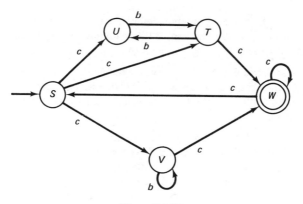

Figure 9.2.12

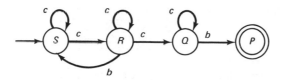

Figure 9.2.13

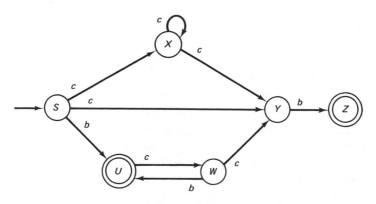

Figure 9.2.14

15. The set of all strings over $\{b, c\}$ with an odd number of b's and an even number of c's.

16. The set of all strings over $\{b, c\}$ in which bc occurs an odd number of times as a substring.

17. The set of all programs in the GOTO language (Section 3.1.2). (The set of WHILE-language programs is not regular; see Exercise 13 of Section 9.4.)

18–24 Prove Theorems 9.2.1 through 9.2.7, respectively. You may make reference to the text. (In the proof of Theorem 9.2.3 there is a bit of complication having to do with reverse-regular grammars. For the proof of Theorem 9.2.7, cite Theorems 9.2.5 and 9.2.6.)

25. Prove that the regular grammar determined from a state graph according to the algorithm in the proof of Theorem 9.1.2 is unambiguous. (*Hint:* Recall Section 8.4.3 on top-down parsing.)

26. (*Difficult*) Prove that for every regular language L, where $\lambda \notin L$, there is for L a grammar G that can be processed by the deterministic parsing automaton in such way that, however long the input tape, the parsing tape never has more than two characters besides the asterisk.

27. (*Abstract and difficult*) Let q be a positive integer and G be a context-free grammar whose start symbol and productions are written on the production tape of the nondeterministic parsing automaton, and suppose that, for every $W \in L(G)$, there is history in which the automaton accepts W in which the parsing tape never has more than q symbols on it besides the asterisk. Prove (as a sort of converse to Exercise 26) that $L(G)$ is regular. Show how to construct one of the five types of representation of $L(G)$ mentioned in Theorem 9.2.3 from G and q.

28. (*Abstract and difficult*) Let G be a state graph with n nodes for a regular language L. Prove that, for any character b in the alphabet, there exists integers $m \geq 0$ and $p \geq 1$ such that $m + p \leq n$ and, for all $x \geq m$, $b^x \in L$ if and only if $b^{x+p} \in L$.

29. Write a computer program to do the second version of the subset algorithm; the input to your program should be a transition graph with (say) alphabet $\{b, c\}$ and with (say) no more than 15 nodes (using whatever data structure you think is appropriate). Have your program halt without a solution, if more than (say) 30 states are needed for the state graph.

9.3 REGULAR EXPRESSIONS

In Section 7.3.3 we introduced formulas for certain sets of strings as a convenient notation [e.g., $\{b^n c^n \,|\, n \geq 0\}$, $\{(b*c)^n (b*d)^n \,|\, n \geq 2\}$, etc.]. We now restrict that notation so as to accommodate the regular languages exclusively. At the same time we systematize it to the point that formulas will represent all and only all the regular languages.

The alphabet for the language of regular expressions includes the alphabet over which strings are composed (which we call the *string* alphabet) and has also: parentheses, the union symbol ($\cup$), the intersection symbol ($\cap$), the set-difference symbol ($-$), the star (*), lambda (λ), the symbol for the empty set ($\varnothing$), and the decimal digits (0, . . . , 9).

Numerals denoting nonnegative integers are made up from the decimal digits in the ordinary way.

Recursive Definition of General Regular Expression: (1) Each character in the string alphabet, λ, and $\varnothing$ are *general regular expressions*. (2) If α and β are general regular expressions and n is a numeral, then $(\alpha) \cup (\beta), (\alpha) \cap (\beta), (\alpha) - (\beta),$ $(\alpha)(\beta), (\alpha)^n,$ and $(\alpha)^*$ are *general regular expressions*. (Often the parentheses can be omitted. Note that this definition is relative to a string alphabet.)

Definition: A *restricted regular expression* is a general regular expression not containing the set difference symbol ($-$) or the intersection symbol ($\cap$).

In some books general regular expressions are called *extended regular expressions*, and restricted regular expressions are called simply *regular expressions*. Historically, the latter came first, having been introduced by S. C. Kleene in 1951 to describe the behavior of nerve nets.

The semantics of general regular expressions is completely concerned with how each expression denotes a set of strings. The operators on such sets that are symbolized in general regular expressions are known to the reader: the Boolean operators (union, intersection, set difference), concatenation $(\alpha)(\beta)$ or $\alpha\beta$, numerical exponentiation $(\alpha)^n$ or α^n and star closure $(\alpha)^*$ or α^*. However, we must now give systematic definitions of concatenation, numerical exponentiation, and star closure, since they are now used in a more general manner than they were in Chapters 7 and 8.

Definition: The *concatenation* of two sets of strings α and β (in order) is the set of all strings that can be formed as a concatenation of a string from α and a string from β (in order). In symbols,

$$\alpha\beta = \{UV \mid U \in \alpha, V \in \beta\}$$

For example, if $\alpha = \{b, bc, bbc\}$ and $\beta = \{c, cc\}$, then $\alpha\beta = \{bc, bcc, bccc,$ $bbcc, bbccc\}$. Note that the string *bcc* is formed in two ways: as *b* concatenated with *cc*, and as *bc* concatenated with *c*.

Also, if $\alpha = \{\lambda, b, bb\}$ and $\beta = \{\lambda, b, bb, bbb\}$, then $\alpha\beta = \{\lambda, b, bb, bbb,$ $bbbb, bbbbb\}$.

However, if $\alpha = \varnothing$ then, whatever β is, $\alpha\beta = \varnothing$. This result is clear from the definition: The set of all strings that result from concatenating a string in α with a string in β is the empty set, since there are no strings in α. Similarly, $\beta\varnothing = \varnothing$.

Recursive Definition of α^n:

$$\alpha^0 = \{\lambda\}$$
$$\alpha^{n+1} = \alpha\alpha^n$$

Note that $\alpha^1 = \alpha$; $\alpha^2 = \alpha\alpha$; and α^n, for $n \geq 3$, is the set

$$\{W_1 W_2 \ldots W_n | \text{each } W_i \in \alpha\}$$

Definition: $\alpha^* = \bigcup_{n=0}^{\infty} \alpha^n$. In other terms, α^* is the smallest set satisfying the following: (1) $\lambda \in \alpha^*$; and (2) for all strings $U \in \alpha^*$ and $V \in \alpha$, $UV \in \alpha^*$.

For example,

$$\{bbb, bbbb\}^* = \{\lambda, b^3, b^4, b^6, b^7, b^8, \ldots\} = \{b^0, b^3, b^4\} \cup \{b^{6+i} | i \geq 0\}$$

In the notation of regular expressions we suppress the braces denoting unit sets. Thus if b is a character in the alphabet, we write simply b instead of $\{b\}$ to mean the unit set of the string b. And we write bc instead of $\{bc\}$; and so on. The omission of the braces is convenient when we use the other operators (e.g., we can write bc^*d in place of $\{b\}\{c\}^*\{d\}$).

Note that $bc^*d = \{bd, bcd, bccd, \ldots\}$. So $\{bc^*d\}^* = \{\lambda\} \cup \{W_1 W_2 \ldots W_n | n \geq 1$, each $W_i \in bc^*d\}$. Examples of strings in the set $\{bc^*d\}^*$ are bd, bcd, $bdbdbd$, $bccccdbd$, and $bcdbcdbccd$.

Having explained the operators, we are now ready to lay down the semantics of general regular expressions: A character of the string alphabet, as a general regular expression, denotes the unit set of the string of unit length made from that character. The general regular expressions λ and $\varnothing$ denote the unit set of the null string and the empty set, respectively. Then every general regular expression denotes a set of strings in accord with the meaning of the operators described above.

When we write "b" we can mean one of three things: a letter of the alphabet, a string of unit length, or the unit set of that string. Confusion need not result, because we can regard a letter of the alphabet as a special case of a string, and we can regard a string as a special case of a set of strings. As a general regular expression, "b" denotes the set according to our semantic formulation, but that does not prevent us from thinking of the other two representations.

We need to state the conventions that permit us to omit parentheses. First, we omit a pair of mated parentheses if there is no operator occurring between them. For example, we write bc instead of $(b)(c)$, b^* instead of $(b)^*$, and $b \cup c$ instead of $(b) \cup (c)$, where b and c are characters in the string alphabet.

Second, we take note of the associative laws

$$\alpha \cup (\beta \cup \gamma) = (\alpha \cup \beta) \cup \gamma$$
$$\alpha \cap (\beta \cap \gamma) = (\alpha \cap \beta) \cap \gamma$$
$$(\alpha\beta)\gamma = \alpha(\beta\gamma)$$

and write $\alpha \cup \beta \cup \gamma$, $\alpha \cap \beta \cap \gamma$, and $\alpha\beta\gamma$ for these sets, respectively.

Except for cases covered by the associative laws, a parenthesis generally occurs between any two Boolean operators. Thus we shall write either $\alpha \cup (\beta \cap \gamma)$ or $(\alpha \cup \beta) \cap \gamma$; $\alpha - (\beta \cup \gamma)$ or $(\alpha - \beta) \cup \gamma$; $\alpha - (\beta - \gamma)$ or $(\alpha - \beta) - \gamma$; and so on.

For purposes of explanation, the operators are divided into priority classes: Star and numerical exponent form class I, concatenation by itself forms class II, and the three Boolean operators form class III. Then parentheses may be omitted between operator occurrences in different classes, with the understanding that the class-i operator occurrence has precedence over the class-j operator occurrence if $i < j$.

For example, we may write $\alpha \cup \beta\gamma^*$ as an abbreviation for $\alpha \cup (\beta(\gamma^*))$. In the following, however, the parentheses are necessary: $(\alpha \cup \beta)\gamma^*$, $(\alpha \cup \beta\gamma)^*$, $\alpha \cup (\beta\gamma)^*$, $((\alpha \cup \beta)\gamma)^*$.

As a notation for regular sets of strings, general regular expressions are quite convenient, for several reasons. First, braces and commas are omitted. Instead of writing $\{\lambda\}$, we write λ. Instead of writing $\{bc, cb\}$, we write $bc \cup cb$. The fact that the unit set of a string is identified with the string itself turns out not to be a source of confusion.

Another attractive feature of general regular expressions is the small number of well-understood operators, together with the knowledge (which we shall obtain by the end of this section) that all and only all regular languages are expressed by them.

The limitations of general regular expressions are important to understand. There is no provision for a variable numerical exponent: We cannot, for example, write $(bc)^n$, although we can write $(bc)^{14}$ and $(bc)^*$. (Our use of n in Section 9.3.1 was as a variable in the metalanguage.) This restriction prevents us from writing down expressions like $b^n c^n$, which, if it is construed to mean $\{b^n c^n \mid n \geq 0\}$, denotes a language that is not regular.

The provision for numerical exponents is not made in some texts. Indeed, numerical exponents are theoretically dispensable; one could write $\alpha\alpha$ instead of α^2, $\alpha\alpha\alpha$ instead of α^3, and so on. We would still be able to express all regular languages.

THEOREM 9.3.1:   For all general regular expressions α and β, the following equations hold:

$$(1)\quad \lambda\alpha = \alpha\lambda = \alpha$$

$$(2)\quad \varnothing\alpha = \alpha\varnothing = \varnothing$$

$$(3)\quad \lambda^* = \varnothing^* = \lambda$$

$$(4)\quad \alpha(\beta\alpha)^* = (\alpha\beta)^*\alpha$$

$$(5)\quad (\alpha \cup \beta)^* = (\alpha^*\beta^*)^*$$

$$(6)\quad \alpha(\beta \cup \gamma) = \alpha\beta \cup \alpha\gamma$$

PROOF: Equations (1), (2), and (3) follow from remarks made in Section 9.3.1. Equations (5) and (6) are left as exercises.

For (4), let $W \in \alpha(\beta\alpha)^*$. Then $W = W_1 W_2$, where $W_1 \in \alpha$ and $W_2 \in (\beta\alpha)^*$. Moreover, either $W_2 = \lambda$ or $W_2 = X_1 X_2 \ldots X_n, n \geq 1$, and each $X_i \in \beta\alpha$.

Case 1. $W_2 = \lambda$. Then $W = W_1 \in \alpha$. So $W = \lambda W \in (\alpha\beta)^*\alpha$.

Case 2. $W_2 = X_1 X_2 \ldots X_n$, each $X_i \in \beta\alpha$. Then each $X_i = Y_i Z_i$, where $Y_i \in \beta, Z_i \in \alpha$. So $W = W_1 Y_1 Z_1 Y_2 Z_2 \ldots Y_n Z_n$. But each of $W_1 Y_1, Z_1 Y_2, \ldots,$ $Z_{n-1}Y_n$ is a member of the set $\alpha\beta$. Since $Z_n \in \alpha$, it follows that $W \in (\alpha\beta)^*\alpha$.

We have thus proved that $\alpha(\beta\alpha)^* \subseteq (\alpha\beta)^*\alpha$. The proof that $(\alpha\beta)^*\alpha \subseteq \alpha(\beta\alpha)^*$ is similar.   ∎

9.3.3 Some Examples

We show how some familiar regular languages can be represented as general regular expressions. Sometimes the natural way to represent a set is to write an expression containing intersection ($\cap$) and set difference ($-$). In these cases, we also give a restricted regular expression, even though the latter is somewhat more remote. Later we show that restricted regular expressions are closer to transition graphs and regular grammars than expressions containing $\cap$ and $-$.

EXAMPLE 1.   The set of all strings over the alphabet $\{b\}$ is b^*; the set of all nonnull strings is $bb^* = b^* - \lambda$. The set of strings over the alphabet $\{b, c\}$ is $(b \cup c)^*$, and so on.

EXAMPLE 2.   The set of strings over the alphabet $\{b, c\}$ having a substring bbb is $(b \cup c)^*bbb(b \cup c)^*$. Thus the set of all strings over the alphabet $\{b, c\}$ not having a substring bbb is $(b \cup c)^* - (b \cup c)^*bbb(b \cup c)^*$. Alternatively, and more subtly, this last set is denoted by the restricted regular expression $(c \cup bc \cup bbc)^*(\lambda \cup b \cup bb)$ and also by $(\lambda \cup b \cup bb) (c \cup cb \cup cbb)^*$.

EXAMPLE 3. The set of all strings over $\{b, c\}$ having an even number of b's is $(c^*bc^*b)^*c^*$ or $c^*(bc^*bc^*)^*$. The subexpression c^*bc^*b denotes the set of all strings with exactly two b's and ending in b.

Note that $(c^*bc^*bc^*)^*$ is not the set of Example 3, since it fails to contain c, cc, ccc, and so on.

EXAMPLE 4. The set of all strings over $\{b, c\}$ whose length is divisible by 3 is $((b \cup c)^3)^*$.

EXAMPLE 5. The set of all strings over $\{b, c\}$ in which all the b's precede all the c's, and where there are an odd number of b's and an odd number of c's is $(bb)^*b(cc)^*c$.

EXAMPLE 6. The set of all strings over $\{b, c, d\}$ with a substring bbb and also a substring ccc (for brevity we write Σ for $b \cup c \cup d$) is

$$\Sigma^*bbb\Sigma^* \cap \Sigma^*ccc\Sigma^*$$

A restricted regular expression is

$$\Sigma^*bbb\Sigma^*ccc\Sigma^* \cup \Sigma^*ccc\Sigma^*bbb\Sigma^*$$

One quickly acquires a facility for writing down general regular expressions to express ideas about sets of strings that naturally come to mind. In this sense, the regular-expression language is a good language to think in when one thinks about regular sets of strings.

Sometimes the general regular expression that one writes down naturally is a restricted regular expression, and sometimes it is not. It is often worthwhile to spend extra effort to get a restricted regular expression, because the algorithms used to obtain therefrom a transition graph, a finite automaton, and so on, are much easier to apply than the corresponding algorithms to obtain them from a general regular expression, as will be explained.

The Expression-to-Graph Algorithm 9.3.4

Definition: A *lambda graph* is a graph that satisfies the definition of transition graph except that each arc is labeled either with a character of the alphabet or with λ. The string *spelled out* by a walk in a lambda graph is the string spelled out from the labels in order, except that λ labels as they occur are omitted; but if all the labels are λ, the string spelled out is the null string.

For example, Fig. 9.3.1 is a lambda graph. The null string is spelled out by the walk S, Q, T. The string bc is spelled out by the walk S, Q, R, Q, T.

In this subsection we show how to construct, from a given restricted regular

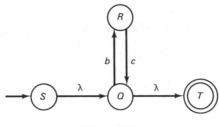

Figure 9.3.1

expression, a lambda graph with the same language. We leave it as an exercise to show how to convert a lambda graph into an equivalent transition graph (i.e., remove all arcs labeled λ).

Definition: A *proper graph* is a lambda graph with a single accepting node, with no arcs leaving this node, and with no arcs entering the start node.

The significant feature of a proper graph is that any walk from the start node to the one accepting node will not repeat either of these nodes. The concept of proper graph is introduced only for the sake of the construction.

EXPRESSION-TO-GRAPH ALGORITHM: We note first that Figs. 9.3.2 to 9.3.4 are proper graphs representing the restricted regular expressions, b, λ, and $\varnothing$, respectively. (By definition, Fig. 9.3.4 is a graph even though it has no arcs.) Graphs for other characters in the alphabet are similar to Fig. 9.3.2.

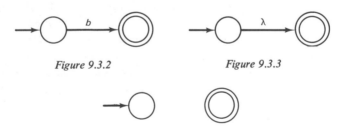

Figure 9.3.2   Figure 9.3.3

Figure 9.3.4

We complete our construction (which follows the recursive definition of *restricted regular expression*) by assuming that we have proper graphs for α (Fig. 9.3.5) and for β, and specifying that the proper graphs representing $(\alpha) \cup (\beta)$, $(\alpha)(\beta)$, and $(\alpha)^*$ are given, respectively, by Figs. 9.3.6 to 9.3.8.

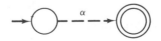

Figure 9.3.5

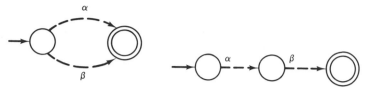

Figure 9.3.6   Figure 9.3.7

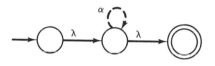

Figure 9.3.8

Note that in this construction the graphs for α and β have been used as parts of a new graph, with the start nodes and accepting nodes sometimes modified to become nonstart nodes and nonaccepting nodes. In Fig. 9.3.7 the accepting node of the graph representing α has been superimposed on the start node of the graph representing β.

We regard $\alpha \cup \beta \cup \gamma$ as an abbreviation for $(\alpha \cup \beta) \cup \gamma$, $\alpha\beta\gamma$ as an abbreviation of $(\alpha\beta)\gamma$, and so on. With this understood, we can apply the algorithm to expressions in which some parentheses are omitted.

An Example 9.3.5

The graph of Fig. 9.3.9 is constructed by the expression-to-graph algorithm to represent $(b \cup c)^*bb \cup (bc)^*$. Note that the subgraph including nodes 1, 2, and 3 represents the subexpression $(b \cup c)^*$; the subgraph including nodes 1, 2, 3, 4, and 7 represents $(b \cup c)^*bb$; the subgraph including nodes 1, 5, 6, and 7 represents $(bc)^*$.

The result of this algorithm can sometimes be simplified by deleting certain λ arcs. For example, in Fig. 9.3.9, nodes 2 and 3 could be joined, eliminating the lambda arc between. However, lambda arcs cannot be eliminated indiscriminately. For example, Fig. 9.3.10 is not equivalent to Fig. 9.3.9: The string bbc is in the language of Fig. 9.3.10, by virtue of the walk 1, 1, 5, 6, 5, 7; but it and other such strings are not in the language of Fig. 9.3.9. By making this careless simplification, we have allowed the string bbc (etc.) to "sneak" into the language.

Similarly, nodes 5 and 7 of Fig. 9.3.9 cannot be made one; otherwise, $bbbc$ (etc.) would sneak into the language. (Actually, nodes 1 and 5 could be made one, although it is not obvious that they can.)

The reason for using proper graphs for the constituent parts in the construction is to make abolutely sure, whatever α and β might be, that the construction at each point does not allow strings to sneak into the language.

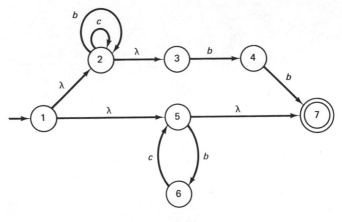

Figure 9.3.9

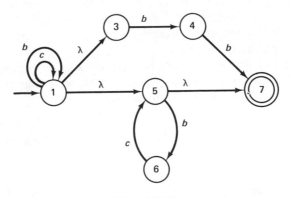

Figure 9.3.10

9.3.6   *More Theorems*

THEOREM 9.3.2:   If a proper graph G is constructed by the expression-to-graph algorithm for a given restricted regular expression α, then $L(G) = \alpha$.

The proof consists of the proofs of the following lemmas, which are left as exercises.

LEMMA 1:   The proper graphs of Fig. 9.3.2 to 9.3.4 represent b, λ, and $\varnothing$, respectively.

LEMMA 2:   If proper graphs whose languages are α and β are as shown, then Figs. 9.3.6 to 9.3.8 are proper graphs and their languages are, respectively, $(\alpha) \cup (\beta)$, $(\alpha)(\beta)$, and $(\alpha)^*$.

There is an algorithm for eliminating lambda arcs, and thereby obtaining an equivalent transition graph from a given lambda graph (Exercise 49). Thus we can say that for any restricted regular expression, there is an equivalent transition graph. Therefore, by Theorem 9.2.3, every restricted regular expression denotes a regular language. We now seek to prove that the same is true of every general regular expression.

THEOREM 9.3.3: Every general regular expression denotes a regular language.

PROOF: By induction on the number of operators in the general regular expression: If a general regular expression has zero operators, it is a restricted regular expression and it denotes a regular language by the remarks above. As an inductive hypothesis, we assume that all general regular expressions with fewer than n operators denote regular languages, and we let α be a general regular expression with n operators.

Case 1. α is $(\alpha_1) \cup (\alpha_2)$. Then since α_1 and α_2 have fewer than n operators, they denote regular languages. Therefore, so does α, by Theorem 9.2.5.

Case 2. α is $(\alpha_1) \cap (\alpha_2)$. The reasoning is similar to that of case 1, using Theorem 9.2.7.

Case 3. α is $(\alpha_1) - (\alpha_2)$. Then $\alpha = (\Sigma^* - \alpha_2) \cap \alpha_1$, where Σ is the union of the alphabets used in α_1 and α_2; so α is regular by Theorems 9.2.6 and 9.2.7.

Case 4. α is $(\alpha_1)^n$. Then, if $n = 0$, $\alpha = \lambda$, which is regular. If $n = 1$, $\alpha = \alpha_1$ and the result is immediate. If $n \geq 2$, $\alpha = \alpha_1 \ldots \alpha_1$ and the result follows by case 5 below (implicitly by mathematical induction on n).

Case 5. $\alpha = (\alpha_1)(\alpha_2)$. α_1 and α_2 are regular, so there are transition graphs for them. These transition graphs are easily converted into proper graphs (Exercise 50). From these a proper graph is constructed according to Fig. 9.3.7, which is a proper graph for α by Lemma 2 in the proof of Theorem 9.3.2. Thus α is regular.

Case 6. α is $(\alpha_1)^*$. The reasoning is similar to case 5, using Fig. 9.3.8. ∎

We remark that the proof just concluded is constructive. It could justify asserting the existence of an algorithm converting a general regular expression into an equivalent transition graph, and an algorithm converting it into an equivalent state graph. The first algorithm would be more unwieldy in execution than the expression-to-graph algorithm, which constructs a transition graph from a restricted regular expression, and the second algorithm would be more unwieldy in execution than the expression-to-graph algorithm coupled with the second version of the subset algorithm. Results in computational complexity suggest that the clumsiness of these algorithms dealing with general regular expressions is unavoidable (see Aho, Hopcroft, and Ullman [1974], Chap. 11).

9.3.7   The Graph-to-Expression Algorithm

Definition: An *expression graph* is a graph that satisfies the definition of a transition graph except that each arc has as a label a general regular expression.

Definition: The set of strings *spelled out* by a walk $\sigma_1, \sigma_2, \ldots, \sigma_{2m+1}$ in an expression graph is the set $\beta_2 \beta_4 \ldots \beta_{2m}$, where, for each i, β_{2i} is the general regular expression that is the label of the arc σ_{2i}. (Recall that, in a walk, σ_{2i+1} and σ_{2i+3} are nodes and σ_{2i+2} is an arc going from σ_{2i+1} to σ_{2i+3}.) For $m = 0$, the set of strings spelled out is $\{\lambda\}$. The *language* of an expression graph is the union of the sets of strings spelled out by all walks from the start node to an accepting node.

For example, Fig. 9.3.11 is an expression graph. The walk S, R, S spells out the set $b^*cb^*b^*cb^*$, which is the set of all strings over $\{b, c\}$ having exactly two c's. The language of Fig. 9.3.11 is the union of $\{\lambda\}$ and the set of all strings over $\{b, c\}$ having an even number of c's and at least two of them.

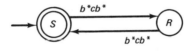

Figure 9.3.11

We assume that the nodes of an expression graph with p nodes are N_1, $\ldots$, N_p. For each i and j, put α_{ij} = the union of all the general regular expressions that are labels of branches going from N_i to N_j. If there are no such branches, then $\alpha_{ij} = \varnothing$.

Clearly, a transition graph or a lambda graph is a special case of an expression graph. Our algorithm for finding a regular expression for a given expression graph G proceeds by (possibly) "splitting" G into several graphs, then simplifying each so that one can write down by inspection a general regular expression for it. The language of G is the union of these general regular expressions.

GRAPH-TO-EXPRESSION ALGORITHM (incompletely specified):   *Stage 1* consists of "splitting" G into graphs $G_1, \ldots, G_m$, where m is the number of accepting nodes of G. If $m = 0$, the general regular expression for L(G) is $\varnothing$ and no further work is done. If $m = 1$, then G_1 is G itself and no splitting occurs. But if $m \geq 2$, then each G_i is like G except that only the ith accepting node of G is an accepting node of G_i.

Stage 2 consists of repeating the following *node-deletion operation* to each of the graphs in turn as often as possible. Select a node N_i other than the start node or the accepting node and delete it and all arcs going to and from it; for each pair of remaining nodes N_j, N_k (including cases where $j = k$) construct a new arc from N_j to N_k labeled $\alpha_{ji}\alpha_{ii}^*\alpha_{ik}$. At the end of stage 2, each graph will have either just one node that is both start and accepting or else will have two nodes, one start and the other accepting.

Stage 3 consists of writing down a general regular expression for each graph. If a graph has a single node N_1 both start and accepting, the general regular expression for that graph is $(\alpha_{11})^*$. If the graph has start node N_1 and accepting node N_2, the general regular expression (see Fig. 9.3.12) is $(\alpha_{11})^*\alpha_{12}(\alpha_{22} \cup \alpha_{21}(\alpha_{11})^*\alpha_{12})^*$.

A general regular expression for L(G) is the union of all *m* of these general regular expressions.

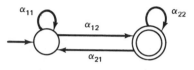

Figure 9.3.12

The simplification of each graph $G_1, \ldots, G_m$ in stage 2 depends on the order in which the nodes are deleted. Since the order is unspecified, the algorithm is incompletely specified. By making a judicious selection each time of the node to be deleted, the human user of this algorithm can save labor and end up with a simpler regular expression.

The problem of node selection in stage 2 is a serious one for somebody who wishes to go to the machine with this algorithm and apply it to graphs as complex as, say, Fig. 9.1.8. If an order for node deletion is specified arbitrarily, the expression that results will be far from optimal.

The graph-to-expression algorithm has another form that is better for possible machine implementation (see, e.g., Hopcroft and Ullman [1979], pp. 33–35, or Salomaa [1969], pp. 10–12).

An Example; Theoretical Discussion 9.3.8

Figure 9.3.13 illustrates the execution of the algorithm. The graph G is split into G_1 with N_1 accepting and G_2 with N_3 accepting. G_1 and G_2 are then simplified. In Fig. 9.3.13 we have omitted arcs whose labels we know equal $\varnothing$. (Omitted, for example, is the arc labeled $bb^*\varnothing$ going from N_1 to N_3, and the loop arc on N_3 labeled $cb^*\varnothing$ in the first graph obtained from G_1, and also in G_2'.) We have also omitted $\varnothing^*$ in the label $c\varnothing^*(b \cup cb^*c)$, since $\varnothing^* = \lambda$ and since $\alpha\lambda\beta = \alpha\beta$.

The general regular expression for G_1' (G_1 after node deletion) in Fig. 9.3.13 is $[bb^*c \cup c(b \cup cb^*c)]^*$. The expression for G_2' is $(bb^*c)^*c[\varnothing \cup (cb^*c \cup b)(bb^*c)^*c]^*$. (From this expression, $\varnothing$ and the union sign following can be deleted.) The expression for L(G) is the union of these two.

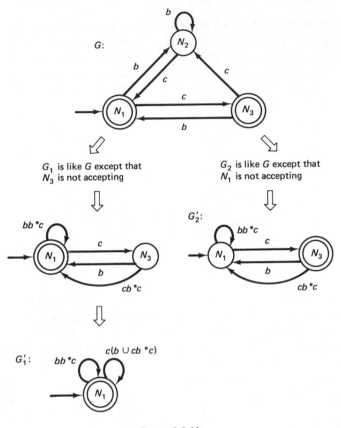

Figure 9.3.13

We note that the graph-to-expression algorithm never brings in intersection ($\cap$) or set difference ($-$) unless these are already present as labels. Hence if the labels of the original graph are all restricted regular expressions, the result of the algorithm produces a restricted regular expression.

THEOREM 9.3.4:   There are algorithms to convert a transition graph into a restricted regular expression representing its language, and vice versa.

The theorem (in one direction) follows in large part from the last remark and Exercises 53 and 54; and (in the other direction) from Theorem 9.3.2 and Exercise 49.

COROLLARY: The following are equivalent for a language L:

1. L is regular.
5. L is denoted by a restricted regular expression.
6. L is denoted by a general regular expression.

(In effect, this is a continuation of the Corollary to Theorem 9.2.3.)

The proof follows from Theorems 9.2.3, 9.3.3, and 9.3.4.

The reader wishing to go somewhat deeper into regular expressions would do well to read Chapter III of Salomaa [1969].

Exercises 9.3.9

In Exercises 1 to 20, write a general regular expression from the verbal phrase without referring to or constructing a transition graph. Write the expression that comes naturally to you at first. Then, if your expression contains $\cap$ or $-$ in it, find a restricted regular expression equal to it. These exercises are arranged approximately in order of increasing difficulty.

1–9. Exercises 17, 19 to 22, and 24 to 27, respectively, of Section 7.3.

10–16. Exercises 11 to 16, and 18, respectively, of Section 9.1.

17, 18. Exercises 32 and 33, respectively, of Section 7.3.

19, 20. Exercises 21 and 22, respectively, of Section 9.1.

21. Where $\Sigma = b \cup c \cup d$, find a restricted regular expression equal to

$$\Sigma^* bcdc\Sigma^* \cap \Sigma^* cdcb\Sigma^*$$

(*Caution:* This is *more difficult* than Example 6 of Section 9.3.3.)

22–31. (*Easy*) Find restricted regular expressions representing the languages of the transition graphs of Figs. 9.1.1 to 9.1.7, and 9.1.9 to 9.1.11, respectively. You may depart from the algorithm if you are sure that your result is correct.

32–35. (*More involved*) The same for Figs. 9.1.12 to 9.1.15, respectively. (*Hint:* If you follow the algorithm, when you come to stage 2, make a judicious selection of the node to be deleted at each step.)

36. (*Much more involved*) The same for Fig. 9.1.8. (*Hint:* The judicious selection of the node to be deleted in each step of stage 2 is even more important in this exercise.)

37, 38. Prove the validity of equations (5) and (6), respectively, of Theorem 9.3.1 (Section 9.3.2). Model your proof after the proof of equation (4) in the text.

In Exercises 39 to 42, prove that the inclusion is valid for all sets α, β, γ, and show by counterexample that equality would not be valid.

39. $\alpha(\beta \cap \gamma) \subseteq \alpha\beta \cap \alpha\gamma$.

40. $\alpha^* \cup \beta^* \subseteq (\alpha \cup \beta)^*$.

41. $(\alpha \cap \beta)^* \subseteq \alpha^* \cap \beta^*$.

42. $(\alpha^* \beta \alpha^*)^* \subseteq (\alpha^* \beta)^* \alpha^*$.

In Exercises 43 to 48, prove the validity of the equation. Note that α and β in Exercises 43 to 45 are sets.

43. $(\alpha \cup \beta)^* = (\alpha^* \cup \beta)^*$.

44. $\alpha^* = \lambda \cup \alpha \cup \alpha^2 \cup \alpha^3\alpha^*$. (Generalize on this equation.)

45. $(\alpha^*\beta)^* = \lambda \cup (\alpha \cup \beta)^*\beta$.

46. (*Difficult*) $[(b \cup c \cup d)^*c \cup d]^*d = [\lambda \cup (b \cup c \cup d)^*c]dd^*$.

47. (*Difficult*) $(c \cup bb^*b)^* = (c \cup bb \cup bbb)^*$.

48. (*Difficult*) $(cb^*c \cup cb^*b)^* = (cc)^* \cup (cc)^*cb(b \cup c)^*$.

49. Write an algorithm for converting a lambda graph into an equivalent transition graph with equally many or fewer nodes.

50. Write an algorithm to obtain an equivalent proper graph from a given lambda graph, such that the result has no more lambda arcs than two plus the number of lambda arcs in the given graph.

51. Complete the proof of Theorem 9.3.2 (Section 9.3.6) by proving Lemmas 1 and 2.

52. Write an algorithm to obtain, from a given general regular expression, an equivalent general regular expression that either is $\varnothing$ or else has no occurrence of the character $\varnothing$.

53. Prove that if the node-deletion operation, as specified in stage 2 of the graph-to-expression algorithm of Section 9.3.7, is applied to a nonstart, nonaccepting node of an expression graph G, then the graph that results is equivalent to G.

54. Prove that if an expression graph has just two nodes, a nonaccepting start node N_1 and accepting node N_2, then the language of the graph is $(\alpha_{11})^*\alpha_{12}(\alpha_{22} \cup \alpha_{21}(\alpha_{11})^*\alpha_{12})^*$, where the α's are as defined in Section 9.3.7.

(Exercises 53 and 54 constitute the bulk of the justification of the graph-to-expression algorithm.)

55. Write a computer program to execute the graph-to-expression algorithm.

9.4 *LANGUAGES THAT ARE NOT REGULAR*

By now the reader should be aware of how tractable regular languages are. They can be represented not only by regular grammars but also by transition graphs, state graphs, and regular expressions, restricted and general. They are closed under all the Boolean operators. And they can be processed by finite-state operations, a great computational advantage. The more advanced theory of finite automata and regular languages reveals even more useful features of regular languages.

Because regular languages can be handled with such facility, it becomes important to be able to tell when a given context-free language is regular and when it is not. Although it is known that there is no such decision procedure (see, e.g., Hopcroft and Ullman [1979], p. 205), we present in this section a way of satisfying ourselves in some cases that a context-free language is not regular, applicable to many of the examples in Chapter 7.

We begin by extending the meaning of the t function in the definition of *finite automaton* in Section 9.2.1. Recall that if the automaton is in state Q at some time step in which it reads an input character b, then it is in state $t(Q, b)$ at the next time step. Alternatively, if Q is a node of a state graph, the unique branch labeled b from Q goes to $t(Q, b)$.

Recursive Definition of transition function, extended concept: For a given state graph,

$$\begin{cases} t(Q, \lambda) = Q \\ t(Q, Wb) = t(t(Q, W), b) \end{cases}$$

Note that this is a legitimate definition, since t has already been defined in cases where its second argument is a string of length 1. It is important to note that this definition is consistent with the original definition of t: For $W = \lambda$, $t(Q, Wb) = t(t(Q, W), b) = t(Q, b)$.

The node $t(Q, W)$ is the unique node that is at the end of the walk in the state graph beginning at node Q and spelling out W. For the proof that follows note that, for any strings W_1 and W_2 and for any node Q in the state graph,

$$t(Q, W_1 W_2) = t(t(Q, W_1), W_2)$$

THEOREM 9.4.1: The language $L = \{b^m c^m \,|\, m \geq 0\}$ is not regular.

PROOF: Suppose that L is regular. Then there is a state graph G, with finitely many nodes, whose language is L. Put $N_0 = $ the initial node of G and, for each $i \leq 1$, put $N_i = t(N_0, b^i)$.

Note that, for $i \neq j$, $b^j c^j \in L$ but $b^i c^j \notin L$. Hence $t(N_0, b^j c^j) \neq t(N_0, b^i c^j)$, since one of these nodes is accepting whereas the other is not. But $t(N_0, b^j c^j) = t(t(N_0, b^j), c^j) = t(N_j, c^j)$ and $t(N_0, b^i c^j) = t(t(N_0, b^i), c^j) = t(N_i, c^j)$. Since $t(N_j, c^j) \neq t(N_i, c^j)$ it follows that $N_j \neq N_i$.

We have proved that, for all i and j, if $i \neq j$, then $N_i \neq N_j$. Thus the state graph G has infinitely many nodes, a contradiction. ∎

The Proof Generalized **9.4.2**

The proof just concluded is more valuable to us than its theorem. Having put some mental effort into understanding this proof, we can with little additional mental effort see that it applies to many other languages. To this end, we can generalize the theorem.

THEOREM 9.4.2:   If for a language L there are two infinite sequences of strings $U_1, U_2, \ldots$, and $V_1, V_2, \ldots$, such that (1) $U_i V_i \in L$ for each i, and (2) $U_i V_j \notin L$ for $i \neq j$, then L is not regular.

PROOF: Suppose that L is regular with (finite) state graph G. From here on the proof is just like the proof of Theorem 9.4.1. We take $N_i = t(N_0, U_i)$, for each i, and then we reason, using V_i in place of c^i for each i, that $N_i \neq N_j$ for $i \neq j$. We conclude there are infinitely many nodes in G, a contradiction.   ∎

We are now in a position to apply Theorem 9.4.2 to show that many languages are not regular. In each case, all we must do is define infinite sequences $U_1, U_2, \ldots$, and $V_1, V_2, \ldots$, satisfying the hypothesis of the theorem:

1. The set of strings over $\{b, (,)\}$ in which the parentheses are mated. Put $U_i = (^i, V =)^i$.

2. $\{b^m c^m d^n e^n \mid m, n \geq 1\}$. Put $U_i = b^i, V_i = c^i de$.

3. L(G-IN), the completely parenthesized propositional calculus in infix notation (Section 7.2.4). Put $U_i = Q^i, V_i = p)^i$, where $Q = {\sim}($. For example, $U_3 V_3$ is the string ${\sim}({\sim}({\sim}(p)))$.

4. L(G-PP), the incompletely parenthesized propositional calculus in infix notation (Section 7.2.4). $U_i = Q^i, V_i = p)^i$, where $Q = {\sim}(p \vee$. For example, $U_3 V_3$ is ${\sim}(p \vee {\sim}(p \vee {\sim}(p \vee p)))$.

As (3) and (4) suggest, any language in which parentheses play their normal role and can be nested arbitrarily can be proved not to be regular by this technique.

5. L(G-PRE), parenthesis-free propositional calculus in prefix notation (Section 7.2.5). Put $U_i = \&^i, V_i = p^{i+1}$.

6. L(G-SUF), propositional calculus in suffix notation (Section 7.2.5). Put $U_i = p^{i+1}, V_i = \&^i$.

7. The set of palindromes over $\{b, c\}$ (Section 7.3.2, Example 4). Put $U_i = b^i c, V_i = b^i$.

Most of the languages that are meaningful in themselves as formal languages, and not just as sets of strings in the abstract, turn out not to be regular. It is somewhat surprising, therefore, that the GOTO language of Chapter 3 is regular (Exercise 17 of Section 9.2).

9.4.3   *Using Other Theorems*

Although Theorem 9.4.2 works in the large majority of cases, we can extend our resourcefulness by keeping Theorems 9.2.5 to 9.2.7 in mind: namely, that the regular languages are closed under the Boolean operators.

8. $L =$ the set of all nonpalindromes over $\{b, c\}$.

PROOF: Suppose that L is regular. Then its complement $\{b, c\}^* - L$ is regular by Theorem 9.2.6. But the latter is the set of all palindromes over $\{b, c\}$, already proved to be not regular (Example 7 of Section 9.4.2). So L cannot be regular.

9. $L = \{b^i c^j \,|\, i \neq j\}$.

PROOF: $\{b^n c^n \,|\, n \geq 0\} = b^* c^* - L = (\{b, c\}^* - L) \cap b^* c^*$. Now $b^* c^*$ is regular. If L were regular, then $\{b^n c^n \,|\, n \geq 0\}$ would be also by Theorems 9.2.6 and 9.2.7, contradicting Theorem 9.4.1. ∎

Our last example uses a more remote idea:

10. $L = \{b^{i^2} \,|\, 1 \geq 1\}$.

PROOF: By Exercise 28 of Section 9.2, if L were regular it would be ultimately periodic. But the set of square positive integers is not ultimately periodic. (In more detail, suppose that the state graph for L has n nodes. Then, by that exercise, there exist $m \geq 0$ and $p \geq 1$ such that $m + p \leq n$ and, for all $x \geq m$, $b^x \in L$ if and only if $b^{x+p} \in L$. But taking $x = n^2$, $b^x \in L$ but $b^{x+p} \notin L$, since the next integral square after n^2 is $n^2 + 2n + 1$. This contradiction shows that L is not regular.) ∎

Languages Not Context-Free *9.4.4*

Another problem that comes up in the advanced literature is that of proving that certain languages are not context-free (i.e., that there are no context-free grammars for them). For example, the language

$$L = \{a^n b^n c^n \,|\, n \geq 1\}$$

is not context-free. The technique for the proof, which works for many languages besides L, can be found in several advanced texts on formal languages (e.g., Ginsburg [1966], pp. 83–85).

Although the proof is beyond the scope of this text, we offer a plausibility argument that L is not context-free, based on the nondeterministic parsing automaton (and Theorem 8.5.3). In order to verify that a string of a's, b's, and c's is in L, the automaton would have to verify that the a's, b's, and c's come in the right order (which is easy) and to verify that there are equally many of each. Assuming that all the a's precede all the b's, which precede all the c's, the automaton could verify that the number of b's equals the number of a's by copying the a's on the parsing tape, and then erasing one for each b that appears. But then all the information about how many b's and a's there are would be gone by the time the c's were being read, so there would be no way to check the number of c's. Similarly, by altering the plan, we could get the machine to verify there are as many b's as c's without any check on the number of a's. Or to verify there are as many a's as c's without any check on the number of b's. But there does not seem to be any way of checking that the number of a's, the number of b's, and the number of c's are all equal.

Similarly, we can argue that the language

$$\{WW \mid W \in \{b, c\}^*\}$$

is not context-free. In order for the parsing automaton to verify that a string $X_1 \ldots X_n X_{n+1} \ldots X_{2n}$ (where each X_i is either b or c) is of the form WW, it would have to verify that $X_1 = X_{n+1}, X_2 = X_{n+2}, \ldots, X_n = X_{2n}$. It must write down $X_1, X_2, \ldots, X_n$ (or information somehow representing this sequence). If n is large it would have to verify that $X_i = X_{n+i}$ for small values of i before it verifies it for large values of i.

But our automaton's mode of operation makes this impossible. When it is reading X_{n+i} for the small values of i, the only way to make the check would be to go back on the tape where it has recorded the corresponding X_i's. In so doing it would have to erase the information about those X_i's for the large values of i, thus annihilating the information it needs later to check the X_{n+i}'s for large values of i.

Although these arguments are convincing on the intuitive level, it is very difficult to make them rigorous. The rigorous proofs that are used to prove that these languages are not context-free use another train of thought.

9.4.5 Exercises

In Exercises 1 to 12, prove that the language is not regular. These are arranged approximately in order of increasing difficulty. Exercises 1 to 7 can be done by an application of Theorem 9.4.2, modeled after the examples in Section 9.4.2. Unless otherwise indicated, m, n, p may be any integers ≥ 0.

    1. $\{b^{m+n}c^m d^n \mid m, n \geq 3\}$.

    2. $\{b^{3m}c^{2m+2n}b^{3n+1} \mid m, n \geq 0\}$.

    3. $\{(d^*b)^m(c^*d)^m \mid m \geq 2\}$.

    4. $\{b^m c^n d^p \mid m, n \geq 1; p = |m - n|\}$.

    5–7. The languages described verbally in Exercises 28, 29, and 31, respectively, of Section 7.3.

    8. $\{b^m c^n d^p e^q \mid \text{either } m \neq n \text{ or } p \neq q\}$.

    9. $\{b^m c^n d^p \mid \text{Either } m = n \text{ or } m = p \text{ or } n = p\}$.

    10. $\{b^m c^n d^p \mid m \neq n \neq p \neq m\}$.

    11. $\{b^m c^n \mid 2 \leq 2m \leq n \leq 3m\}$.

    12. $\{b^m c^n \mid m > 0; \frac{2}{5} \leq n/m \leq \frac{3}{5}\}$.

    13. The set of all programs of the WHILE language (Section 3.3.1).

THEOREM 9.4.3: If for a language L there are two infinite sequences of strings $U_1, U_2, \ldots$, and $V_1, V_2, \ldots$, such that (1) $U_iV_i \in L$ for each i, and (2) either $U_iV_j \notin L$ or $U_jV_i \notin L$ for $i \neq j$, then L is not regular.

14. Prove Theorem 9.4.3.

15. Prove that $\{b^m c^n \mid m > n\}$ is not regular.

16. Prove that $\{b^m c^n d^p \mid$ either $m < n$ or $m < p$ or $n < p\}$ is not regular.

17. (*Difficult*) Prove that $\{(d*c)^m(c*d)^m \mid m \geqq 1\}$ is not regular.

18. (*Difficult*) Just for variety, prove that $\{(cd*)^m(c*d)^m \mid m \geqq 1\}$ *is* regular.

I Euclidean Algorithm: Correctness Proof

Generally, one proves that a specified organized set of commands is an algorithm for a specified class of answerable questions by proving two things: (1) for every set of inputs representing a question in the class, execution will eventually terminate; and (2) the output upon termination is a correct answer to the question represented by the inputs. This procedure is permissible here because the Euclidean algorithm, so called, clearly satisfies the other conditions of the definition.

In the formal proof below we shall make use of the following elementary properties of divisibility in the domain of the nonnegative integers.

1. If $w = y + z$, then any divisor both of y and of z is also a divisor of w.

2. The same if $w = y - z$.

3. If w is a common divisor of y and z, and u is the greatest common divisor of y and z, then w is a divisor of u.

4. If v is a divisor of w, and w is a divisor of v, then $w = v$.

5. For $w \neq 0$, w is a divisor of 0, but 0 is not a divisor of w.

The proof has several lemmas, some of which are proved by course-of-values inductions (see Appendix V).

THEOREM AI.1: The Euclidean algorithm, so called, is an algorithm for finding the greatest common divisor of two given positive integers.

PROOF FOR THE SUBTRACTION VERSION: Let x_1, x_2 be two positive integers, taken as inputs. Assume that execution produces the sequence

$x_1, x_2, x_3, \ldots.$ We prove that the execution eventually terminates by noting that all the terms of the sequence are nonnegative, and showing that the sequence is decreasing. To this end, we prove the following:

LEMMA 1: If x_{i+1} is calculated (i.e., if termination has not yet occurred), then $x_i > 0$.

Proof: x_1 and x_2 are positive. An examination of the algorithm shows that there is no way that negative numbers can be computed from nonnegative numbers. Hence $x_i \geqq 0$, if x_i is calculated. If, moreover, x_{i+1} is calculated, then $x_i \neq 0$, so $x_i > 0$.

LEMMA 2: For any i for which a value of x_{i+3} is calculated, $\text{MAX}(x_{i+2}, x_{i+3}) < \text{MAX}(x_i, x_{i+1})$.

Proof:

Case 1. $x_{i+1} > x_i$. Then $x_{i+2} = x_i < x_{i+1}$ and $x_{i+3} = x_{i+1} - x_{i+2} < x_{i+1}$, from which the inequality follows.

Case 2. $x_{i+1} = x_i$. Then $x_{i+2} = 0$, execution halts, and no x_{i+3} is computed.

Case 3. $x_{i+1} < x_i$. Since $x_{i+1} > 0$, $x_{i+2} = x_i - x_{i+1} < x_i$. x_{i+3} equals either $x_{i+1} - x_{i+2}$ or x_{i+1}; in either case, $x_{i+3} < x_i$. The required inequality again follows.

LEMMA 3: Execution eventually terminates.

Proof: Definite $y_i = \text{MAX}(x_{2i-1}, x_{2i})$, for each i for which x_{2i} exists. By Lemma 2, the sequence $y_1, y_2, \ldots$ is a strictly decreasing sequence of nonnegative integers. But such a sequence cannot be infinite. It follows that the x sequence from which the y sequence is taken is also finite, completing the proof of Lemma 3.

Assume now that $x_1, x_2, \ldots, x_n$ is the complete sequence produced from inputs x_1, x_2 with $x_n = 0$ and x_{n-1} as output. Let d be the greatest common divisor of x_1 and x_2. The proof of Theorem AI.1 will be complete when we have proved that $d = x_{n-1}$.

LEMMA 4: For each i, $1 \leqq i \leqq n - 1$, d is a divisor of x_i.

Proof: The proof is by mathematical induction on i. For $i = 1$ or 2, the statement follows by the definition of d.

Assume as an inductive hypothesis that Lemma 4 is true for all $i < i_0$, where $3 \leqq i_0 \leqq n - 1$. Thus d divides both x_{i_0-2} and x_{i_0-1}. We must prove that d divides x_{i_0}.

Case 1. $x_{i_0-2} < x_{i_0-1}$. Then $x_{i_0} = x_{i_0-2}$, so d divides x_{i_0}.

Case 2. $x_{i_0-2} \geqq x_{i_0-1}$. Then $x_{i_0} = x_{i_0-2} - x_{i_0-1}$. Since d divides both x_{i_0-2} and x_{i_0-1} it divides x_{i_0}.

By mathematical induction, Lemma 4 follows.

LEMMA 5:   For each i, $1 \leqq i \leqq n$, x_{n-1} is a divisor of x_i.

Proof: Clearly, x_{n-1} is a divisor of both x_{n-1} and $x_n = 0$. We complete the proof by proving that, for each i, $1 \leqq i \leqq n - 2$, if x_{n-1} is a divisor of both x_{i+1} and x_{i+2}, it is a divisor of x_i. (Thus the proof is a course-of-values induction on j, taking $j = n - i$.)

Assume then that x_{n-1} is a divisor of both x_{i+1} and x_{i+2}. From the statement of the algorithm, either $x_{i+2} = x_i$ or $x_{i+2} = x_i - x_{i+1}$. From either equation we infer that x_{n-1} is a divisor of x_i, concluding the proof of Lemma 5.

We can now complete the proof of the Theorem. Since x_{n-1} is a divisor of both x_1 and x_2, it is a divisor of their greatest common divisor, d. But d is a divisor of x_{n-1} by Lemma 4. Hence, $x_{n-1} = d$. ∎

Labyrinth Algorithm: Correctness Proof

We are faced with a difficulty in this proof that we did not have with the proof for the Euclidean algorithm. The issue is command number (5): we must demonstrate that, whenever the executor is called upon to execute this command, there will be a unique yellow edge leaving his present position. Until we do so, we have no right to say that the labyrinth algorithm, so called, is a procedure, let alone an algorithm.

Then we must also prove that the procedure always terminates with an affirmative answer if there is a vertex labeled T in the graph, and with a negative answer if there is no such vertex.

By a *step* we mean the time during which the person moves along an edge in execution of the algorithm. (This stipulation is in accord with the discussion of the term *step* in Section 1.1.2.) We note that during any step, the edge traversed changes color: Either it is uncolored and is colored yellow, or it is yellow and is colored red. A red edge is never traversed.

For $s \geqq 0$, let P_s be that node which is the person's position at the completion of step s for $s \geqq 1$, or node A for $s = 0$. A number $n = n(s)$ and nodes and branches are defined for s as follows. $E_1(s), \ldots, E_n(s)$ are all the edges that are yellow at the completion of step s, in the order they were colored yellow. $N_0(s) = A$, and, for each i, $1 \leqq i \leqq n$, $N_i(s)$ is the node visited just after coloring $E_i(s)$ yellow. The sequence $N_0(s), E_1(s), N_1(s), \ldots, E_n(s), N_n(s)$ is called the *sequence for step s*.

Definition: An *almost-loop-free walk of length $n \geqq 0$* is a walk $U_0, D_1, U_1, \ldots, U_{n-1}, D_n, U_n$, where (if $n \neq 0$) the part $U_0, \ldots, U_{n-1}$ is a path, and $D_n \neq D_i$ for $i \neq n$. [U_n may or may not equal some U_i, for $i \neq n$. Thus an almost-loop-free walk either is a path (i.e., is loop-free) or else has a single loop involving the last node.]

Lemma 1: For each $s \geq 0$ (assuming that s steps have been executed), $N_{n(s)}(s) = P_s$, and the sequence for step s is an almost-loop-free walk from A to P_s. (In particular, if there are no yellow edges in the graph, $P_s = A$.)

(Lemma 1 justifies our thinking of a piece of string along the yellow edges from A to P_s, mentioned in Section 1.2.4.)

PROOF BY SIMPLE MATHEMATICAL INDUCTION ON s (SEE APPEN-DIX V): For $s = 0, P_0 = A$, and the sequence is the null path at A, which clearly satisfies Lemma 1.

Assume as an inductive hypothesis that Lemma 1 is true for s and that step $s + 1$ has been taken. The proof that Lemma 1 is true for $s + 1$ breaks down into six cases according to which command is taken at step $s + 1$ (i.e., the five possibilities of the search phase, or the return-affirmative phase). In what follows, "n" is an abbreviation for $n(s)$.

Case 1. Possibility (1) $(P_s = T)$. Then step $s + 1$ is determined by the return affirmative phase, which we consider below.

Case 2. Possibility (2) $[P_s \neq T, P_s = N_n(s)$ and another yellow edge leaves P_s besides $E_n(s)]$. Then the sequence for $s + 1$ is $N_0(s), E_1(s), N_1(s), \ldots N_{n-1}(s)$, which satisfies Lemma 1, since $N_0(s), \ldots, N_n(s)$ satisfies it.

Case 3. Possibility (3). The fact that possibility (2) does not hold implies that the sequence for step s, which by inductive hypothesis is an almost-loop-free walk, is a path, Furthermore, $P_s \neq T$. Let E_{n+1} be the first uncolored edge leaving $N_n(s)$ clockwise from $E_n(s)$, and N_{n+1} the node at the other end of E_{n+1}. Then $N_0(s), \ldots, N_n(s), E_{n+1}, N_{n+1}$ is the sequence for step $s + 1$ and satisfies Lemma 1.

Case 4. Possibility (4). A halt occurs and there is no step $s + 1$.

Case 5. Possibility (5). The proof here is the same as for Case 2.

Case 6. The return-affirmative phase. The proof is again the same as for Case 2.

Thus in all cases the sequence for step $s + 1$ satisfies Lemma 1, completing the proof by mathematical induction. ∎

Lemma 2: If $s + 1$ steps have been executed, then either $n(s + 1) = n(s) + 1$ or $n(s + 1) = n(s) - 1$; and for all i, $0 \leq i \leq \text{MIN}(n(s), n(s + 1))$, $N_i(s) = N_i(s + 1)$, and (for $i \neq 0$) $E_i(s) = E_i(s + 1)$. (In other words, the sequence for step $s + 1$ is formed from the sequence for step s either by adding an edge and a node, or deleting an edge and a node, at the end. Thus the string is either lengthened or shortened at the end, but otherwise remains as it was.)

Lemma 2 can be quickly verified by going through each of the six possible ways step $s + 1$ is executed.

COROLLARY: Let step x be the last step before step s such that the sequence for step x is shorter than the sequence for step s. Then the sequence for step x is

$$N_0(s), \ldots, E_{n(s)-1}(s), N_{n(s)-1}(s)$$

LEMMA 3:   If execution is in the search phase with $P_s \neq T$, and if the sequence for step s is not a path, then the yellow edge $E_n(s)$ was the edge traversed during step s, and the command from possibility (2) is executed for step $s + 1$.

PROOF: Since the sequence for step s is an almost-loop-free walk that is not a path (i.e., has a loop), $N_n(s) = N_j(s)$ for some $j < n$. The edge $E_{j+1}(s)$ is yellow, different from $E_n(s)$, and leads from $N_n(s) = N_j(s)$.

Now suppose that $E_n(s)$ is not the edge traversed during step s. Letting $t - 1$ be the last step whose sequence was shorter than the sequence for step s, it follows that $t < s$. Then, from the corollary to Lemma 2, we can infer that at step t the edge $E_n(s)$ was colored yellow and $P_t = N_n(s) = P_s$. By definition of $E_1(s), \ldots, E_n(s)$, the edge $E_j(s)$ was colored yellow before step t; furthermore, $E_j(s)$ was yellow at step t, since by the labyrinth algorithm an edge cannot go from yellow to nonyellow and then back to yellow. Since $P_t = P_s \neq T$, the command of possibility (2) would have been executed at step t, leaving $E_n(s)$ red, which then could not be yellow for step s, a contradiction. ∎

LEMMA 4:   If step s has been executed and is not a halt, then step $s + 1$ is uniquely determined. (Hence the so-called labyrinth algorithm is a procedure.)

PROOF: It suffices to prove (a) that in the search phase if none of the possibilities (1) through (4) holds, then there is a unique yellow edge leaving P_s; and (b) in the return-affirmative phase if $P_s \neq A$, then there is a unique yellow edge leaving P_s.

By Lemma 1, if $P_s \neq A$, there is at least one yellow edge leaving P_s. By Lemma 3, in the search phase if $P_s \neq A$ and there is more than one yellow edge leaving P_s, possibility (2) would hold. So if possibilities (1)–(4) do not hold in the search phase, the yellow edge leaving P_s is unique.

In the return-affirmative phase, if $P_s = T$ (the first step of the return-affirmative phase), step s must be the first time at this node and hence the walk is a path (i.e., has no loop). Therefore, the yellow edge leaving P_s is unique. Since subsequent steps contract the walk, no new edges are traversed, the walk is always a path, and the yellow edge leaving P_s is always unique until A is reached. ∎

LEMMA 5:   Execution eventually terminates.

PROOF: At each step either an uncolored edge is colored yellow or a yellow edge is colored red. If there are n edges in the graph, execution cannot last more than $2n$ steps. ∎

LEMMA 6:   If execution halts in the search phase, all nodes have been visited.

PROOF: If step s is a halt, $P_s = A$. If there are any yellow edges in the graph, the sequence for step s is not null. $N_0(s) \neq N_1(s)$ since, by the definition of the term *graph*, the edge $E_1(s)$ must connect two distinct nodes. Hence $n > 1$, $E_1(s) \neq E_n(s)$, and there are two yellow edges at $P_s = A = N_0(s) = N_n(s)$. Possibility (2) would be in operation and a halt would not occur. Hence at the halt there are no yellow edges in the graph.

Suppose N is a node that has not been visited. Then since the graph is connected, there is a path $U_0, D_1, U_1, \ldots, U_{n-1}, D_n, U_n$, where $U_0 = A$ and $N = U_n$. Since U_0 has been visited but U_n has not, there must be an i such that U_i has been visited but U_{i+1} has not. The edge D_{i+1} must be uncolored (otherwise, U_{i+1} would have been visited). Suppose that U_i was visited for the last time just before step t. The execution of that step could not have been in response to possibility (1) since that would have transferred execution to the return-affirmative phase. Possibility (2) is also excluded, since then at least one other yellow edge would have been left there without an opportunity to color it red (since there is no return to U_i).

But then the command for possibility (3) would have been executed, since there was at least one uncolored edge leading from U_i. One of these would have been traversed and colored yellow and would have remained yellow, since there is no return to U_i. This contradicts our previous observation that no nodes remain yellow at a halt, completing the proof of Lemma 6 by reductio ad absurdum. ∎

THEOREM AII.1:   The so-called labyrinth algorithm is an algorithm for the following problem: Does there exist a node labeled T in a given connected graph, situated in a plane, having one node labeled A at which search must begin, with one of the edges at A designated as the leading edge?

PROOF: Lemma 4 tells us that the organized set of commands is a procedure. Lemma 5 tells us that the procedure always halts. And from Lemma 6, we can easily conclude that the question is always answered correctly. ∎

Basic Issues **III**
of Formal Languages

This appendix, which is elementary enough to be read right after Chapter 1, covers some linguistic matters that are relevant to a discussion of algorithms. After contrasting the general nature of formal languages and natural languages, it explains the syntax and semantics of formal string languages, focusing temporarily on a sample language of declaratives. It then goes on to discuss command languages for expressing algorithms, of which programming languages are the chief examples.

NATURAL AND FORMAL LANGUAGES AIII.1

A *natural language* is any language used for general communication in a community, and often exists in both spoken and written forms. It comes into being as the result of a slow, unpredictable, and unplanned process, and never ceases to change. Most of us are aware that Old English became Middle English, which became modern English; we are also aware of the changes that have taken place in modern English since the Elizabethan period, when Shakespeare's plays were written.

Natural languages of complex societies are themselves complex, and any rules by which they can be understood are difficult to formulate precisely and difficult to apply once they are formulated. Getting a computer to handle a natural language such as English is such an immense job that, to date, success has been achieved only by severely limiting the subject matter and situational context from which the material may be taken.

In contrast, a *formal language* is created for intensive use with a specific, precisely delineated set of purposes in view. Usually, it is created in written form only, all at once, either by a single person or by a group of people; it may be modified, but only by a conscious act. The rules by which a formal language is understood are precise, and are created as parts of the language itself. As a consequence, formal languages (even a complicated language such as FORT-RAN) are simpler and more easily understood than most natural languages.

There are two major areas in which formal languages are used: symbolic logic and programming. The development of formal systems of symbolic logic in the early twentieth century was a culmination of a century-old movement toward greater precision by the mechanization of the logic of mathematical reasoning. Formal programming languages came into being when it became necessary in the middle twentieth century to express thoughts to a machine with a new order of complexity. At first it was necessary to have a formalized language (machine code) in terms of which a machine could be mechanically instructed. Later it was discovered that programming languages could be made more human (i.e., "user-oriented"). But even then, because of the desirability of machine translation of the user-oriented languages into machine code, the new programming languages had to be formal languages.

We have something to gain by looking at both the class of languages of symbolic logic and the class of programming languages under the common heading of *formal languages*. By studying in detail some simple languages of symbolic logic and some simple programming languages, we achieve an understanding of some important aspects of formal languages in general. (However, this book presupposes no previous exposure to symbolic logic.)

Although we are interested in developing formal languages for algorithms, we should keep in mind that whatever can be done in a formal language can be done in a natural language. For example, in Section 1.2.2 we wrote the Euclidean algorithm in English. Many algorithms in the later chapters are also written in English, because their formalization would offer no advantage.

AIII.2 STRINGS OVER AN ALPHABET

An essential feature of formal languages is the absolute rigidity of specification made possible by restricting what can be said. All the formal languages used in this book are in a certain subclass of the formal languages, the class of formal string languages, whose general structure we now describe.

Definition: An *alphabet* is a finite set of characters. A *string over an alphabet* is a sequence of characters from the alphabet (repetition of characters being allowed) written from left to right without separation. We include a single character as a string of length 1, and the null string λ (i.e., the string of length zero).

The condition that strings are written from left to right is an arbitrary one reflecting the convention used in our part of the world. If this direction were changed to right to left, top to bottom, or bottom to top, no significant change in the concept of string would result.

Definition: The *concatenation* of two or more strings is a new string that consists of the old strings in order, written together without spaces between. If U_1 and U_2 are, respectively, the first and second strings, this concatenation is written as U_1U_2. $U_1U_2U_3$ is the concatenation of U_1, U_2 and U_3; and so on.

For example, if the alphabet is the set $\{b, c, d\}$, then *bccbd*, *d*, and *ccbdcc* are strings over this alphabet. The concatenation of these strings (in order) is the string *bccbddccbdcc*.

Definition: V is a *substring* of W if $W = U_1VU_2$ for some U_1, U_2. If $U_1 = \lambda$, then V is a *prefix* of W. If $U_2 = \lambda$, then V is a *suffix* of W. If $V \neq W$ (i.e., if either $U_1 \neq \lambda$ or $U_2 \neq \lambda$), then V is a *proper substring* of W. The string V is a *proper prefix* of W if it is a prefix and $V \neq W$ (i.e., if $U_1 = \lambda$ but $U_2 \neq \lambda$). It is a *proper suffix* if it is a suffix and $V \neq W$ (i.e., if $U_2 = \lambda$, but $U_1 \neq \lambda$).

Definition: A *string language* is a language all of whose occurrences are strings of characters over its alphabet.

Written natural languages, as well as many formal languages, can be thought of as string languages. But if we take this point of view toward the English language, we must allow for an alphabet of well over 50 characters. Capital letters must be distinguished from lowercase letters, punctuation signs must be included, and the space between words must be a member of the alphabet. An English sentence can be conceived of as a string of characters over this enlarged alphabet.

The alphabets of formal string languages are sometimes much simpler. In many formal languages (e.g., the foundational programming languages and the formalism of functional expressions) the space does not have to be regarded as an alphabetic character, since the meaning of a string is determined without regard to any spaces.

Some formal languages are not string languages, for example, languages allowing subscripting or superscripting of their alphabetic characters: If the occurrence 2^2 is to be distinguished from the string 22, it cannot be called a string.

However, subscripting and superscripting can easily be accommodated to a string organization. For example, 2^2 can be rewritten as $2\uparrow2$ or $\uparrow(2, 2)$ to make it a true string.

Some important languages cannot be readily revised to become string languages. A language of maps and a language of blueprints (with a firm set of conventions as agreed to, say, by a committee of experts) are certainly formal languages, as we have been using the term. But neither of these could be converted into a string language without a radical change of character. The concepts we use in handling string languages will not apply to formal languages such as these.

One important nonstring language is the language of flowcharts for computer programs, a variety of which is used in Chapter 3. Although a flowchart can be readily translated into a string language (i.e., a programming language whose programs are strings), the flowchart language itself is a two-dimensional language. Like the languages of maps and blueprints, it can be revised to become a string language only by radically changing its character.

AIII.3 A SAMPLE FORMAL LANGUAGE

We now present a simple illustrative formal string language which we call the language of *plus, times, greater-than, and equals,* or PTG&E. It is simpler than most formal languages, and (except for the present purpose of illustration) it is not useful.

Following a procedure widely used in presenting a formal language, we first enumerate the alphabet, then define certain sets of strings called *syntactic categories,* and finally, state what each string in each syntactic category means. A syntactic category in a formal language is like a part of speech in ordinary language (noun, verb, etc.). We shall give a more precise explanation of the notion of *syntactic category* at the end of this section.

1.   The alphabet of PTG&E has the following seven characters:

$$/ \quad + \quad * \quad (\quad) \quad > \quad =$$

These characters are named, respectively, stroke, plus, asterisk, left parenthesis, right parenthesis, greater-than, and equality.

2. The syntactic category of *numeral* is the set of all strings consisting exclusively of strokes. Examples:

$$/$$

$$////$$

3. The syntactic category of *operator* is the set of just two strings, the single character $+$ and the single character $*$.

4. The syntactic category of *expression* is the set of strings defined recursively as follows:

a. A numeral is an *expression*.

b. The result of concatenating, in order, a left parenthesis, an expression, a right parenthesis, an operator, a left parenthesis, an expression, and a right parenthesis is an expression.

c. Nothing is an expression unless its being so follows from (a) and (b).

We have here a recursive definition. A word of explanation is in order before we proceed with the exposition of the language PTG&E. In part (b) of the definition of "expression," the term "expression" itself occurs. Although it might appear that the definition is circular, in reality it is not. A string is an expression if (and, by part c, only if) we can prove it to be so using parts a and b. Part b simply tells that expressions that are not numerals can be made up from shorter expressions by means of parentheses and operator signs.

For example, by parts a and b,

$$(///) + (///)$$

is an expression, since it is the concatenation of left parenthesis, the numeral ///, right parenthesis, plus, left parenthesis, the numeral /// and right parenthesis. Similarly,

$$(/)*(////)$$

is an expression. And then, using these results, we conclude that the following is also an expression:

$$((///) + (///)) + ((/)*(////))$$

We can use paragraph 4 (together with paragraphs 1 to 3) to tell whether any given string is or is not an expression. For example, none of the following is an expression:

$$(x)*(///)$$
$$(/) + (//) + (///)$$
$$/ + //$$
$$(/) + (/) = //$$

In each case we can see clearly that there is no way of showing that the string is an expression by using parts a and b.

Note the strictness of this definition of expression in excluding $/ + //$ because it lacks parentheses. Also, the string $(/) + (//) + (///)$ is excluded from the category of expression, although each of the following is included:

$$((/) + (//)) + (///)$$
$$(/) + ((//) + (///))$$

We now proceed with the exposition of the language PTG&E.

5. The syntactic category of *relation* is the set $\{=, >\}$.

6. The syntactic category of *sentence* is the set of all strings made up by concatenating, in order, an expression, a relation, and an expression.

Thus there are five syntactic categories in PTG&E: numeral, operator, expression, relation, and sentence. Our one remaining task is to explain what the strings in each syntactic category mean.

7. A numeral *denotes* that positive integer equal to the number of its strokes: / denotes the number one, // denotes the number two, and so on. The operator + *denotes* the operation of addition of positive integers; * *denotes* multiplication.

8. Each expression denotes a positive integer as determined by the following recursive stipulation: An expression of the form $(E_1) + (E_2)$ *denotes* the sum of the positive integer denoted by E_1 and the positive integer denoted by E_2; an expression of the form $(E_1) * (E_2)$ *denotes* the product.

9. The relation $=$ *denotes* the equality relation over the positive integers; $>$ *denotes* the greater-than relation.

10. A sentence of the form $E_1 = E_2$ *denotes* the proposition that the expressions E_1 and E_2 denote the same positive integer. A sentence of the form $E_1 > E_2$ *denotes* the proposition that the positive integer denoted by E_1 exceeds the positive integer denoted by E_2.

11. A sentence of the form $E_1 = E_2$ is *true* if and only if E_1 and E_2 denote the same positive integer. A sentence of the form $E_1 > E_2$ is *true* if and only if the positive integer denoted by E_1 exceeds the positive integer denoted by E_2. A sentence is *false* if and only if it is not true.

This concludes our account of the language PTG&E.

It should be noted that the language PTG&E has been set forth by sentences in the English language. A language used in describing another language in this way is called a *metalanguage*. A metalanguage often has symbols of its own that are not part of the language that it describes. For example, the symbols E_1 and E_2 are metalinguistic symbols; they stand for expressions in the language PTG&E, but they are not symbols *in* PTG&E. They are used in the metalanguage of PTG&E to talk about PTG&E.

A *syntactic category* of a formal language is generally a set of strings that (1) is defined by a certain pattern (syntax), (2) has a common kind of meaning relationship to things outside the language (semantics), and (3) is referred to in the formulation of the language. The syntactic categories of all useful formal languages are recursive sets, in the sense of Section 1.1.6.

AIII.4 SYNTAX AND SEMANTICS

There are generally three parts in the study of a language: syntax, semantics, and pragmatics. The first two are important in this book and will now be discussed. Later, pragmatics will be discussed briefly for the sake of completeness.

The *syntax* of a language deals with relationships among strings of the language, apart from any relationships to things outside of the language. It is concerned, for example, with relationships among strings in the various syntactic categories. Paragraphs 1 through 6 in the description of PTG&E are simply syntactic statements, characterizing elements of the language in terms of other elements of the language without reference to things outside the language.

A *grammar* for a language is a systematic presentation of its syntax. Thus in a language of strings, the grammatical rules are sufficient to determine whether any given string is a member of any given syntactic category. For example, paragraphs 1 through 6 constitute a complete grammar of PTG&E. The rules of a grammar for the English language should perhaps be sufficient to determine that "They goes home" is not in the syntactic category of sentence, but "They go home" is.

This book is concerned with grammars for formal languages: informal grammars for formal languages in Chapters 3 and 4, and formal grammars (specifically, *context-free grammars*) in Chapters 7 and 8.

The *semantics* of a language deals with relationships of elements in the language to a *field of objects*, or *reference field*. It makes it easier for us to think of the semantic relationship if we assume that the field of objects is completely separate from the language. We make this assumption throughout the book, except for one part in Chapter 6, where we find ourselves investigating the peculiar phenomenon of a sentence that talks about itself.

Paragraphs 7 to 11 specify the semantics of PTG&E, making use of the fact that the syntax has already been dealt with. In presenting a formal language, it is generally best to specify the syntax completely before treating the semantic concepts.

The field of objects to which PTG&E refers is the set of positive integers. The relationship between a string in a syntactic category and an object is called *denotation*. For example, a numeral denotes a number. (In this book we have adhered to this usage of the terms *numeral* and *number*, because the distinction between the two is an important one.)

More generally, every expression of PTG&E denotes a positive integer. The precise explanation of which positive integer each expression denotes is given recursively and assumes that the reader is familiar with addition and multiplication in the domain of the positive integers.

Note that there is redundancy in paragraphs 7 to 10. Paragraph 8, explaining the denotation of an expression, could be removed since what it says follows from paragraph 7, telling what numerals and operators denote.

Paragraph 10 states that a sentence denotes a proposition. Some theorists would prefer to leave this paragraph out, since the semantics of sentences is covered well enough by paragraph 11.

Paragraphs 9 to 11 constitute a three-way redundancy, in that any one of these paragraphs makes the other two superfluous. Exactly which paragraph one selects is perhaps a matter of taste.

A certain metaphysical issue tends to come up when one attempts to deal with the semantics of any mathematical theory. The most natural way to talk about what such a theory refers to is to assume the existence of mathematical entities such as numbers and operations and relationships over numbers. This assumption is clearly present in our presentation of paragraphs 7 to 11. Paragraph 10 also presupposes the existence of another abstract entity, a proposition. But then, as we have noted, paragraph 10 is dispensable.

The metaphysical position that any abstract entities, including mathematical entities, exist in the same sense that concrete objects exist is traditionally known as *Platonism*. Many philosophers (traditionally known as *nominalists*) dispute this tenet, and some issue an outright denial that abstract entities exist. We do not think it necessary at this point to espouse any position in this controversy. We must have a distinction between numbers and strings in our language (i.e., numerals) that denote numbers; our motive in taking an implicit Platonistic position is to express the important semantic relationship as simply as possible. (For a good exposition of this philosophical issue, we recommend Quine [1953], pp. 1–19.)

We suggest that readers decide how to think about the entities denoted by numerals. They can think of them as abstract entities, or as objects of thought, or as symbols in a different language, or in any other way. All we ask is that the semantic relationship be acknowledged.

AIII.5 PRAGMATICS; IMPERATIVES

While syntax is concerned with linguistic elements (such as strings) in themselves, and semantics is concerned with the relationship of these linguistic elements to objects in a reference field, pragmatics is a three-term relationship: it involves the linguistic elements, the objects in the reference field, and the circumstances in which the linguistic elements occur. These circumstances include the time and place, the agent who issues the linguistic element (e.g., by saying or writing it), the intended recipient of it as a communication (who hears or reads it), and so on.

Pragmatics is important in understanding many uses of natural languages, such as persuasion and the expression of attitudes and emotions, well beyond our present discussion. It is worth noting briefly that there are certain words and phrases in ordinary language whose meaning is understandable, in the most common and simple of circumstances, only in pragmatic terms. Examples of these are "you," "I," "left," "right," "here," "these," "today," "yesterday," and "tomorrow." For example, each of the following sentences may be true or false depending on who says (or writes) it, when, and where: "Your hat is on the rack." "Battery Park is over there, just to the left of the Statue of Liberty." "It is snowing today." Clearly, the truth or falsity of any such sentence goes beyond semantics, since it depends on the circumstances of its utterance.

The language PTG&E (as we stated) has no pragmatics: Sentences are true and false, and other strings denote or fail to denote objects, without regard to the circumstances of their occurrence. This concludes our discussion of pragmatics.

All sentences of PTG&E are declaratives (i.e., are either true or false).

Other sentences (as we learned in grammar school) may be imperative, interrogative, and exclamatory. Exclamatory sentences are of no interest in this book. We have discussed interrogatives, or questions, in Section 1.1.1, as the origin of our interest in algorithms. Imperatives are important to us as the ingredients of algorithms.

A command is an imperative sentence that directs the addressee (hearer or reader) to carry through a specified course of action. Not all imperative sentences are commands. "Do not write the number eleven," for example, is an imperative that serves to place a limit on the freedom of choice of the addressee, but does not direct him to act. In fact, any negative imperative has this property, and hence is not a command. Another example is, "Feel free to write the number eleven," which is roughly equivalent to saying, "You may write the number eleven." It merely grants permission, leaving the addressee to make up his or her own mind what course of action to take.

The rules of a logical derivation are permission-granting imperatives. For example, the rule "q may be derived from p and p-implies-q" does not command anyone using the logical system to derive q. It simply gives one permission to do so provided that one has first derived p and p-implies-q. (The rules of formal computation of Section 4.6 and the context-free productions of Chapter 7 are of this nature.)

One may regard some of the imperatives of a nondeterministic procedure (see Section 1.1.5) as permission-granting imperatives, namely, those applying to situations in which the executor may choose among alternatives. A command is the only kind of imperative allowed in an algorithm, since any other kind would violate the condition of determinism. The foundational programming languages, like most programming languages, are formal languages of commands only.

Because everything of a fundamental nature that we said about the syntax of declaratives (e.g., about the sample language PTG&E) applies to formal languages of commands, no sample language of commands will be given in this section. The language of commands to a Turing machine (Chapter 2) and the two foundational programming languages (Chapter 3) serve as examples.

Although the full meaning of an imperative requires pragmatics (since the identity of the addressee is essential to its meaning), we shall not require a full account of the meaning of the commands in our languages, getting by with syntax and semantics only. Thus pragmatics is not used in this book.

THE SEMANTICS OF COMMANDS AIII.6

When a command is obeyed and executed, the reference field is usually (but not always) modified. More to the point, given the reference field before execution, and given the command, the reference field after execution is determined. In this subsection (which contains material not needed for reading other parts of this book), we suggest that an algorithmic command denotes a function. This idea comes up in the advanced topic of the semantics of programming languages.

In the execution of an algorithm, the reference field includes whatever is mentioned in the algorithm. It must include everything modified by the executor and everything outside the algorithm that determines his or her action. It therefore includes the input and everything written by the executor up to termination. The written algorithm itself, however, is not part of the reference field. (The idea of an algorithm modifying itself during execution is not absurd, but this possibility is excluded in this discussion for the sake of simplicity.)

We introduce now the important concept of the *total state* of the reference field of an algorithmic language. Two total states are distinguished from one another if there is a difference between the two that is discernible in some way by the execution of some algorithm in the language. Thus, if the reference field has many places where numbers are written, and if at certain times a number in one of these places differs from the number in the same place at a previous time (even if all the numbers in the other places are the same), the two total states for those two times are different. This concept of *total state* is conceived abstractly. It does not matter, for example, whether a person executes the algorithm on a blackboard or on paper, since implementation differences do not affect the important aspects of the execution of an algorithm. Thus the set of all total states for paper-and-pencil computation is the same as the set of all total states for blackboard-and-chalk computation if the algorithm being executed is the same.

The concept of the total state of the reference field has an important relationship to the deterministic property of algorithms. First, the total state of the reference field before the first step of execution is determined by the inputs. Second, given the total state at any time, if one step of the algorithm is executed, the total state immediately after execution is determined. Consequently, given the input and given any positive integer t, the total state after the tth step of execution (if a termination has not occurred before then) is determined.

With this concept of total state we arrive at an interesting formulation of the semantics of algorithmic commands:

Definition: A command *denotes* a function f over the set of all total states of the reference field, where, for each total state S of the reference field just before execution of the command, $f(S)$ is the total state of the reference field just after execution.

For example, suppose that we are executing an algorithm in which there are three spaces, A, B, and C, in which nonnegative integers are written. Let us assume that these three spaces constitute the entire reference field and that the total state is determined given the three nonnegative integers in these three respective spaces. A command in the algorithm might be: "If the number in space A exceeds the number in space B, erase the number in space C and write zero in its place." Letting f be the function this command denotes, if S is the total state with 7, 4, and 2 in spaces A, B, and C, respectively, $f(S)$ equals the total state with 7, 4, and 0 in these respective spaces.

If we consider a program in machine code run on a computer, the reference field is the set of all storage positions and registers in the computer that are used by the program. A total state is a vector of values for these respective storage positions and registers.

We must emphasize our assumption here that the program does not modify itself. Our elementary semantic analysis does not apply without further complication to programs that modify themselves during execution.

A program in any computing language that requires any kind of translation before machine execution is more difficult to discuss.

If each of two commands constitutes an algorithm step, the two can be joined together to form a new command that takes two algorithm steps. For example, consider the two commands: (1) "If the number in A exceeds the number in B, put zero into C"; and (2) "Double the number in B." Joining them in order we get a single command: "If the number in A exceeds the number in B, put zero into C; then (in either case) double the number in B." This new command denotes a function g which bears a well-known relationship to the functions f_1 and f_2 denoted by (1) and (2), respectively; g is the *composition* of f_1 and f_2, since, for all S, $g(S) = f_2(f_1(S))$.

The algorithm as a whole can be regarded as a compound command, since it is an organized set of commands, although much more is involved in obtaining this compound command from its parts than the idea of the above paragraph. The algorithm denotes a function ϕ such that, for any S, if S is the total state at the beginning, $\phi(S)$ is the total state at the halt. The problem of determining this function ϕ from a given program (well beyond the scope of this book) is one of the fundamental problems in the advanced topic of the semantics of programming languages.

Appendix

IV Critique of Algorithms; Computational Complexity

This appendix will help round out the discussion of the concept of algorithm in Chapter 1 by investigating the various criteria by which we decide between competing algorithms for the same problem. These include static criteria (based on the algorithm itself, as conceived and written) and dynamic criteria (based on what happens during execution). The latter have given rise to the theory of computational complexity, the word "complexity" being used to denote the classification of problems according to the amount of time and memory the most efficient algorithm for each problem requires in execution. The classification of problems is quite difficult; the analysis of the algorithms themselves is a necessary part of the pursuit of that goal, and also important in its own right.

AIV.1 STATIC CRITERIA

Before a computer begins to do something for us, we must do several somewhat difficult things. We must think up an algorithm for our problem, and perhaps discuss it with other people. We must write a program from the algorithm. After that, we may have debugging to do. Since the intellectual labor between the posing of a problem and a successful program is considerable, we should do whatever we can to make it less tedious, less time-consuming, less error-prone, more enjoyable, and more enlightening. In evaluating algorithms, and in choosing among them for possible computer application, this consideration should be foremost, and efficiency of execution should be secondary.

For this reason we focus on static criteria for the length of this section, delaying the discussion of the theoretically more exciting execution criteria.

There are several static criteria, which, although apparently similar, may compete with one another in some situations. We now list four of them:

1. *The criterion of brevity.* A shorter algorithm probably gives rise to a shorter computer program, taking less time for a person to write and less time for a computer to compile.

2. *The criterion of intuitive clarity.* Quite often we have reason to consider algorithms that we have no reason to execute. For example, it may be necessary merely to convince ourselves that an algorithm exists for a class of questions, without getting the answer to any particular questions in the class. In that case, rather than be concerned with efficiency of execution, we should look for an algorithm that gives us the understanding we require as efficiently as possible. If implementation is ever called for, we can modify the algorithm for efficiency of execution.

This criterion is important throughout this book and in many other theoretical expositions, where algorithms are presented with the purpose of communicating an understanding of the subject matter and without any claim of efficiency of execution.

3. *The criterion of insightfulness.* In working to understand an algorithm for a particular problem, we may gain an insight that facilitates a more general understanding. Moreover, the ideas that we learn may help us design algorithms for other similar problems.

This criterion is important not only in an academic setting, but in a practical programming setting as well. A programmer who learns after he has completed a job that modifications are needed can generally apply the insights he has gained in doing the job the first time in a relatively quick rewrite.

4. *The criterion of structure.* Many programmers and teachers of programming have emphasized the need for "structured" programs—that is, for a style of writing programs that have fewer and less consequential errors to begin with and are at the same time more easily debugged. Without attempting to go into the various controversies that have arisen in this matter, we can say that an algorithm that by its nature tends to yield a well-structured program is to be preferred for computer application.

These four criteria are related to one another. A briefer algorithm tends to be clearer intuitively, although there are exceptions. An algorithm that is clearer intuitively is quite often more insightful. An algorithm that has a better structure tends to be clearer intuitively and more insightful, although possibly not as brief. Other such observations could be made.

When computer application is intended in the form of a computer program that will run only a few times, these four static criteria should dominate our considerations. On the other hand, when programs are written to be run many times, dynamic criteria (efficiency of execution) should dominate.

AIV.2 FEASIBILITY OF EXECUTION

When we evaluate an algorithm on the basis of execution, we are compelled to divide our considerations into two stages. In the first stage, we must consider whether execution is feasible at all, given the kind of inputs we wish to use and given the computing capacity of the executor (person, computer, etc.). Only when we know the algorithm is feasible for our needs can we begin to ask about its efficiency. For example, suppose that we wish to get a computer to answer certain questions as fast as possible. If the fastest algorithm for the problem requires an amount of memory that no computer has, that algorithm must be rejected in favor of a slower algorithm with feasible memory demands.

When the computing power in a given situation is severely limited, considerations of feasibility become critical. Suppose, for example, that we wish to prescribe an algorithm by which a person can mentally divide two numbers, given by decimal numerals, and obtain the quotient to two significant figures. (For example, if she were told to divide 880,000 by 3.7, her answer should be 240,000.)

Let us state the specifications for this algorithm in greater detail. The person doing the calculation may neither write nor use a calculator. She reads the two decimal numerals, each having no more than, say, 10 digits, and is allowed to stare at them as she goes through her mental calculation. Execution must be fairly quick (say within 1 or 2 minutes) for whatever numerals are read. The algorithm must be fairly easy to learn by a person of average intelligence, power of concentration, and background in arithmetic, and must be such that once the person has learned it she remembers it for use the next time, even though several years (say) may go by before she uses it again. In particular, the person should not have to rehearse the algorithm before using it each time.

Such an algorithm might be practical and quite useful to some people. Although the considerations are different, as much thought is needed to design the algorithm as to design a small program for a computer, since one must make sure that it works for all inputs in the included range under the stated limitations of the executor.

Our discussion of this situation has the same purpose as the discussion of the labyrinth problem in Section 1.2; limited computing capacity in each case leads to a peculiar algorithm. Clearly, the study of such peculiar restrictive computing situations is far from the main purpose of this book.

AIV.3 COMPUTATIONAL COMPLEXITY

This theory has much to tell us about both feasibility and efficiency in the execution of various algorithms. While the theory of computability is concerned with the question of whether a problem has an algorithm at all, computational complexity is concerned with how efficient an algorithm it has: the amount of resources—time, memory, energy, money, and so on—that must be expended to execute for various inputs. The two principal resources used in any execution are time and memory. The other resources are dependent on these and, for that reason, omitted from theoretical consideration.

Although computational complexity is not a principal concern of this book, we devote the remainder of this appendix to it, to help round out our presentation of the concept of algorithm and to give the reader a glimpse into this advanced topic.

The complexity theorist begins by measuring the size of a written input to an algorithm. If the inputs are strings, the input size is generally taken to be the total input length (i.e., the total number of characters in all the input strings). He proposes to measure the quantity of resources used during execution as a function of input size, facing the difficulty that this quantity depends on the kind of implementation. Thus he seeks to establish functions T and S such that, if i is the size of the written input, $T(i)$ is an upper bound on the amount of time it takes to execute the algorithm with that input, and $S(i)$ is an upper bound on the amount of memory (or space) used. The resource functions T and S are called a *time function* and a *space function*, respectively, for the implemented algorithm.

Since only general knowledge is desired, algorithms are classified not strictly according to these functions but according to their orders of magnitude. In particular, if one implemented algorithm has the functions $T(i) = 3i^2$ and $S(i) = \log_2(i)$ and another implemented algorithm for the same problem has $T'(i) = 6i^2$ and $S'(i) = 4\log_2(i)$, these are regarded as equivalent since T differs from T', and S from S', by a proportionality constant.

Furthermore, algorithms are classified on the asymptotic properties of the resource functions. For example, if a time function for one implemented algorithm is $3i^2 + 10,000$ and a time function for a second algorithm for the same problem is $i^{5/2} + 100$, and these cannot be improved, the first of these algorithms is declared to be the faster by the complexity theorist, since for i sufficiently large the second algorithm takes much longer.

Let us examine this example more closely. For any $r > 0$ there is a value of i_0 such that, for all inputs of size greater than i_0, the second algorithm takes more than r times as much time as the first. Thus, except for finitely many inputs, the first algorithm is more than r times as fast as the second. And this is true no matter how large r may be.

But although the first algorithm is asymptotically faster than the second, it does not follow that the first algorithm will be chosen in a practical situation, even if speed is the dominant consideration. The value of i must exceed 49 before $i^{5/2} + 100$ exceeds $3i^2 + 10,000$. This means that the first algorithm is faster only for inputs of 50 characters or longer. If the practitioner wants to compute only for inputs of less than 50 characters in length, he would be foolish in this case to use the algorithm that the theorist has judged to be the more efficient.

In spite of the possible discrepancy with practical considerations, there is good reason for the complexity theorist to classify resource functions in the way that he does. By assuming the equivalence of functions that are within a proportionality constant of one another, he is able to disregard theoretically insignificant variations, such as minor changes in a computer program, or the fact that one machine is faster than another machine. And by looking at the asymptotic properties of these resource functions, he is able to pass judgments that go beyond the particular usage that the algorithms may happen to have at present.

Ultimately, what the theorist is after is not a classification of implemented algorithms but a classification of problems themselves. To turn to our previous example where we considered a certain problem P and two distinct implemented algorithms, one with functions $T(i) = 3i^2$ and $S(i) = \log_2(i)$ and the other with functions $T'(i) = 6i^2$ and $S'(i) = 4\log_2(i)$, either one of these implemented algorithms shows that the problem can be computed with "time on the order of i^2" (or "quadratic time") and with "space on the order of $\log_2(i)$" (or "log space"). The complexity theorist would then carry on research either to find an implemented algorithm that was essentially faster or required essentially less memory, or else to prove that no such algorithm existed. If he succeeded in proving the latter (as sometimes happens), he would have succeeded in establishing the time complexity classification and the space complexity classification of the problem, a notable theoretical achievement.

The kind of complexity we are discussing here is "worst-case" complexity. The resource functions for an algorithm are an upper bound on the resources used, and hence tell us that things will not be worse than that. Although this kind of analysis dominates the field of computational complexity, there are many theoreticians who also like to give "average-case" analyses of algorithms (i.e., resource functions that indicate how the algorithm performs on the average). Such analyses are useful to practitioners who wish to consider algorithms that perform quite well for most inputs, but behave badly for a few exceptional inputs. Clearly, the practitioner should have both a worst-case analysis and an average-case analysis before he decides to use such an algorithm.

AIV.4   COMPLEXITY AND ALGORITHM SELECTION

There are problems for which several different algorithms are practical, depending on the input size. Sorting is a good example. There are several rather simple sorting algorithms that are used to order lists, all of which in the worst case take an amount of time proportional to the square of the input size. (In most cases, the input size is proportional to the length of the list to be sorted.)

But there are other more complicated algorithms that have the advantage that their time of execution is proportional to $i \log(i)$. (For this sort of statement, we need not indicate what the base of the logarithm is, since logarithms in one base are proportional to logarithms in another base.) It is easy to see that, whatever the constants of proportionality C_1 and C_2, $C_1 i^2 > C_2 i \log(i)$ for values of i sufficiently large [since $\log(i)/i$ approaches 0 as i gets arbitrarily large].

Sorting situations vary, so that both kinds of sorting algorithms are used. (For further details on computational complexity and sorting, see Chapter III of Aho, Hopcroft, and Ullman [1974] and Knuth [1973].) The algorithms that take quadratic time are often chosen because of the brevity of the program.

There are many algorithms that are perfectly natural for their problems, but whose time complexity is an exponential function. For the sake of this discussion, let us say that an exponential function f_e is one satisfying an equation of the form

$$f_e(i) = C^{i^k}$$

where C and k are real constants, $C > 1$ and $k > 0$. For example, 2^i and $(1.1)^i$ are both exponential functions of i. It is well known that if f_e is an exponential function and f_p is a polynomial function with nonnegative values [i.e., $f_p(i) = a_n i^n + \ldots + a_1 i + a_0 \geq 0$ for all nonnegative integers i, $a_n \neq 0$, $n \neq 0$], then $f_e(i) > f_p(i)$ for all but finitely many nonnegative integers i. Exponential functions increase quite rapidly in value as their argument increases.

We remarked in Section AIV.3 how the classification of functions by their asymptotic properties sometimes yields peculiar results. The same is true when we compare certain exponential functions with certain polynomial functions, for example, the particular functions $f_e(i) = (1.1)^{\sqrt{i}}$ and $f_p(i) = i$. The immediately preceding paragraph tells us that $f_e(i) > f_p(i)$ for all but finitely many i, and that $f_p(i)$ increases quite rapidly as i increases. However, the finitely many values of i for which $f_e(i) \leq f_p(i)$ include all integral values of i up to 9161. Although this is only a finite set of values, it may be an important set of values. Furthermore, although $f_e(i)$ generally does increase rapidly with i, one has to get rather large values of i before that starts to happen. For example, $f_e(1024)$ is approximately 21.1.

Complexity theorists have judged algorithms with exponential time and space functions to be unsatisfactory, because their resource requirements increase so fast with the input size i. Practitioners who are interested in these algorithms for only small values of i, however, might find some of them perfectly satisfactory.

Complexity theorists are interested in broad classifications of algorithms and problems based on time and space functions. In their investigations they have uncovered many new efficient algorithms for some problems, and also proofs of limitations on improvement for other problems. These impressive discoveries have been quite helpful to people programming for practical situations with practical ends in view. But the final choice of algorithm in a practical situation must always take into account the specific nature of that situation, and cannot be based simply on its complexity classification.

AIV.5 EFFICIENCY OF THE EUCLIDEAN ALGORITHM

Of the two versions of this algorithm (see Section 1.2.2), the remainder version, which we now analyze, is quite efficient. Figure AIV.5.1 is a flowchart for a subprogram based on it, in which the inputs Z and W are two positive integers. REM(Z, W) means the remainder when Z is divided by W [e.g., REM(95, 11) = 7].

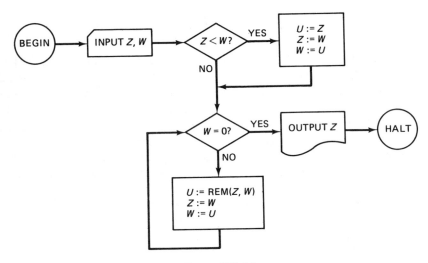

Figure AIV. 5.1

This flowchart can easily be converted into machine code or an assembly language program on any computer. All numbers in this program are integers and all operations are integer operations.

Let us first describe in detail how a computer program written from this flowchart will execute the remainder version of the Euclidean algorithm. Suppose that $x_1, x_2, \ldots, x_n$ is the sequence obtained by the algorithm, with $x_n = 0$. Then input W is x_2, Z is x_1. If $x_1 \geqq x_2$, then the loop is entered for the first time with $Z = x_1$ and $W = x_2$; but if $x_1 < x_2$, the loop is entered for the first time with $Z = x_2$ and $W = x_3 = x_1$.

Execution goes through the loop as long as $W \neq 0$. At any time the remainder is computed, $Z > W$. If $Z = x_{j-1}$ and $W = x_j \neq 0$, then execution proceeds through the box, during which U is computed as x_{j+1} (the remainder when x_{j-1} is divided by x_j). The value x_j is then put into Z and x_{j+1} into W.

[The program takes advantage of the fact that in the remainder version of the Euclidean algorithm, for all $j \geqq 3$, $x_j < x_{j-1}$ if x_j exists. Thus after the first step, one need not check for $x_{j-1} < x_j$.

As a matter or fact, checking for $x_1 < x_2$ is not necessary either, since in that case $\text{REM}(x_1, x_2) = x_1$, which is what we want x_3 to be. But we prefer to have the program make this check; although it makes the program longer, it does not add substantially to execution time in any case.]

We shall establish a space function and a time function for this algorithm. To fix our ideas, we shall assume that numbers in the computation are represented in binary. Put $\delta(x)$ = the length of the binary numeral for x [e.g., $\delta(15)$ = 4, $\delta(16) = 5$]. We let i be the input size: $i = \delta(W) + \delta(Z)$, taking here the values of the variables W and Z at the beginning of the program. Since W and Z never increase, i is always an upper bound on $\delta(W) + \delta(Z)$.

We consider first the operation of obtaining $\text{REM}(Z, W)$ for a given Z and W. One is inclined to say that this operation takes one division time, so is a constant. But this would assume that W and Z are within the limits of integer representation in some given machine. Complexity theorists would not be content with the restriction of Z and W to a finite set of positive integers. They would insist on an analysis that would apply for arbitrarily large inputs.

One way to find the remainder is to divide Z by W using the long-division algorithm in binary. This division consists of a number of steps, each consisting of subtracting Z times a power of 2 from W. Each such step takes an amount of time bounded by a quantity proportional to $\delta(W)$. The number of steps is at most $\delta(Z) - \delta(W) + 1$. For the entire division, therefore, there is a constant c_2 such that the amount of time is bounded by $c_2 i^2$. (Exactly how we would get the computer to do this long division for very large numbers we leave to the reader.)

The amount of space needed to find the remainder in this way is not very much. Besides the place for W and the place for Z, one needs an extra register with as much space as Z. Multiplying W by a power of 2 can be done by shifting W leftward in this register.

(The amount of space we need to do long division on paper is not so limited; it is perhaps proportional to i^2. However, this is because, as we proceed, a lot of information is left on the paper that could be erased.)

A space function for this implemented algorithm is now easy to ascertain. Since the remainder from any division is always less than the divisor, the numbers produced by the execution never get larger than what they were at the beginning. Besides W, Z, and U, an extra register is needed for finding the remainder. Since none of these four storage positions ever needs more than i binary places, the amount of storage is bounded by $4i$.

The train of thought establishing a time function for this implemented algorithm is more involved. A large part of the work is in determining a bound on the number of times the loop will be executed. But before we get to that, let us ask: How much time is spent inside the loop each time?

For most machines, as long as inputs W and Z are within the limits of integer representation, the amount of time spent in the loop is constant. However, complexity theorists would insist on an analysis that could determine a time function that applies even when the inputs are larger than the largest integer represented by a machine word, for any fixed machine.

Three things are done in the loop: (1) finding the remainder, (2) setting Z to W, and (3) setting W to U. The last two take an amount of time that is at most proportional to the number of digits in the numbers involved. Since these are each bounded by i (the numbers do not increase), there is a constant c_1 such that the amount of time to do both (2) and (3) is bounded by $c_1 i$.

We have already seen that the amount of time to find the remainder is bounded by $c_2 i^2$. Thus the amount of time through the loop each time is bounded by $c_2 i^2 + c_1 i$ and (taking $c_3 = c_1 + c_2$) by $c_3 i^2$.

By looking at the flowchart, we note that the amount of time spent outside the loop is, in any case, less than the amount of time spent during the longest time in the loop. Hence we adopt the subgoal of finding an upper bound B on the number of times through the loop; $(B + 1)c_3 i^2$ will be a time function for the program.

AIV.6 NUMBER OF TIMES IN THE LOOP

We find we can concentrate on the case $x_1 > x_2$ (i.e., input Z > input W) for most of our analysis. In the case $x_1 = x_2$, the machine is in the loop only once ($n = 3$, since $x_3 = 0$); and in the case $x_1 < x_2$, $x_3 = x_1$ and execution proceeds from there on as in the case $x_1 > x_2$. These other cases are easily accommodated later (namely, in the proof of Theorem AIV.6.1).

For the sequence $x_1, \ldots, x_n$ with $x_1 > x_2$, the number of times in the loop equals $n - 2$. For $1 \leq j \leq n - 2$, $x_{j+2} = \mathrm{REM}(x_j, x_{j+1})$; a quotient q_{j+2} and remainder x_{j+2} are uniquely determined from x_j and x_{j+1}, where

$$x_j = q_{j+2}x_{j+1} + x_{j+2} \qquad \text{and} \qquad 0 \leq x_{j+2} < x_{j+1}.$$

We must refer in our present analysis to the quotient q_{j+2} although it is not used in the algorithm.

LEMMA 1:   If $x_1 > x_2$ then, for $1 \leq j \leq n - 2$, $x_{j+2} < x_{j+1}$ and $q_{j+2} \geq 1$.

PROOF: We prove both assertions simultaneously by mathematical induction on j (see Appendix V). Lemma 1 is true for $j = 1$, by definition of x_3 and q_3.

Assume now that Lemma 1 is true for j, and that $j < n - 2$. We must prove that $x_{j+3} < x_{j+2}$ and $q_{j+3} \geq 1$. We have

(1) $x_{j+1} = q_{j+3}x_{j+2} + x_{j+3}$

(2) $0 \leq x_{j+3} < x_{j+2}$

Since $j + 2 < n$, $x_{j+2} > 0$. Since $x_{j+3} < x_{j+2} < x_{j+1}$, we see from (1) that $q_{j+3} \geq 1$, which completes the inductive step, and the proof of Lemma 1 by mathematical induction on j. ∎

LEMMA 2: If $x_1 > x_2$, then, for $1 \leq j \leq n - 2$, $x_{j+2} < \frac{1}{2}x_j$.

PROOF: Applying Lemma 1, $x_j = q_{j+2}x_{j+1} + x_{j+2} \geq x_{j+1} + x_{j+2} > 2x_{j+2}$. Hence $x_{j+2} < \frac{1}{2}x_j$. ∎

Lemma 2 tells us that the numbers in the sequence are decreasing by at least a certain rate. Using this fact, we are able to place a limit on the length of the sequence, given the magnitude of x_1.

It is convenient to write $\lceil y \rceil$ to mean the smallest integer not smaller than the real number y. Then $\lceil \log_2 x_1 \rceil$ is the smallest integer p such that $2^p \geq x_1$.

LEMMA 3: If $x_1 > x_2$, then $n \leq 2 \lceil \log_2 x_1 \rceil + 1$.

PROOF: By Lemma 2, if x_{2p+1} exists, then $x_{2p+1} < x_1/2^p$; if, furthermore, $2^p \geq x_1$, then $x_{2p+1} = 0$, since it must be a nonnegative integer.

Putting $p = \lceil \log_2 x_1 \rceil$, we therefore see that either x_{2p+1} does not exist or $x_{2p+1} = 0$. In either case $n \leq 2p + 1$. ∎

THEOREM AIV.6.1: For some constant c, a time function for the Euclidean algorithm (as implemented via the flowchart of Fig. AIV.5.1) is ci^3 (where i is the input size).

PROOF: We seek first to bound L, the number of times the machine goes through the loop.

Case 1. $x_1 = $ input Z $>$ input W $= x_2$. Then $L = n - 2 \leq 2 \lceil \log_2 (x_1) \rceil - 1 < 2i - 1$ (using Lemma 3 and the fact [see Section AIV.5] that $\lceil \log_2 (x_1) \rceil \leq \delta(x_1) < i$).

Case 2. input Z $<$ input W. When the loop is entered the first time, Z has the value $x_2 = $ input W, and W has the value $x_3 = x_1 = $ input Z. We look at the sequence $x'_1, x'_2, \ldots, x'_n$, produced by the Euclidean algorithm, where $x'_1 = x_2$ and $x'_2 = x_3$. As in case I, $L = n - 2 < 2i - 1$.

Case 3. input Z $=$ input W. Then $L = 1 \leq 2i - 1$.

Thus in all cases, $L \leq 2i - 1$. (In other words, $2i - 1$ is the value of B we decided to find at the end of Section AIV.5.) Since the amount of time in the loop each time is bounded by $c_3 i^2$, a time function for the program $= (2i - 1 + 1)c_3 i^2 = 2c_3 i^3$. The theorem follows with $c = 2c_3$. ∎

(A more searching analysis yields a bound on the number of times through the loop equal to $\lceil \log_\phi (\sqrt{5}\, x_1) \rceil - 2$, where $\phi = (1 + \sqrt{5})/2$, which is about 1.62 [see Knuth (1969), p. 130]. This bound, although significantly smaller than the one we have deduced [see Lemma 3], would improve our time function only by decreasing the proportionality constant.)

AIV.7 EFFICIENCY OF A COMPETING ALGORITHM

We have seen that the Euclidean algorithm can work in "cubic time." Most practical programmers might be more interested in the fact that a program on a machine working on inputs within the integer limits of the machine word size takes an amount of time bounded by a constant times the logarithm of the smaller of the two input values. (The proof of this assertion is similar to our proof in Sections AIV.5 and AIV.6. One must reformulate Lemma 3 of AIV.6 in terms of x_2 in place of x_1.) Of course, they would be interested in knowing what the constant is.

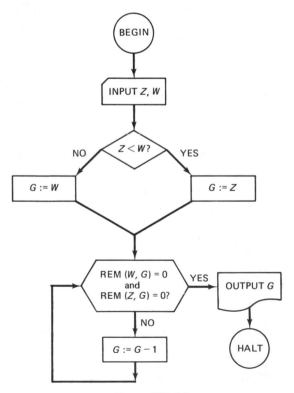

Figure AIV. 7.1

It is interesting to compare the Euclidean algorithm with the obvious trial-and-error algorithm for finding the greatest common divisor G of two given positive integers W and Z, shown in the flowchart of Fig. AIV.7.1. By this algorithm, G is first set to the smaller of the two inputs and tested for being a common divisor. If that fails, G is successively decremented by one until it is a common divisor.

As we begin to analyze this program, we observe that the number of times through the loop in the worst case equals one less than the smaller of the two input numbers. (The worst case occurs when the greatest common divisor is 1.) We have already noticed (at the beginning of this subsection) that the number of times through the loop of the Euclidean-algorithm program is bounded by a constant times the logarithm of the smaller number. The loops are comparable, because they each involve at least one division (to get the remainder). We see immediately that the Euclidean algorithm is generally much more efficient than the algorithm of Fig. AIV.7.1.

If we wish to determine a time function for Fig. AIV.7.1, we can say that the smaller input number is $\leq 2^{i/2}$, for input size i. (We continue to assume the binary system.) Let ki be the maximum time outside the loop. Since the division time (time to find the remainders) is bounded by a constant times i^2, we can say that the time of execution is bounded by $ci^2 2^{i/2} + ki$, for constants c and k. Although we can make a minor improvement in this time function, we cannot get a time function that is not exponential.

All in all, the remainder version of the Euclidean algorithm is more efficient than the program of Fig. AIV.7.1 as judged by any of the criteria we have discussed in this section. On this the practitioner and the complexity theorist would agree, as they do in most cases.

Recall that in Section 1.2 we concentrated on the subtraction version of the Euclidean algorithm. This version is quite inefficient as judged by execution time, since the number of subtractions may be as large as the larger of the two input numbers. (This happens when the smaller of the two input numbers equals 1. A rare case, but these complexity functions must take the worst case into consideration. To adjust the algorithm to give a quick answer in this case, or any finite set of similar cases, would still leave the worst-case number of subtractions proportional to the larger number.) However, the subtraction version of the Euclidean algorithm was focused on in Section 1.2 because of its operational simplicity, subtraction being a simpler operation than division, and moreover being a part of the algorithm for division. This kind of consideration is closer to the concerns of this book than is efficiency of execution.

V Proofs by Mathematical Induction

There are two varieties of proof by mathematical induction used in the mathematical literature. One of these, simple induction, is frequently used in elementary mathematics in establishing arithmetic formulas and properties of numbers. The other, course-of-values induction, is useful in proving properties of structures (such as graphs, formulas of symbolic logic, and algorithms).

Although the purpose of this appendix is to elucidate the several proofs in this book using course-of-values induction, we begin by explaining simple induction, mostly for the sake of comparison.

AV.1 SIMPLE INDUCTION

A proposition to be proved by mathematical induction must be of the following form, or else must be reinterpreted so as to be of this form: "For all integers n in the set α, $P(n)$." The set α is most frequently the set of all nonnegative integers, whose smallest element is 0, or the set of all positive integers, whose smallest element is 1. The set α can be any set of integers having a smallest element i_α and containing all integers greater than it, for example the set of all integers greater than or equal to 10.

Format for simple induction. First, one proves $P(i_\alpha)$, where i_α is the smallest integer in α. This step is called the *basis* of the induction. Second, one proves for an unspecified integer $n \in \alpha$ that the assumption $P(n)$ (the *inductive hypothesis*) implies $P(n + 1)$. The second step is called the *inductive step*. Having completed both the basis and the inductive step, one concludes: For all $n \in \alpha$, $P(n)$.

Assuming that the reader has had some experience with this type of proof and needs no persuasion about its validity, we proceed with two examples.

PROPOSITION AV.1.1.   If a function f satisfies (1) $f(0) = 1$, and (2) $f(n + 1)$ $= 2f(n) + 1$ (for all $n \geq 0$), then, for all nonnegative integers n, $f(n) = 2^{n+1} - 1$.

PROOF BY MATHEMATICAL INDUCTION ON n: $f(0) = 1 = 2^{0+1} - 1$. Now assume that $f(n) = 2^{n+1} - 1$. By (2), $f(n + 1) = 2(2^{n+1} - 1) + 1$ $= 2^{(n+1)+1} - 1$.

[Therefore, by mathematical induction, for all nonnegative integers n, $f(n) = 2^{n+1} - 1$.] ∎

Explanation: The brevity of the proof is justified by the assumption that the reader is familiar with proofs by simple induction. Note that α is the set of all nonnegative integers, $i_\alpha = 0$, and $P(n)$ is the equation

$$f(n) = 2^{n+1} - 1$$

Thus $P(0)$ is the equation $f(0) = 2^{0+1} - 1$, which is the basis of the induction, established in the short first paragraph of the proof.

The inductive hypothesis is $P(n)$, that is, the assumption that $f(n) = 2^{n+1} - 1$ (for an unspecified nonnegative integer n). In the second paragraph the inductive step is completed by proving that the inductive hypothesis implies $P(n + 1)$, that is, that

$$f(n + 1) = 2^{(n+1)+1} - 1$$

The basis and the inductive step having been completed, the third paragraph, in brackets, simply draws the conclusion. The proof could be shortened further by deleting this last paragraph, with the end-of-proof sign placed at the end of the second paragraph. The reader who is familiar with proofs by mathematical induction would realize that the basis and inductive step are complete and the statement of the theorem follows. This practice is followed in the next proof and thereafter.

Note that the preceding proof by simple mathematical induction parallels what is in effect a recursive definition of the function f in the statement of Proposition AV.1.1. (Such a recursive definition is called a *primitive recursion* in Chapter 4.)

PROPOSITION AV.1.2.   For every positive integer n, the sum of the first n odd positive integers equals n^2.

PROOF BY MATHEMATICAL INDUCTION ON n: $\sum_{i=1}^{1} (2i - 1) = 1$ $= 1^2$. Now assume that $\sum_{i=1}^{n} (2i - 1) = n^2$. Then $\sum_{i=1}^{n+1} (2i - 1) = \sum_{i=1}^{n} (2i - 1)$ $+ 2(n + 1) - 1 = n^2 + 2(n + 1) - 1 = (n + 1)^2$. ∎

AV.2 COURSE-OF-VALUES INDUCTION

The only difference between simple induction and course-of-values induction is a difference in the inductive step, the inductive hypothesis being somewhat more involved in the latter. We again assume that α is the set of all integers greater than or equal to i_α.

Format for course-of-values induction. First, one proves $P(i_\alpha)$. Second, one assumes, for an unspecified integer $n_0 > i_\alpha$, that, for all n, if $n < n_0$ and $n \in \alpha$, then $P(n)$. One proves that this assumption (the *inductive hypothesis*) implies $P(n_0)$ (the *inductive step*). Having completed both the basis and the inductive step, one concludes: For all $n \in \alpha, P(n)$.

Like simple induction, course-of-values induction is most generally used where α is either the set of all nonnegative integers or the set of all positive integers.

In spite of its seemingly more difficult inductive hypothesis, the intuitive justification of the new principle is no more difficult than the intuitive justification of simple induction. The new principle is useful where, in order to prove in the inductive step that $P(n_0)$, it is not sufficient merely to refer to the fact that $P(n_0 - 1)$; one must refer to the fact that several or all of the elements of α less than n_0 have the property P. One can therefore regard the principle of course-of-values induction as a generalization of the principle of simple induction.

A course-of-values induction was used in Appendix I in the proof of Lemma 4 (about the Euclidean algorithm). There, to prove that d divides x_{i_0} in the inductive step, we had to refer not only to the fact that d divided x_{i_0-1} but also to the fact that d divided x_{i_0-2}. The proof of Lemma 5 also was a proof by course-of-values induction.

The proofs of Propositions AV.2.1, AV.3.1, and AV.3.2 will further illustrate the format of course-of-values induction.

PROPOSITION AV.2.1:   If a function f satisfies

(1) $f(1) = 1$, and

(2) $f(2n) = f(2n + 1) = 2f(n)$, for $n \geq 1$,

then, for all positive integers $n, f(n)$ equals the largest power of 2 not greater than n.

PROOF BY MATHEMATICAL INDUCTION ON n: $f(1) = 1 = 2^0$. So $f(1) =$ the largest power of 2 not greater than 1.

Now assume that $n_0 > 1$ and, for all $n < n_0, f(n) =$ the largest power of 2 not greater than n.

Case 1. n_0 is even. If $n_0 = 2i$, by inductive hypothesis, $f(i) = 2^j$, where $2^j \leq i < 2^{j+1}$. From this we get $2^{j+1} \leq 2i = n_0 < 2^{j+2}$. So $f(n_0) = 2f(i) = 2^{j+1}$ is the largest power of 2 not greater than n_0.

Case 2. n_0 is odd. If $n_0 = 2i + 1, f(i) = 2^j$, where $2^j \leq i < 2^{j+1}$. From this we get $2^{j+1} + 1 \leq 2i + 1 = n_0 < 2^{j+2} + 1$. Since both n_0 and $2^{j+2} + 1$ are odd, $n_0 < 2^{j+2}$. Hence $f(n_0) = 2^{j+1}$ is the largest power of 2 not greater than n_0. ∎

PROOFS ABOUT TREES AV.3

To illustrate our remark that proofs by course-of-values induction are frequently appropriate in proving properties of structures, we introduce the binary tree, a rather simple structure from the theory of graphs. This concept is one of several in this book to be introduced by recursive definition, which always leads naturally to proofs by course-of-values induction.

Generally, a recursive definition begins by enumerating the smallest (or simplest) objects in the class being defined and proceeds by describing exactly how the larger objects in the class are constructed from smaller objects. The recursive definition is always understood to be complete: no object is in the class unless its being so follows from what is said. In the following definition, the completeness clause is explicitly written in parentheses, but in other recursive definitions, the completeness clause is tacitly understood.

Recursive Definition of *binary tree:* A single node (with no edges) is a *binary tree*, of which the node is both the *root* and a *leaf*. If T_1 and T_2 are binary trees with no parts in common, the graph that results by taking a new node N, connecting it by an edge to the root of T_1, and connecting it by another edge to the root of T_2 is a *binary tree*. The *root* of the new tree is N, and its *leaves* are the leaves of T_1 and the leaves of T_2. (Nothing is a binary tree unless its being so follows from this definition.)

A binary tree is a special kind of graph (see Section 1.2.3).

Figure AV.3.1 is a binary tree, with the vertex labeled 15 as the root and nodes labeled 1, 2, 4, 6, 8, 10, 11, and 13 as leaves. Binary trees are generally drawn this way, with the root at the top, leaves at the bottom, and each path from the root to a leaf going generally downward.

Note that the binary tree of Fig. AV.3.1 is formed by taking the binary tree T_1 with root at 9 and leaves 1, 2, 4, 6, and 8; the binary tree T_2 with root at 14 and leaves 10, 11, and 13; and a new node 15, which is joined to the root of T_1 and to the root of T_2. T_1 and T_2, in turn, are each formed in a similar way, and so on.

PROPOSITION AV.3.1: A binary tree with n leaves has $2n - 2$ edges.

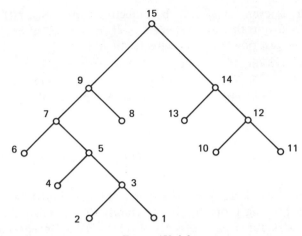

Figure AV. 3.1

PROOF BY MATHEMATICAL INDUCTION ON n: By definition, a binary tree must have at least one leaf. If a binary tree T is formed from binary trees T_1 and T_2, each of these must have at least one leaf, so T must have at least two leaves. A binary tree with one leaf, therefore, must be a single node with zero edges. Thus Proposition AV.3.1 is true for $n = 1$.

Assume now, for $n_0 > 1$ and for all $n < n_0$, that all binary trees with n leaves have $2n - 2$ edges. Let T be a binary tree with n_0 leaves. T must be made up from T_1 and T_2 as stated in the definition (since $n_0 > 1$). If T_1 has n_1 leaves and T_2 has n_2 leaves, then $n_1 + n_2 = n_0$, and $n_1, n_2 > 0$; thus $n_1, n_2 < n_0$. By the inductive hypothesis, therefore, T_1 has $2n_1 - 2$ edges and T_2 has $2n_2 - 2$ edges. Since T has two edges that are not part of either T_1 or T_2, the number of edges in T is $(2n_1 - 2) + (2n_2 - 2) + 2 = 2n_0 - 2$. ∎

The kind of argument just concluded is sometimes called a *structural induction*. In general, one proves that all structures in a certain class have a certain property by proving (1) that all structures in the class with the smallest size have the property, and (2) that if all structures smaller than a given size have that property, then all structures with that size also have the property. In so doing, one makes use of the fact that all sufficiently large structures in the class are made up in some uniform way from smaller structures also in the class. We conclude with a similar argument.

Definition: The *height* of a binary tree is the length of a longest path (see Section 1.2.3) from the root to a leaf.

PROPOSITION AV.3.2: The height of every binary tree is less than the number of its leaves.

PROOF: Where T is a binary tree, let $HE(T)$ and $LE(T)$ be the height and the number of leaves, respectively, of T. The proof is by mathematical induction on the number $LE(T)$, which must be a positive integer. If $LE(T) = 1$, then T must have zero edges and so $HE(T) = 0$.

Assume now, for $n_0 > 1$ and for all $n < n_0$, that $LE(T) = n$ implies that $HE(T) < n$. Let T_0 be a binary tree with n_0 leaves. Since $n_0 > 1$, T_0 must be made up from T_1 and T_2 each with fewer leaves. If $N_{01}, \ldots, N_q$ is a path from root to leaf in T_1, N_0 is the root of T_0, and E is the edge from N_0 to N_{01}, then $N_0, E, N_{01}, \ldots, N_q$ is a path from root to leaf in T_0, whose length is one more than the length of the original path in T_1. Similarly, any path from root to leaf in T_2 can be extended to a path, of length one more, from root to leaf in T_0. Furthermore, all paths from root to leaf in T_0 are formed in this way. Thus the longest path from root to leaf in T_0 is longer by one than the longest of all paths from root to leaf in T_1 and T_2. It follows that $HE(T_0) = MAX(HE(T_1), HE(T_2)) + 1$, Without loss of generality, we assume that $HE(T_1) \geq HE(T_2)$, so that

$$(1) \quad HE(T_0) = HE(T_1) + 1$$

Since $LE(T_2) \geq 1$, and $LE(T_0) = LE(T_1) + LE(T_2)$,

$$(2) \quad LE(T_1) + 1 \leq LE(T_0)$$

Since $LE(T_1) < n_0$, $HE(T_1) < LE(T_1)$ by inductive hypothesis; thus

$$(3) \quad HE(T_1) + 1 < LE(T_1) + 1$$

Putting (1), (3), and (2) together, we get $HE(T_0) < LE(T_0)$. Thus the fact that every binary tree with less than n_0 leaves has fewer edges implies that the same is true of every binary tree with n_0 leaves.

Proposition AV.3.2 follows by mathematical induction. ∎

VI The Diagonal Method

The method of proof used in Chapter 6 to establish the undecidability of the halting problem is quite pervasive. It is interesting to observe some other applications of the same method. But first let us review informally the proof in Section 6.1.

The proof of the Lemma of Section 6.1.1 in outline is the construction of a program P_2 under a certain hypothesis which leads to a contradiction. P_2 begins by "looking" at the Gödel number of a program (the initial value of X1). Let us simplify and say that P_2 looks at a program.

Thus P_2 is constructed so that whenever it looks at any program P' it halts if and only if P' does not halt when it looks at itself. We see that this is a contradiction when we take $P' = P_2$ (i.e., when we have P_2 look at itself); it halts when it looks at itself if and only if it does not halt when it looks at itself.

This proof is often called a "proof by the diagonal method" (although this might not be the best name) because of its resemblance to Cantor's proof that there are more real numbers between 0 and 1 than there are positive integers.

AVI.1 A FAMOUS PROOF BY GEORG CANTOR

The proof, also by contradiction, goes as follows. Suppose there are as many positive integers as there are real numbers x such that $0 \leq x < 1$. (The inclusion of 0 and the exclusion of 1 is a matter of convenience.) Then there would be a one-to-one correspondence (or bijection) between the two sets, that is, a function ϕ such that (1) for every positive integer n, $0 \leq \phi(n) < 1$; (2) if $n \neq m$

then $\phi(n) \neq \phi(m)$; and (3) for every real number x, $0 \leq x < 1$, there is an integer n such that $\phi(n) = x$.

Following Cantor, we consider the decimal expansions of these real numbers. For each n, we put $\phi(n) = a_{n1}a_{n2}a_{n3} \ldots$, where each a_{nt} is a decimal digit.

We think of these numbers in an array:

$$.a_{11}a_{12}a_{13} \ldots$$

$$.a_{21}a_{22}a_{23} \ldots$$

$$.a_{31}a_{32}a_{33} \ldots$$

$$\cdot$$
$$\cdot$$
$$\cdot$$

Looking along the diagonal of this array, we construct a number $y = .b_1b_2b_3$ as follows: For each n,

$$b_n = \begin{cases} a_{nn} + 2 & \text{if } a_{nn} \leq 6 \\ a_{nn} - 2 & \text{if } a_{nn} \geq 7 \end{cases}$$

Clearly, $0 \leq y < 1$. Also, the sequence of digits $b_1, b_2, b_3, \ldots$ is different from any of the sequences $a_{n1}, a_{n2}, a_{n3}, \ldots$, since it differs in the nth term: $b_n \neq a_{nn}$. Also, since there is a difference of two between these digits, it follows that $\phi(n) \neq y$.

So, by the diagonal method we have constructed a new number, demonstrably not equal to any of the numbers corresponding to the integers, contradicting the assumption that this was a one-to-one correspondence. It follows that there is no such one-to-one correspondence. Since it is possible to put the positive integers into one-to-one correspondence with a subset of the reals in the interval (i.e., map the positive integers to these reals by an injection), there are, in a sense defined by Cantor, more of these reals than there are positive integers.

RUSSELL'S PARADOX AVI.2

The diagonal argument appears at several crucial places in the foundations of mathematics. During the latter part of the nineteenth century, a crisis emerged in the movement that sought to lay a logical foundation for mathematics. Several paradoxes were discovered, constituting what some considered a threat to the entire movement. The argument behind all these paradoxes was essentially the same, and was similar to Cantor's diagonal argument and to our proof of the lemma for the unsolvability of the halting problem.

The logician Bertrand Russell began his most important work with a concern for these paradoxes. His book, Russell [1919], is a good exposition of them. We discuss next one of the paradoxes that bears Russell's name and is in effect a simplified version of all the others.

We are all familiar with the concept of *set*. Sets can sometimes have other sets as members: for example, the set of all sets having exactly two members, or the set of all sets having infinitely many members.

A principle of set existence states that any property of things determines a set, namely the set of all and only all those things that have that property. We are using the term *thing* to denote all entities that exist, including sets. A *property* is any statement we might make about a thing. We stipulate only that a property be definite: Each thing must either have that property or not.

Some sets can be members of themselves. For example, the set of all infinite sets is a member of itself, since there are certainly infinitely many infinite sets. On the other hand, many sets are not members of themselves, such as the set of all physical objects.

Now, being a member of itself is a property of sets. Some sets have this property, others do not. This property itself determines a set, namely the set of all self-members. But then the property of not being a member of itself also determines a set. This last set R we call *Russell's set*: the set of all sets that are not self-members.

The rule for R is as follows. For all sets x, $x \in R$ if and only if $x \notin x$.

The paradox arises when we ask if R is a member of itself. Assume first that $R \in R$. Then, by the rule, $R \notin R$, a contradiction. On the other hand, assume that $R \notin R$. Then, again by the rule, $R \in R$, again a contradiction.

We know that either $R \in R$ or $R \notin R$. But in either case, we get a contradiction. We made no arbitrary assumption; all our reasoning was based on supposedly valid principles. The result is therefore called a paradox.

Russell's paradox indicates that the principles and concepts in terms of which we have just reasoned cannot be completely correct. Russell himself sought to correct the difficulty by introducing the theory of types. He postulated a ground level consisting of objects that are not sets, or things of type zero. Next, there are things of type one, which are sets of objects. Only objects can be members of sets of type one. Then there are things of type two, which are sets of things of type one. And so on. In general, things of type $i + 1$ are sets of things of type i. For Russell, no set could have as a member anything except one of the immediately lower type.

Also, Russell declared it meaningless to talk of a thing of type i being a member of a set of type j, unless $j = i + 1$. In particular, he declared that it was meaningless to talk of a set being a member of itself, or to talk of a set not being a member of itself.

Other logicians have sought less drastic means of avoiding Russell's paradox. But in any consistent set theory, the principle that every property determines a set must be limited in some way or another. Otherwise, Russell's set could be defined by the diagonal argument, yielding a contradiction.

Epimenides was a Cretan of classical times who was reported to have said, "All Cretans are liars." Such an assertion tends to refute itself. If anyone had any reason to believe what Epimenides said, he would then have reason also to believe (depending on the precise meaning of the word "liar") that Epimenides was lying when he said it.

We get a sharpened version of this paradox by considering the sentence that follows:

The italicized sentence in Section AVI.3 *of the book "Elementary Comput-ability, Formal Languages, and Automata" is false.*

Clearly this sentence is talking about itself, and for that reason is quite pointless. Be that as it may, it is a declarative sentence. Furthermore, all its terms have a clear meaning, so it is natural to assert that it must be either true or false. So we ask, is it true or is it false?

If we assume that the sentence is true, we arrive quickly at the contradiction that it is false. Similarly, if we assume that it is false, we get the contradiction that it is true. The reasoning is reminiscent of the proof of Lemma 1 in Section 6.1.1 and Russell's paradox. (If we were willing to use a demonstrative pronoun, a simpler sentence would suffice, namely, "This sentence is false.")

Since the paradox has to do with the fact that the sentence talks about itself, the contradiction can be avoided if we can somehow declare that such sentences are meaningless. Russell thought that the theory of types offered the best solution to this paradox as well as the others. But other logicians have discussed the matter in different terms, of whom the most noteworthy has been Alfred Tarski (see Tarski [1936]).

The Epimenides paradox is a semantical paradox. As explained in Appendix III, the semantics of declarative sentences is concerned with denotation of terms and the truth of sentences. A principle that most formal linguists and logicians adhere to is that we cannot hope to construct a consistent formal language that contains its own complete semantics. If we try to construct such a language, we are almost sure to admit a sentence like the italicized sentence and the language will thereby become inconsistent.

But this does not mean that we cannot deal with semantics in a formal way. Suppose that we have a language L without any semantics, called an *object language*, dealing only with objects outside the language. We can go on to for-malize the semantics of L by constructing a new, essentially richer, language M, called the *metalanguage* of L. M is essentially richer because it has everything that L has, but in addition has the semantics of L.

As an example, let L be the formalism of functional expressions. Certainly, there is no way to make semantical statements about L in L itself. We did make many semantical statements about L in Chapter 4, but we did so informally in the English language (augmented by technical symbols).

If we had found it helpful (which we did not), we could have constructed a formal metalanguage M for L in Chapter 4, which would have contained formal expressions of such thoughts as the following: "If the equation $f(0) = 10$ is true and $f(S(x)) = S(S(f(x)))$ is true for all positive-integer values of the variable x, then the function symbol f denotes a total function." It would take us too far afield to discuss the actual construction of M.

We think of the language M as being one level up from L, since it must be a richer language. If we had constructed M in a fully formal fashion, we might want to go on to deal formally with the semantics of M. To do so we would have to construct M', the metalanguage of M, or the *meta-metalanguage* of L. And so on. We would thus get a hierarchy of languages, quite in accord with the theory of types.

We note without explanation that the proof of Gödel's incompleteness theorem (mentioned briefly in Section 5.1.1) is similar to the Epimenides paradox. The proof proceeds by assigning Gödel numbers to any formal system sufficiently rich to contain the theory of nonnegative integers. It then shows that the various aspects of proving formulas can be dealt with as definable predicates, and culminates in showing that a formula F can be constructed which, in effect, asserts that F itself is unprovable. It follows that, under the assumption that the formal system has nothing wrong with it, it can admit a proof neither of F nor of the denial of F. There is a significant difference, however, between Gödel's theorem and the Epimenides paradox: Gödel's theorem does not mention truth at all, but the distinct (although related) notion of provability. Despite the similarity of its proof to a paradox, Gödel's theorem is not a paradox.

AVI.4   A RECURSIVE FUNCTION NOT PRIMITIVE-RECURSIVE

We have mentioned without proof that Ackermann's function and the Ackermann–Péter function (see Section 4.3) are total and computable but not primitive-recursive. We now construct a function by the diagonal method which we can prove to have these properties.

Recall that a function f is in the class of primitive-recursive functions if and only if there is a sequence of functions $f_1, f_2, \ldots, f_n$ such that (1) each f_i is definable from the successor function and (for $i > 1$) functions preceding it in the list, either by explicit definition or primitive recursion; and (2) $f = f_n$.

Let us now enumerate all functions obtainable this way. For the sake of convenience, we shall represent all functions other than the successor S by the function variables $f_1, f_2, f_3, \ldots$. No other function variables and no function constants other than S are used. The first definition defines a function f_1, the second f_2, and so on.

We progressively define classes $C_1, C_2, \ldots$ of primitive-recursive functions as follows: Put $C_0 = \{S\}$. Then put $C_1 =$ the union of C_0 with the set of all functions definable by explicit definition from S in 100 characters or less. (The entire definition must be no more than 100 characters. The number 100 here is arbitrary.) Then let C_2 = the union of C_1 with the set of all functions definable by a primitive-recursive definition from functions in C_1 by means of a primitive recursion of 200 characters or less.

The definition for all the C's is given recursively: For each $i \geqq 1$, $C_{2i+1} = C_{2i} \cup \{\psi \mid \psi$ definable from functions of C_{2i} by an explicit definition of $(2i + 1)100$ characters or less$\}$, and $C_{2i+2} = C_{2i+1} \cup \{\psi \mid \psi$ definable from functions of C_{2i+1} by a primitive recursion of $(2i + 2)100$ characters or less$\}$.

We can easily devise a procedure to write down the new definitions for each set C_x so as to be sure that no functions belonging to C_x will be left out. It is clear that every primitive-recursive function will be in some C_x.

We thus have a procedure to write down a sequence of functions (together with their definitions) including all the primitive-recursive functions: $S, f_1, f_2, f_3, \ldots$. Functions, indexed as they are defined, will be repeated in this sequence (since a function has many different definitions), but every primitive-recursive function will appear somewhere in the list.

Furthermore, each primitive-recursive function as defined is effectively calculable, as we have observed. So, given numbers i and x, we can effectively obtain the numerical value of $f_i(x, x, \ldots, x)$. (The number of x's in this expression is the number of arguments of the function f_i as defined.)

We are now ready to define our function by the diagonal method. We put

$$\phi(i) = f_i(i, i, \ldots) + 1$$

By the remarks made above, ϕ is a total and computable one-argument function. And if f_j is any one-argument primitive-recursive function, $\phi \neq f_j$, since $\phi(j) \neq f_j(j)$. ϕ is therefore the function that we set out to construct.

It should be noted that this proof turns on the fact that the primitive-recursive functions are total functions. We can generalize on what we have proved. For any effectively enumerable set of total and computable functions, there exists a total and computable function not in the set. Furthermore, the function can be defined from the enumeration.

The reader might be tempted to speculate on the possibility of a paradox by using this argument. Indeed, if one could effectively enumerate all and only all the total and computable functions, one could define a total and computable function that is not in the list, which would be a contradiction. But as a matter of fact, what we have here is not a paradox but a proof that there is no effective enumeration of all and only all the total and computable functions (each accompanied by the algorithm for calculating it). Any effective enumeration that includes all of these functions must include partial functions as well.

Thus we have the explanation for an assertion made without justification in Chapter 1, namely, that any formalism for all algorithms must contain some procedures that sometimes fail to halt. (We are making what seems to be a reasonable assumption based on experience, that the procedures of any formalism are effectively enumerable. Indeed, if we found something whose set of expressible procedures is not effectively enumerable, we would probably not call it a formalism.)

AVI.5 COMPUTATIONAL COMPLEXITY

Definition: A *time-cycle complexity measure* of a program in the GOTO language that computes a total n-argument function f is a total one-argument function h such that, for each n-tuple $(i_1, i_2, \ldots, i_n)$ of nonnegative integers having a total of s decimal digits when represented as numerals in the GOTO language, the number of time cycles used whenever the machine executes P to compute $f(i_1, \ldots, i_n)$ is no greater than $h(s)$. We assume for convenience that h is monotonic: For $s_1 \leqq s_2, h(s_1) \leqq h(s_2)$.

Since the amount of time consumed during a time cycle can be arbitrarily large (see Section 3.2.2) a time-cycle complexity measure is not necessarily a time function for the program, as defined in Section AIV.3.

For example, let P be the GOTO-language program of Section 3.4.2 that computes multiplication with respect to the variable sequence X, Y, W (Fig. 3.4.4). To obtain a time-cycle complexity measure for this program, we first note that for any (i_1, i_2), the number of time cycles when inputs X and Y are initially set to i_1 and i_2, respectively, equals

$$3 + i_2(4 + 4i_1)$$

To get a function h, we must convert this expression into one involving the total number of digits s in the decimal representations of i_1 and i_2. The function h must give us an upper bound on the number of time cycles in a computation, and fortunately does not have to tell us the exact number. Since i_1 and i_2 are each less than 10^s, we can take

$$h(s) = 3 + 10^s(4 + 4 \cdot 10^s)$$

This is an exponential function, and clearly no alternative analysis would give us a function that is less than exponential. Thus the number of time cycles needed to complete a computation run is exponential in the input size. A similar analysis reveals that the same is true for addition in the GOTO language.

It is well known that both addition and multiplication can be done faster than that: The algorithms of grade-school arithmetic allow addition to be done in time that is linear in the input size, and multiplication in time proportional to the square of the input size (with improvements achieved by advanced research).

Neither algorithm is directly available in either of our foundational programming languages, since there is no way in these languages of picking out a decimal digit from a number in storage in one time cycle.

For this reason, the foundational programming languages are not good vehicles for the study of computational complexity, as we have mentioned. But although the result of this subsection will be lacking in significance, the method of proof is used for similar, more significant theorems of computational complexity, which we find too difficult to be worth an adequate explanation in this book. (See Aho, Hopcroft, and Ullman [1974], Chap. 11.)

We recall that an arbitrary program in the GOTO language is converted into special form (see Section 5.2.1) by a mere change of variables and labels. The program in special form, therefore, operates in exactly the same way for each choice of corresponding inputs, time cycle by time cycle. For this reason, we can restrict our attention to programs in special form.

THEOREM AVI.5.1: If h is any computable total one-argument function, there exists a computable total one-argument function f_h such that no program in the GOTO language computes this function with time-cycle complexity h.

PROOF: Let f_h be defined as follows. For each nonnegative integer x, (1) if x is not the Gödel number (see Section 5.2.1) of a program in special form, then put $f_h(x) = 0$; (2) if x is the Gödel number of a program P in special form, let s be the number of decimal digits in the numeral representing x, and put $f_h(x) =$ one plus the value that the variable X2 assumes at time cycle $h(s)$, or at the halt if it occurs sooner, when the program P is run with X1 initialized at x and all other variables initialized at zero.

Given x, we can effectively tell whether it is the Gödel number of a program, and if so, to construct the program. Then where s is the number of decimal digits of x, we can hand-simulate the program to $h(s)$ time cycles or to the halt if that occurs sooner. In any case, the value $f_h(x)$ is algorithmically determined. Thus f_h is a total and computable function.

Let P_0 be any program for computing the computable function f_h. We may assume that P_0 is in special form, computing this function with respect to the variable sequence X1, X2, and has the Gödel number x_0. Let s_0 be the number of decimal digits in the numeral representing the number x_0. Now $f_h(x_0) =$ the value of X2 at the halt, when P_0 is run with X1 initialized at x_0, however the other variables are initialized, and hence when these other variables are initialized to zero. By definition of f_h, however, $f_h(x_0)$ does not equal the value of X2 at time cycle $h(s_0)$ or at the halt if that comes before. It follows that P, when run with X1 initialized at x_0, requires more than $h(s_0)$ time cycles to reach a halt. Thus no program in the GOTO language computes f_h with time-cycle complexity h. ∎

There is another aspect of this theorem that shows that it lacks significance in its present form. Complexity theorists generally would not be satisfied with the function f_h unless they were sure there were infinitely many inputs for which a program fails to compute f_h with time-cycle complexity h (even if they were interested in time-cycle complexity, as opposed to time complexity, which they probably would not be). It is possible to restate the theorem and rework the proof to get this effect, but that would take us too far from our train of thought.

AVI.6 SPACE COMPLEXITIES

Our final observation is the application of the diagonal method to space complexities.

Definition: The *amount of storage used* by a program run up to the tth time cycle is $\sum_{i=1}^{n} s_i$, where n is the number of variables and s_i is the *amount of storage used* by ith variable (i.e., the number of decimal digits of the decimal representation of the maximum value the ith variable assumes in the run), up to the tth time cycle.

Definition: A *space complexity measure* of a program P that computes a total n-argument function f is a total one-argument function h such that, for each n-tuple $(i_1, \ldots, i_n)$ of nonnegative integers having a total of s decimal digits when represented as decimal numerals, the amount of storage used up to the halt when the machine runs the program to compute $f(i_1, \ldots, i_n)$, with variables other than input variables initially set to zero, is no greater than $h(s)$. For convenience, h is assumed to be monotonic.

The following theorem is quite similar in spirit to Theorem AVI.5.1; it has little substantive significance in the theory of computational complexity, but is a simplified version of other theorems that are significant. The proof has the same outline as the proof of Theorem AVI.5.1 but has significant differences in detail.

THEOREM AVI.6.1: If h is any computable total one-argument function, there exists a computable total one-argument function f_h which no program in the GOTO language computes with space complexity h.

PROOF: The function f_h is defined as follows. For each nonnegative integer x, (1) if x is not the Gödel number of a program in special form, then put $f_h(x) = 0$; (2) if x is the Gödel number of a program P in special form, assuming that P is run with X1 initially set to x and all other variables set to zero, put $f_h(x)$ equal to one plus the value that the variable X2 assumes at the first time cycle in which (a) there is a halt, (b) the total configuration (see Section 5.2.2) of the computation is an exact repetition of the total configuration at some previous time cycle, or (c) the storage used by the program run up to that time cycle exceeds $h(s)$, where s is the number of decimal digits in the numeral representing x. Note that possibility (b) occurring first implies that execution never terminates and the storage never exceeds $h(s)$.

To show that f_h is a total function, we must verify that in any run of a program, one of the three conditions (a), (b), or (c) must occur. The crucial observation is that in any infinite run of a program (i.e., one without a halt), either the storage used must exceed $h(s)$ or else the machine must repeat a total configuration, since there are only finitely many total configurations whose total storage is limited by $h(s)$. From this it follows that after some finite amount of time one of the three conditions will occur. The value of $f_h(x)$ is determined by hand-simulating P to that point, so f_h is computable.

Now let P_0 be any program in the GOTO language for computing f_h. We assume that P_0 in special form computes f_h with respect to the variable sequence X1, X2; and has a Gödel number x_0, where s_0 is the number of decimal digits in the numeral representing x_0.

From the definition of f_h, P_0 when computing $f_h(x_0)$ will require more than $h(s_0)$ decimal digits of storage. For if the halt were to occur before the storage exceeds $h(s_0)$, we would have $f_h(x_0)$ equal to one plus the value of X2 at the halt, contradicting the stipulation that X2 has the value $f_h(x_0)$ at the halt. Hence P_0 does not compute with space complexity h. ∎

Bibliography

AHO, A. V. (ed.) [1973] *Currents in the Theory of Computing.* Englewood Cliffs, N.J.: Prentice-Hall.

AHO, A. V., J. E. HOPCROFT, and J. D. ULLMAN [1974]. *The Design and Analysis of Computer Algorithms.* Reading, Mass.: Addison-Wesley.

AHO, A. V., and J. D. ULLMAN [1972]. *The Theory of Parsing, Translation, and Compiling,* Vol. 1. Englewood Cliffs, N.J.: Prentice-Hall.

AHO, A. V., and J. D. ULLMAN [1973]. *The Theory of Parsing, Translation, and Compiling,* Vol. 2. Englewood Cliffs, N.J.: Prentice-Hall.

AHO, A. V., and J. D. ULLMAN [1977]. *Principles of Compiler Design.* Reading, Mass.: Addison-Wesley.

ALEKSANDER, I., and F. K. HANNA [1975]. *Automata Theory: an Engineering Approach.* New York: Crane Russak.

ARBIB, M. A. [1969]. *Theories of Abstract Automata.* Englewood Cliffs, N.J.: Prentice-Hall.

BAASE, S. [1978]. *Computer Algorithms: Introduction to Design and Analysis.* Reading, Mass.: Addison-Wesley.

BACKHOUSE, R. C. [1979]. *Syntax of Programming Languages: Theory and Practice.* London: Prentice-Hall.

BAR-HILLEL, Y. [1964]. *Language and Information: Selected Essays on their Theory and Application.* Reading, Mass.: Addison-Wesley.

BECKMAN, F. S. [1980]. *Mathematical Foundations of Programming.* Reading, Mass.: Addison-Wesley.

BOOK, R. V. [1973]. "Topics in formal language theory." In Aho [1973], pp. 1–34.

BOOLOS, G., and R. JEFFREY [1974]. *Computability and Logic.* Cambridge: Cambridge University Press.

BOOTH, T. L. [1967]. *Sequential Machines and Automata Theory.* New York: Wiley.

BORODIN, A. [1973]. "Computational complexity: theory and practice." In Aho [1973], pp. 35–89.

BOYER, C. B. [1968]. *A History of Mathematics.* New York: Wiley.

BRAINERD, W. S., and L. H. LANDWEBER [1974]. *Theory of Computation.* New York: Wiley.

BURKS, A. W. [1980]. "From ENIAC to the stored-program computer: two revolutions in computers." In Metropolis, Howlett, and Rota [1980], pp. 311–344.

BURKS, A. W., and J. B. WRIGHT [1953]. "Theory of logical nets." In Moore [1964], pp. 193–212. Originally in *Proceedings of the IRE 41*, 1357–1365.

CHOMSKY, N. [1956]. "Three models for the description of language." *IEEE Transactions on Information Theory 2*, 113–124.

CHOMSKY, N. [1957]. *Syntactic Structures.* The Hague: Mouton.

CHURCH, A. [1936a]. "An unsolvable problem of elementary number theory." In Davis [1965], pp. 88–107. Originally in *American Journal of Mathematics 58*, 345–363.

CHURCH, A. [1936b]. "A note on the Entscheidungsproblem." In Davis [1965], pp. 108–115. Originally in *Journal of Symbolic Logic 1*, 40–41, 101–102.

CHURCH, A. [1956]. *Introduction to Mathematical Logic*, Vol. 1. Princeton, N.J.: Princeton University Press.

CLARK, K., and D. COWELL [1976]. *Programs, Machines, and Computation.* London: McGraw-Hill.

CLEAVELAND, J. C., and R. C. UZGALIS [1977]. *Grammars for Programming Languages.* New York: Elsevier/North-Holland.

CONWAY, J. H. [1971]. *Regular Algebra and Finite Machines.* London: Chapman & Hall.

DAVIS, M. [1958]. *Computability and Unsolvability.* New York: McGraw-Hill.

DAVIS, M. (ed.) [1965]. *The Undecidable.* Hewlett, New York: Raven Press.

DAVIS, M. [1973]. "Hilbert's tenth problem is unsolvable." *American Mathematical Monthly 80*, 233–269.

DENNING, P. J., J. B. DENNIS, and J. E. QUALITZ [1978]. *Machines, Languages, and Computation.* Englewood Cliffs, N.J.: Prentice-Hall.

ECKERT, J. P., JR. [1980]. "The ENIAC." In Metropolis, Howlett, and Rota [1980], pp. 525–539.

EILENBERG, S. [1974]. *Automata, Languages, and Machines*, Vol. A. New York: Academic Press.

ENGELER, E. [1968]. *Formal Languages: Automata and Structures.* Chicago: Markham.

ENGELER, E. [1973]. *Introduction to the Theory of Computation.* New York: Academic Press.

GAREY, M. R., and D. S. JOHNSON [1979]. *Computers and Intractability: A Guide to the Theory of NP-Completeness.* San Francisco: W. H. Freeman.

GINSBURG, S. [1966]. *The Mathematical Theory of Context-free Languages.* New York: McGraw-Hill.

GÖDEL, K. [1931]. "On formally undecidable propositions of *Principia Mathematica* and related systems, I." Translated from the German by E. Mendelson. In Davis [1965], pp. 4–38. Originally appeared in *Monatshefte für Mathematik und Physik 38,* 173–198.

GOLDSTINE, H. H. [1972]. *The Computer from Pascal to von Neumann.* Princeton, N.J.: Princeton University Press.

GRIES, D. [1971]. *Compiler Construction for Digital Computers.* New York: Wiley.

GROSS, M., and A. LENTIN [1970]. *Introduction to Formal Grammars.* New York: Springer-Verlag.

HAMLET, R. G. [1974]. *Introduction to Computation Theory.* New York: Intext.

HARARY, F. [1969]. *Graph Theory.* Reading, Mass.: Addison-Wesley.

HARRISON, M. A. [1965]. *Introduction to Switching and Automata Theory.* New York: McGraw-Hill.

HARRISON, M. A. [1978]. *Introduction to Formal Language Theory.* Reading, Mass.: Addison-Wesley.

HARTMANIS, J. [1978]. *Feasible Computations and Provable Complexity Properties.* Philadelphia: Society for Industrial and Applied Mathematics.

HENNIE, F. C. [1968]. *Finite-State Models for Logical Machines.* New York: Wiley.

HENNIE, F. [1977]. *Introduction to Computability.* Reading, Mass.: Addison-Wesley.

HERMES, H. [1969]. *Enumerability, Decidability, Computability.* Translated from the German by G. T. Hermann and O. Plassman. New York: Springer-Verlag.

HOPCROFT, J. E., and J. D. ULLMAN [1969]. *Formal Languages and their Relation to Automata.* Reading, Mass.: Addison-Wesley.

HOPCROFT, J. E., and J. D. ULLMAN [1979]. *Introduction to Automata Theory, Languages, and Computation.* Reading, Mass.: Addison-Wesley.

JONES, C. B. [1980]. *Software Development: A Rigorous Approach.* London: Prentice-Hall.

JONES, N. D. [1973]. *Computability Theory: An Introduction.* New York: Academic Press.

KAIN, R. Y. [1972]. *Automata Theory: Machines and Languages.* New York: McGraw-Hill.

KLEENE, S. C. [1936]. "General recursive functions of natural numbers." In Davis [1965], pp. 236–253. Originally published in *Mathematische Annalen 112,* 727–742.

KLEENE, S. C. [1952]. *Introduction to Metamathematics.* New York: D. Van Nostrand.

KNUTH, D. E. [1968]. *The Art of Computer Programming,* Vol. 1. Reading, Mass.: Addison-Wesley.

KNUTH, D. E. [1969]. *The Art of Computer Programming*, Vol. 2. Reading, Mass.: Addison-Wesley.

KNUTH, D. E. [1973]. *The Art of Computer Programming*, Vol. 3. Reading, Mass.: Addison-Wesley.

KORFHAGE, R. R. [1966]. *Logic and Algorithms*. New York: Wiley.

KURKI-SUONIO, R. [1971]. *A Programmer's Introduction to Computability and Formal Languages*. Princeton, N.J.: Auerbach.

LEVY, L. S. [1980]. *Discrete Structures of Computer Science*. New York: Wiley.

LEWIS, H. R., and C. H. PAPADIMITRIOU [1981]. *Elements of the Theory of Computation*. Englewood Cliffs, N.J.: Prentice-Hall.

LEWIS, P. M., II, D. J. ROSENKRANTZ, and R. E. STEARNS [1976]. *Compiler Design Theory*. Reading, Mass.: Addison-Wesley.

LOECKX, J. [1972]. *Computability and Decidability: An Introduction for Students of Computer Science*. New York: Springer-Verlag.

MACHTEY, M., and P. YOUNG [1978]. *An Introduction to the General Theory of Algorithms*. New York: Elsevier/North-Holland.

MANNA, Z. [1973]. "Program schemas." In Aho [1973], pp. 90–142.

MANNA, Z. [1974]. *Mathematical Theory of Computation*. New York: McGraw-Hill.

MAUCHLY, J. W. [1980]. "The ENIAC." In Metropolis, Howlett, and Rota [1980], pp. 541–550.

McNAUGHTON, R., and S. PAPERT [1971]. *Counter-free Automata*. Cambridge, Mass.: MIT Press.

METROPOLIS, N., J. HOWLETT, and G. ROTA (eds.) [1980]. *A History of Computing in the Twentieth Century*. New York: Academic Press.

MEYER, A. R., and D. M. RITCHIE [1967]. "The complexity of LOOP programs." *Proceedings of the 22nd Association for Computing Machinery National Conference*, pp. 465–469.

MINSKY, M. L. [1967]. *Computation: Finite and Infinite Machines*. Englewood Cliffs, N.J.: Prentice-Hall.

MOORE, E. F. [1956]. "Gedanken-experiments on sequential machines." In Shannon and McCarthy [1956], pp. 129–153.

MOORE, E. F. (ed.) [1964]. *Sequential Machines: Selected Papers*. Reading, Mass.: Addison-Wesley.

MORRIS, C. W. [1938]. *Foundations of the Theory of Signs*. Vol. 1, No. 2, of the *International Encyclopedia of Unified Science*. Chicago: University of Chicago Press.

NELSON, R. J. [1968]. *Introduction to Automata*. New York: Wiley.

PAZ, A. [1971]. *Introduction to Probabilistic Automata*. New York: Academic Press.

PÉTER, R. [1967]. *Recursive Functions*. Translated from the German by I. Földes. New York: Academic Press.

POST, E. L. [1936]. "Finite combinatory processes. Formulation I." In Davis [1965], pp. 288–291. Originally in *Journal of Symbolic Logic 1*, 103–105.

POST, E. L. [1947]. "Recursive unsolvability of a problem of Thue." In Davis [1965], pp. 292–303. Originally in *Journal of Symbolic Logic 12*, 1–11.

QUINE, W. V. [1953]. *From a Logical Point of View: 9 Logico-Philosophical Essays.* Cambridge, Mass.: Harvard University Press.

RABIN, M. O. [1963]. "Probabilistic automata." In Moore [1964], pp. 98–114. Originally in *Information and Control 6*, 230–245.

RABIN, M. O., and D. SCOTT [1959]. "Finite automata and their decision problems." In Moore [1964], pp. 63–91. Originally in *IBM Journal of Research and Development 3*, 114–125.

ROGERS, H., JR. [1967]. *Theory of Recursive Functions and Effective Computability.* New York: McGraw-Hill.

ROSSER, J. B. [1939]. "An informal exposition of proofs of Gödel's theorem and Church's theorem." In Davis [1965], pp. 223–230. Originally in *Journal of Symbolic Logic 4*, 53–60.

RUSSELL, B. [1919]. *Introduction to Mathematical Philosophy.* London: Allen & Unwin. Also, New York: Macmillan.

SALOMAA, A. [1969]. *Theory of Automata.* Oxford: Pergamon Press.

SALOMAA, A. [1973]. *Formal Languages.* New York: Academic Press.

SAVAGE, J. E. [1976]. *The Complexity of Computing.* New York: Wiley.

SCHMIDT, E. M., and T. G. SZYMANSKI [1977]. "Succinctness of descriptions of unambiguous context-free languages." *SIAM Journal on Computing 6*, 547–553.

SHANNON, C. E., and J. McCARTHY (eds.) [1956]. *Automata Studies.* Princeton, N.J.: Princeton University Press.

SHEPHERDSON, J. C., and H. E. STURGIS [1963]. "Computability of recursive functions." *Journal of the Association for Computing Machinery 10*, 217–255.

STANAT, D. F., and D. F. McALLISTER [1977]. *Discrete Mathematics in Computer Science.* Englewood Cliffs, N.J.: Prentice-Hall.

STOY, J. E. [1977]. *Denotational Semantics.* Cambridge, Mass.: MIT Press.

TARSKI, A. [1936]. "The concept of truth in formalized languages." In *Logic, Semantics, Metamathematics*, translated by J. H. Woodger, revised edition edited with introduction and index by John Corcoran. Indianapolis, Ind.: Hackett, 1981, pp. 152–278. Originally in *Studia Philosophica 1*, 261–405.

TARSKI, A., A. MOSTOWSKI, and R. M. ROBINSON [1953]. *Undecidable Theories.* Amsterdam: North-Holland.

TENNENT, R. D. [1981]. *Principles of Programming Languages.* London: Prentice-Hall.

TRAKHTENBROT, B. A. [1963]. *Algorithms and Automatic Computing Machines.* Translated from the Russian by J. Kristian, J. D. McCawley, and S. A. Schmitt. Lexington, Mass.: Heath.

TURING, A. M. [1936]. "On computable numbers, with an application to the Entscheidungsproblem." In Davis [1965], pp. 115–151. Originally in *Proceedings of the London Mathematical Society* (*Ser. 2*) *42*, 230–265.

ULLMAN, J. D. [1973]. "Applications of language theory to compiler design." In Aho [1973], pp. 173–218.

VAN HEIJENOORT, J. [1967]. *From Frege to Gödel: A Source Book in Mathematical Logic, 1879–1931*. Cambridge: Mass.: Harvard University Press.

WANG, H. [1963]. *A Survey of Mathematical Logic*. Amsterdam: North-Holland.

WHITEHEAD, A. N., and B. RUSSELL [1910]. *Principia Mathematica*, Vol. 1. Cambridge: Cambridge University Press.

WILKES, M. V. [1957]. *Automatic Digital Computers*. New York: Wiley.

YASUHARA, A. [1971]. *Recursive Function Theory and Logic*. New York: Academic Press.

Index of Symbols

Index